D0392103

LIBRARY AUTOMATION

McGRAW-HILL SERIES IN LIBRARY EDUCATION

Jean Key Gates, Consulting Editor
University of South Florida

Gates INTRODUCTION TO LIBRARIANSHIP

Heiliger and Henderson LIBRARY AUTOMATION: EXPERIENCE, METHODOLOGY, AND TECHNOLOGY OF THE LIBRARY AS AN INFORMATION SYSTEM

Katz INTRODUCTION TO REFERENCE WORK: VOL. I, BASIC INFORMATION SOURCES

Katz INTRODUCTION TO REFERENCE WORK: VOL. II, REFERENCE SERVICES

LIBRARY AUTOMATION: Experience, Methodology, and Technology of the Library as an Information System

Edward M. Heiliger

Professor of Library Science
Director, Kent Center for Library Studies
School of Library Science
Kent State University

Paul B. Henderson, Jr.

Director, Systems & Data Processing
Allis Chalmers Manufacturing Co.

McGraw-Hill Book Company

New York St. Louis San Francisco Düsseldorf Johannesburg Kuala Lumpur London Mexico Montreal New Delhi Panama Rio de Janeiro Singapore Sydney Toronto

LIBRARY AUTOMATION: EXPERIENCE, METHODOLOGY, AND TECHNOLOGY OF THE LIBRARY AS AN INFORMATION SYSTEM

Library of Congress Catalog Card Number 77-137128

07-027888-1

234567890MAMM7987654321

This book was set in Vladimir by John C. Meyer & Son, and printed on permanent paper and bound by The Maple Press Company. The designer was Marsha Cohen; the drawings were done by John Cordes, J. & R. Technical Services, Inc. The editors were Samuel B. Bossard and Ellen Simon. Annette Wentz supervised production.

CONTENTS

PREFACE vii

INTRODUCTION xi

PROLOGUE 1

PART I EXPERIENCES IN LIBRARY AUTOMATION 7

1. Acquisition 25
2. Cataloging 37
3. Reference 53
4. Resource Control 67
5. Processing Control 77
6. Administrative Processes 93

PART II METHODOLOGY OF LIBRARY AUTOMATION 105

7. Identification and Definition 119
8. Analysis and Specification 127
9. Design and Development 135
10. Installation and Operation 153

PART III TECHNOLOGY FOR LIBRARY AUTOMATION 159

11. Hardware 189
12. Software 203
13. Concepts 215

PART IV THE PROSPECTS FOR LIBRARY AUTOMATION 235

14. Library Automation in the 1970s 239

BIBLIOGRAPHY 255

BIBLIOGRAPHY SUBJECT INDEX 317

INDEX 327

PREFACE

The goal of this book, *Library Automation: Experience, Methodology, and Technology of the Library as an Information System,* is to provide a perspective of the library functions that have been or might be mechanized or automated, an outline of the methodology of the systems approach, an overview of the technology available to the library, and a projection of the prospects for library automation.

There is concern in every library for the proper handling and control of a veritable flood of material and for the prompt and convenient fulfillment of service demands. That concern is matched by excitement about the possibilities for effective use of the computers and communications network in many library functions. Knowledge, the library's stock-in-trade, is being generated at an unprecedented rate and sought after with unprecedented intensity. Technology, the driving force behind the library's problems and one hope for future solution, is being advanced to unprecedented levels.

In an environment of such impelling need and tremendous opportunity, the future of the automated library lies not in any one feature, but rather in a balance among concepts, equipment, tradition, and talent. Preoccupation with any one aspect leads to fruitless research, unattainable expectations, unjustified fears, or a deep sense of frustration. Conceptual solutions have not been devised for some important problems. Equipment cannot perform some essential functions. Historical library processes are not adequate to all demands. The supply of educated, experienced, and willing talent is insufficient. The scope and intensity of the problem and the spectrum of disciplines, techniques, and devices emphasize the importance of the need and the opportunity.

The apparent sophistication and complexity of data systems and data processing equipment often obscure a very basic and essentially simple logical foundation. The computer is not a magic machine—it cannot now be creative or innovative beyond the programs prepared for it by human reasoning and skill, and it should not be expected to be so in the next decade. Neither is the computer a malevolent brain working to our detriment—if it were, we would get far more help in relieving man from his burdens. Mathematical technology provides an intricate and remarkably productive discipline; chemical technology yields strange and wonderful products; information technology offers access to knowledge and control—all from simple processes and powerful concepts. These technologies, like elephants, are best viewed in broad perspective rather than intimate detail. The benefits of mathematics, chemistry, information, and elephants are available to those who come to them knowing what they want and why—only the scientists, engineers, analysts, programmers, and mahouts need approach the detail.

The librarian must become knowledgeable of many subjects and confident in that knowledge, but it is neither possible nor desirable to become an expert in everything. The details presented here exemplify the essential ideas that have emerged from experiences with a variety of applications in libraries and in many different fields. The present focus is on the "what" and "why" which can be expected to persist rather than the "how" and "when" which will surely continue to change.

A new vocabulary and the beginning of insight need to be exercised and nourished by exploration and observation. There is a wealth of data about mechanization and automation in current publications and a world of surprising problems and innovations in the processing and control systems of every library; both are available for the asking.

This book is organized into four parts to emphasize the distinctive, but related, features of the experiences, methodology, technology, and prospects for library automation.

Part I, "Experiences in Library Automation," is a reflection of the past and present efforts to bring together the need for better, faster, and more reliable processing of physical objects and data with the opportunities for use of the techniques and devices of mechanization and automation. It provides a bridge between the familiar ground of library processes and the less familiar ground of computers and automation.

It is not possible to mention, much less explain, all the efforts to rationalize and improve library processes. The intent is, rather, to identify the highlights and offer a perspective that places the library in the context of a system. In this view, the evidences of past successes, failures, and mere changes reveal a pattern that discloses some of the reasons for those results. The story of library automation is not yet complete, but, by analogy, the forest is beginning to appear, and the individual trees are beginning to seem less important.

There are other views of library automation. Some have been overtaken by the advance of technology, others by the increase in understanding that attends the passage of time and the process of introspection. For the student there is a reading list with each chapter; for the scholar there is an extensive bibliography. The references have been selected predominantly from the writings of the past decade; there is little from earlier times that is meaningful in the current context except to the specialist who can recognize the essence of contemporary technology in the initial gropings by the pioneers of past decades and centuries.

Part II, "Methodology of Library Automation," provides a guide to the vocabulary, concepts, and techniques of the systems approach in the perspective appropriate to a librarian rather than in the detail needed by a systems analyst or programmer. There is still far more art than science in the practice of systems design. It is still true, and it is expected to remain true for some time, that a subtle mix of education, experience, imagination, and sensitivity is needed in systems development. In this presentation, the prevailing methodology is presented as it is interpreted from the evidence of many practitioners.

The methodological synthesis presented must be adapted to the particular goals and environment and personnel of each library. If copied literally, it is most likely to lead to an excess of detail, for each project is partially done when it is started and the mark of a good design is preservation of the good features that already exist and alteration or elimination of the weaknesses.

Part III, "Technology for Library Automation," presents an overview of the hardware, software, and concepts that constitute the means to mechanization and automation.

There is already a bewildering array of devices and techniques, and it is probable that more, rather than less, variety will be available in the immediate future. The presentation is therefore addressed to the understanding of the very simple and logical pattern that lies just behind that bewildering array. It is assumed that the approach will be to define *what* is needed and then decide *how* to accomplish that established goal; it is expected that the practice of selecting an interesting device or technique and then considering how the library can use it will soon cease. It is, accordingly, appropriate first to comprehend the objectives to be served, then to consider what is needed in relation to human skills, hardware, software, and conceptual capabilities, and finally to select the resources and techniques that are appropriate.

There are few good presentations of this approach. The current professional journals rather than existing books are recommended as sources for confirmation that technology is becoming a servant to management and is ceasing to be the master. Every librarian is encouraged to acquire a sound knowledge of the technological vocabulary and to establish a broad perspective of the essential capabilities of the hardware, software, and concepts of information technology.

Parts I, II, and III are supported by an extensive glossary of terms. It is, perhaps, unfortunate that communication is hampered by vocabulary problems, but, in a deeper sense, that is the chief problem in knowledge transfer that the library seeks to serve. The librarian is thus faced with the utter necessity of comprehending familiar processes in unfamiliar ways and discoursing in alien terms. There is an illusion that the library/systems match can be formulated by anyone who will provide the interdisciplinary link. In fact, the librarian and analyst are complementary, not alternative—each must recognize the basic vocabulary of the other in order that the librarian can concentrate on *what* is needed and the analyst on *how* to do it.

Part IV, "Prospects for Library Automation," is a summary of the most likely advances in library automation in the next decade. Past forecasts and the pace of technological development and innovation in the past decade suggest that there is a high risk of overestimating the ability for practical and economic exploitation of new concepts and an equally high risk of underestimating the advances in devices. In line with the proposition that needs rather than opportunities are primary, the interpretation is focused on probable advances in service rather than possible introduction of new hardware. The library does not appear to be a mere variation on other institutions, and the most important new hardware is foreseen as response to library needs rather than application of available equipment features.

We must express our gratitude and appreciation to our professional colleagues at Allis-Chalmers Manufacturing Company and the dean, faculty, and staff of the School of Library Science and the library at Kent State University; to Cloyd Dake Gull for his advice and assistance; to Lawrence Berul and Mrs. Carol Steffan for help on the glossary; to Mrs. Virginia Spahr and Mrs. Joyce Mueller for assistance in preparing the bibliography; and to our wives for help and encouragement.

Edward M. Heiliger
Paul B. Henderson, Jr.

INTRODUCTION

In past applications of computer technology to the library, effort has been concentrated on the use of equipment to do existing tasks in more efficient ways—an approach that is aptly termed *mechanization.* Too little thought has been given to realizing the full potential of the machinery by changing traditional methods that were developed to conform to the limited capabilities of the precomputer years. It is this broader view of the challenge of information technology that merits the term *automation.*

Henry Dubester[1] recently referred to the present state of library automation as the "second generation." While some libraries continue to live with first-generation manual systems, he envisions the third generation as that in which libraries would be recognizably different because of the new technology.

This view of library data system "generations" mirrors the prevailing view of hardware generations. The first (vacuum tube) generation involved massive equipment, slow processing, and frequent human intervention and was suitable only for isolated processes and specialized applications. The second (transistor) generation provided order-of-magnitude advances in size and speed and confirmed the opportunities for system continuity. Despite the advances, this equipment could not provide sufficient capability to do more than mechanize processes designed for human efforts. The third (integrated circuit) generation offers the speed, capability, and diversity of functions sufficient to provide the technical elements for automation. A fourth generation is expected to emerge in the mid-1970s. The technology is not yet clear but will probably be based on large-scale integrated circuits and may include laser and holographic techniques for data storage.

It is typical for old practices to persist for several years after the equipment has changed. This "generation lag" emphasizes the inability to exploit technological advances until time, education, and experience provide perspective, competence, and proof of feasibility, practicality, and economy. The change from the second to the third generation of hardware is not yet completed, and the system changes that will come when libraries begin to move to their third generation

[1] Henry Dubester, address before the Joint Meeting of chapters of the Special Libraries Association and the American Society for Information Science, Cleveland, Ohio, Feb. 19, 1969.

are expected to be more profound and even more difficult for librarians than the current change. The time is close at hand when there must be a decision on what to keep and what to discard in our traditional methods.

The student who aspires to a career in librarianship must become conversant with both the structure and the content of the library and the logic and capability of information technology and must be prepared to accommodate the impact of that technology without losing contact with either the historical or the social context of the library. The students in the graduate library schools today will be needed to help in the transition to the third generation and will be expected to use information technology to good advantage. This book is for them, for the practicing librarian who seeks to maintain an up-to-date knowledge of the field and the changes in it, and for the library board member, the university administrator, the college president, the school principal, the company manager, and other nonlibrarians who must understand the new problems of the library in transition.

Library Automation is designed to provide an introductory exposition of automation in practice, in theory, and in prospect to those who are familiar with the objectives and purposes of the library and seek to comprehend and improve its functioning.

There is no assumption of either background or expertise in information technology. The concepts and approaches are developed from the foundation of library terminology and practices; the advanced student can proceed rapidly through the preliminary discussions to considerations of applications and prospects. The individual details of application and equipment will doubtless present some unexpected results, pleasant and otherwise, in the next decade. Some problems will seem to disappear as particular solutions are found to be especially well suited to library needs. Other problems will grow and intensify because the basic goal of library service is not trivial and the inherent problems of processing library data are both complex and intricate. The basic logic which has emerged from the first decade of efforts to exploit the computer will persist as a foundation on which to build and as a guide to further advance to those who can recognize what is essential and lasting among many details that are trivial and transitory.

LIBRARY AUTOMATION

PROLOGUE

Progress in the development of human institutions and activities over the span of recorded history has been neither steady nor consistent. In many fields of endeavor there has been noted an accelerating pace, alternating periods of intense activity and relative quiet, and even occasional periods of retreat to earlier practices. The quiet periods have varied in length from the centuries of the Dark Ages to the years of the Great Depression. The bursts of innovation have involved whole continents, as in the industrial revolution; whole countries, as in Japan; and whole industries, as in electronics. The pattern of fluctuations is especially apparent where there is a high order of involvement of technology and consequent emphasis on the interaction of people with machines.

Photography took one hundred twelve years to move from discovery to commercial application, the telephone fifty-six, radio thirty-five, radar fifteen, and television twelve. The pace continues and even quickens; the transistor appeared in products only five years after its laboratory demonstration.

The burst of activity that leads to a higher plateau of attainment reflects the interaction of several driving forces.[1] Creative efforts provide new concepts and new devices in response to perceived needs and to discovered opportunities. Assimilation of previous developments and consideration of successes and failures suggest the basis for novel applications and new combinations. Finally, experience, education, and communication bring together the necessary constituents for a new advance.

These periodic assaults of innovation are sufficient to overcome the inclination to resist change

[1] "Knowledge in itself is sterile. When you have a combination of knowledge, understanding, and imagination, you begin to reach a desired result," Dr. C. Stark Draper, director, M.I.T. Instrumentation Laboratory, Boston College Seminar on Innovative Technology, Boston, May 1969.

and to cherish traditional practices. There is a risk in change, especially when several different topics must be integrated to form a novel pattern. Discontent with existing patterns may facilitate acceptance, but change requires an active proponent.

When the impetus for change arises from a perceived need, the recognition does not occur to all practitioners at the same time. Those who are especially perceptive or are operating near the limits of system capability are most likely to recognize the problem and begin the search for a solution. One or a few of the first effective solutions will gain acceptance and attain dominance even if the margin of value over later offerings is insignificant.[2]

When technological opportunity is the driving force, the transfer from the theoretical to the practical realm is inhibited by the lack of demand for a solution to a pressing problem. Acceptance is likely to be relatively slow; better solutions rather than the earlier solutions can be expected to prevail. Since the exploratory and introductory period prior to widespread acceptance and use is relatively long, there is ample time for reappraisal and reflection and a consensus of acceptance from which to consider the next step forward.[3]

When both the demand and the opportunity for innovation are acute, the result is not necessarily the prompt and precise determination and application

[2] It is common practice in major military and space projects to pursue simultaneously several alternative approaches to critical problems and to use whichever solution is first available. Gaseous diffusion for refining uranium, solid propellants for rockets, pressurized water for nuclear reactors, and pure oxygen atmosphere for space capsules were used because they were available—they have been confirmed as successful but are not always the best solutions either technically or economically.

[3] The long and expensive search for the right design of the supersonic transport (SST) is a current example of technology looking for a suitable problem to solve. Not even the urgency of international competition can justify acceptance of a first marginal solution.

of the optimum solution. When high enthusiasm for a new technology finds an eager demand for change, the merits of careful evaluation are likely to be forgotten. In due time the harsh realities of failure and the oppressive burden of cumbersome detail combine to reintroduce the perspective otherwise offered by the cautious and skeptical.

When technology is incomplete or inadequate to the demands, the early overextended applications that fail or attain only minimal acceptance leave an attitude resistant to further developments. As in the physical sciences, new concepts and discoveries lead to the recognition that old ideas, even successful old ideas, are not valid under all conditions. The old ways prevail wherever they provide useful solutions and are only supplanted where the boundaries of validity and utility have been reached or passed. With greater sophistication, broader experience, and better equipment the risks of failure are reduced but not eliminated, and the enthusiasm for further and faster advance persists despite occasional setbacks. Finally, the insight provided by new tools and concepts begins to reveal why the successful ideas are successful, where new demands and new opportunities are touching the further limits of capability and validity, and how the features may be modified to open new realms of operation.

The period of rapid advance does not long persist. When the innovators become occupied with practical problems, the driving force is removed, and the pace slows. Technical, social, and economic forces again become dominant and introduce a new period of readjustment and refinement.

Libraries, long before the advent of computers or of rapid mass communications, experienced such bursts of activity. Time and again human ingenuity has solved or minimized the problems created by growth and change and responded to the challenge of opportunities offered by new technology. Most of the procedural features of the library in the mid-twentieth century were devised, tried, and proven in a process of innovation and experimentation. Many that were demonstrated to have great utility are now recognized to have definite limitations. Nevertheless, they will persist until the essential elements that have made them successful are identified and understood and a better means is perfected to accomplish the same ends.

The early growth of population, when thousands rather than millions or billions of people were involved, made it necessary to supplement oral traditions. The audiences grew more rapidly than the storytellers could be trained—a phenomenon now recurring in educational institutions. The demand for better, faster, and more reliable interchange of knowledge was, in time, met by a new supply technology for memory and communication. The development of written languages and printing greatly increased the scope of recorded knowledge and greatly accelerated the speed of its dissemination. A dedication to universal education in most industrially developing countries fostered the establishment of libraries to nourish the hunger for new ideas and new modes of expression. These conditions have so encouraged the generation of knowledge that the stock of ideas has become an increasing burden to manage and disseminate.

The problems of bulk and quantity called forth intensive efforts to reduce the mass of materials to manageable size and convenient shapes and to provide faster and more precise means for locating a few items of interest from a vast collection.

The introduction of commercial computers in the mid-1950s in the United States and soon thereafter in all other countries suggested to many users the possibility of fruitful applications in areas other than ballistics and payroll computations. The immediate efforts centered upon attempts to mechanize the manual processes that were successful but burdensome. It was apparent by the early 1960s that the mere mechanization of manual procedures was of limited value. Attention shifted to automation. For the library this meant casting the purposes of the library into the framework of rigorous logic wherein the technology might be exploited as the means to a useful end rather than a goal in itself.

The great promise of a computation and communications network has proved very difficult to fulfill. There is little doubt that computers, communications, and the library belong together and no further doubt that the union is hard to consummate. There has been notable progress in many areas and several clear indications that the results will justify the costs, but the dreams of quick success are gone. The reality of the need for great insight and more careful evaluation is apparent.

PART I
EXPERIENCES IN LIBRARY AUTOMATION

The efforts to use machines in the library began long before computers or even punch-card equipment became available. The limited but nonetheless real success of early equipment simply accelerated the efforts and accented the interest. The introduction of computers for scientific computation and for commercial record keeping in the early 1950s brought the possibilities for substantial mechanization to the attention of libraries. The introduction of improved process capabilities and of random-access storage in the early 1960s marked the beginning of a decade of intensive mechanization efforts and the prelude to automation.

The 1970s offer promise of meaningful automation if the methods of information technology can be adapted to the needs of the library. The first and foremost problem is to determine *what* the library is trying to accomplish in terms that can be related to *how* the available and prospective technology can be used.

A variety of experiments, some monumental failures, and many worthwhile advances have provided sufficent experience to indicate that a library is not one but three systems and that the needs and opportunities for mechanization and automation are revealed in:

1. *Technical processes* that are directly concerned with the acquisition of library materials, their cataloging in preparation for later use, and reference to the accumulated holdings
2. *Control processes* that are applied to the resources employed by the library, the handling of library materials, and processing of data about them
3. *Administrative processes* concerned with the organizational structure of the library and its operational activities

These processes are applicable to every library and to every library data system—manual, mechanized, or automated. They are especially critical when integrated control is to be established over both the administrative and technical processes.

The technical processes of acquisition, cataloging, and reference are the most fundamental of library functions. By comparison, control and administration are reflections of the institutional attributes of the library whereas the technical processes relate to its reason for being.

The acquisition function seeks to discover what materials exist that might fulfill the library's objectives, to select and order those best suited to the library's purposes that have not yet been acquired, to receive shipments, to claim all materials that fail to arrive, to preserve and replace the holdings, and to process the materials to the cataloging function.

Acquisitions mechanization has been very popular. Interest in further progress and eventual automation is strong for several reasons. There are many apparently similar uses of computer-based data systems in business and industry, and many people have encouraged librarians to borrow the techniques and devices that have been successful. Librarians are attracted to mechanized and automated acquisitions by the obvious advantages in eliminating typing of book orders, consolidating many individual files, producing multiple copies of the current consolidated file or portions thereof for automatic claiming, monitoring service being rendered by various suppliers, and providing statistics about all phases of acquisitions work. The jobbers and publishers with whom libraries deal are also turning to machines to supplant manual data processing for reasons of speed and economy. There will be savings in time, money, and scarce talent for the libraries that can make common use of the standard numbering system, computer-to-computer communications, and other devices and techniques.

The cataloging function seeks to describe individual and collective characteristics of the items, the sources of their creation, their physical embodiment, their location, and their possible future interest. The essential purpose is to inform potential users of the existence and character of the item. In so doing, cataloging forms new combinations of ideas and data and thereby adds to the body of recorded knowledge. Inevitably, cataloging influences the very processes it serves.

Mechanization and automation experience has touched on all the areas of technical processes, but most time and effort have been devoted to cataloging. The national libraries have been instrumental in advancing the broadest concerns for national library services. The British Museum Library of England, the Deutsche Nationalbibliothek of Germany, and the National Library of Canada have made noteworthy contributions to their countries and to worldwide library concerns. The universities have been aggressive in their quest for better library service for a rapidly growing student population.

In the United States, the Library of Congress led the major efforts beginning with an original definitive study of automation[1] and culminating in an established standard for computerized cataloging in the MARC (Machine-Readable Cataloging) program. The work of the National Library of Medicine in its MEDLARS (Medical Literature Analysis and Retrieval System) program, although concentrated on the analysis of medical journal literature for *Index Medicus,* has provided a significant operational prototype. Other aspects of the national concern are reflected in active programs at the National Agricultural Library (N.A.L.) and the Library of the U.S. Department of the Interior. The results of these cooperative and complementary efforts will be important to automation of technical processes in all libraries.

The work of many countries is exchanged and enhanced by international cooperative efforts such as the Anglo-American Conference on the Mechanization of Library Services held at Oxford University in 1966 and the activities of the International Federation for Documentation (FID).

The American Library Association provides a sustained contribution through the activities of its Information Science and Automation Division, the publication of the *Journal of Library Automation,* and many articles in other journals of the Association. The American Society for Information Science and its journal and the Special Libraries Association, with its *Special Libraries,* have been actively publishing articles on library automation for many years, and their members have made major contributions in the

[1] U.S. Library of Congress, *Automation and the Library of Congress,* 1963.

concept, development, and testing of many mechanization and automation applications. Automated cataloging owes much to pioneering libraries such as in the University of Illinois in Chicago, Stanford University, Harvard University, Florida Atlantic University, and the University of Chicago.

The reference function seeks to fulfill the ultimate goal of the library—to make accessible to an inquiring mind the accumulated knowledge of other minds and times.

The inclusion of reference work in technical processes is at variance with the traditional approach, which has grouped public service areas together. In practice, reference librarians are more concerned with cataloging and acquisitions than with circulation, and in the automated library the reference librarian is a key user of automated records. The professional nature of reference work also relates more closely to book selection, cataloging and classification, and the bibliographic aspects of library work than to the control processes such as circulation, inventory, and work control.

Both book selection and reference assistance can benefit greatly from rapid and precise data processing and ready access to computerized records of all kinds. The widespread availability of the catalog by printed or visual display, bibliographic listings, and computer control of certain reference materials and statistics are of particular interest to the reference librarian. Reference works are now appearing in machine-readable form, and the reference librarian is entering a new phase as an information retrieval expert. Dialogue with the user of the library has always been a problem, but also a vital process; dialogue with the computer and, more importantly, dialogue with the data by means of the computer and communications network will become a common experience. In due time, the veteran librarian will have to introduce the user to the computer for the most successful treatment of the question at hand.

In the technical processes area, librarians are concerned with the large problem of converting existing records into a machine-readable store. These records have been created over a period of many years by a corps of people using changing rules. The records are not accurate and often reflect the lack of inventory effort in the very large libraries. This problem is compounded when related libraries, such as in the City University of New York, try to develop a common computerized record. All units contributing to a store must maintain certain standards, and they must abide by the basic structure of the system. Once this is accomplished, each unit benefits greatly, as does the total system. As in regular input to a computer record, accuracy is a necessity. The newer equipment for input is helping to attain this accuracy by allowing recognition and correction of errors before the copy gets into the computer. On-line correction of the record is to be welcomed.

Output from the computer record has been a major concern to libraries because of the cost of handling "hard copy" printed output. Economical "soft copy" displays using cathode-ray tubes (CRT) or televisionlike devices offer promise of fast and economical output, but printed copy will always be with us. Print image storage on microforms and ultramicroforms is much more compact than hard copy storage and simplifies wide distribution. Miniprint and regular hard copy can be obtained, but microforms, with suitable viewers, are acceptable substitutes for hard copy in certain applications such as union catalogs.

The control processes apply to technical processing as well as administration and public services.

Resource control concerns personnel, funds, space, and equipment and is closely related to the administrative processes. Personnel data which are stored in the computer can be sorted, rearranged, and summarized to yield the kind of information that is not now available even though the data are in the manual files. Information in library budgets and funds within the budget must be provided in a variety of ways. The library's needs differ from those of the business office, and this must be considered in structuring the access methods to the computer store of fund data. The burden of the complexities of space usage and allocation can be reduced by routine data processing. Equipment inventory is a considerable matter in a library, with tables, chairs, stacks, typewriters, etc., having to be accounted for at regular intervals. Computers are already helping with this and promise to do much more.

Processing control covers bibliographic inventory, work control in the processing area, and serials control. It applies to the movement and storage of all library materials from first receipt to final disposition, and it provides the basis for all inventory and location controls as well as the means to systematic control of work flow, department workloads, and personnel allocations.

Serials control is an important problem in most libraries. The continuing process of receipt and the continuing need for follow-up and claiming for issues not received are sufficiently different from the usual processes to introduce numerous opportunities for loss of control and of accuracy.

In this regard, serials control involves some of the time constraints of industrial and commercial inventory control while retaining all the special aspects incident to the distinguishability and uniqueness of each item. Copies of the serials record are needed in many places for many purposes and should be accurate and current. Each branch of a large library or library system can have a union serials list for its system and for nearby systems through interchange of lists, but printed lists are clearly an imperfect means for distributing the needed data. Supplementary data are provided by frequent current serials lists with up-to-date receipt information, claiming notices, statistics on serials service, binding information, aid in routing serials, serials circulation information, and serials orders. The record can also show which serials are indexed and by what indexing service, which have their own indexes as a help in determining which serials will be kept, which will be bound, and perhaps, which even need to be checked in.

Circulation control includes circulation, bindery, reserves, shelf reading and inventory, handling of overdues and fines, and hold requests.

The common image of a library is of an unchanging place with everything in its proper location, also unchanging. This is a false image. A library has a constantly changing inventory problem. Library materials circulate, are used in the library, go to the bindery, are reclassified, move to new shelf locations with expansion of the collection, and continually change location in many other ways. The problem is further complicated by the unique character of each item and the frequent need for identifying it briefly with a reader, who is also unique in his needs.

The computer, with its great capacity for filing and sorting, can help in the processing of inventory data of both library materials and equipment. Circulation, shelf reading, and checking periodical shelves for bindery preparation are all inventory processes of a sort. Circulation control can be automated to eliminate filing of book cards and slipping, to reduce errors through automatic reading of book and reader identification information, and to speed the book back to the shelf. Overdue notices can be automatically produced and circulation data made widely available through listings and displays. With on-line access to the data, reserve work in academic libraries will come under computer control for the first time, giving a more accurate picture of that important segment of circulation work.

Inventory of the library holdings is a difficult and complex problem, and new techniques to simplify the annual chore are badly needed. Special devices and machine-readable numbers for each piece and for each area promise some relief.

The administrator must have his finger on the pulse of the entire library. Immediate access to records about the activities in finances, personnel, circulation, acquisition, serials, cataloging, and reference would be of great use to any administrator. Misunderstandings by users of the library, brought to the administrator in a sometimes forceful way, could often be straightened out by prompt and accurate access to basic records. Judgment on awarding contracts to jobbers, preparation of budgets, planning of facilities and personnel, and other activities are dependent upon data, and the the busy administrator can be assisted and supported by good accessible records.

It is a curious thing that library interest in automation has centered on those aspects of the library's work which are least familiar to computer people: circulation, serials control, and cataloging. Most help has been given by the computer people in book ordering and fund control, and this has often been in situations where the computer center serves not only the library but also the business office and registrar. In some businesses, such as insurance and credit companies, patron files are common, but libraries do not seem to have gained from the experience. Inventory control by computer is commonplace, but not simple, in every large company, and the techniques, suitably adapted to the library environment, will be of increasing benefit. Library experience usually comes from computer applications to one phase of the library's work. Sometimes this is related to a plan that speaks for complete automation, but unfortunately it is not usually a complete plan.

Libraries are forever adapting to their own uses equipment that has not been designed for libraries. They have often done this cleverly and have contrived ways of making the equipment very useful. With the advent of the computer, history is repeating itself. The scientists and engineers have their own grand designs which do not always relate to the pleas of the marketing people who often see the customers' needs more clearly. Fortunately, the general-purpose digital computer is admirably suited to the logical demands of many library requirements. Peripheral equipment, such as input and output devices, needs to be more specialized and probably will be provided soon after it becomes clear just what is needed.

GLOSSARY

ABSTRACT: an epitome or summary of a document. An abstract may be locative, illative, indicative, or informative to specify the place where the original document may be found, to specify the general nature of the material in the document, to specify all pertinent material in and about the original document, or to outline the content of the original document.

ACCESS: (1) a device or method whereby a document may be found. (2) Permission and opportunity to use a document. (3) A coordinate for finding a document.

ACCESSION: to register acquisitions.

ADDED ENTRY: a secondary entry—that is, any entry other than the main entry.

ALPHABETIC SUBJECT CATALOG: a catalog limited to subject entries and the necessary references, alphabetically arranged.

ALPHABETIC-CLASSED CATALOG: a catalog with entries under broad subjects alphabetically arranged and subdivided by topics in alphabetic order.

ANALYTICAL SUBJECT ENTRY: a subject entry for part of a work, sometimes also called an *analytic.*

ANNOTATED: supplied with annotations—that is, critical notes and commentaries.

AREA SEARCH: an examination of a large group of documents to segregate those documents pertaining to a general class, category, or topic. Screening.

ARRANGEMENT: order of index terms or items of information in a system.

ARRAY: (1) an ordinal arrangement of informational materials. (2) A set of mutually exclusive coordinate subclasses totally exhaustive of a class, derived by its division according to some one characteristic.

ASYNDETIC: without cross references, said of a catalog.

AUTHOR ENTRY: catalog entry under the name of the author or under the heading which, according to the rules for author entries, corresponds to it.

AUTO-ABSTRACT: to select an assemblage of key words from a document, commonly by an automatic or machine method, for the purpose of forming an abstract of the document.

AUTO-ENCODE: to select key words from a document by machine for the purpose of developing search patterns for information retrieval.

AUTO-INDEX: to select key words from a document by machine for the purpose of developing index entries.

AUXILIARY PUBLICATION: the process of making data available by means of specially ordered microforms or photocopies. Auxiliary publication usually presupposes that the materials have not been published before, though the term is sometimes applied to publication of out-of-print books.

AUXILIARY SYNDESIS: the accessory apparatus, e.g., cross reference, which is used to supplement indexing sequence so as to reveal other relations.

BATTEN SYSTEM: a method of indexing invented by W. E. Batten, utilizing the coordination of single attributes to identify specific documents. Sometimes called the "peek-a-boo" system because of its method of comparing holes in cards by superimposing cards and checking the coincidence of holes.

BIBLIOGRAPHY: (1) an annotated catalog of documents. (2) An enumerative list of books. (3) A list of documents pertaining to a given subject or author. (4) The process of compiling catalogs or lists.

BOOK NUMBER. a symbol, usually consisting of a combination of letters and figures, which serves to identify a given book among others bearing the same class number and, at the same time, to place books bearing the same class number in the desired order on the shelves, by author, title, edition, and the like. When used to arrange books alphabetically by author, it is called author number or author notation.

BOUND: (Coordinate indexing). joined in modification of the meaning of a commonly used term. For example, "free energy" is a *bound* term (unit concept) while "free" and "energy" may be *free* terms in the same coordinate indexing system.

BROWSABILITY: the degree to which an indexing system lends itself to unsystematic or random searches. This ability is of interest or use to the searcher even though it may not produce a logical answer to the search question.

BROWSE: to investigate, without design, the contents of a collection of books or documents.

CALENDAR: a chronologically arranged sequence of documents pertaining to a single author, subject, series, or class.

CALL NUMBER: the class number and the book number by which the location of the book on the shelf is indicated.

CARD CATALOG: a catalog made up of cards, each usually bearing a single entry. The card catalog is to be distinguished from the printed catalog, in book form, and the sheaf catalog, which consists of sheets brought together in portfolios.

CATALOG: (1) a register or compilation of items arranged methodically, usually with sufficient description to afford access. (2) To register or compile a list of documents with sufficient description to afford access.

CATCHWORD INDEX: one which uses a significant word from a title or text to index an item.

CATEGORY: (1) a comprehensive class or description of things. (2) A logical grouping of associated documents. (3) A class or division formed for purposes of a given classification. In faceted classification special distinctions are made between categories, classes, facets, and phases.

CHAIN INDEX: an alphabetic index wherein a heading is provided for each term or link for all the terms used in a subject heading or classification.

CHECK LIST: an enumeration of documentary holdings with a minimum of organization and bibliographic information.

CLASS: (1) a group having the same or similar characteristics. (2) A major subdivision of a category.

CLASS NUMBER: a symbol applied to a book, etc., indicating the class to which it belongs in the classification system used by the library.

CLASSED CATALOG: a catalog arranged by subject according to a systematic scheme of classification. Also called "class catalog," "classified subject catalog," and "systematic catalog."

CLASSIFICATION: a distribution into groups. A systematic division of a group of related subjects. A schedule for the arrangement or organization of documents.

CLASSIFICATIONIST: one who makes classification schedules. A theorist who organizes and divides documents according to a specific criterion.

CLASSIFIED INDEX: an index characterized by subdivisions of hierarchic structure. An index using or displaying genus-species (class-subclass) relationships.

COINCIDENCE: intersection or conjunction of two or more concepts.

COLLECTION: when a group of items is brought together connoting a common set, it is dubbed a "collection," and the term "collection" itself implies some orderly storage, often chronologically by size, class, or subject.

COLON: (1) a device used in the UDC (Universal Decimal Classification) to link related class terms. (2) A device used in Colon Classification to separate successive foci. Later, in Colon Classification, a device to introduce the energy facet.

COLON CLASSIFICATION: a faceted classification scheme developed by S. R. Ranganathan.

COMPENDIUM: an abbreviated summary of the essentials of a subject—specifically, a book containing such treatment.

CONCEPT COORDINATION: (1) the use of documentation techniques employing analysis and indexing of items in terms of elemental unit concepts (rather than in terms of either hierarchic or free combinations of concepts), thus permitting retrieval of information by means of the flexible combining (coordination) of concepts during retrieval. (2) A system of multidimensional indexing with single concepts to define a document uniquely.

CONCORDANCE: an alphabetic list of words and phrases appearing in a document, with indications of the context of such words and phrases in the text.

CONJUNCTIVE: pertaining to the joining or coupling of two documents, words, phrases, or elements of information to express a unity. Being neither disjunctive nor collateral.

COPY: (1) a reproduction of a document. (2) To reproduce information in a new location replacing whatever was previously stored there and leaving the source of the information unchanged. (3) To duplicate.

CORPORATE NAME: the name of a corporate body as distinguished from the name of a person.

CORRELATION: (1) a systematic or reciprocal connection—sometimes, the establishment of a mutual or reciprocal relation. (2) Physically or statistically relating items which have a high degree of association.

CORRELATIVE INDEX: an index enabling selection of documents or cross references to them, usually unrelated by hierarchic organization, by correlation of words, numbers, or other symbols.

CROSS REFERENCE: a reference or direction made from one term or one part of an index to another related term or part.

DESCRIPTOR: (1) an elementary term. (2) A simple word or phrase used as a subject.

DEWEY DECIMAL CLASSIFICATION (DC): classification system developed by Melvil Dewey and used extensively to determine the arrangement of books on library shelves.

DICTIONARY: (1) words arranged alphabetically and usually defined. (2) A lexicon in alphabetic order.

DICTIONARY CATALOG: a catalog in which all entries are interfiled to form a single alphabet, as in a dictionary.

DIMENSIONAL STABILITY: the quality of retaining dimensions with varying conditions of temperature, humidity, etc.

DOCUMENT: (1) an instrument having recorded information regardless of its physical form or characteristics. (2) Recorded and grouped information capable of being handled and read by human beings.

DOCUMENT CARD: a unit card. A card carrying all the bibliographic and index information for an item. Used in edge-notched card systems as well as in serially searched files.

DOCUMENTATION: (1) the science of collecting, storing, and organizing recorded informational materials or documents for optimum access. (2) Includes the activities which constitute special librarianship plus the activity or distribution. (3) Selection, classification, and dissemination of information. (4) The science of ordered presentation and preservation of the records of knowledge serving to render their contents available for rapid reference and correlation. (5) The procedure by which the accumulated store of learning is made available for the further advancement of knowledge. (6) The art of facilitating the use of recorded, specialized knowledge through its presentation, reproduction, publication, dissemination, collection, storage, subject analysis, organization, and retrieval. (7) Collection and conservation, classification and selection, dissemination and utilization of all information.

DUPLICATE ENTRY: entry of the same subject matter under two distinct aspects of it.

EDITION: the whole number of copies of a publication printed at any time or times from one setting up of type. An impression, issue, or printing is the whole number of copies printed at one time.

ENTROPY: the unavailable information in a group of documents. The degree of disorganization in an informational assemblage.

ENTRY: (1) a record of a document in a catalog, list, or index. (2) A posting.

ENUMERATIVE CLASSIFICATION: a classification based on a list of the individual subjects to be included.

EPITOME: a concise summary; a brief statement of the contents of a work.

FACET: an aspect of orientation of a topic.

FACETED CLASSIFICATION: classification schemes whose terms are grouped by conceptual categories and ordered so as to display their generic relations. These categories of "facets" are standard unit-schedules, and the terms, or rather the notation for the terms from these various unit-schedules, are combined at will in accordance with a prescribed order of permutation or combination.

FACSIMILE: (1) a precise reproduction of an original document; an exact copy. (2) a hard-copy reproduction.

FALSE-DROP: (1) a citation that does not pertain to the subject sought. An alien, usually in a manipulative or coordinate index. (2) A document identification irrelevant to the question because of extraneous combination of descriptors.

FEEDBACK: partial reversion of the effects of a given process to its source. Control of a system by the output of the system—that is, a self-correcting or self-compensating control.

FICHE: a card:

FREE: (Coordinate indexing). Alone, not bound or joined to a separate modifier. See *bound.*

FUNCTOR: a logical element which performs a specific function or provides a linkage between variables.

GAP: a hiatus in a collection, commonly of serials or regularly issued proceedings.

GENERAL REFERENCE: a blanket reference in an index or catalog to the kind of heading under which one may expect to find entries for materials on a certain subject or entries for particular kinds of names. Also called "general cross reference" and "information entry."

GENERIC: pertaining to a genus or class of related things.

GENERIC TREE: index terms arranged by increasing or decreasing specificity (generality), for example, human, man, boy, Larry.

GENUS: a class of similars divisible into two or more subordinate classes or species.

HEADING: the word, name, or phrase at the beginning of an entry to indicate some special aspect of the document (authorship, subject content, series, titles, etc.).

HIERARCHIC: (1) arranged in serial rank rather than ordinal position. (2) Pertaining to a generic classification or organization of materials.

HIT: term used in mechanized retrieval systems to represent an apparent answer found by the machine.

IMPRINT: (1) the place of publication, the name of the publisher, and the date. (2) The title, author, and other information stamped on the spine of a book.

INDEX: (1) a file of locators for documents or information. (2) That which specifies, indicates, or designates the information, contents, or topics of a document or a group of documents. Also a list of the names or subjects referring to a document or group of documents. (3) To prepare an organized or systematic list which specifies, indicates, or designates the information, contents, or topics in a document or group of documents.

INDEX ENTRY: the part of an index which covers a specific index term.

INDEX FILE: data used to represent the collection of items and their contents and define a location of information in the collection. An index should be more manageable (smaller) than the collection itself and its growth rate should be less.

INDEX TERM: a word or phrase used to designate a concept.

INDEX TRACING: all the index terms listed concerning one item.

INDEXING: (1) indexing pertains to the process of implementing and maintaining the index file to the collection. (2) The task of relating information in a document to the procedure and methods of searching.

INTERCALATE: to file or insert, as in a card catalog.

INTERFIX: a device to signal relationships between concepts. Thus for a series of compounds $A, B, C, \ldots$, insertion of the interfixes 1 and 2 (for example, $A_1, B_1, B_2, C_2, \ldots$) signals that the compounds with the same numerical interfix are in one mixture and those with a different one are in a different mixture.

ITEM: (1) in an index, the reference to the document. (2) A unit of correlated data relating to a single entity such as a person or a document, or an object or a class of objects. (3) A generic term for a document or other record. (4) Any set considered as a single unit for indexing purposes. (5) Since a document can be described in so many specific ways, the word "item" has been applied to include anything which can be indexed.

KEY: a group of characters which identifies a record or item.

KEY WORD: grammatical element which conveys the significant meaning in a document. A word indicating a subject discussed in a document.

KEY WORD IN CONTEXT INDEX: a listing, usually of titles or significant sentences from an abstract, with the key words put in a fixed position within the title or sentence and arranged in alphabetic order in a column.

KWIC: an acronym which stands for "key word in context." Listings are made by the key word in the title.

KWIC INDEX: an abbreviation for key word in context index.

KWOC: an acronym which stands for "key word out of context." Listings are made by the key word followed by the full title.

LANGUAGE: (1) a defined set of characters which are used to form symbols, words, etc., plus the rules for combining these symbols, words, etc., for meaningful communication; e.g. English, Russian, etc. (2) In particular, a combination of a vocabulary and rules of syntax.

LATTICE: the network of interrelationships between specific subjects.

LEXICON: an ordered vocabulary with definitions. When the alphabet is used to order the vocabulary, the lexicon is a dictionary.

LIBRARY OF CONGRESS CLASSIFICATION (L.C.): classification scheme developed by the Library of Congress to arrange its collection.

LITERATURE SEARCH: a systematic and exhaustive search for published material bearing on a specific problem or subject, with the preparation of abstracts for the use of the researcher; an intermediate stage between reference work and research, and differentiated from both.

LOG: a registry of items, e.g., an accession list.

MAIN ENTRY: a full catalog entry, usually the author entry, giving all the information necessary to complete identification of a work. In a card catalog this entry bears also the tracing of all the other headings under which the work in question is entered in the catalog.

MANIPULATIVE INDEX: an index in which manipulation other than turning pages, reading entries, following cross references, and locating documents is necessary. Mechanized indexes using punch cards, and the various coordinate indexing systems are examples.

MARC: Machine-Readable Cataloging (Library of Congress acronym).

MICROCOPY: a facsimile of substantially reduced size. A microtext.

MICROFORM: a generic term for describing any miniaturized form containing microimages. Microcards, microfiche, microfilm, and aperture cards are all microforms.

MICROPRINT: printing, reproductions of printing, or other documents of reduced size on opaque paper.

MNEMONIC: assisting or intended to assist human memory. A mnemonic term is usually an abbreviation and thus should be easy to remember.

MODULANT: an interfix; a standardized suffix added to the root of a word (Ruly English) to bring out the different aspects of a word's basic meaning (U.S. Patent Office).

NOTATION: an arbitrary device to indicate the contents or location of a document.

OFFPRINT: a separate; an excerpt, as a magazine article, separately printed.

OPEN-ENDED: (1) unlimited vocabulary of a system. (2) Being possessed of the quality by which the addition of new terms, subject headings, or classifications does not disturb the preexisting system.

PAMPHLET: a short work commonly bound as a single fascicle and published as a separate issue. Unlike a reprint or separate, a pamphlet is not a part of a larger work.

PERMUTED INDEX: an index in which key terms are selected from the title of a document and are displayed in the index in exact context with other words in the title. An index entry is made for each key word in the title.

PERTINENCE: pertinence is a factor which relates a retrieved item to its question, entered in a way which allows ordering of either items or questions in relation to each other.

POST: (1) to transfer an indicial notation from a parent or main entry to individual analytic entries; for example, to type the proper catalog entry and number at the top of a group of catalog cards. (2) (Coordinate indexing). To put the accession number of a document under each entry representing a coordination term.

QUALIFIED HEADING: a heading followed by a qualifying term which is usually enclosed in parentheses, e.g., Composition (Art), Composition (Law).

QUESTION: area, study, project, request, interest, query, search criteria.

RANK: a measure of the relative position in a series, group, classification, or array.

REDUNDANCY: use of more words or symbols than needed to convey the thought. An excess of rules and syntax whereby it becomes increasingly likely that mistakes will occur.

"REFER FROM" REFERENCE: an indication, in a list of subject headings, of the headings from which references should be made to the given heading; it is the reverse of the indication of a "see" or "see also" reference.

REFERENCE: (1) a direction from one heading to another. (2) An indication referring to a document or passage.

RELATIVE INDEX: an alphabetic index to a classification scheme in which all relationships and aspects of the subject are brought together under each index entry.

RETRIEVAL: (1) techniques of searching an index file or document collection for information. (2) The act of finding again, recovery, retrospective searching, and securing of documents. The act of going to a specific location and returning with an item.

RETRIEVALS, FALSE: the library references which are not pertinent to, but are vaguely related to, the subject of the library search and are sometimes obtained by automatic search methods.

ROLE: a code designator which indicates the use of an individual term in the tracing list of a document.

ROTATIONAL INDEXING: correlative indexing wherein each term is "rotated" so as to file in the first position.

RULY ENGLISH: English in which every word has one and only one conceptual meaning and each concept has only a single word to describe it. Terms proposed by S. Newman of the U.S. Patent Office to develop certain index codes.

SCAN: to examine every reference or every entry in a file routinely as part of a retrieval scheme.

SCOPE NOTE: a statement giving the range of meaning and scope of a subject heading or descriptor and usually referring to related or overlapping headings.

SEARCH: to examine a series of items until one with a desired property is found.

"SEE" REFERENCE: a reference from a term or name under which no documents are entered to that used in place of it.

"SEE ALSO" REFERENCE: a reference to a less comprehensive or otherwise related term.

SELECTIVE DISSEMINATION OF INFORMATION (SDI): a dissemination scheme which screens all input documents and automatically sends to each information user all documents relevant to his work.

SELF-ORGANIZING: capable of spontaneous classification.

SEMANTICS: word meanings.

SEPARATE: a reprint of special copy of an article, chapter, or other part of a larger publication. Distinguished from pamphlet in that it was originally issued in a larger publication.

SOURCE DOCUMENT: the original paper on which are recorded the details of a transaction.

SPECIFIC ENTRY: entry of a document under a heading which expresses its special subject or topic, as distinguished from the class or broad subject including that special subject or topic.

SPLIT CATALOG: a library catalog in which the different varieties of entry (e.g., subject, author, title) are filed in separate alphabets.

STRING: a sequence of characters without regard to the internal structure of the sequence; a group of sequenced items in a sort.

SUBJECT AUTHORITY CARD: a card which, in addition to citing the authorities consulted in determining the choice of a given heading, also indicates the references made to and from related headings and synonymous terms.

SUBJECT CATALOG: a catalog consisting of subject entries only.

SUBJECT HEADING: a word or group of words indicating a subject under which all material dealing with the same theme is entered in an index or catalog of bibliography or arranged in a file.

SUPPLIED TITLE: the title composed by the cataloger to indicate the nature and scope of the monographic work under study.

SYNDETIC: having entries connected by cross references. A coordination of two or more related documents.

SYNOPSIS: an essential summary of actions. In fiction, the argument of a story.

SYNTAX: relationship of words. The rules governing sentence structure in a language.

SYSTEM, PEEK-A-BOO: an information retrieval system which uses peek-a-boo cards, i.e., cards into which small holes are drilled at the intersections of coordinates (column and row designations) to represent document numbers.

SYSTEM, UNITERM: an information retrieval system which uses uniterm cards. Cards representing words of interest in a search are selected and compared visually. If identical numbers are found to appear on the uniterm card undergoing comparison, these numbers represent documents to be examined in connection with the search.

TAG: a unit of information which is a unique member of a restricted set used for the purpose of denoting some quality of associated information.

TAXONOMY: the science of classification. Also, the study of the names and naming of items in generic assemblies.

TELEGRAPHIC ABSTRACTS: a special abbreviated style of abstract, commonly considered suitable for machine input (used by J. W. Perry).

TELEREFERENCE: a method for consulting catalogs from a remote location, consisting of a closed-circuit television system for viewing the catalog, a relay for finding the part of the catalog to be examined, and mechanical handling equipment for moving the catalog cards or pages about.

TERM: (1) a word used in an index. (2) In an index, the subject heading or descriptor. (3) A term is used to describe an item for the purpose of storing it in or retrieving it from a storage and retrieval system. (4) Descriptor, variable, aspect, concept, characteristic, attribute, talent, parameter, value, data.

THESAURUS: a lexicon, more especially where words are grouped by ideas; a grouping or classification of synonyms or near synonyms; a set of equivalent classes of terminology.

TITLE ENTRY: the record of a work in a catalog or bibliography under the title.

TRACING: in a card catalog, the record on the main entry card of all the additional headings under which the work is represented in the catalog. Also, the record on the main entry card or on an authority card of all the related references made. In coordinate indexing, a listing of the descriptors, Uniterms, etc., applied to a specific document.

TRANSFORM: to derive a new body of data from a given one according to specific procedures, often leaving some feature invariant (e.g., "meaning").

TRANSLATE: to transform information (e.g., from one code to another or from one natural language to another) in a way which preserves meaning.

UNION CATALOG: an orderly compilation of the holdings of two or more libraries, presumptive of cooperation between the libraries.

UNITERM: a word, symbol, or number used as a descriptor for retrieval of information from a collection; especially, such a descriptor used in a coordinate indexing system. Related to *aspect card, descriptor, coordinate indexing, docuterm.*

UNITERM INDEXING: a form of index display developed by Mortimer Taube which utilizes single descriptors, called Uniterms, to define a document and which facilitates the manual coordination of these descriptors.

UNIVERSAL DECIMAL CLASSIFICATION (UDC): an expansion of Dewey Decimal Classification started by P. Otlet in Brussels. It is sometimes referred to as the Brussels system.

WEED: to discard currently undesirable or needless materials from a file.

CHAPTER 1
ACQUISITION

Acquisition is defined as the discovery, searching, selection, ordering, and receiving of all kinds of library materials, whether they be books, journals, films, newspapers, pamphlets, or microforms. Some of these processes are bypassed to some degree in the case of gifts, block purchases, blanket orders, government documents, college catalogs, and corporation reports, but a high proportion of library acquisitions do follow the entire routine.

DISCOVERY

Every library user, and certainly every librarian, discovers the need for certain items that are available in the vast array of materials being offered by publishers and distributors. This discovery may come through reading of reviews, conversation, perusal of the item itself, publishers' announcements, dealers' catalogs, bibliographies, library catalogs, or through personal knowledge of the work of the author. There are today more reviews; more conversation at more meetings; improved communications media; improved access to the items themselves through approval services, at convention exhibits, and at better bookstores; a plethora of attractive publishers' announcements coming through more efficient mailing lists; more and better dealers' catalogs made possible by higher book prices and improved means of producing the catalogs; significant new bibliographic sources produced by the new scholarship; commercially produced library catalogs of many fine collections; increased knowledge of who is doing what; increased travel by intellectually alert people; and increasing numbers of professional associations and their meetings providing opportunity for personal contact. Discovery of the existence of a publication through one or another of these contacts often results in a recommendation to the library for purchase. This leads to the "searching process" in the library.

SEARCHING

Searching has two goals: one, to find out whether the library already has the item, and the other, to find out where and when the item can be obtained and at what price.

Automatic searching hits its first roadblock in the notoriously inaccurate and incomplete form in which the requests are received. A well-designed data system can provide better access to bibliographic data for the requester and, carried to the ultimate, could make all requests perfect and searching completely automatic. In practice, there will always be a residue of requesters who will not bother to be accurate or complete, and they will require assistance. The searcher must use a wide variety of sources and considerable imagination just to obtain data usable in either human or machine processing. This involves the consultation of library-created files and other files, both of which are beginning to appear in machine-readable forms as reference and bibliographic tools. Library-created files include the shelf list, the catalog, the processing files, and the circulation files (including circulation, reserve, and bindery). The "other files" now include MARC (Machine-Readable Cataloging) tapes and *Books in Print* on tape as well as the *National Union Catalog* and the thousands of bibliographic and reference tools traditionally used in searching.

The hope is that the book is in print. If it is, the order process can begin. If the book is out of print, the usual procedure is to search catalogs of out-of-print dealers or to hire out the job of searching. If the job is done in the library, a computer record of out-of-print materials can be assembled from these catalogs, ready for searching and listing. Desiderata lists can be maintained in the computer for constant matching with the out-of-print computer file, and for exchange and order lists.

Searching is affected by the whole matter of blanket orders for all or part of a publisher's output and by special arrangements with jobbers, publishers, foreign dealers, and out-of-print agents. Unfortunately, all publishers do not honor blanket-purchase arrangements. The tendency in some cases for very popular titles is to use the existing supply for other outlets. One means of combating this would be an automatic check by the computer, using the *Books in Print* tape, asking that all titles listed by the publisher in question be checked against the library's records.

One jobber presently maintains selection profiles of certain libraries it serves and sends on approval all incoming books which fit these profiles. Another supplier has indicated that a return of a certain percentage of books supplied in this fashion indicates a need for revision of the profile in order to improve the service. If a library is part of a system of libraries which has a central store of bibliographic information in a computer, it would often be necessary to consult this record. New York and Ohio are planning statewide systems, the former for public libraries and the latter for college and university libraries. When these are completed and operating effectively, the participating libraries will find their searching problems greatly reduced.

SELECTION

Selection work can benefit greatly from an automated data system. The computer cannot, by itself, decide that a certain item should be chosen for addition to the collection. However, it can be instructed to prepare orders for items by certain publishers or for all items tagged as having plus reviews in *Choice, Kirkus, Booklist,* and other reviewing journals. Library of Congress (L.C.) MARC files and others which are tagged for display of author, date, language, and other bibliographic elements can also provide listings arranged according to the chosen elements for selection consideration. If one knows he wants all books coming out by a certain author, on a certain subject or combination of subjects, in a certain language, or published in a certain country, the computer-based system can be used to identify such books as they appear and automatically order them. The individual library stands to benefit from the size and quality of the machineable records available to it, whether through purchase of such records or availability because of the library's membership in a library system supplying such records.

The selector, whether he is a branch librarian, a professor in a building distant from the university library, a divisional librarian far from technical processes, or an engineer in an industrial laboratory, can benefit from remote access to library records. At the present time the important files needed in selection and order work are usually one of a kind and are not available to the public. The public catalog, the official catalog, the shelf list, the orders-outstanding file, the being-considered file, gift listings, and block-purchased listings are of interest to the selector because he must often assess the desirability of his item in terms of other similar things in the collection or on order. The lack of immediate availability of such files to the selector means that 25 percent or more of the requests come back marked "already in the library." The selector may be discouraged from contributing to the selection process by the need to go some distance to consult a large card catalog or to ask an acquisitions librarian for help even in a matter as important as planning a new course or developing a new area of collection.

The listing of gifts and block purchases, already mentioned, is greatly facilitated by a listing of author, title, date, and location code—needed input that is readily available.

The backlog problem in many libraries is assuming astonishing proportions. The computer can be used to help reduce this problem by the quick listing of less needed backlog material until more help is available for cataloging.

The problem of out-of-print books also faces the selector. *Books in Print* now appears in tape form. Many books not in print are becoming available through photographic reproduction. Perhaps a *Books Not in Print* list can be prepared on tape, at least for more recent titles. For hard to secure originals, dealers' catalog information could be fed in, with prices, to give a more up-to-date picture of the market. The decision to buy or not to buy an out-of-print book may depend on price and availability, acceptability, and availability of photographic reproduction. This information can be available to the selector quickly and easily through computerized data.

Selectors in libraries that belong to a system of libraries may be supplied computer-produced lists including titles from standing orders from a selection center. In the ultimate case, the selection process is completely centralized, and local library selection processes are eliminated.

The selector often needs up-to-date knowledge of the current status of the book budget, especially when considering purchase of an expensive item or a large number of items. If the library's business operations are automated, the book, periodical, and binding budget situation is immediately available by breakdown of the figures by branch and department and by comparisons with previous years' expenditures.

The statistical capability of the computer for analyzing library records offers further help to the selector. Usage statistics from automated circulation, for instance, can provide information indicating shortages or lack of use of certain classes of material. Statistics on time required to acquire and catalog a book can help in appraising the availability of the book for early needs. Statistics on relative expenditures for subject areas can be revealing of omissions or bias in meeting the holdings objectives.

ORDERING

Order work, as distinct from selection work, has many clerical tasks which lend themselves to automation. Such jobs as typing of book orders all day, every day, are tedious for humans but easy for the computer. Manual ordering requires a variety of files which must be maintained at considerable expense in time and effort and which are highly susceptible to filing errors. Order work done with a computer maintains one file for everything, and the computer does the filing. Location and status data can be updated as items move through work process, providing knowledge of each item's whereabouts and recording the time required for the completion of each process. Regular and frequent printouts or displays can provide access to any desired data without a need to consult closed files in nonpublic areas.

A wealth of statistics can be gleaned from a computerized order operation. Which jobber is giving the best service? Are promised discounts being given? How are departments and branches spending their money in relation to the fiscal year requirements? What proportion of orders are out of print? Is it better, timewise, to order through a foreign agent? These are examples of questions which can be better answered in a computer-based system than in a manual system.

RECEIVING

Receiving involves matching the items with the invoices accompanying the shipment, returning the wrong items, claiming missing items (after checking against a copy of the original order), and reporting damage. Property marks must be put on the items received as soon as possible to reduce the danger of pilferage. Separation of different kinds of materials takes place at the receiving point. Purchased books, serials, documents, gifts, and special materials are each treated differently in work process and must be identified as belonging to one group or another. This is commonly considered clerical work, but in a large library some of the demands for subjective judgment are formidable.

Gifts must be set aside for further consideration, as all items in a gift are seldom accepted for inclusion in the library's collection. Books received on approval must also be set aside. Following this consideration, the accepted items are incorporated into the appropriate groups listed above.

Rush status has to be indicated with appropriate follow-through in the work process. The computer can aid in assuring proper handling of rush items if rush status is indicated. Notes on progress through work flow can be reported frequently by the computer, thus helping to prevent stalling. Lists of the rush items which are destined for reserve use by an ordering professor might reveal that his students seldom read assignments or that he needs more copies for the more difficult and more lengthy reading assignments.

Nonarrival of an ordered item must be recognized in time to remedy the situation before it is too late. Automatic recognition can be achieved, providing the computer is instructed as to the time limits to be imposed. Between this recognition and the automatic claiming notice prepared by the computer, there should be manual intervention to determine the validity of the situation. A railroad strike, natural disasters, or some other valid reasons for delay can be considered by a member of the library staff appointed to review the claiming situation each day. The computer will write the claiming notices and alert the librarian of the "irregulars" situation. The latter, which come according to the convenience of the publisher, often do have a recognizable pattern of publication. The computer can print out an assessment of the "irregulars" condition at regular intervals, pinpointing those that should be evaluated.

In addition to claiming, the computer can store and make available for output a variety of acquisitions information. Each succeeding generation of equipment provides better output, both in quantity and quality. Each is having its effect on library methods and procedures, and there is every indication that each will have a more profound effect on the rate and amount of change in traditional library practices. The advent of readout from the computer record and the on-line updating of that record promise to decrease present worries about ways and means of improving printout and reducing costs of printout. In a large library, the concentration in one computer file of all data concerning items ordered but not yet in the catalog requires either frequent printout or readout capability. This printout can be a sizable list, and, if updated and brought out weekly, the cost will be substantial. Microfilm printout, with possible conversion to other forms, is potentially suitable for massive files, whereas slave typewriters operating from magnetic tape offer possibilities for shorter lists.

Computer-controlled photocomposition equipment, if already available for catalog printout, can be used very effectively in the acquisitions area since the need for upper and lower case and other typographical refinements is not as great as in cataloging. The number of outputs (printouts or readout stations) is not as great either. The release from unique files confined to work areas is a great thing, of course, and the more accessible the data can be in the main library or elsewhere, the better it is.

Accessibility to the computerized records in other libraries holds great promise since knowledge of what another library is buying can be very useful, especially in the case of rare and expensive items. Common support of an out-of-print data bank could eliminate searching of dealers' catalogs, and access to other libraries' processing files could alert the library to another library's acquisition of the item.

IDENTIFICATION

The assignment of sequential numbers to each item accepted for the library's collection must be made as soon as convenient. These unique control numbers may be assigned to all items to help in keeping track of their movement through work process and in everyday work after they have been processed. These numbers are for convenience of control and will remind the many librarians of the accession numbers which were convenient for many manual applications. Such numbers have been limited to books, but can and should cover all materials.

Identification for acquisitions also concerns the total input of data at the time of ordering and the accuracy with which the process can be accomplished. Althought MARC copy provides the information needed after the receipt of the item, it does not have all the data needed for acquisitions, such as price, supplier's name and mailing address, etc. A standard input code for acquisitions can supplement the MARC data. At present, coding sheets prepared by the acquisitions librarian are handed to a key-punch operator or a paper-tape machine operator. This is less satisfactory than typing onto magnetic tape, which makes visual proofing and correction procedures possible before input into the computer.

In addition to the sequential numbers needed for internal control mentioned above, consideration must be given to both the L.C. card numbers and to the book numbering system being developed by publishers both here and abroad. The latter, called Standard Book Numbering (SBN), has been developed through the cooperative efforts of the American Book Publishers' Council, A.L.A., and many other organizations. A booklet describing SBN[1] states, "There has been a general consensus that with the increasing use of computers in the ordering and supplying of books some kind of standard book numbering is both necessary and urgent. . . ." It was decided that it would be impossible to combine SBN with the L.C. catalog card number system because of the necessity of serving the publishers' internal needs and L.C.'s internal needs. The SBN is always nine digits in length, and the nine digits are always divided into three parts. The first part identifies the publisher, the second part, the title or edition (if there is more than one). The two parts always total eight digits. The third part, one digit, is called the check digit, which insures against error in manual transcription. The sample SBN given in the aforementioned Bowker booklet is 8436-1072-7, with 8436 identifying the publisher, 1072 the book, and the 7 serving as the check digit. (The most common form of check digit permits detection of an error in a single digit or transposition of two adjacent digits. To construct the

[1] *Standard Book Numbering,* Bowker, New York, *c* 1968, p. 13.

check digit, alternate digits are multiplied by 2 and added to the sum of all other digits. Then the units position is subtracted from 10.) A tenth digit for indicating country is being reserved for future developments. Present international collaboration includes England, which started a year earlier than the United States. Other countries have expressed an interest.

The L.C. card numbering system until recently has always had a seven-digit system starting with two digits for the year the cards were published. The new L.C. card numbers do not use the first two digits for the year. The importance of L.C. card numbers for library automation is the fact that they are entry numbers for using MARC tapes for computerized cataloging data. They are also useful, of course, for ordering cataloging data not on MARC tapes. L.C. has proved the usefulness of a numbering system for ordering L.C. cards, and this has provided impetus for development of the SBN for ordering books.

Although SBN is limited to books, there has been discussion[2] of unique numbers for serial titles and for articles appearing in serials. From the library point of view, numbers of issues, too, would be helpful for claiming missing issues and ordering duplicate issues.

The problem of the use of the SBN for internal library uses in an automated library has been posed. Numbers needed internally by the library for control purposes are assigned to many books not covered by SBN and to other library materials and need be only sequential numbers applied when the need arises. SBN was designed for publishers, and librarians can make whatever use of it they can.

SUGGESTED READING LIST

Brody, Arthur: "Bro-Dart Industries' Experience with Electronic Data Processing," *Proceedings of the 1965 Clinic on Library Applications of Data Processing* Graduate School of Library Science, University of Illinois, Urbana, 1966 pp. 65–78.

Cox, Carl R.: "The Mechanization of Acquisition and Circulation Procedures a the University of Maryland Library," in *IBM Library Mechanization Symposium,* Endicott, N.Y., 1964, pp. 205-236.

[2] ALA San Francisco Conference, luncheon sponsored by Bowker and Co., June 1967.

Culbertson, Donald S.: "The Costs of Data Processing in University Libraries: in Book Acquisition and Cataloging," *College and Research Libraries,* **24**: 487-498, November 1963.

Ferris, H. Donald: "Automated Procedures at Purdue University Library: Order Department," in Theodora Andrews (ed.), *Meeting on Automation in the Library—When, Where, and How, Purdue University, 1964, Papers,* Purdue University, Lafayette, Ind., 1965, pp. 39-42.

Flora, Betty: "High School Library Data Processing," *Journal of Library Automation,* **2**: 10-19, March 1969.

Hayes International Corporation: *Automated Literature Processing, Handling, and Analysis System—First Generation,* Redstone Scientific Information Center, Redstone Arsenal, Ala., 1967. AD 658081.

Heiliger, Edward: "Florida Atlantic University Library," *Proceedings of the 1965 Clinic on Library Applications of Data Processing,* University of Illinois, Urbana, 1966, pp. 92-111.

Kozlow, Robert D.: *Report on a Library Automation Project Conducted on the Chicago Campus of the University of Illinois,* University of Illinois, Urbana, 1966.

Minder, Thomas L.: "Automation—The Acquisitions Program at the Pennsylvania State University Library," in *IBM Library Mechanization Symposium,* Endicott, N.Y., 1964, pp. 145-156.

Moore, Evelyn A., Estelle Brodman, and Geraldine S. Cohen: "Mechanization of Library Procedures in the Medium-sized Medical Library: III. Acquisitions and Cataloging," *Medical Library Association Bulletin,* **53**: 305-328, July 1965.

Nelson Associates, Inc.: *Centralized Processing for the Public Libraries of New York State: A Survey Conducted for the New York State Library,"* Theodore Stein Co., New York, 1966.

Norris, Ned C.: "Computer Based Acquisitions System at Texas A and I University," *Journal of Library Automation,* **1**: 1-12, March 1968.

Rift, Leo R.: *Automation of Standing Order Acquisitions Procedures at Bowling Green State University,* Bowling Green, Ohio, 1966.

Schultheiss, Louis A.: "Data Processing Aids in Acquisitions Work," *Library Resources and Technical Services,* **9**: 66-68, Winter 1965.

Schultheiss, Louis A., Don S. Culbertson, and Edward M. Heiliger: *Advanced Data Processing in the University Library,* Scarecrow Press, New York, 1962, 388 pp.

Scott, Jack W.: "An Integrated Computer Based Technical Processing System in a Small College Library," *Journal of Library Automation,* **1**: 149-158, September 1968.

Stein, Theodore: *Centralized Book Acquisition for New York State; Proposed Computer System: Part 1, System Definition; Part 2, System Design, Submitted to the New York State Library by Theodore Stein,* New York State Library, Albany, N.Y., 1967.

Stevens, Norman D., ed.: "The National Program for Acquisitions and Cataloging: A Progress Report on Developments under the Title II C of the Higher Education Act of 1965," *Library Resources and Technical Services,* **12**: 17-29, Winter 1968.

Swenson, Sally: "Flow Chart of Library Searching Techniques," *Special Libraries,* **56**: 239–242, April 1965.

Warheit, I. A.: "File Organization of Library Records," *Journal of Library Automation,* **2**: 20–30, March 1969.

Wedgeworth, Robert: "Brown University Library Fund Accounting System," *Journal of Library Automation,* **1**: 51–65, March 1968.

CHAPTER 2
CATALOGING

The cataloger describes an item and indicates its logical place among thousands, perhaps millions, of other items. The description is intended to capture all the pertinent data about the item and to reveal its content, appearance, source, and relation to other items. The catalogers' description is, ideally, written with all present and future potential users in mind; the shortcomings of such message writing are obvious and serious.

This chapter is concerned with development of the library's cataloging records, with the experiences and potential uses of computer-based cataloging records, and with problems of conversion from a manual operation to a computer-based system. The library's cataloging records include the cataloging messages themselves; the author, subject, and title authority files needed for a properly structured catalog; and a method for filing the messages in a way acceptable to the user of the catalog. The use of the computer-stored record involves consideration of more subject depth, a variety of catalogs produced from one catalog record, multiple copies of catalogs for wide distribution, easier updating of the catalog record, and the use of other computerized stores of cataloging data.

STANDARDS

The national libraries typically provide the leadership in efforts toward standardization and mechanization in cataloging. The British MARC (Machine-Readable Cataloging) plan, the Deutsche Nationalbibliothek computerized catalog, and the work of the Bibliographical Institute at the Royal Library in Stockholm are notable examples. In the United States, the Library of Congress (L.C.) is the standard, but not the only, source for cataloging data. Depending on the type and size of the library, cataloging copy is available for 40 to 90 percent of their materials. L.C. copy is available from proof sheets, cards, the *National Union Catalog,* MARC computer tapes, and certain library journals. The *National Union Catalog* incorporates cataloging copy acceptable to L.C. for non-L.C. items that have been cataloged by cooperating libraries. For other non-L.C. cataloging, book-form catalogs of other libraries are becoming increasingly available. Local and regional banks of computerized cataloging data are now being created by groups of libraries using the MARC input format to standardize the input.

Traditionally, libraries have tended to alter cataloging copy to suit their own needs, arguing that their cataloging needs are not the same as those of the huge L.C. In the field of classification it is particularly true, but the present trend of libraries to convert to the L.C. classification indicates a willingness to go along with most aspects of that classification. Automation will provide the means and rising costs will provide the pressure to force libraries to use standard cataloging copy and to do less of their own tailoring. At last the specter of thousands of catalogers around the country cataloging the same books may diminish.

The L.C. has also taken the lead in standardizing cataloging data for input to computer records. This was done first on an experimental basis in the MARC I program. Toward the end of 1966 the first tapes containing machine-readable cataloging copy were sent to the sixteen libraries chosen to be MARC participants. Computer programs were provided to enable the libraries to print out a bibliographic listing with all tags and fields displayed, a brief author-title listing, and 3 by 5-in. catalog cards. For other output, the libraries had to provide their own programming. In a report issued in June, 1968, uses of the MARC tapes by the participants included production of book catalogs, catalog cards, and selected bibliographic listings. Bibliographic information about 44,000 English language monographs had been put into machine-readable form.

As a result of experiences with the MARC pilot experiment, the MARC input format has been improved. MARC II tapes became available on a commercial basis to all libraries in April, 1969 and with the experience of more libraries may develop into the prevailing input standard.

PROCEDURE

Cataloging of perhaps half or more of all items is done according to an elaborate set of rules called the Anglo-American Cataloging Code. This uniformity of method is important for library automation since it will make it possible for libraries to contribute to and draw from common data banks.

The catalogers' messages are traditionally written on a 3 by 5-in. card. The message includes a call number (classification number for subject plus an author number) used to place a book on the shelves near other books on the same subject. This is usually a unique alphanumeric code and sometimes quite long. The author's full name is also given, sometimes including his birth and death dates. The author's first initial and a short title may be included to provide a short author, short title listing. Place and date of publication, the name of the publisher, subject headings, series statements, number of pages, illustrations, maps, etc., are included when applicable. The L.C. card number is now the unique identifying number for MARC tape entry; non-L.C. cataloging now must also have unique numbers for entry to the library's data bank.

The catalog is now appearing in a variety of computer-produced formats in addition to the 3 by 5-in. card form. Book form is the most common of these, with various reductions in type size. Microfilm output from the computer provides a variety of microform catalogs as well as a new route to hard-copy format.

FILING

Library filing is a very complicated matter. The American Library Association (ALA) rules for filing fill a small book, and all the rules in the book are exceptions to the first rule. The University Library Information Systems (ULIS) Project at the University of Illinois in Chicago in the early 1960s determined that it was impractical to write programs which would enable the computer to file according to the ALA Filing Rules. During the fall of 1963 when the ULIS system was tried at Florida Atlantic University, several compromises were allowed, and the work was successfully completed. The filing used in the 1964 edition of the FAU computer-produced book catalog was found to be acceptable. The easy scannability of the pages of the book catalog helped make the simplified filing rules acceptable.

Catalog filing is largely a problem of adding the new items in correct sequence in both computer and manual filing, since deletions from the catalog record are relatively infrequent. Filing for circulation and acquisition is somewhat more difficult because of the dynamic character of these files. As the catalog grows larger, the input phase encompasses only new materials, whereas output increases as the size of the catalog increases. The General Electric study for the ULIS project emphasized the high cost of filing and maintenance in the card catalog. The shift of filing work to the computer was an important element in the estimate that the computerized library would cost approximately the same as a manual system but would offer many new services and make many old ones more efficient.

In manual filing, the librarian recognizes certain subtle features of the messages being filed and automatically compensates for them. In filing by title initial articles, the differences between *Mc* and *Mac,* Roman numerals, historical subdivisions, and other complicated filing matters are related in the brain of the filer. The computer does not offer a corresponding ability unless each and every aberration is identified and precisely accommodated in the program logic. *The* at the beginning of any title will be ignored in filing if the computer is told that this must be done. *Mc* and *Mac* can be together or apart, as one wishes, but the computer must be so instructed. Catalogers have themselves fought a battle against the increasing complexity of filing rules. Computer use will insist on simplification of the rules.

Computer filing offers unparalleled flexibility. If a library wishes to try an arrangement by date instead of by author under each subject heading, the computer can quickly make the shift. A manual change of a card catalog to accomplish this would be a major effort. In effect, the arrangement of the catalog can be by any elements or combinations of elements in the bibliographic entry.

DESCRIPTION OF SOURCE

Librarians have chosen the author as the key element in their message writing and the author's name as the main entry. Complications arise in choosing a consistent form for the author's name, whether the real name or pseudonym or a corporation, and in making appropriate cross references to the preferred form. Traditionally, librarians maintain "author authority" files which give the accepted usage for every author's name.

The publisher is the source of the document itself and is an important element in the cataloger's description. Publishers establish reputations for excellence in certain fields, and librarians must consider indication of the publisher as an important part of their message. Computerized cataloging makes it possible to use both the author and publisher as retrieval and output keys.

DESCRIPTION OF EMBODIMENT

The storage of millions of items of varying size, shape, and material creates tremendous problems for the librarian. If the cataloger describes each item with this in mind, such identification can help in solving some of the problems. Compact storage of seldom-used items may call for identification by size, so that items of like size can be put together. The cataloger recognizes that library materials appear as microforms, phonodiscs, audiotapes, sheet music, art prints, maps, manuscripts, and others and enters form facts in the message. Computerization of cataloging now makes it possible to sort any of these elements or combination of them and to produce unique listings hitherto unavailable. Listings of microform materials on seventeenth-century English literature, biographies of George Washington containing portraits, and available prints by Degas, all could be supplied.

DESCRIPTION OF CONTENT

The bibliographic elements provide the key to the content of an item being cataloged. Subject depth provides keys to the storage of knowledge, with the computer aiding the user in his search.

With capability of a subject approach to computerized cataloging, librarians have hoped for "see," "see also," "see from," and "see also from" cross references which would enable them to request the computer to build in appropriate cross references when a new subject was added.

The last edition of *Subject Headings Used in the Dictionary Catalogs of the Library of Congress* was published by the U.S. Government Printing Office using computer tape for printing control. The required programming was not well suited to a library with a computerized catalog, and reprogramming is underway to improve the compatibility. Some libraries, while waiting for this development, use the printed L.C. subject heading list with the book catalog to provide cross-reference aid.

The subject approach to computer-stored library data has developed a large literature of its own. This literature is concerned with ways and means of providing access to the knowledge stored in books and other storage media, as contrasted with the general subject identification provided by present library practices. This is not only a matter of depth of subject analysis but also of structuring the data in such a way that there can be an efficient dialogue between the user and the computer. The first obvious result of this structuring effort has been the creation of thesauri for special fields. These thesauri are essentially subject heading lists but include some elements of classification. This trend will probably continue but will eventually lead to a hierarchic superthesaurus, which will be usable by all. In the meantime, L.C., the National Library of Medicine, (N.L.M.), and the National Agricultural Library (N.A.L.) are cooperating in developing a common subject approach. N.L.M. with its MEDLARS (Medical Literature Analysis and Retrieval System) experience, L.C. with its MARC project, and the N.A.L. automation efforts should give this cooperative effort considerable computer orientation.

Librarians using the Dewey classification have always made use of the index to the classification as an aid in subject cataloging. The schedule outline, the G. K. Hall publication of the Boston University Library index, and the numbers indicated for some of the entries of the L.C. subject heading list are of some help. Computerization should be designed to provide a subject key for whatever classification scheme is used.

Much of the early effort devoted to cataloging automation by pioneering libraries was devoted to questions of content and tagging for retrieval. L.C. cataloging is overly elaborate for some types of libraries, such as school libraries and small public libraries, and not elaborate enough for many special libraries. The decision has generally been to accept L.C. cataloging as it is and tag it for the different uses to be made of it. In planning MARC, questions posed about tagging were concerned with possible approaches by many kinds of libraries, including the L.C. itself. The tagging has been designed so that a library user has an option of readout or printout listings by individual elements such as author, title, subject, date, publisher, etc., thus making MARC an adaptable standard for input of cataloging data for different kinds of libraries.

DESCRIPTION OF ENVIRONMENT

The cataloger has avoided incorporating nonbibliographic types of information in his output. The price of a book, the source of purchase, the type of binding, the use of plastic jackets, the physical condition of the book, loss rate, critical evaluations, and similar items of information have not been considered appropriate for cataloging purposes.

A new look at the information about each item of library material can provide new insights. Do we need answers to such questions as: Do books with plastic jackets wear better and circulate oftener than books without jackets? Should part of the record be a listing of critical reviews showing plus or minus ratings? Should each book have a short summary? Should separates from conferences, proceedings, prepapers, and even journal articles be treated as individual items by the catalogers? Should the number of analytics be greatly increased? Information of any sort added to the cataloging record can be correlated with other information to help the librarian to do a better job.

CONVERSION

The conversion of cataloging records from the present records stored on cards involves consideration of the accuracy of the present records, methods for converting the cataloging data into a form usable by the computer, consideration of the desired order of filing, and the decisions related to tagging the bibliographic data so as to provide the variety of outputs that will be required of the system.

Conversion of the cataloging records of a large library system to computer store is a costly, time-consuming task that must be planned with care. The steps in such a conversion start with editing and coding of the copy at hand. If the pressures of time and cost have restricted the work of catalog maintenance and updating, the copy may well have been produced decades ago by poorly trained catalogers using incomplete instructions under weak controls. Careful coding using a standard such as MARC II for the format keeps proofreading time down and the number of corrections to a minimum. The input process should allow preliminary proofreading at the input point and provide frequent proof copy to permit correction and control before the items being cataloged pass along the production line. On-line correction of proof is ideal for work flow and will undoubtedly become common practice. After the corrections have been made, the computer sorts and merges the new additions into the total record and conducts a limited editing job using stored authority files. The catalog is then ready for a wide variety of printouts. An extensive study of this process, with cost figures, is available in *Catalogs in Book Form*[1] by Cartwright and Shoffner.

The mechanics of conversion can start with microfilming the shelf list after hours. The resulting microfilm record can be reproduced on hard copy for use in editing and coding and should be kept as a safeguard until the computer record is complete. The computer catalog, when it is complete, can be duplicated at any time for safekeeping.

The condition of the catalog to be converted, the number of locations (in branches, departmental libraries, etc.) in which copies may be located, and labor costs in the area are pertinent cost factors. A study of conversion prospects for the City University of New York Libraries showed that conversion of the best libraries in the system first would greatly ease the job of converting the poorer and newer members of the system.[2] Sharing of a common store can make a significant difference in conversion costs. If the item has already been

[1] Kelley L. Cartwright and Ralph M. Shoffner, *Catalogs in Book Forms,* Institute of Library Research, University of California, Berkeley, 1967, 69 pp., illustrations.

[2] United Aircraft Corporate Systems Center, *Preliminary Job Description for Preparation of Union Catalog for CUNY,* technical proposal submitted to the City University of New York, United Aircraft Corp., Farmington, Conn., 1967.

cataloged elsewhere in the system, it need only be tagged to become a part of a new catalog. Coding, proofreading, and correction are eliminated.

PRESENTATION

The libraries have contributed to several significant developments in computer output. The *MEDLARS Story* describes the GRACE system in this way: "He pushes the START button and GRACE begins to 'set' type by extracting a line at a time in coded form from the magnetic tape, manipulating and decoding the information, and photographically recording composed three-column pages of INDEX MEDICUS on the film in the magazine."[3] The specifications for MEDLARS II, issued on July 1, 1967, indicate that GRACE will still be with us; "major MEDLARS publications are produced on GRACE (Graphic Arts Composing Equipment), a photocomposition device that converts information from magnetic tape into latent typographical images on photo-sensitive paper and film. . . . Since present plans call for retention of GRACE, the proposed system must be able to produce output typeset by GRACE."[4] GRACE has been recognized as a significant contribution to the printing business.

Another library contribution has been the development of the first upper/lowercase computer print chain. In 1963, the libraries at Florida Atlantic University, Yale University, and the University of Toronto cooperated with IBM in developing such a chain. The three libraries established eighty-eight common characters, and each library selected its own pattern for the remainder of the one-hundred-twenty-character set. This print chain doubled the time needed by the computer to print out, and there was a substantial monthly charge for the special circuitry needed to operate the chain on existing computers. A careful consideration of the real value of uppercase versus upper/lowercase presentation based on a user test at Florida Atlantic University

[3] U. S. Public Health Service, *The Medlars Story at the National Library of Medicine,* 1963, p. 46.

[4] *Function Systems Specifications for the National Library of Medicine,* prepared through the cooperative efforts of Auerbach Corporation and the Task Force for New Computer Implementation, National Library of Medicine, National Library of Medicine, Washington, 1967.

indicated a strong preference for uppercase only. The larger letters were easier to read in the predominantly finding-list kind of use of the catalog. The second edition of the FAU catalog in 1966, using the uppercase chain, was only half again as large, even though the number of titles was doubled. The larger type enabled the lines to be put close together without harming readability. One by-product of this was the discovery that it is easy to experiment with format for computer printout.

Paper printout from the computer has certain drawbacks, the chief of which are the limited number of copies (six), the awkward size of the folding sheets, and the slow speed (as compared with microfilm). The first objection can be overcome by using reproducing masters for duplication. The most interesting possibilities at the moment involve bringing computer copy onto microfilm and from there to various kinds of presentation. Several different systems are being introduced. Electron-beam recording provides printing speeds up to 30,000 lines per minute and encompasses uppercase, lowercase, boldface type, size variations, and the automatic merging of background graphics such as printed forms. The decoding and display of data from magnetic tape to the face of a cathode-ray tube (CRT) permit the use of photographic recording of 16-millimeter roll microfilm at rates up to 90,000 characters per second. With the microfilm in hand from either system, there are these possibilities: (1) use a microfilm high reduction catalog; (2) convert the microfilm to hard copy; (3) convert the microfilm to miniprint for copy resembling the miniprint edition of the British Museum Catalog; (4) convert to microfiche; or (5) convert to ultrafiche.

The present state of the art is not quite ready for everyday use of many CRT tubes for readout. Costs have not settled, and dialog methods are being developed. There is no doubt that in the future much of the consultation of the computer store of information will be handled this way. In the meantime, we must emphasize printout techniques.

Cost and use studies of all the possibilities are badly needed. Such studies promise to be difficult. What is the value to a user of having access to the catalog from a distant point? How much more cataloging can be done if the catalogers do not have to file (and revise filing) in the card catalog? How much time is saved in searching and checking reserve lists if the selector examines a remote-access catalog first? What values are lost if a reader depends on a convenient copy of the catalog and does not come to the library in person? Does the increased amount of browsing by catalog in the new environment make up for the browsing lost by not going to the library as often? With reference to this, perhaps widespread availability of catalogs actually brings more people to the library. Cost studies must have standardized methods so that comparisons can be made. The cost of cataloging a book may or may not include a small bit of the salaries of the head of technical services and the director of the library. Comparing cataloging costs is meaningless unless libraries use common approaches to their cost studies.

Decisions on the variety of output desired have caused interested libraries to reexamine the function of the catalog. The first question to be asked is, "Is the library catalog primarily a finding tool or a bibliographic tool?" The answer should be that it is both, but very largely a finding tool. The conclusion to be drawn from this is that much of the cataloging information is wasted on most users. Most readers can be satisfied with a one-line, short author, short title, date and call number entry. A computer catalog can have all items tagged for this short-form printout, thus greatly reducing the size, cost, and complexity for most users of the catalog. Frequent printouts in this format can also reduce the number of supplements to the catalog. This does not in any way reduce the amount of cataloging in store. It just permits a special kind of printout. The bibliographic needs can be satisfied by less frequent editions of the entire catalog and other bibliographic sources.

The approach to the catalog is by author, title, or subject. It is possible to list all materials by each of these approaches and interfile in one complicated order, called a dictionary catalog by librarians. It is possible to have separate catalogs for each approach or to combine authors and titles in one catalog and have subjects in another. The latter seems to hold more promise for computer catalogs by reducing the amount of programming needed for the complicated filing in a dictionary catalog. Authors and titles combined do not present much difficulty. It is possible to bring out catalogs of holdings in different subjects regularly or irregularly. This can be done by selecting pertinent subject headings and/or appropriate shelf list numbers and printing out all items listed under them. Time limitations can also be used to restrict the size of such special subject catalogs. In a field such as a rapidly developing science, materials older than a certain number of years would be harmful rather than helpful. Printout of bibliographies might have language, country, or even publisher restrictions, with the possibility of including only those items which have maps or illustrations, bibliographies and/or indexes, or which appear only on film, records, tapes, or in microforms. The experience of the N.L.M. has shown that subject bibliographies produced for customers from their MEDLARS computer records can be made available to other potential users at low cost.

Progress has been made on the main problems of the computerized catalog: filing, input methods, conversion techniques, standardization of the content, and improving output appearance, usability, and cost.

In *filing,* dividing the catalog has lessened the problem, and the book-form catalog has a scannable quality which makes it easier to use. The ability to present listings in order must include arrangements not only by author, title, and subject but also by date, publisher, and place. Other elements in the cataloging description such as maps, illustrations, etc., may also be involved.

Input methods are tending to avoid the keypuncher and his inevitable mistakes and to use machinery which will record directly onto magnetic tape or disc in a way that allows recognition of errors and correction of copy as the input is being prepared. The latter greatly lessens the proofreading job. Transposition of L.C. copy from MARC tape to the computerized cataloging store of the local library is a simple matter, easing the input problem for a considerable portion of the cataloging being accumulated by the local library.

Conversion of records is a matter of correcting and updating those records as well as of coding them for input. The existence of MARC now provides a format for the proper storage of the records and one that will be compatible with other libraries. The cost of conversion can be shared by cooperating libraries, each of which can take responsibility for preparing input for a segment of the whole.

Standardization of the content has also been achieved by MARC in such a way that each library using MARC will be able to decide on the selection it makes from the array offered by L.C. The effort by the national libraries to integrate the subject approach promises to provide a broader standard for subject matter. This will go hand in hand with the development of special subject thesauri, which will eventually be amalgamated with the national system to make a superthesaurus.

Improving output appearance, usability, and cost is of major concern, particularly cost. The most promising development in this area is the new capability to print out onto microfilm instead of paper at much greater rates of speed, thus saving a high percentage of computer time. Frequent complete new editions of the library catalog in various forms taken from the microfilm hold real possibilities. Output format can be changed easily for experimentation in achieving a better appearing and more usable catalog.

SUGGESTED READING LIST

Angell, Richard S.: "On the Future of the Library of Congress Classification," *Proceedings of the Second International Study Conference on Classification for Information Retrieval, Elsinore, Denmark, 14-18 September, 1964,* Munksgaard, Copenhagen, pp. 101-112, 118-119.

Artandi, Susan: *An Introduction to Computers in Information Science,* Scarecrow Press, Metuchen, N.J., 1968.

Avram, Henriette D.: *The Philosophy behind the Proposed Format for a Library of Congress Machine-readable Record,* Institute on Information Storage and Retrieval, University of Minnesota, Minneapolis, 1965.

Avram, Henriette D., and Julius R. Droz: "MARC II and COBOL," *Journal of Library Automation,* 1: 261-272, December 1968.

Balfour, Frederick M.: "Conversion of Bibliographic Information to Machine Readable Form Using On-line Computer Terminals," *Journal of Library Automation,* 1: 217-226, December 1968.

Becker, Joseph: "Using Computers in a New University Library," *ALA Bulletin,* 59: 823-826, October 1965.

Bregzis, Ritvars: "The Bibliographic Information Network, Some Suggestions for a Different View of the Library Catalog, Brasenose Conference on the Automation of Libraries, Oxford, England, 1966," in John Harrison and Peter Laslett (eds.), *Proceedings of the Anglo-American Conference on the Mechanization of Library Services,* Mansell, London, 1967.

Cartwright, Kelley L., and Ralph M. Shoffner: *Catalogs in Book Form: A Research Study of Their Implications for the California State Library and the California Union Catalog, with a Design for Their Implementation,* Institute of Library Research, University of California, Berkeley, 1967, 69 pp., illustrations.

Chapin, Richard E., and Dale H. Pretzer: "Comparative Costs of Converting Shelflist Records to Machine Readable Form," *Journal of Library Automation,* **1**: 66-74, March 1968.

Costello, John C., Jr.: *Coordinate Indexing,* Rutgers, New Brunswick, N.J., 1966.

Courtright, Benjamin: "The Johns Hopkins University Library," *Proceedings of the 1966 Clinic on Library Applications of Data Processing,* Graduate School of Library Science, University of Illinois, Urbana, 1966, pp. 18-33.

Cox, Nigel S. M., and Michael W. Grose: *Organization and Handling of Bibliographic Records by Computer,* Archon, Hamden, Conn., 1967.

De Gennaro, Richard: "A Computer Produced Shelf List," *College and Research Libraries,* **26**: 311-315, 353, July 1965.

Fasana, Paul J.: "Automating Cataloging Functions in Conventional Libraries," *Library Resources and Technical Services,* **7**: 350-363, Fall 1963.

Griffin, Hollis: "Automation of Technical Processes in Libraries," *Annual Review of Information Science and Technology,* vol. 3, Interscience-Wiley, New York, pp. 241-262.

Gull, Cloyd Dake: "How Will Electronic Information Systems Affect Cataloging Rules?" *Library Resources and Technical Services,* **5**: 135-139, Spring 1961.

Hammer, Donald P.: "Problems in the Conversion of Bibliographic Data—A Keypunching Experiment," *American Documentation,* **19**: 12-12, January 1968.

Heiliger, Edward: "Florida Atlantic University Library," *Proceedings of the 1965 Clinic on Library Applications of Data Processing,* Graduate School of Library Science, University of Illinois, Urbana, 1965, pp. 92-111.

International Business Machines Corporation: *Report of a Pilot Project for Converting the Pre-1952 National Union Catalog to a Machine Readable Record,"* Council on Library Resources, Rockville, Md., 1965.

Johnson, Richard: "A Book Catalog at Stanford," *Journal of Library Automation,* **1**: 13-50, March 1968.

Kilgour, Frederick G.: "Library Catalogue Production on Small Computers," *American Documentation,* **17**: 124-131, July 1966.

Kountz, John C.: "Cost Comparison of Computer versus Manual Maintenance," *Journal of Library Automation,* **1**: 159-177, September 1968.

Kozumplik, W. A., and R. T. Lange: "Computer-produced Microfilm Library Catalog," *American Documentation,* **18**: 67-80, April 1967.

Lazorick, Gerald J.: *Proposal for Conversion of Shelflist Bibliographic Information to Machine Readable Form and Production of Book Indexes from Shelflist,* State University of New York, Buffalo, N.Y., 1966.

Palmer, Foster M.: "Conversion of Existing Records in Large Libraries, with Special Reference to the Widener Library Shelflist, Brasenose Conference on the Automation of Libraries, Oxford, England," in John Harrison and Peter Laslett (eds.), *Proceedings of the Anglo-American Conference on the Mechanization of Library Services,* Mansell, London, 1967.

Perreault, Jean M.: "Approaches to Library Filing by Computer," *Proceedings of the 1966 Clinic on Library Applications of Data Processing,* Graduate School of Library Science, University of Illinois, 1966, pp. 47-90.

———: "Computerized Cataloging: The Computerized Catalog at Florida Atlantic University," *Library Resources and Technical Services,* **9**: 20–34, Winter 1965.

———: "On Bibliography and Automation: or How to Reinvent the Catalog," *Libri,* **15**: 287–339, 1965.

Phillips, Arthur H.: *Computer Peripherals and Typesetting,* Her Majesty's Stationary Office, London, 1968.

Richmond, Phyllis A.: "Note on Updating and Searching Computerized Catalogs," *Library Resources and Technical Services,* **10**: 155–160, Spring 1966.

Ruecking, Frederick H., Jr.: "Bibliographic Retrieval from Bibliographic Input: the Hypothesis and Construction of a Test," *Journal of Library Automation,* **1**: 227–238, December 1968.

Schultheiss, Louis A., Don S. Culbertson, and Edward M. Heiliger: *Advanced Data Processing in the University Library,* Scarecrow Press, New York, 1962.

Simonton, Wesley C.: "The Computerized Catalog: Possible, Feasible, Desirable?" *Library Resources and Technical Services,* **8**: 339–407, Fall 1964.

Stromberg, Donald: "Computer Applications to Book Catalogs and Library Systems," *Proceedings of the 1966 Clinic on Library Applications of Data Processing,* Graduate School of Library Science, University of Illinois, Urbana, 1966, pp. 195–210.

Swanson, Don R.: "Dialogues with a Catalog," *Library Quarterly,* **34**: 113–125, January 1964.

U. S. Library of Congress, *Automation and the Library of Congress,* Washington, 1963.

Warheit, I. A.: "File Organization of Library Records," *Journal of Library Automation,* **2**: 20–30, March 1969.

Weber, David C.: "Book Catalog Trends in 1966," *Library Trends,* **16**: 149–164, July 1967.

Weinstein, Edward A., and Virginia George: "Computer-produced Book Catalogs: Entry Form and Content," *Library Resources and Technical Services,* **11**: 185–191, Spring 1967.

Weiss, Irwin J., and Emilie V. Wiggins: "Computer-aided Centralized Cataloging at the National Library of Medicine," *Library Resources and Technical Services,* **11**: 83–96, Winter 1967.

CHAPTER 3
REFERENCE

The reference librarian is the chief user of the library's catalog and serials records, provides an important liaison function between the user and the library collections, and uses the entire collection in his search for information. The ability to understand the user's need and to find the appropriate messages to fill that need constitutes the essense of reference work. The user rarely asks his question in a specific manner, and the reference librarian must clarify requests ranging from the very simple to the impossibly complex. Careful judgment is required in making the decision on how to treat each question and how to convey the final result. The resulting dialog is important. Its techniques must be examined carefully by those expecting to develop successful dialog between the user and a computer store of information.

An important element of reference work is the reference collection of indexes, handbooks, manuals, encyclopedias, and other tools. The use and selection of these tools is a specialty of the reference librarian, and efficiency in their use goes hand in hand with ability to communicate with the library user.

REFERENCE SERVICE

The ability to extract bibliographies from a computerized record has great attraction for the reference librarian. There are frequent requests for a list of the books that the library has on a certain subject or combination of subjects or by a certain author. Such a list may have restrictions such as "only the books published in the last ten years" or "only books published in England on the subject" or "exclude all books in foreign languages." Such restrictions are no problem for the computer if proper structuring of the data was provided by the design.

The reference librarian should be an influential member of the library staff team which is considering how the system is to be used.

All elements of the bibliographic entry are available for all logical purposes, but not every library will want them all. To provide the ability to sort by language when the library has no interest in works other than in English would be foolish. The special library with intense interest in a small collection often makes decisions very different from those made by a large general library or a school library. The system must be designed to provide what is needed by each library from the available common data.

Bibliographies compiled for the reference librarian often are useful to others. The National Library of Medicine (N.L.M.), in its MEDLARS (Medical Literature Analysis and Retrieval System) project, has discovered this and circulates regularly a list of bibliographies such as the *Index to Dental Literature, Index of Rheumatology, Cerebrovascular Bibliography,* and other bibliographies that have resulted from search requests.

The many serials indexes, such as *Index Medicus, Readers' Guide to Periodical Literature,* the *Engineering Index,* and the *Education Index,* are important reference tools. Each refers to its respective serials in its own way, but reference librarians tend to favor segregation of serials from the general collection and arrangement in a way that is independent of the regular classification arrangement. To locate the file of a journal on the shelves with the books on the same subject requires a lot of walking in a big library. The individual user, however, can appreciate having the journals as well as the books on his subject in the same area. There are times, too, when the reference librarian would appreciate this arrangement, when the nature of the question sends him to the shelves rather than to the indexes. Individual volumes of serials occasionally have their own indexes, which provide much greater depth than the indexes which cover many serials, making the shelf approach more appropriate. A list of all the periodicals on a given subject can be compiled easily by computerized serials records if a subject structure is built into the serials file. In general, the reference librarian has more orientation to journal *articles* than to journal *titles,* reflecting the emphasis of the indexing journals. From the point of view of computer analysis, identification of each article would provide much more precise retrieval.

The problem of repeat questions is now handled in some libraries with a special card file. The reference librarian on duty writes the question on a card and indicates where the answer was found. The next librarian to come on duty scans the new cards and files them away. There is the possibility, with on-line access to the computer, of keeping such a file in computer store. Before tackling a new question, the reference librarian could search the record for any previous similar question and readout or printout the results of the past effort.

In college, university, and school libraries there is a close relationship between the teacher and the reference librarian, although it is not always recognized. The good reference librarian does try to find out what is coming at him as the result of teaching assignments, but he is never very successful. A computer store of data about all courses being given on campus, including dates, subject matter, reading assignments, and other pertinent facts, would be extremely helpful to the reference librarian and to the student. A Monday morning look at what is coming up during the week's teaching would alert the reference personnel and give them time to prepare for what is sure to come. It could also enable the reference librarian to alert a given professor as to library offerings (or shortcomings) related to his teaching activity.

Estimates have shown that the reference staff in some libraries make approximately half of the total use of the catalog. This means that the quality of reference service is strongly affected by the adequacy and availability of the catalog. A computer-produced book catalog can save the staff many trips to the card catalog, and such catalogs available throughout the library would lessen the reference burden. Finding lists would reduce the bulk sufficiently so that a subject or author catalog could be carried about the library during the search. Pages of such a catalog can also be duplicated for searching or for future use for bibliographies, footnotes, etc.

As in other areas of the library's work, statistics are important. How many and what type of questions are being asked? How much reference time is being used to answer questions, compile bibliographies, do selection work, read shelves, weed the vertical file, etc.? What tools are used the most, the least, in answering questions?

Which reference librarians seem most efficient at handling certain types of questions? Which contribute most to the selection of reference tools? The computer can do a great deal by manipulating whatever input is provided. Careful consideration should be given to what is wanted in the way of reference statistics in planning the input and the system structure.

REFERENCE AIDS

Many librarians have gained an insight into the possibilities of computer usage through association with data-retrieval work. Lawrence Berul makes the distinction well: ". . . data is generally used to characterize material which is easily quantifiable, nonabstract, and which can be formatted; conversely, information is material which is conceptual, descriptive, usually narrative, and may be judgmental, and is not easily quantifiable or formattable."[1] Perhaps information about information falls somewhere in between. Fact retrieval calls for a depth of subject analysis which our catalogs have not attempted. Reference tools are designed for fact retrieval; information retrieval, based on use of a computer, means more tools that enable the reference librarian to get to the facts.

Reference librarians make little use of many materials because they are not indexed. This includes certain important books, secondary periodicals, newspapers, and special collections of materials. Computerized access to a bibliographic data store by many libraries and scholars will encourage subject analysis, perhaps not to the depth of a well-indexed book, but it will put the item into the stream of accessible knowledge. Cooperative effort by libraries, publishers, and authors will be needed to accomplish such an effort. Library networks can share input and output; publishers can provide data usable by the networks and encourage authors to index, to use descriptive titles, and to provide abstracts helpful to the cataloger. Descriptive titles facilitate automatic indexing on the basis of the meaningful words in the title. Key-word-in-content (KWIC) indexes such as *Chemical Titles*

[1] Lawrence Berul, *Information Storage and Retrieval: A State of the Art Report,* 1964, available from the Clearinghouse for Federal Scientific and Technical Information, paragraph 2.2.4. AD 630 089.

are widely used because they can be produced quickly and at a reasonable cost. A by-product of a computerized catalog can be a KWIC index based on titles or subject headings for limited groups of materials. The chief drawback is that many titles do not have the right words to enlighten anyone as to the contents of the work. Descriptive subtitles can be provided for bibliographic purposes, and perhaps in time, optical scanning equipment will pick key words from the table of contents.

Some traditional reference tools are now being produced by a computer. *Index Medicus* and the *New York Times Index* are examples. The effort to produce the *New York Times Index* is the first step in developing an automated information-retrieval system to be called the *New York Times* Information Bank. This real-time system will eliminate the "morgue," with the clippings stored on microfiche. Remote terminals will be used to interrogate the large computer about the information in store. A no-charge service for *New York Times* customers will enable libraries to call into the system from outside.[2]

Some very expensive reference aids are available only on magnetic tape. They present difficult problems such as who will pay for them (the library, the computer center, or the college most concerned) and how can they be used. The solution on one large university campus[3] for subscribing to an expensive business service on computer tape was for the library and the College of Business Administration to share the subscription cost, the computer center to do the searching and printout, and the library to own the tape and store it in the computer center. Both the library and the College of Business Administration could request the searches and participate in them if they wished.

Certain reference materials which are not purchased, but which are received free if requested, must be asked for regularly. Examples of these are college catalogs, annual reports of corporations, and municipal, state, and county documents. The computer can recognize renewal time and write a request for renewal. Reference files of uncataloged materials such as pamphlets and clippings can be better controlled by generating a one-line short author, short title, and

[2] New York Times, *The New York Times Information Bank, a Real-time, Interactive Information Retrieval System,* from a five-page brochure dated Mar. 26, 1969.
[3] Kent State University.

subject entry for the computer. This can make the files more useful and can aid in the frequent culling necessary for such files. It can also help in determining possible permanent value of any items in the file.

SELECTIVE DISSEMINATION OF INFORMATION (SDI)

The referral to accumulated knowledge can be examined in terms of the degree of voluntary control exercised by the user. The initial receipt of data is typically involuntary, as in kindergarten and elementary education and in first introductions to new topics. With increased exposure, the pattern becomes more and more subject to the volition of the user. Perhaps the ultimate expression of this process is reflected in the reference librarian, but there remains, nevertheless, a measure of potential surprise in the quest.

It has been presumed that a profile of known interests could be used to guide a quasi-involuntary flow of data about new items of probable interest. This process is best represented as selective dissemination of information (SDI).

The reference librarian, concerned with the library users' quests for information, seems to be the logical person to assist with the use of the computer in notifying users of the arrival of new materials of interest to them. Reading-interest profiles based on the subject used in subject cataloging can be stored in the computer. As new materials come in and subject headings are assigned, the computer can match the profile with the subject headings and print out a notice to the user telling him that the particular item has arrived. Good SDI systems provide feedback showing whether the user has actually made use of the item. If he repeatedly ignores a certain part of the profile, the computer informs the librarian, who then discusses the possibility of deleting that subject with the user. Updating a profile is also important if a user's new and changing interests are to be served.

Industry libraries have made most use of SDI. All kinds of libraries can consider the possibility. Such a personalized notification service could have its appeal for university professors, serious users of the public library, and school teachers, as well as researchers in all fields. Current tapes with proper subject alignment for journals, technical reports, documents, and whatever other library material, as well as books, could also be used for SDI.

Studies by Wolfe and Herner, Bivona, and Julius Frome have stressed the problem of vocabulary in making matches,[4] noting that persons involved in applied research were more responsive to SDI than those in pure research,[5] and stating that low cost can be achieved by making SDI a by-product of existing computerized services.[6]

A variant of SDI for individuals is SDI for groups working on the same project, with the profile designed for the group's needs. This reduces costs but also reduces service to the individual. Costs depend on the number of new additions to the data base, the number and complexity of the profiles, and the equipment used. A high cost for one purpose might be cheaper than a low cost for another. Studies are needed on the worth of SDI for different kinds of library situations.

ORIENTATION

At present, orientation for the user of the library is nothing more than a quick tour of the facilities and/or a descriptive pamphlet telling of the library's services. An occasional university has a brief course on use of the library, brief lectures by the library staff members to groups of graduate students on the library's resources in their major subject, and special tours for subject specialists.

The reference librarian has an opportunity to take the reader by the hand and lead him through the maze, an opportunity the reader seldom takes advantage of. In a large university to do this just once during the year for each student would require a very large reference staff. It would be an interesting experience to sell each student one hour of reference time and use the money to provide reference staffing to handle the crowd. One hour's paid use would undoubtedly lead to other hours of free use, much to the embarrassment of the understaffed library.

[4] William A. Bivona, *Selective Dissemination of Information: Pilot Test at U. S. Army Natick Laboratory, Final Report,* vol. 1. Information Dynamics Corp., Reading, Mass., 1967. AD 654 997.

[5] M. A. Wolfe, and Sol Herner, "SDI System for the U. S. Public Health Service, Office of Pesticides," *Journal of Chemical Documentation,* 7: 138–141, August 1967.

[6] Julius Frome, "An Experimental Approach to Current Awareness," *Journal of Chemical Documentation,* 7: 135–137, August 1967.

The reference librarian will probably be the key person in the education of the reader in the use of the computer for information retrieval. The reference librarian may be saying to the reader, "If you haven't found your answer in *Index Medicus,* perhaps you can consult the MEDLARS record with the computer. *Index Medicus* has a subject depth of only three per article, and the computer-stored record has nine. Here is the input keyboard and readout screen. This is the way you conduct your query. . . ." In the meantime, the reference librarian tries *Biological Abstracts* or some other likely source for help. Eventually, the computer search can jump from one data bank to another, and everything can be accomplished by one orientation lesson for the reader. When this time comes, the reader may have his contact with the computer in his own office and do his searching from there. The immediate future, however, promises only computer approach to a fringe area of total information, and the reference librarian will continue to be the professional searcher and guide.

Computer-produced catalogs, multiple copies of serials lists, processing information lists, and circulation lists produced daily by the computer can all help in the general orientation of the reader once he knows that these aids exist. It will be part of the reference librarian's job to acquaint the reader with these lists. When readout is available, on-line query can help provide the same information about the location of materials in an even more effective way because the records will be updated on line and will therefore be more up to date.

Computerized instruction in the use of the library, or something like a "management game" (based on computer reaction to a given situation), will undoubtedly be useful in library orientation. Computerized instruction can capitalize on the readers' special interests and can be a most effective teaching machine. The "management game" approach could give the reader a dramatic look at the excitement of a reference librarian's job when he is in quest of information.

Faculty and graduate research in a large university (or network of colleges and/or universities), research efforts within a large company, or government research activity are frequently of immediate interest to a user of a library. Access to computer-stored information about such research should be part of the readers' orientation. The reference librarian now knows much about the technical report literature and the government indexes thereto. He should try to capture on tape information about research in the institution his library serves and about research in related institutions if possible. The special librarian needs control of internal research literature as well as external. Orientation here may be limited by security problems for both defense and proprietary reasons.

The librarian needs orientation too. The average librarian does not seem to have a feeling for machinery, and thoughts of a computer do not seem to fit into his ideal library. One university library hired a librarian knowledgeable in computer matters whose first two years of work were to be devoted to staff orientation toward computerization. Another involved the entire library staff in flow charting the work of this library in computer terms. Many libraries have encouraged their staff members to attend meetings devoted to library automation and to visit libraries involved in automation efforts. Such meetings have been well attended. Orientation is also provided by the library journals, which are publishing many articles on library automation. Other journals, such as the *Journal of the American Society for Information Science* and *Datamation,* are also being read by automation-minded librarians.

SUMMARY

The primary interest of librarians in library automation has been in the use of the computer for acquisitions, cataloging, and circulation work. Information retrieval has seemed to be less applicable within the present state of the art. Directly and indirectly, however, librarians have helped in the development and dissemination of retrieval concepts. The development of the Rapid Selector at the U. S. Department of Agriculture Library in the forties, the advanced curriculum at the library school at Western Reserve University, the organization of the American Documentation Institute (ADI), the contribution of knowledge about subject heading lists, and classification and complex filing have all had an important influence on the development of information science. Graduate curricula in information science are now being offered in many schools; linguists, psychologists, scientists, and computer specialists, as well as librarians, have become involved in the total effort.

Financial support from the Council on Library Resources (Ford Foundation) and the National Science Foundation during the last ten years has made research and real progress possible.

Computer-based systems have provided a variety of concordances, indexes, and special tools. KWIC indexes are usually permuted on titles, but the possibility of permuting subject headings has been seriously considered. ULIS[7] (University Library Information Systems Project of the University of Illinois) compared permuting on titles and permuting on subject headings and decided the latter would be more useful in the general library situation where titles are less specific. Permutation on subject headings is not practical for an entire collection, but is a promising means of dealing with limited special areas of the collection.

Character recognition and optical scanning have not yet been perfected to a point where key words in tables of contents, indexes, and abstracts can be extracted for expanded subject analysis, but there is reasonable hope for such capability. The speed with which this might be done will give the reference librarian more up-to-date access to much information as well as the means to treat subject analysis in great depth.

The reference librarian can do surprising things in fact retrieval with the World Almanac and a few other low-priced, well-analyzed reference tools. When the literature reaches a certain stage, as in chemistry, and the problems in production, storage, and use get out of hand, resort to a computer becomes practical. The special librarians working in industry libraries, in university departmental libraries assisting large research projects, in special departments in large public libraries, and in many government research libraries are meeting the challenge of the flood of new literature (especially in science and technology). The vast technical report literature, with indexes like STAR (Scientific and Technical Aerospace Reports), USGRDR (United States Government Research and Development Reports), TAB (Technical Abstract Bulletin), and NSA (Nuclear Science Abstracts), is largely ignored by many general reference librarians but is most important to special librarians. Beyond this are enormous stores of data that

[7] Louis A. Schultheiss, Don S. Culbertson, and Edward M. Heiliger, *Advanced Data Processing in the University Library,* Scarecrow Press, New York, *c* 1962, p. 37.

need better organization before librarians can get to them. In some cases it is being realized that librarians have something to offer in solving the problems of organizing this data. Librarians should be alert to this and give the benefit of their knowledge and experience in organizing such data for use.

The dialog between the reference librarian and the user seeking information has its parallel in the dialog between the user seeking information and the computer store of information. In the latter case the reference librarian will certainly be a user and will undoubtedly be helping other users. The conversion of library cataloging, serials, acquisition, circulation, and administrative records to computer store will have an even greater effect on the reference librarian.

Service at the reference desk often involves the compilation of lists of books and other library materials, usually by subject, sometimes by author. The computer can compile such lists very quickly, with refinements impractical in a manual search. Date, place, publisher, language, and other elements in the cataloging record can become restrictions, individually or in combination. It thus becomes possible, for instance, to list all materials in the collection published since 1955 in London, in French, by Macmillan, with authors by the name of Smith. The MARC (Machine-Readable Cataloging) program of the Library of Congress is structured for this, a bit more than average libraries would ever require.

Reference librarians use serials literature extensively. The many commercial indexes are the keys to this literature. Each index has its own way of identifying a given serial. A decision is made to identify such a journal as that of the American Medical Association as *JAMA, Journal of the American Medical Association,* or *American Medical Association Journal.* Lists of journals or different subjects can be as varied as the subject headings and classification numbers assigned. The future promises to lead to journal articles rather than to journal titles, and to secondary journals not now indexed.

The handling of certain reference materials such as college catalogs, corporation reports, vertical file materials, and microform materials promises to become more effective. The computer can automatically request new issues on specified dates, can make short author, short title listings of pamphlet materials, and can record holdings for large microform collections in such a way that the user will have new approaches to the material. Storing of reference questions for retrieval in case of "reports" will call for a look at the computer file before starting a complex search, while the analysis of the library's reference work will show how long it takes to find answers, what subjects are most used, and which librarians tend to answer certain types of questions.

SUGGESTED READING LIST

Atwood, Ruth: "An Index to Medical Book Reviews: A Computer Experiment," *Bulletin of the Medical Library Association,* 55: 66–69, January 1967.

Chen, Ching-Chic, and E. Robert Kingham: "Subject Reference Lists Produced by Computer," *Journal of Library Automation,* 1: 178–197, September 1968.

Darling, Louise: "Information Retrieval Projects in the Bio-Medical Library, University of California, Los Angeles," *Proceedings of the 1966 Clinic on Library Applications of Data Processing,* Graduate School of Library Science, University of Illinois, Urbana, pp. 91–123.

DOD User Needs Study, Phase K: Final Technical Report, vols. I and II, Auerbach Corp., Philadelphia, May 1965. 1151 TR-3.

Haas, Warren J.: "Statewide and Regional Reference Service," *Library Trends,* **12**: 407–410, January 1964.

Hickey, Doralyn, "Bridging the Gap between Cataloging and Information Retrieval," *Library Resources and Technical Services,* **11**: 173–183, Spring 1967.

Kuney, Joseph H., "Publication and Distribution of Information," *Annual Review of Information Science and Technology,* vol. 3, Interscience-Wiley, New York, 1968, pp. 31–59.

Licklider, J. C. R., "Man-Computer Communication," *Annual Review of Information Science and Technology,* vol. 3, Interscience-Wiley, New York, 1968, pp. 201–240.

Podrick, R. G.: "Automation Can Transform Reference Services," *Ontario Library Review,* **51**: 145–150, September 1967.

Schultz, Claire K., "Automation of Reference Work," *Library Trends,* **12**: 413–424, January 1964.

Shera, Jesse: "Automation and the Reference Librarian," *R. Q.,* **3**: 3–4, July 1964.

Swanson, D. R.: "Scientific Journals and Information Services of the Future," *American Psychologist,* **21**: 1005–1010, November 1966.

Swanson, Rowena: *Move the Information,* U. S. Air Force Office of Scientific Information, Arlington, Va., 1967. AD 657 754.

Taylor, Robert S: *Studies in the Man-System Interface in Libraries, Report No. 3: Question-Negotiation and Information-seeking in Libraries,* Center for the Information Sciences, Lehigh University, Bethlehem, Pa., July 1967. AD 659 468.

Terrant, Seldon W., Jr., and J. L. Wood: "Operational Computer-based Systems at the Chemical Abstracts Service," *Proceedings of the 1966 Clinic on Library Applications of Data Processing,* Graduate School of Library Science, University of Illinois, Urbana, 1966, pp. 124–166.

Weil, Cherie B.: "Automatic Retrieval of Biographical Reference Books," *Journal of Library Automation,* **1**: 239–249, December 1968.

CHAPTER 4 RESOURCE CONTROL

The library is directly comparable with other businesses in the necessity and importance of controlling its resources. The needs and problems in careful utilization of space and equipment, thoughtful dealing with employees, suppliers, and patrons, and prudent administration of financial and legal activities are mirrored in thousands of other organizations. With due attention to those details the concepts, procedures, and devices used by other businesses can be copied in the library with far greater assurance of validity and success than applies to the more specialized technical processes.

It is very likely that all the pertinent characteristics of interest about all resources are already being observed and recorded. Unfortunately the data are not usually established in a form consistent with other data and not in such a way as to facilitate access to the data, except for the original user.

As with the technical processing data, there is need for a clear recognition that the generation and retention of the data are separate from, but related to, the use of the data. Any changes in input introduce questions of completeness and consistency, whereas changes in use are clear and direct—if only a good base of data is maintained.

SPACE

Space is the library's most inflexible resource. Mechanization and automation alter the requirements for space and the traffic relationships among the departments as well as provide the data system to support utilization studies and expansion and rearrangement plans.

There are standards for library arrangements of space and area needed per reader, per worker, per thousand volumes, etc. Planning figures include projections of future numbers of students, growth of graduate programs, and so on. Relations between the different needs and levels of past usage can be projected to provide estimates of future requirements.

Branch building must be related closely to the community served. Analysis of reference and circulation usage by persons living in the area being considered for a new building and/or location can be based on registration and other circulation records. Changing neighborhoods are with us, and the computer can help in judging population trends.

Space needs in the special library are affected by the percentage of business done on the telephone (it is usually high) and by the related effect of numbers of readers and their workspace preferences. Space limitations perhaps more than economics force consideration of heavy use of microforms and of the need for ordering technical report literature when it is requested rather than storing it for possible use.

Arrangements of space within a library will be affected by automation. Access to the catalog, serials file, and other records from many points in the library has dominated traffic patterns, but catalogers will no longer need to be physically near a central card catalog. Traffic between floors will be minimized, making upper floor spaces more self-sufficient. System-wide availability of computerized records may well reduce the number of people actually coming to the library on campus, the main and branch libraries in public library systems, and the industrial libraries, at the same time increasing the use of the library and requiring considerable differences in space needs and arrangements. The possibility of self-circulation with circulation stations throughout the library should reduce the main circulation area, prevent queuing, and change traffic patterns.

EQUIPMENT

Libraries have two inventory problems: equipment inventory and inventory of library materials. Equipment inventory is usually done annually, and inventory of library materials is seldom, if ever, done in some of the larger libraries because of lack of time and staff. The manual method of equipment inventory involves checking the inventory list against the pieces of equipment themselves, each of which has an affixed number relating to the appropriate number on the inventory list. This is a large, dreaded job, ending with a desperate search for the missing items. Tables, chairs, filing cabinets, shelves, office equipment, microform readers, film projectors, and map cases are just a part of the list of standard library equipment.

There is need for a portable direct-reading device to read the inventory number from each piece of equipment, recording quickly and accurately each item. Designated areas could be assigned ID numbers as well. Reading of the area number and the item number would be correlated, just as the patron's number and the book's ID number are read together at the circulation station. Searching through endless inventory sheets to identify items, particularly those which have been moved since the last inventory, would be eliminated. In an institution of which the library might be only a part, an institution-wide inventory using this system would clear up some mysteries occasioned by the unrecorded change of equipment between the library and other areas.

Storing of control data about equipment is also useful in other ways. Deterioration measured by the discard rate of different equipment items can be useful in planning replacements and in judging brand quality. Studies of use of equipment could be made by using a data collection machine in an area, feeding, for example, a table's ID card and a reader's ID card into the machine before and after use. Usage of microfilm readers and listening and film-viewing equipment and the relative popularity of lounging areas and regular reading areas, smoking and nonsmoking areas, elevators and escalators, and individual studies and tables can be measured when changing conditions require assessment of equipment and facility use. The computer can keep track of such use and alert the librarian to changes.

PERSONNEL

Manual files of personnel records yield data about individuals but not about the staff as a whole. Such files also emphasize current staff. Weeding of records of staff no longer with the library is necessary to save space. Records of persons who have applied for positions and were not hired receive even less attention. The great value of the computer-based personnel records is the ability to analyze the staff by a predetermined set of values and continue control of the older files for comparative purposes and for reconsideration of previous applicants.

The traditional manila folders housed in filing cabinets provide superb access to individual records, but it is difficult to secure from these files the answers to such questions as the following: What percentage are over fifty years old? How many are clerical workers? What percentage have a college education? How many have a graduate degree in library science? How many are specialists in children's work? How many speak Spanish or some other foreign language? What percentage belong to the American Library Association (ALA) or other professional organization? How many have an interest in data processing? Who can take shorthand? What percentage have children? Which had college majors in a scientific field? These are questions which could be answered easily from a properly constructed personnel data system, and the data would be fully accessible in accordance with security rules. Specific concerns for an individual may still call for a review of all the pertinent documents. But the data such as that related to the above questions plus such things as age, names of persons giving references, and any other items the library felt the need for would be available. A constant review of persons considered for positions is called for in light of new needs for staff. Information about such persons could be stored for display at any time for a position opening in cataloging, for example, where the applicant has had the following qualifications: five years of experience, some experience in serials cataloging, a knowledge of German, and some experience in MARC (Machine-Readable Cataloging) II input methods. Such access could give a quick review of any potential candidate who had been previously interviewed but for whom no position had been available at the time.

Staffs change, administrators come and go, and it becomes difficult to respond to a request for information about someone who used to work in the library. A minimum record can be maintained in machine-readable form, with room for indication of the quality of the work done by each person. This takes almost no space and is easily accessible. Activities of staff members, committee memberships, association activities, workshop and conference attendance, publications, and research are examples that might have interest for the administrator. A look at the computerized record of any staff member could show sick leave taken, vacation scheduling, overtime, work efficiency record, and probationary period status. These and other useful items can be kept for prompt access in the personnel data file.

SUPPLIERS

The external business relationships of a library are concerned with all types of suppliers' equipment, and services in addition to books and other library materials. For purposes of good management, the importance of the item or service being provided is matched by concern for the supplier.

There is regular need for data about supply sources, performance, reliability, and cost, as well as a continuing flow of data about individual transactions. In this regard, the library is not unique, and the methods, procedures, and controls used by other businesses can be borrowed and adapted to the library needs.

USERS

Data about the *user* of the library can certainly be a resource in achieving the library's main objective—assisting the user. The basic data is readily available, and it can be analyzed in hundreds of helpful ways, alone and in relation to catalog, circulation, and acquisitions information. Many librarians argue that we are in more need of information about nonusers of the library. Fruitful comparisons between user files in the library and similar data banks elsewhere could be made to improve the library's effort to attract more readers.

The users of the library can be studied to advantage by the administrator, with analysis by age, occupation, sex, and any other characteristics it seems important to put in the record. If an SDI (Selective Dissemination of Information) system is set up for serious readers, with reading profiles developed for each, these profiles can be analyzed by the computer and studied by the administrator to help him achieve a better understanding of his public. Use of the library by certain segments of the population can be studied. Is TV decreasing fiction reading by housewives? Are white readers showing any interest in the new literature on the importance of the Negro in American history? Are the new efforts by Professor Jones to increase his students' reading having any effect? Has the change from divisional reference to centralized reference increased or decreased the number and quality of reference questions asked? What has decentralization of the high school library done to overall use of library materials? Has the aid given the engineering department on their Apollo Applications literature searches increased the use of library materials? These are kinds of questions that might arise in different kinds of libraries, questions that could be answered by administrators having at their command library records in computer store. There might be a tendency to develop data banks with more and more information for more and more purposes, as the U. S. Census Bureau has done. As the end result would be to give better service to the individual reader, this might not meet with too much resistance on the part of the library patron. The matter of privacy in computer banks of information will be of real concern to some people, and the records must be protected against any type of abuse. What one reads is one's own business, and it is his right to insist on privacy if he wishes it. Safeguards can be provided.

FINANCIAL AND LEGAL RECORDS

Financial and legal records can be maintained in such a way as to yield a wide variety of information when it is needed. The book budget, which usually includes expenditures for books, binding, and periodicals, is a complicated matter, and questions about its status are many and frequent. Expenditures for books are divided in different ways by different libraries. In whatever way the division is made, information is needed about the amount that is allotted and how much has been spent against each allotment.

The tempo of spending sometimes needs speeding up and sometimes needs slowing down. The administrator needs to know the current status so that he can help keep the flow of spending adjusted to his staffing situation and to the needs of the library and its users.

Appraisal of the spending of book money can be aided by analysis of trends in book prices, of requests to buy in certain subject (or geographical) areas, of service given by book suppliers, of publishing trends, and of the effectiveness of the book-selection process.

The business office usually makes different uses of the library's financial records. Its main concern is paying bills. As a result of this, both the business office and the library keep separate records of library expenditures, each for its own purpose. Computerization makes possible the use of one record for both, with an output designed for all needs of both users. In budget preparation, comparisons with past years' expenditures, with financial statistics of the parent institution, and with library use statistics are very helpful to the administrator. With neighboring libraries that are also computerized, library administrators can spot trends in expenditures and use that can be very helpful in budget justification. Price rises of journals and books in an inflationary situation need to be documented when a budget is proposed.

Periodicals are demanding a higher and higher proportion of the book budget, and the administrator has a hard time appraising this increase. The prices of journals are going up very rapidly, and the number of new journals is keeping pace with the development of new fields of research and with the establishment of new associations. New printing machinery and new publishing methods aggravate the problem. The increasing need for the newest information puts more pressure on periodicals in many fields. All of this forces the administrator to watch and consider the periodicals part of the book budget. The computerized record can help keep this situation in hand by informing the administrator of price increases. Indexes and special services related to periodicals are becoming more numerous and more expensive. Whether these are handled as periodicals or as reference materials, they must be watched.

CONCLUSION

Resource control is an important feature of library automation. The computer, with its ability to store, analyze, and make more available information about the library's resources, can make for a better organized and more efficient library. People, money, space, and equipment have been treated in this chapter. The people who work in the library and the people who use the library are key elements in any library. The computer can yield much additional valuable information if the data now stored in manual files is transferred to computer storage. Meaningful comparisons of this computerized personnel data with other data in the computerized library can also yield significant information. Instant financial data at his fingertips has always been a dream of the librarian. The ability to follow price trends of library materials, to know accurately what kind of service the library is getting from suppliers, and to be able to check on fulfillment of promises to give certain discounts has been needed by librarians. This now becomes possible. Budget planning and justification becomes easier. Space use is changing because of the effect of the newly computerized activities. The computer also has the potential for helping in the study of space utilization problems. Related to this is the equipment occupying much of the space. Inventory control of equipment can be handled by computer methods in a way that yields significant information about space use. It can also help decide on the most useful type of equipment, the best brands to buy, and the arrangement of what is bought. The inventory itself can be simplified by reading the data about each piece into the computer along with machine-readable identification of the area in which the equipment is located.

SUGGESTED READING LIST

Burkhalter, Barton R., ed.: *Case Studies in Systems Analysis in a University Library,* Scarecrow Press, Metuchen, N.J., 1968. Note: Included to show the kind of studies that could be made much more easily in a computer-based library situation.

Courtwright, Benjamin: "The Library as an Inventory System," *Progress Report on an Operations Research and Systems Engineering Study of a University Library,* Johns Hopkins University, Baltimore, Md., 1963, pp. 123–144.

Gentle, Edgar C., Jr., ed.: *Data Communications in Business, an Introduction,* American Telephone and Telegraph Co., New York, c. 1965.

Kurmey, William J.: "Management Implications of Mechanization," *C.A.C.U.L. Workshop on Library Automation, University of British Columbia, 1967,* Canadian Association of College and University Libraries, Ottawa, 1967, pp. 116–123.

Morse, Philip M.: *Library Effectiveness: A Systems Approach,* M.I.T., Cambridge, Mass., 1968, 207 pp.

Nugent, William R.: "Statistics of Collection Overlap at the Libraries of the Six New England State Universities," *Library Resources and Technical Services,* **12:** 31–36, Winter 1968.

Parker, Ralph H.: "Concept and Scope of Total Systems in Library Records," *Data Processing in Public and University Libraries,* Drexel Information Science Series, vol. 3, Spartan, Washington, 1966, pp. 67–77.

——: "Library Records in a Total System, Brasenose Conference on the Automation of Libraries, Oxford, England, 1966," in John Harrison and Peter Laslett (eds.), *Proceedings of the Anglo-American Conference on the Mechanization of Library Services,* Mansell, London, 1967, pp. 33–45.

Pearson, Karl M., Jr.: *Providing for Machine-readable Statistical Data Sets in University Research Libraries,* Systems Development Corporation, Santa Monica, Calif., 1968, p. 157. SP-3155.

Studer, William J.: "Computer-based Selective Dissemination of Information (SDI) Service for Faculty Using Library of Congress Machine-readable Catalog (MARC) Records," doctoral dissertation, Graduate Library School, Indiana University, Bloomington, Ind., 1968, p. 253.

University of British Columbia Library: "U.B.C. Library and the School of Librarianship Are Making Computer-based Study of Library Use Patterns in a Large Academic Community," *PNLA Quarterly,* **31:** 238, April 1967.

Watson, William: "Library Automation: A Primer on Some of the Implications," *C.A.C.U.L. Workshop on Library Automation, University of British Columbia, 1967,* Canadian Association of College and University Libraries, Ottawa, 1967, pp. 135–146.

Zuckerman, Ronald A.: *Optical Scanning for Data Collection, Conversion and Reduction,* Los Angeles County Public Library, Los Angeles, 1967, p. 54. PB 179 765.

CHAPTER 5
PROCESSING CONTROL

Processing work in libraries is traditionally defined as that part of the library's function concerned with acquiring library materials and preparing them for use. This chapter emphasizes the control aspects related not only to technical processing but to movement of library materials in and out of the library and to the maintenance of the holdings. Processing control is thus defined as (1) bibliographic control—concerning authority files, classification standards, and bibliographic content; (2) inventory control—encompassing location, movement, and physical inventory of library materials; (3) serials and documents control—reflecting the special control provision applicable to the history of each serial and document, the complexity of content, and the frequent irregularity of receipt; and (4) circulation control—addressing the dynamic movement of materials beyond direct control of the library.

BIBLIOGRAPHIC CONTROL

Bibliographic control is concerned with the structure and the controls within which technical processing deals with individual items. Thus, the emphasis is on the characteristics of control for similar items and for similar characteristics of different items.

The principal elements of bibliographic control are consistency and completeness. The means to consistency are provided by authority files and classification. Completeness concerns the bibliographic entry itself and the bibliographic coverages of material in the collection.

Authority files for subjects and authors are of real importance in the proper organization of bibliographic data in a library. *Subject authority files* usually rely on the *Subject Headings Used in the Dictionary Catalogs of the Library of Congress* or, for smaller libraries, the Sears list. The size of the L.C. subject heading list might lead one to believe that it would cover all knowledge. However, the development of special vocabularies in special fields has been very rapid in recent years and now extends to much greater scope and depth than the standard list. The medical field has developed MESH (Medical Subject Headings) at the National Library of Medicine (N.L.M.). The Engineers Joint Council and the Department of Defense have collaborated to develop a large engineering thesaurus. One of the chief problems of coordinating work on library automation between our "national libraries" is the development of a national subject authority list upon which all can rely. The same words have different meanings in different fields. Identification of a word must be conditioned to reflect field specialties and perhaps to provide for referral to microthesauri of whatever size is necessary to the details of the chosen field.

Author authority is important because of the obvious desirability of putting all of the works of an author under the same form of his name. A typical example is that of Mark Twain. If all his works were listed under both Samuel Clemens and Mark Twain, the size of the catalog would increase, and the cataloger's work load would be greater. Part of the titles under one name and part of them under the other would be confusing to the reader, and he might miss one or the other.

Corporate authors are often complex, and delineation becomes even more important. Changes occur in author authority, as when a woman author marries or an author assumes a pseudonym, and the file must be adjusted. Such adjustments can be easier in mechanized or automated files because the computer can change data entries much faster and more easily than physical records can be changed.

Title authority must be established when the title is used as main entry instead of the author.

Classification structures are assigned to aid in logical grouping of similar items as well as to assure physical grouping of the items in storage. Classification numbers are usually constructed as subject numbers followed by author numbers. For physical handling, this puts the books in subject order on the shelves, a fact much appreciated by all, except the subject specialist who cannot see the reasoning behind a general classification which most libraries use. Chemists do not like the division between pure and applied chemistry. Educators do not like to see John Dewey's works filed with philosophy, or books on the teaching of a subject with the subject; they want them with the education books.

The physical limitation of a single positional sequence is not applicable to the logical data about the item. Any desired number of sequences can be established and arranged in any desired pattern. In this way it would be easy to have the copies located wherever it is most convenient and at the same time under a central control system. If the medical library wanted to take over a book hitherto located in the home economics library, it is necessary only to indicate the change in location—all previous identity codes are still valid because location is a descriptive attribute, not an inherent aspect of identity.

Classification for placing books on library shelves and classification of knowledge have always been two different things. Library classifications have supplemented classification work with subject headings, thus making up for the fact that a book must go on the shelf in only one location.

The modern searcher for information sees all this in a rather primitive way. He is trying to use the computer and computerized fields for his searching, but the structuring of those files is based on traditional library files. Dialogue between the searcher and the computer can produce the bibliographic references that will contain the information needed. Unless a classification scheme is devised for every question asked, a ridiculous possibility, there must be dialogue. Jumping from one part of a hierarchic arrangement to another in the dialogue must be efficient, using as little of both the searcher's time and the computer's time as possible.

Librarians are presented many problems to solve in the efforts to take full advantage of technological opportunities Should the bibliographic content be the same as in a manual system? What purpose does the catalog serve? Could the computerized catalog be the source of many different catalogs, each serving a different purpose? What elements of the cataloging entry should be tagged to enable the computer to generate a variety of listings?

Bibliographic coverage is not complete in a manual system. Some file materials, such as college catalogs, are not cataloged but are heavily used in most libraries. The computer can order new editions on schedule and put in claims for those not received. Microform collections often include large numbers of publications which the library has not cataloged. Better access to these can be obtained. Many libraries depend on outside agencies to index special collections of materials such as Human Relations Area Files and do not catalog them. Much of the good work done in creating such files is wasted because of the limited indexing system. United States government and United Nations documents are often not cataloged, and the indexes which are used as a substitute fall short of what is needed. Few newspapers are indexed, and most libraries rely on the *New York Times* and the *Wall Street Journal* because they are indexed. Local newspapers may be clipped, and a few may be saved. Microfilming makes saving them more feasible and therefore more worth indexing.

There is a growing exchange of book catalogs as they become more common and an increase in union catalogs as libraries seek the benefits of sharing a large central computerized catalog. The work of preparing proper cataloging and indexing for materials not now covered can be shared by all, and all can reap the benefits.

The statistics aspect of bibliographic control encompasses selection, acquisitions, and cataloging and includes analysis of the collection.

In the acquisitions area, statistical analysis can give accurate, up-to-the-minute information on service being given by suppliers, jobbers, and publishers. Work studies can provide data on the time needed for searching, the percentage of requests returned marked "already in library," and the extent of input slowdown resulting from personnel problems. Budget statistics are of great importance in acquisitions. There is a need to adjust the work flow to the requirements of the budget year and to balance the selection work with the state of book budget allocations.

Cataloging statistics are considered a more accurate measure of the growth of the library than acquisitions statistics, even though many items are not cataloged. After classification, there can be referral back to the acquisitions record to determine average prices of books in different fields. The cataloging done can be analyzed in as many different ways as the cataloging data is tagged for retrieval. What percentage of the cataloging is of recent materials? What of retrospective materials? What percentage of cataloging is of foreign language materials and what languages? In what subject areas are the materials being cataloged?

Cataloging is expensive. Ways of cutting cataloging costs concern library administrators. A better knowledge of the cataloging time needed to process different types of books is needed. Work statistics can be provided by automatically informing the computer as each book moves through cataloging. It might be discovered that technical books or foreign language books take more cataloging time than art or music books, thereby affecting decisions to purchase heavily in foreign language and technical books. If cataloging checkpoints indicate that cataloging of phonodiscs is very time consuming, such statistics might well result in deferring purchase of phonodiscs or a decision to hire another cataloger.

The size of a cataloging backlog in a computerized library can be easily measured by asking the computer for a counting (or list) of all items received but not cataloged. A similar counting of the short title listing of block purchases and gifts could also be provided. The catalog department needs accurate figures on which to base its budget requests and measure its ability to keep pace with the library's acquisition program. The number of books being cataloged, the percentage of difficult materials handled, the regularity of the flow of cataloging work, the percentage of "rush" items, accomplishment in reclassification, withdrawal work, changing of incorrect cataloging records, authority work, and searching are all cataloging matters needing statistical analysis which the computer can provide.

INVENTORY CONTROL

The manual inventory of library materials is a far more complex matter than that of library equipment. The number is far greater, the numbering system more complicated, the dislocation greater, and the physical area where an item may be found is constantly changing.

Manual methods call for taking a drawer of the shelflist, with its cards arranged by call number, to the appropriate shelf area and checking the cards against the items on the shelf. For those items not on the shelf, cards are removed from the shelflist (a unique file in constant use) for searching against various files, such as circulation, overdues, binding, mending, missing, and reserve files. If an item does not appear on the shelf or in any of these files, the shelflist card or a copy thereof must be kept aside for further searches at later dates. Finally, replacement of the shelflist cards is subject to filing errors. All of this refers only to inventory of cataloged items that are included in the shelflist. There are many materials, such as documents, microform materials, films, prints, maps, college catalogs, corporation reports, vertical file materials, unprocessed gifts and block purchases, which are often not in the shelflist. These represent an even more difficult inventory problem.

These undesirable characteristics arise directly from the limitations of physical placement and apply equally to data which has been removed from the machinable file and embodied in cards, listings, or catalogs. If flexibility is to be retained, the rigidity of physical embodiment must be avoided.

It is commonly said of large libraries that the entire staff could be used doing nothing but taking inventory or trying to locate items reported missing by those who have searched unsuccessfully for things they want. This is an exaggeration, but it does explain why many libraries do not take inventory. As a result, their records become less and less accurate, and library efficiency decreases. Shelfreading (keeping the books on the shelves in order according to call number) is done by all libraries, because a book out of place is almost as good as lost. Inexperienced help for shelving and shelfreading makes location control a difficult matter.

Today, mechanization is of some help in the inventory process. Shelflists and printouts of books in circulation, books at bindery, books on reserve, and books on interlibrary loan can be available—either at shelf during inventory or at a more convenient place than in work areas. New search lists can be prepared any time, and appearance of a missing item can be monitored at the circulation point.

SERIALS CONTROL

Each serial has its own history, sometimes a very long one. During its lifetime it may have changed names, period of issuance, or other characteristics. It may or may not have its own indexes, and it may be indexed by an indexing service or by a government agency. The library finds serials an important source of both current and retrospective information. It collects back files as well as subscribes to current issues, and an accurate knowledge of its holdings is important.

The user of serials becomes accustomed to a certain form of entry in an index he frequently uses; or he has found periodicals listed in a certain way in the library catalog; or he has seen them listed in *Union List of Serials* form. In automation the problem of form of entry becomes very important. In a computerized library the serial title should correspond with the cataloging practice and have adequate cross references to lead the searcher to the appropriate form. Those checking in serials soon accommodate themselves to this practice, even though at first it may seem somewhat awkward. The user of a commercial or government index can be led by a cross reference to the cataloging form if it differs from the index form. Standardization is badly needed.

Irregular journals, such as the European journal that comes out only when sufficient material has been gathered to warrant a new issue, present a real problem. Regular journals can have check-in cards prepared ahead by the computer, based on the publishing and delivery schedule. These cards can be pulled from a tube file and fed back into the computer for updating both the serials holdings record and the current serials record.

With irregulars, however, each issue must be input at the time of receipt by manual intervention. This may be solved by on-line check-in using a CRT (cathode-ray tube) and a light pencil or through character reading of key information printed on the journal. In the meantime, manual inputting develops a computer record that can provide multiple copies of holdings lists, current lists, subject lists, bindery lists, orders, union lists and claiming notices, exchange lists, and desiderata lists.

New modes of storage may well emphasize the individual article sought rather than the journal title. At present, the journal title, volume and number, date, and pages are only aids in finding the article which the user has found listed in an index, a bibliography, footnotes, in proceedings, a reference, or has heard about. There is talk of the elimination of journals, to be replaced by articles contributed to a central store from which copies could be easily reproduced on demand. This would undoubtedly bring to the attention of readers articles of interest now appearing in journals they would not have read regularly or which were not indexed in the indexes covering journals in their fields of interest. Ultramicrostorage may also make feasible convenient extensive files of journals for the researcher, reader, professor, or student in his own office or home.

Such files must be everchanging if they are kept up to date, however, and the retrieval of data from them will need abstractors, indexers, indexes, and machinery for rapid handling of information about the messages in microstorage.

An increasing percentage of the budget is going for serials, and the library must monitor the prices and service received on serials. The computer can help in this by reporting on service and by comparing prices offered with prices received. A list of claiming notices sent, compared with those sent the previous year when the contract was handled by another jobber; budget breakdowns by subject to appraise the overall support for different subject areas; lists of current serials, including cover date of latest issue received, date received, and if late, how late the issues usually arrive; holdings lists indicating volumes and issues held for each title, including location; bindery lists, periodical orders, and circulation information if serials are circulated, are all possible outputs from an off-line batch-processed operation. The same information can be summoned onto a screen for on-line reading and for addition and correction.

The well-known indexes to serials, such as *Reader's Guide to Periodical Literature, Education Index,* etc., are now being joined by computer-produced indexes, such as the *Index Medicus, Chemical Titles,* etc. Tape versions of these new indexes usually extend subject coverage beyond that in the printed version. Off-line use of such tapes can mean storage and use of tapes in the computer center or wherever the computer is. On-line use could take place from the output station in the library. The searching process may be much more effective if the questioner is with the librarian to participate in the dialogue with the computer.

There are many areas of investigation today where the serial literature is of great importance, particularly in science and medicine. In almost all fields, the serial literature is increasing. The value of this literature is great to the librarian if it is accessible. This accessibility can be enhanced by computer-stored knowledge of the location of each volume of a journal in the respective libraries. Large libraries with branches, regional and county systems, school systems, and industry and government often have widely scattered collections of serials. Computer storage of information about serials can provide quick aid to help the librarian locate the journal needed. Facsimile transmission can now help in transmitting copies of articles, making the computerized central serials record even more useful.

Constant monitoring of the use of serials can help in resolving the problems of storage and access to back files of serials. Treatment of secondary journals, those not indexed or of minor importance, can also be considered in terms of their use. Are they ephemeral? Are they worth checking in? Are they worth binding?

The inventory process for serials is a must because of the binding problem. Assignment of machine-readable control numbers to each serial as it arrives will help in inventory as well as circulation and routing. Frequent exposure of the unbound serials to the machine can alert the staff to missing numbers, and replacement procedures can be instituted. Materials at bindery can be charged to bindery through automated circulation procedures and will show up in the daily circulation printouts (or in readout) as being at bindery. A tentative due date can be assigned to help the reader calculate the time of return from the bindery.

The average serial article is short enough to make it attractive for photoduplication in hard-copy form. This should cut down on the need for circulating serials and on the loss of serials from the shelves. The effect of lowering or raising the cost of copying could be measured in a properly automated serial operation. Some library users are beginning to create files of important serials articles in their offices and at home. Such activity can be related to an SDI system if journal articles in certain areas are treated in the data base in the library. The resultant match against the reader's interest profile will alert the reader to possible additions to his file.

Subject lists of serials are often requested of the library. "What magazines do you have in biology?" is a typical question. Subject headings for the serial as a whole make it possible to print lists without tedious manual compiling. Fields such as biology and chemistry can be combined in the list and segmented to cover one part of the catalog or any combination of parts. A list of the serial publications of a given association is an example.

DOCUMENT CONTROL

United States government documents are frequently given separate treatment. Each document is part of a series by one government agency. In this sense, they can be considered serials in that they come out at intervals (regular or otherwise) and are kept together on the shelf. They are indexed in the *Monthly Catalog* each month and cumulated annually. The Documents Office classification number accompanies the invoice, and the documents are shelved by this number. Important to automation is the fact that the *Monthly Catalog* index gives a sequential number which must be referred to in the main part of the catalog in order to find the full data. These sequential numbers continue through the year and, by the addition of year prefixes, can become unique numbers for circulation inventory control.

The problem facing most libraries in handling documents is whether to integrate documents into the regular collection or to maintain a document department, or to compromise between the two. If integration is chosen, documents are given full cataloging treatment if suitable, and serials treatment otherwise. Cataloging is expensive, and the number of documents received is large. Because of this, many libraries handle all documents in a documents department and rely on the *Monthly Catalog* and the Documents Office classification scheme for a cheap and fairly serviceable arrangement, although a select few documents, principally reference items, are cataloged. The indexing method provided by the *Monthly Catalog* is not consistent with the L.C. subject heading list. If it were, it would be reasonably easy to include in the bibliographic search the documents which would help solve the major problem of achieving more effective use of documents even when they are segregated.

The handling of other documents—state, municipal, county, United Nations, and foreign—presents even more severe problems. Perhaps each unit of government could assume responsibility for contributing a standardized record of its output to a central data store.

The flood of near-print material generated by government agencies that does not find its way into existing channels of publication and indexing can be very important, both for current use and for historical purposes. A central data record informed of the existence of a new document would assist in recognition of important new materials. This will never be fully achieved, because in government, as in industry, there are "proprietary" materials or undigested materials that will not be put into a central record. Much good near-print material could be salvaged by an earnest effort to supply central data records with bibliographic information.

The present effort of the L.C., the National Agricultural Library (N.A.L.), and the N.L.M. to integrate the subject approach to their materials might well involve those who do the *Monthly Catalog* indexing. Indexing may be an art and cataloging may be a science, but perhaps the creative aspects of one can be tied to the order of the other to assist in the creation of what must come—a total store of knowledge usable by everyone. At the present time the *Monthly Catalog* indexers treat U.S. Department of Agriculture publications as do the catalogers of the N.A.L. The same system for both would prevent duplication of work at the source and greatly facilitate the end use.

CIRCULATION CONTROL

Control of the daily movement of thousands of books and other library materials, each of which is a distinctive unit, is a complex matter. Each item must return to its place in exact relation to other items on the shelf. As the total collection expands day by day, the actual physical spot to which a book must be returned cannot be assured.

There is a myth that library materials are arranged by subject. It is quite likely that in a given library a significant percentage is arranged by periodical title, document-issuing agency, type of microform, artist's name, arbitrary numbering system, publishers' numbers, classification systems, and various miscellaneous schemes. Added to this are rare book and other special collections, uncataloged gifts and block-purchase materials, and reserve collections. From the point of view of control, the problem of what circulates and what does not must be solved and safeguards established for those items which are not to be circulated. For automated circulation the system used to identify each piece must be able to restrict circulation according to the library's circulation policy.

In the public library, statistics from circulation records can pinpoint the type and volume of reading in different areas of the city. This can be helpful in establishing new branches, developing bookmobile service, and considering staffing changes in old branches. Sex, age, and other characteristics of readers and the relation of these factors to types and subjects of materials being circulated can yield data of interest to the book selectors. Who keeps books out overtime? It may be a few readers who are not too well organized, in which case it might pay to concentrate on these in an effort to reduce the overdue problem. How late are overdue books usually returned? It may be that a change in the loan period would be advisable. Do commuters have special problems in getting books back on time and should they be given special consideration? These and many other circulation problems can be solved more easily with appropriate statistics.

College and university libraries often do as much as half of their circulation in the reserve library. This type of circulation has not yet come under computer control, except for indication that the item has been removed from regular circulation and put on reserve. The advent of on-line techniques, direct-reading devices, and readout capability promises control of reserve circulation that will help in the analysis of reserve reading. Faculty have a way of reserving books which are never used. The relative security of the reserve library situation and the advantage of always being able to reach the book for his own use motivate the professor to put more books on reserve than he should. The restricted lending situation makes life difficult for many students, especially for those doing work in the same field for a different professor for different purposes. Reserve books should be only those which are under immediate pressure. Computerized reserve circulation can do a great deal to analyze reserve book use and indicate clearly that many books on reserve should not be there, but be under less restricted use. Shortage of copies in reserve use is often a problem, and the computer can indicate that certain titles have an inadequate number of copies to meet demand. Buying duplicate copies for reserve use is expensive. Those copies bought limit the purchase of other books. An accurate estimate of reserve needs is important. Present manual methods do not provide this.

Circulation statistics also provide aid in such matters as assessing the value of a change in exit control measures, the use of a rental collection, the need for longer opening hours, and scheduling of circulation help. When self-circulation stations become feasible, statistics will help in assessing the value of certain locations for such stations. Interlibrary loan statistics can be handled either through circulation or reference. If handled through the circulation department, loans can be part of the circulation records. A book checked out for this purpose can be so identified for the searching reader. Separate listings can be printed out for study. Analysis by subject, borrowing library, etc., can be made by the computer for any time period desired. Overall circulation statistics can be kept for analysis for longer periods of time.

CONCLUSION

Care must be taken to incorporate authority controls (author, subject, and title) in computerized processing. Classification is important, and the completeness of the bibliographic entry itself is a subject of concern. Decision on the uses to which the bibliographic data will be put must be made in structuring the system.

The library is recognized as a complicated inventory problem both for equipment and for library materials, particularly the latter. The computer can store inventory information in such a way as to greatly ease the work effort when inventory time comes. Many libraries that have abandoned materials inventory may be able to go back to it.

Serials cause certain unique problems in library automation, and some solutions are available. (1) Consistency in form of entry and standardization in the title used for a given serial are provided by using the L.C. cataloging form and making cross references to it from other forms. This ties serials in with cataloging and makes union lists and interlibrary loan easier. (2) Indexing services, whether by the publisher of the serials, a commercial indexer, or government indexers, promise improvement and reduction of duplicate indexing effort. (3) Computerization promises to lead toward emphasis on the article rather than the serial itself. (4) Irregular journals await on-line check-in for more efficient handling. (5) On-line control of all serials offers hope for service on current serials, where the question often is, "Has the last issue of *X Journal* come in?" (6) Serials holdings records are being widely distributed. (7) Binding of journals benefits from printout of binding lists, automatic claiming, inventory assistance, and recording of binding requirements on tape. (8) Analysis of serial use assists in relegating certain journals to secondary status and helps identify the heavy-use years for more efficient storage. (9) Printout of subject lists of serials saves reference time. (10) Union lists are created in great variety by drawing from a common store on computer tape. Without such a store, multiple copies of serials lists from individual library computer stores are exchanged. (11) Routing statistics help determine the number of subscriptions needed and provide a check on routing movement. A consistent stall in a certain in-basket might change priorities or generate hurry-up notices for the offender.

Better indexing of documents; better coverage of state, municipal, county documents; and cooperative effort to get information about near-print document materials into the record are promised. For United States government documents, the *Monthly Catalog* practice of assigning a unique number for each document can assist in a computerized subject approach to those documents. The computer may also tend to integrate documents with other materials by providing up-to-date cataloging data for documents from a central store.

Circulation control benefits from the accuracies resulting from automatic reading into the computer record by the use of data collection machinery, from the elimination of filing of book cards and slipping of books, and from automatic production of overdue notices. Work is speeded up, there are fewer errors, and drudgery is reduced. Self-charging, control of noneligible borrowers, and automated reserve circulation are soon to be with us.

Statistical control is important in all areas of the library's work. The computer's ability to count and sort enables it to provide a variety of statistics based on the data it has stored. The librarian must only make it clear what he needs in the way of statistics and the computer programmer can arrange for it. Statistics alone may prove to justify computerization. Such information as the following can come easily from the computer records: a frequent reckoning of the service being given to the library by each supplier; how long it is taking to catalog different kinds of materials; which journals are arriving late; who is reading what; and what special talents members of the library staff have. Administration of the library can be based largely on facts for the first time.

SUGGESTED READING LIST

Alanen, Sally, David E. Sparks, and Frederick G. Kilgour: "A Computer-monitored Library Technical Processing System," *American Documentation Institute: Proceedings of the Annual Meeting,* vol. 3, Adrianne Press, Woodland Hills, Calif., 1966, pp. 419–426.

American Standards Association, Sectional Committee on Standardization in the Field of Library Work and Documentation, Z39: *American Standard for Periodical Title Abbreviations,* ASA, New York, 1964, 19 pp.

Becker, Joseph: "Automating the Serial Record," *ALA Bulletin,* 58: 557–558, June 1964.

———: "Circulation and the Computer," *ALA Bulletin,* 58: 1007–1010, December 1964.

Bishop, David, Arnold L. Milner, and Fred W. Roper: "Publication Patterns of Scientific Serials," *American Documentation,* **16**: 113–121, April 1965.

Brown, W. L.: "Computer Controlled Charging System at Essendon Public Library," *Australian Library Journal,* **16**: 231–239, December 1967.

Cammack, Floyd, and Donald Mann: "Institutional Implications of an Automated Circulation Study," *College and Research Libraries,* **28**: 129–132, March 1967.

Computerized Circulation Summary, Arizona State University, Tempe, Ariz., 1965, 3 pp.

Culbertson, Don S.: "Computerized Serial Records," *Library Resources and Technical Services,* **9**: 53–58, Winter 1965.

Curran, Ann T.: "The Mechanization of the Serial Records for the Moving and Merging of the Boston Medical and Harvard Medical Serials," *Library Resources and Technical Services,* **10**: 362–372, Summer 1966.

DeJarnett, L. G.: "Library Circulation Control Using IBM 357's at Southern Illinois University," in *IBM Library Mechanization Symposium, 1964, Endicott, N.Y.*, IBM Corp., White Plains, N.Y., 1965, pp. 77-94.

Flannery, Anne, and James D. Mack: *Mechanized Circulation System, Lehigh University Library, Bethlehem, Pa., Center for Information Sciences,* Library Systems Analysis, report no. 4, Lehigh University, 1966, 17 pp., appendices.

Geller. William: *An Optical Character Recognition Research and Demonstration Project,* Council on Library Resources, Washington, 1968. ED 019 974.

Hammer, Donald P.: "Automated Procedures at Purdue University Library Serials Department, Including Binding," in Theodora Andrews (ed.), *Meeting on Automation in the Library—When, Where, and How, Purdue University, 1964, Papers,* Purdue University, Lafayette, Ind., 1965, pp. 26-35.

Harris, Michael H.: "The 357 Data Collection System for Circulation Control," *College and Research Libraries,* **26**: 119-120, 158, March 1965.

Jones, H. W.: "Computerized Subscription and Periodicals Routing in an Aerospace Library," *Special Libraries,* **58**: 634-658, November 1967.

Kennedy, Robert A.: "Bell Laboratories' Library Real-time Loan System (BELLRELL)," *Journal of Library Automation,* **1**: 128-146, June 1968.

Lebowitz, A. I.: "AEC (Atomic Energy Commission) Library Serial Record: A Study in Library Mechanization," *Special Libraries,* **58**: 154-159, March 1967.

McCormick, Jack: "The Use of an Optical Scanner in a Small Research Library," *The LARC Reports* (1) **31**: 26-34, December 1968.

McCoy, Ralph E.: "Computerized Circulation Work: A Case Study of the 357 Data Collection System (Southern Illinois University)," *Library Resources and Technical Services,* **9**: 59-65, 1965.

Nolan, K. P., et al.: "Mechanized Circulation Controls," *Special Libraries,* **59**: 47-50, January 1968.

Skelton, Margaret W., and Richard R. Haefner: *A Computer Program for Library Journals,* E. I. DuPont de Nemours and Co., Savannah River Laboratory, Aiken, Ga., 1965, 55 pp. DP-970.

Trueswell, Richard W.: "Two Characteristics of Circulation and Their Effect on the Implementation of Mechanized Circulation Control Systems," *College and Research Libraries,* **25**: 285-291, July 1964.

———: "A Quantitative Measure of User Circulation Requirements and Its Possible Effect on Stack Thinning and Multiple Copy Determination," *American Documentation,* **16**: 20-25, January 1965.

Vdovin, George, et al.: *Serials Computer Project: Final Report,* University of California, San Diego, LaJolla, 1964.

CHAPTER 6
ADMINISTRATIVE PROCESSES

The administrator has some concern with all processes in the library, but certain aspects of organization and operation are his special province. Automation, in particular, is necessarily so pervasive of all functions that it must be treated in the broadest possible terms. No library exists in isolation, and administrative concerns which extend beyond the library are extremely important to the success of any effort leading to and sustaining library automation. The administrator must deal with the computer center, other users of the computer center, larger institutions of which the library is a part, the network, automation activities of professional associations, data bases available and being developed elsewhere, and significant library-related activities of companies supplying hardware, software, and systems planning.

Mechanization efforts have been carried out within the traditional organizational and operational structure. The availability of proven automation capabilities will force libraries to make major changes for economic reasons. Only a few libraries have used computers to good advantage, and most will find themselves faced with the need and opportunity to jump from manual operations to automation.

The tendency has been to mechanize circulation or serials or acquisitions, depending on the need of the moment. Now it is evident that there must be an overall plan for the automation of the library and that each development toward that end must fit the ultimate objective and provide an immediate detailed plan to guide and measure results.

The administrator is concerned with rapid access to the library's records. The system must be able to handle a heavy flow of data and a large number of queries more or less simultaneously and do it in a way that is acceptable and convenient to the user and at a reasonable cost. The administrator wants up-to-date records, and the system must be planned to receive and process new data promptly and accurately.

Communication is extremely important in library automation because there is need to share activity with other libraries and to achieve access to other data bases provided by government and industry. This implies a need for standardization of techniques and development of equipment suitable for libraries. The administrator must help in the creation of such standards and encourage manufacturers to undertake development of needed equipment. Finally, the administrator must encourage the design of software that is responsive to library needs, preferably in terms that permit sharing, for uniqueness is an expensive luxury if there is any available alternative.

ORGANIZATION

There is continuing conflict between the custodial and the service functions of the library. The conflict centers on the personnel most directly concerned with the library as a collection of books and other materials as distinct from the library as an information store. Libraries have had to introduce reference departments staffed with librarians who are information-oriented. These reference librarians have become the principal users of the catalog, an important factor in book selection, the prime contact with the public, and without doubt an increasingly important factor in library service. In contrast, the organizational separation of acquisitions and cataloging from reference and circulation has tended to isolate a portion of the technical processing staff from the users' needs and attitudes. Finally, the relationship between libraries and the public they should serve is not usually ideal; libraries in educational institutions are not properly integrated with the teaching program, and public libraries are inadequately staffed.

Better library organization is not the solution to all these problems, but combined with judicious use of automation technology, reorganization can accomplish a great deal. Clerical work in libraries should be eliminated or done by clerical help. The computer is well suited to tasks which people find routine, boring, and too demanding. A new organization pattern might include a *data services department* staffed by a few computer-oriented librarians, a systems person or two, programmers, and typists. Input of all data, whether from a cataloging, acquisitions, reference, circulation, or administration center, that cannot be done directly on-line would be done by this department. Relations with the computer center (or operation of it, if the library has its own computer), output control, and distribution would be the responsibilities of this department. Inventory, exit, control, shelf reading, stack maintenance, reading-area control, shelving activities, serials and documents check-in, and invoice checking are all possible activities for this department.

A *professional services department* could include the professional work being done in acquisitions, cataloging, and reference, thus making reference an integral part of cataloging and book selection.

An *administrative services department* would include personnel work, statistical planning, report writing, budget control, and other professional aspects of the library administration. In this area, too, clerical functions would be taken over by a data services department.

The need for reaching the library's public more effectively could be met by a *liaison services department.* Librarians staffing this department would be few in number, experienced, and representative of a variety of subject specializations. Formulation of reading interest profiles for computer-based SDI (selective dissemination of information) systems and the feedback to improve the system would be part of the responsibility of the department. Contact with individual users (such as professors in educational libraries), research groups, organizational users, etc., would be the principal function of this department.

The responsibility of the library to provide access to the whole storehouse of knowledge must become easier to fulfill. Ready access to knowledge stored elsewhere, microstorage in the library, and improved reproduction facilities will make the custodial responsibility somewhat easier to live with. The computer/communications-based library network will definitely improve access to remote materials. If the network involves joint development of data bases and standards, the data services department will need a section responsible for coordination with other network members, for development of common standards, and for computer relationships.

Information science, documentation, and other new disciplines concerned with information retrieval started because of the tremendous increase in the growth of knowledge, the desperate need for more effective literature searches in research and development work, and the inadequacies of libraries and the commercial indexing services. The scientists faced with information problems often discounted library capabilities and sometimes did not even consider them. The *American Society for Information Science* (previously the *American Documentation Institute*) helped in bringing information seekers together with librarians. The basis for the togetherness was the computer and what it could do to help solve information problems. This resulted in a mix of scientists, computer specialists, psychologists, linguists, librarians, and a sprinkling of researchers in the humanities and social sciences who had information problems. KWIC (Key-word-in-context) indexes, subject data banks, thesauri, and considerable new knowledge about using the computer to search data banks have been forthcoming. For libraries, the result should be increased emphasis on the reference function, valuable new reference tools usable only with a computer, availability of data banks, and a whole new area of library cooperation.

OPERATIONS

Efficient operation of the library depends on accurate knowledge of what is transpiring in the library. In the past this knowledge has been very uncertain. Concerned members of the library staff might state with some assurance that a certain jobber was giving good service, but they would be unable to say just how good or whether it was better than the service provided by another jobber. The administrator might like to know what persons were most active in assisting the library in its book-selection effort. A good guess by the acquisitions people would bring up a few names, but nothing approaching an appraisal of the total situation. Is cataloging slowing down since certain staff changes occurred? How much, and where? Data collection in all areas of the library and storage of these data to yield up-to-date and accurate information about the library's operation will facilitate more efficient library administration.

In the past, the administrator has been unable to deal directly with pertinent data. With automation much of what is needed can be obtained directly from the computer record. At other administrative levels horizontally as well as vertically, operations will be based on more complete, more current, and more accurate data. A decision by the catalogers to file by date under subject headings might hinder the reference librarians or the public in their use of the catalog. Circulation and reference statistics, not cataloging statistics, are needed to reveal this story. The elimination of error-prone work, such as filing, typing book and periodical orders, preparing binding lists, printing overdue notices, compiling bibliographies, listing budget figures, and preparing statistical compilations of various sorts, makes for more efficient operations in other departments.

STAFFING

The projected data services department should have responsibility for orientation of the entire staff to library automation. The understanding and cooperation of the librarians in the professional, administrative, and liaison areas are essential to success in automation because the entire library is necessarily affected. The administrator can encourage attendance at association meetings, automation workshops, and new courses on library automation being offered by library schools. New staff members for the library and the computer center who have some orientation to library automation are also helpful. Circulation of journals such as the *Journal of Library Automation,* the *Journal of the American Society for Information Science,* and *Datamation* is essential to the preservation of professional competence.

RELATIONS WITH THE COMPUTER CENTER

It is increasingly likely that the library will be relying on a computer center that serves not only the library, but other areas as well. Such reliance may be diminished by small satellite computers that can perform much of a library's work, or it may be increased by installation of new super computers serving a large area.

The computer center, as distinct from a data processing center, is more closely related to academic than administrative activities on campus. The computer center is still a changing and developing organization in most places, and the library depending on it should work to understand and improve it.

Computer centers serving libraries have assigned one or more analysts or programmers completely to library work or alternatively have assigned one phase of the library's work along with nonlibrary projects. Both approaches have their drawbacks. In the first case there is awareness of the side effects of data systems in any one area of the library's work. Loss of such a person from the computer center staff, however, can be a serious matter for the library. In the second case with assignments to circulation, cataloging, serials, acquisitions, and administration, there is danger of lack of coordination among them in developing a true system. Another approach, now being used successfully by the universities of British Columbia,[1] is to develop systems departments in each library. Cooperation between these departments has been of great assistance in automation development in each library.

Pressures on the computer center by other customers is often a problem. In a university or school situation, the needs of the registrar at registration time or the needs of the business office at payroll or budget time can overwhelm the computer center. Certain library files must always be available regardless of other pressures. The library administrator and/or the head of the data services department must make this clear to the computer center and regularly monitor the performance.

The satellite computer in dispersed data processing centers, with backup provided by a large computer elsewhere, promises the best and most economic solution, and it will make a data services department much more necessary.

DATA BANKS

The library administrator must now add to his concerns the collections of computer-based data known as data banks. They already exist in real estate and insurance companies, census and credit

[1] University of British Columbia, Simon Frazer University, and the University of Victoria.

bureaus, and in libraries. The MARC data bank at the Library of Congress and the MEDLARS data bank at the National Library of Medicine are well known. Two extensive listings of data banks are the Science Associates list, "Directory of Computerized Information in Science and Technology," and A.L.A.'s "Data Banks, with special reference to Data Bases in the Social Sciences and Humanities" (in preparation for A.L.A. publication in 1971). The National Science Foundation and the Federal Libraries Committee work on data bank development and provide a well-qualified service on current data about technology and practices. Many firms offer commercial data bank service. EDUCOM (Interuniversity Communications Council) provides active leadership in the identification of file resources and has begun to take a census of data banks on the campuses of universities belonging to EDUCOM. Libraries are creating many specialized data banks which will serve other libraries' needs and some for their own needs only. A college catalogs listing is an example of the former, circulation files the latter.

If the data bank is bibliographic in nature, libraries should try to influence its development by recommending use of library standards, such as those represented by the MARC program. The advice of librarians, particularly on the matter of the subject structure, is often sought by those planning such data bases. Anyone planning a thesaurus in a special field can benefit from examining existing subject heading lists both for structure and content. Someday we may have a superthesaurus which will cover all fields and will be used by everyone. Until then, special thesauri appear to be necessary. Each reference tool is a data bank, of course, and computer-stored data banks are often printed out and become regular reference tools.

More and more reference tools will be generated from computer banks because the updating process is so much easier. The printout version, such as *Index Medicus,* often includes only part of the total store. Access to the total store can be had only by computer search. *Index Medicus* could be printed out to the total subject depth of nine levels instead of the present three, but the bulk of the printout would be much larger. The use of microfilm printout and conversion from that to other reduced forms may simplify the problem.

NETWORKS

There now appears no doubt that library automation development will be deeply involved in communications networks. The library administrator will be involved in the establishment and operation of networks and must also consider the potential of commercial networks. The intended goal of such a network is apparent in this quotation about Western Union: "Today, Western Union's ultimate goal is to consolidate its record communications services into one, integrated, computer controlled system providing common switching facilities, which will enable a customer to obtain access to the particular service or services that he needs at any given time. To this end, four computer centers located in New York, Chicago, San Francisco, and Mahwah, New Jersey have been completed, with three in operation and the fourth becoming operational currently. These centers route messages, switch circuits, adjust transmission speeds and convert codes between systems, collect data, and handle billing functions. W. U. is currently programming and testing a large capacity, multiple access computer to interconnect its systems and services on an even broader scale."[2] Whether this, like present Bell Telephone services, will be restricted because of expense remains to be seen.

The library aspects of information networks are presented in recent works by Joseph Becker and Wallace Olsen in the 1968 *Annual Review of Information Science and Technology,*[3] the EDUNET (EDUCOM Network) report,[4] and Norman Meise's recent work on the design for an automated national library system.[5] The programs at the National Library of Medicine,[6] the Ontario Universities Bibliographic Center, and the Ohio Colleges Library Center[7] are also of interest.

[2] *Dow Digest,* Sept. 1969, pp. 61-62.

[3] American Society for Information Science, *Annual Review of Information Science and Technology,* vol. 3, Encyclopaedia Britannica, Chicago, 1968, pp. 289-327.

[4] Interuniversity Communications Council, *EDUNET. N. U.,* Wiley, New York, 1967.

[5] Norman Meise, *Conceptual Design of an Automated National Library System,* Scarecrow Press, Metuchen, N.J., 1969.

[6] Charles J. Austin. "Transmission of Bibliographic Information: Brasenose Conference on the Automation of Libraries, Oxford, England, 1966," *Proceedings of the Anglo-American Conference on the Mechanization of Library Services,* Mansell, London, 1967. pp. 143-149.

[7] Duncan Wall. *The Ontario Universities Bibliographical Center,* a progress plan dated September 1968, 43 pp. For copy, contact author at Kent State University Library.

Library networks might concern themselves with (1) shared data banks of cataloging information; (2) central serials records for member libraries; (3) interlibrary loans; (4) transmission of graphic materials; (5) access to special data banks; (6) locating out-of-print materials; (7) book selection; (8) statistics of member libraries; (9) fact retrieval in special areas; (10) exchange of duplicates lists; (11) exchange of want lists; (12) guiding collection development; (13) sharing of library materials; (14) planning for better service at the same or lower cost; (15) automation developments in the national libraries and other networks.

The administrator confronted by the possibility of a network must be able to contribute certain knowledge about his own institution to the network planners. The budget, the size of the collection and staff, characteristics of the public served, cataloging situation (size of backlog, classification used, variants of L.C. cataloging, condition of the catalog), and serials and documents handling rules are all important. The degree of automation already achieved and details about this will be needed. Each library has problems and some idea of priorities for solving them. The network planners must discover the restrictions that will hinder network development. Political, financial, and technical restrictions are possibilities for any network planner. He must discover the opportunities within these constraints with the assistance of the librarians and other key people in each member institution.

CONCLUSION

Mechanization puts machines to work to do the same things that were previously done manually. Computers and telecommunications now encourage total automation and a fresh approach to library operation. The organization and operation of the library and the administrator's relation to the world outside the library are subject to change. In the library, organization will tend to group clerical duties together and relate them to the computer, which excels at this kind of work. Professional activities will also be more closely drawn together in order that operations may be conducted where accurate, up-to-date information is always available. Administration, both vertically and horizontally, will benefit by easy access to information about activities at all levels and in every area.

Outside the library, the administrator must relate to computerized activities in other parts of the larger organizations; must maintain a close relationship with the computer center; become involved in automated library network planning at the city, state, regional, national, and international levels; understand the computer activities of his suppliers; and watch the offerings of business concerns that sell automation equipment, offer software services, make systems studies, and maintain data bases.

SUGGESTED READING LIST

American Library Association: *The Library and Information Networks of the Future,* prepared for U.S. Air Force Systems Command, Rome Air Development Center, Chicago, 1963, 43 pp. AD 401 347.

BALANCE (Bay Area Libraries Associated Network for Cooperative Exchange): A Report on Computerized Procedures, Bay Area Library Working Committee, San Jose, Calif., 1966, 78 pp.

Becker, Joseph: "The Future of Library Automation and Information Networks," *Library Automation, A State of the Art Review,* American Library Association, Chicago, 1969, pp. 1–6.

———: "Using Computers in a New University Library," *ALA Bulletin,* **59**: 823-826, October 1965.

The Biomedical Communications Network: Technical Development Plan, National Library of Medicine, Bethesda, Md., 1968.

Bregzis, Ritvars: "The Bibliographic Information Network: Some Suggestions for a Different View of the Library Catalog: Brasenose Conference on the Automation of Libraries, Oxford, England, 1966," in John Harrison and Peter Laslett (eds.), *Proceedings of the Anglo-American Conference on the Mechanization of Library Services,* Mansell, London, 1967, pp. 128–142.

Brown, G. W., et al., eds.: *EDUNET: Report of the Summer Study on Information Networks Conducted by the Interuniversity Communications Council (EDUCOM),* Wiley, New York, 1967, 440 pp.

Budington, William S.: "National Information Networks (with discussion)," *Law Library Journal,* **60**: 379–87, November 1967.

Covill, George W.: "Librarian + Systems Analyst = Teamwork?" *Special Libraries,* **58**: 99–101, February 1967.

Cox, N. S. M., et al.: *Computer and the Library: The Role of the Computer in the Organization and Handling of Information in Libraries,* Archon, Newcastle-upon-Tyne, 1966, 96 pp., bibliography.

DeGennaro, Richard: "The Development and Administration of Automated Systems in Academic Libraries," *Journal of Library Automation,* **1**, (1): 75-91, March 1968.

Fussler, Herman H., and Charles T. Payne: *Annual Report 1966/67 to the National Science Foundation from the University of Chicago Library: Development of an Integrated, Computer-based, Bibliographical Data System for a Large University Library,* University of Chicago Library, Chicago, 1967.

Geddes, Andrew: "Data Processing in a Cooperative System—Opportunities for Service, (Nassau Library Systems)," in John Harvey (ed.), *Data Processing in Public and University Libraries,* Drexel Information Science Services, vol. 3, Spartan Books, Washington, 1966, pp. 25–35.

Gull, Cloyd Dake: "Automated Circulation Systems," *Library Automation: A State of the Art Review,* American Library Association, Chicago, 1969, pp. 138–148.

Hammer, Donald P.: "Scheduling Conversion," in John Harvey (ed.), *Data Processing in Public and University Libraries,* Drexel Information Science Series, vol. 3, Spartan Books, Washington, 1966, pp. 103–123.

King, Gilbert W., et al.: *Automation and the Library of Congress,* Library of Congress, Washington, 1963, 88 pp.

Licklider, J. C. R.: *Libraries of the Future; Based on a Study Sponsored by the Council on Library Resources, Inc. and Conducted by Bolt, Beranek, and Newman, Inc.,* M.I.T., Cambridge, Mass., 1965, 219 pp., bibliography.

Lorenz, John G.: "The Communication Network: An Academic Library and the Dissemination of Knowledge," *Dedication of the University Library,* Bowling Green State University, Bowling Green, Ohio, February 1968, pp. 19–27.

National Advisory Commission on Libraries: "Library Services for the Nation's Needs: Toward Fulfillment of a National Policy," *ALA Bulletin,* **63**: 67–94, January 1969.

National Agricultural Library: "Pesticides Information Center, N.A.L. Will Convert 5,000 Herbicide Records into Machine-readable Form," *IAAID Quarterly Bulletin,* **12**: 147, October 1967.

Nugent, William R.: "NELINET—the New England Library Information Network," *Congress of the International Federation for Information Processing (IFIP), 4th, Edinburgh, 5–10 August, 1968, Proceedings,* North-Holland Publishing, Amsterdam, 1968, pp. G28-G32.

Parker, Ralph H.: "Not a Shared System: An Account of a Computer Operation Designed Specifically and Solely for Library Use at the University of Missouri," *Library Journal,* **92**: 3967–3970, November 1, 1967.

Pflug, Gunther, and Bernhard Adams, eds.: *Elecktronische Datenverarbeitung in der Universitatsbibliothek Bochum,* Bochum, West Germany, 1968, 147 pp.

Price, Derek J. De Solla: "Networks of Scientific Papers," *Science,* **149**: 510–515, July 30, 1965.

Reily, Kevin D.: "Nature of Typical Data Bases," Institute of Library Research, University of California, Los Angeles, 1967, 51 pp.

Rice University: "Rice University Developing Regional Communication and Information Exchange Connecting Eighteen Gulf Coast Area Academic Institutions," *Scientific Information Notes,* **10**: 1, June-July, 1968.

Stuart-Stubbs, Basil: "Automation in a University Library from the Administrator's Viewpoint," *C.A.C.U.L. Workshop on Library Automation, University of British Columbia, 1967,* Canadian Association of College and University Libraries, Ottawa, 1967, pp. 124–134.

Takle, K. G.: "Operating Information Retrieval Satellite," *Special Libraries,* 58: 644-650, November 1967.

Troutman, Joan C.: *Inventory of Available Data Bases,* University of California, Institute of Library Research, Los Angeles, Calif., 1967, 55 pp.

Warheit, I. A.: "The Mechanization of Libraries," *1967 IEEE International Convention Record,* Institute of Electrical and Electronics Engineers, New York, 1967, pp. 44-47.

Wedgeworth, R.: "Brown University Library Fund Accounting System," *Journal of Library Automation,* **1**: 51-65, March 1968.

PART II
METHODOLOGY OF LIBRARY AUTOMATION

The process of definition, analysis, development, installation, use, and evaluation that is known as the systems approach has been notably successful in guiding the introduction of technology to important areas of man's life and activities. Systems methodology has been especially beneficial when intense human involvement is linked to applications at the very frontiers of knowledge and capability. The systems approach is itself an instance of close and systematic interaction of man with his logic and his machines.

The successful application of a new technology to an existing discipline requires an appreciation of the historical context of the problem and the existing institutions.

The library reflects the forces that have led man to record and preserve whatever he finds to be interesting and useful, to refer to that accumulation, and to attempt to comprehend both the facts and the significance of the historical record. Many institutions participate in the storage and retrieval functions of a complex society; the library is distinguished both by the materials it processes and by the services it renders.

The designation as a library is not usually applied unless the materials processed have their value in use rather than in consumption, are essentially intellectual rather than economic, are more important for their content than their physical embodiment, and remain useful for long periods of time, although some are "current awareness" items of ephemeral value. Many items fulfill these conditions and are readily accepted by some, but not all, libraries. Each of these aspects finds favor as the basis for specialization and provides the distinguishing characteristics of stores, banks, museums, broadcasters, and publishers; the generality and diversity of a library is well marked by all of them.

The bridging of the gap between contributors to the stock of knowledge and the recipients of it is performed, in part, by many institutions. Speeches, newspapers and magazines, radio and television, and the stage and screen each provide a link, with strong emphasis on the initiative of the recipient.

Individual preferences and nonstandard products are the classical basis for a rambling search and selection process. The shopping trip and mail-order catalog are the counterparts to browsing through library stacks and through the card file; uncertainty about what is wanted and what is available favors the use of the wish book and index rather than direct handling of the physical object.

Apart from the selection of materials to be processed and a modest effort toward standardization, the library is a passive receiver. A diversity of materials and a wide range of forms, shapes, sizes, and weights are accepted in order to amass an effectively complete body of material in anticipation of future use.

As the individual materials are accumulated, the library must endeavor to minimize the effect of unwieldy and inconvenient physical characteristics. The transition from treatment on an individual basis to processing as a member of a collection is a feature of critical importance. Little can be done with a single physical object; there is no natural or optimal form or shape, and any change is expensive. A collection, however, especially a large collection, can be organized into convenient subgroups containing materials that have similar properties. An effective degree of control and standardization can be attained even though the incoming materials are physically diverse and uncontrolled.

The development of an integrated plan and program for automation can provide visibility of many worthwhile opportunities.

There are four levels of concern in a systems project. The first is the level of *needs* for data to support operational controls and management decisions. Second is the level of *concepts* of an approach to satisfaction of the need. Third is the level of technical, administrative, and control *processes.* Fourth, and last, is the level of *resources* to implement the processes.

Too many projects begin at the lowest level in terms of particular human and mechanical capabilities; all too few ever give serious consideration to all the levels in order, from needs to resources. Mechanization, at its simplest, substitutes mechanical resources for human resources without change of the processes.

Mechanization, at its best, includes modification of the processes to remove the features that were oriented to manual use. Automation, at its worst, is just mislabeled mechanization; at its best, it encompasses new concepts to better serve the needs and introduces the processes and resources best fitted to those concepts. Automation does not imply elimination of human resources in favor of machines, but rather the choice of concepts and processes that use both human and machine resources in the tasks best suited to each.

From a variety of choices, it is possible to assign priorities to elements that offer early returns. Size, sequence, and leverage are important factors in selecting projects. In general, larger projects afford greater opportunities dependent, of course, on the degree of improvement that is technically and operationally attainable. When the output of one system is used as input to another, it is usually advantageous to work "downstream" to take advantage of the controlled outputs rather than to work "upstream" against the uncontrolled and changing inputs. Not all projects are immediately and directly beneficial. Some are worth doing because they are necessary to legal and financial control and others because they provide the necessary preconditions to other directly beneficial projects.

If the technology does not provide the full scale of desired capability, an interim solution to some portions can be provided with the recognition that enhanced capability can be accommodated whenever it becomes available. It is important to develop some feasible and practical solution to each major problem before undertaking a commitment to implement a new system. It can be expected that improved elements will be developed and can be utilized, but systems that assume a technological "breakthrough" or development of a new device are best treated as research and development rather than implementation efforts.

When it is assumed that the boundaries of a problem are precise and unchanging, the solution is constrained to an equally precise form. Such precision is appropriate to mechanization, but neither necessary nor desirable under the broader view of automation. Few current processes are static and, with a firm conception of the logic involved, it is feasible and practical to include dynamic features in a system which encompasses a variety of processes. The economics of such an approach are unfavorable if a single process is involved. Whatever the technology, the cost of generality is real and nonzero and must be amortized over many uses if the final economic result is to be favorable. The economic advantage in automation is dependent upon the development of many uses for the same data, many applications of the same logic, and long-term use of a basic foundation with minor adaptation whenever needed.

A machine, whether as simple as a light switch or as complex as a computer, has a relatively limited repertoire of functions. There is far more similarity between the switch with one or two functions and the computer with fifty or a hundred than between the computer and the human brain. The combination of a few score basic commands offers a rich and powerful vocabulary with many useful sequences. The problems in exploiting such a device are to find logical similarity that can be repeated and to eliminate or minimize diversity or reserve it for manual processing. In a data system, the logical foundation is potentially very extensive. Within the limits of practical and economic operations there are increasing opportunities to ease human burdens of mass and detail and to extend the use of human cognitive abilities.

Capabilities for improved service and prospects for lower unit costs are not assured simply by expressions of confidence and dedication. Logic and the devices that perform logical operations offer many capabilities and many opportunities for misuse of them. Careful planning, competent personnel, and sound professional library and system effort are all essential.

It has been often repeated that successful computer-based systems were beneficial because of the improvements in work flow and the simplification of the manual processes rather than because of the computer itself. That conclusion may be overdrawn—there are some things that a computer can do better than any person—but the essential truth remains, and every library can and should look for system improvements long before automation becomes a feasible, practical, and economic reality.

The systems approach is actually quite simple and direct. Its four phases can be described as follows.

The *identification and definition* phase establishes an understanding of the objectives, the policies, the responsibilities, and the importance of the problem among all those concerned with the project.

A continuing *review and evaluation* effort by the system users reveals needs that might be served. A regular *development and experimentation* effort by the system designers indicates opportunities for exploitation of technology. Together these two efforts establish an environment that fosters new ideas, identifies significant needs and opportunities, and lays the foundation for effective communication and collaboration.

An *initiation request* begins the effort in problem identification. The *survey* includes, in appropriate detail, a review of the problem, its environmental setting, the controlling influences, and a description of previous efforts, of current activities, and of the goals to be attained.

The resulting *problem definition* is the statement of the problem as it is recognized and the guide to all subsequent work.

The preliminary efforts in analysis may be conducted in parallel with the identification in order to ensure an appropriate basis for later work or simply to reduce the total time span of the systems project.

The *analysis and specification* phase provides a precise view of the demands to be met by the system and a recommendation of the best approach to a solution. This effort considers five specific topics and yields two end products.

A statement of *criteria* stipulates the requirements that must be met, the restrictions that must not be violated, and the objectives to be sought. *Quantification* of the demands imposed from outside the system reveals the interfaces[1] that must be maintained and the identity and rates of flow of both objects and data across the interfaces.

The requirements and the possibilities are reflected by the *alternatives* that are formulated to express possible approaches.

[1] The electrical convenience outlet represents a fine example of an interface design that allows power generation and distribution to proceed independent of appliance design. The incompatibility of foreign electric razors to American power sources highlights the cost of incomplete interface independence.

Intuition as well as formal techniques of modeling, demonstration, and simulation provides a spectrum of choices. The *selection* process narrows the alternatives to a single recommended approach by considering the feasibility, practicality, and economics of each alternative. The final step provides an *exposition* of the purpose, approach, and system targets.

The results of the analysis are documented in a *system specification,* and the suggestions for conduct of the project are expressed in a *system proposal.*

The *system design and development* phase establishes the characteristics that will be apparent to the user. The most important questions are *what* the user must do relative to input and output and *what* the system will provide or accomplish. The technical details of *how* the inputs are handled and the outputs are created need be considered only to the level necessary to assure that some suitable process is available. Further development of the internal processes is unnecessary and undesirable until agreement about the external features has been established with the user.

The *functional characteristics* of a design encompass the basic function of the system, the object and data flows, and the operational activities. The *performance characteristics* provide for consideration of scope, size, availability, and response. The *component selection* considers variability, speed, and consistency in establishing a choice of human machine processors for each activity.

The *development specification* reflects the design and establishes the requirements for the development of procedures to guide human processing and the development of programs to control machine processing. The *logic* of manual procedures, expressed in *instructions,* is presented in formal *manuals. Training specifications* provide the basis for development of a staff competent to use the system.

The *logic* of machine programs, expressed in *programs,* is corrected with the aid of the computer in a process popularly known as *debugging.*

The final products of this phase are *test and installation specifications* to guide the efforts needed to assure that the development is completed and the system is ready for operational use.

The *installation and operation* phase is the culmination of the systems effort and the moment of truth for the entire project.

A variety of *test* strategies are available to facilitate the proof of the design approach and the development results. The major challenge in testing is to complete the integration of many elements that are individually complete and workable but may be collectively incompatible.

The *installation* includes conversion of any existing data files, a proof of the new system in parallel with the old, and a routine time trial to establish both comparative and absolute indices of availability and response.

The *release for production* is a certification of the system for regular *operation* and must provide a definitive appraisal of the degree of attainment of the system objectives and of fulfillment of the evaluation criteria.

The *maintenance specification* closes the project effort with a completion report and the maintenance specifications to guide the continuing use of the system.

It should be recognized that any attempt to explain how a specialist conducts his work will appear to be both incomplete and excessively wordy. The impression of incompleteness can be dispelled if a clear distinction is drawn between *what* is to be accomplished during the system development and the details of *how* the forms and techniques are employed. The impression of wordiness is more critical; every project is unique in some details and obvious in others. The discussion of the systems approach touches upon the whole spectrum in order to establish a perspective of the processes and to clarify the vocabulary. It should not be assumed that an appreciation of the whole pattern conveys the knowledge and expertise of an analyst or programmer.

Every library will have need for assistance in major system projects.

Major projects are best done under firm control and a tight schedule. There are peak demands for a variety of skills that cannot be met internally even in the largest libraries. The best strategy is to maintain a regular staff of well-qualified personnel sufficient in number to meet all continuing needs and to obtain outside assistance for specialty skills and peak demands.

In a typical major systems project, the effort should be almost equally balanced between the systems staff (internal and outside) and the user departments. Without close and continuing involvement of the users, the system may be technically competent, but the likelihood of full acceptance and real success is poor. The work balance will not be equal at every stage of the project, of course, since the level of effort will vary widely, and the user involvement should be kept nearly stable throughout.

GLOSSARY

ACCURACY: the degree of freedom from error, that is, the degree of conformity to truth or to a rule. Accuracy is contrasted with precision; e.g., four-place numbers are less precise than six-place numbers; nevertheless a properly computed four-place number might be more accurate than an improperly computed six-place number.

ACRONYM: a word formed from the first letter or letters of the words in a name, term, or phrase, e.g.; *algo*rithmic *l*anguage, *for*mula *tran*slator, *co*mmon *b*usiness-*o*riented *l*anguage.

ALGEBRA, BOOLEAN: a process of reasoning or a deductive system of theorems using a symbolic logic and dealing with classes, propositions, or on-off circuit elements. It employs symbols to represent operators such as AND, OR, NOT, EXCEPT, IF . . . THEN, etc., and to permit mathematical calculation. Named after George Boole, famous English mathematician (1815–1864).

ALGORITHM: a prescribed set of well-defined rules, or process, for the solution of a problem in a finite number of steps, e.g., a full statement of an arithmetical procedure for evaluating sin X to a stated precision.

ALPHABET: an ordered set of unique representations, called characters, e.g., the alphabet 0 and 1, the twenty-six letters of the English alphabet, and the complete American Standard Coded Character Set.

ALPHAMERIC (also alphanumeric): a generic term for alphabetic letters, numerical digits, and special characters which are machine-processable.

ANALYSIS: the methodical investigation of a problem and the separation of the problem into smaller related units for further detailed study.

APPLICATION: the system or problem to which a computer is applied. Reference is often made to an application as being either of the computational type, wherein arithmetic computations predominate, or of the data processing type, wherein data handling operations predominate.

ARTIFICIAL LANGUAGE: a procedure-oriented language suited for stating information for computer storage and processing.

AUTOMATION: (1) the implementation of processes by automatic means. (2) The theory, art, or technique of making a process more automatic. (3) The investigation, design, development, and application of methods of rendering processes automatic, self-moving, or self-controlling.

BATCH PROCESSING: a system approach to processing where similar input items are grouped for processing during the same machine run.

BLOCK DIAGRAM: a diagram of a system, instrument, computer, or program in which selected portions are represented by annotated boxes and interconnecting lines.

CENTER, DATA PROCESSING: a computer installation providing data processing service for users, sometimes called customers, on a reimbursable or nonreimbursable basis.

CHARACTER RECOGNITION: the technique of reading, identifying, and encoding a printed character by optical means.

CHECK: a process of partial or complete testing of the correctness of machine operations, the existence of certain prescribed conditions within the computer, or the correctness of the results produced by a program. A check of any of these conditions may be made automatically by the equipment or may be programmed.

CHECK-SUM: the sum used in a summation check.

COLLATE: to compare and/or merge two or more similarly ordered sets of items into one ordered set.

CONTROL DATA: one or more items of data used as control to identify, select, execute, or modify another routine, record, file, operation data value, etc.

CYBERNETICS: the theory of control and communication in the machine and the animal.

DATA: a general term for the symbols used to refer to or to describe an object, idea, condition, situation, or other factors. Data are represented by numbers, letters, and other characters, by images, and by physical states.

DATA COLLECTION: the act of bringing data from one or more points to a central point.

DATA PROCESSING SYSTEM: a network of machine components capable of accepting information, processing it according to man-made instructions, and producing the computed results.

DATA, TEST: a set of data developed specifically to test the adequacy of a computer run or system. The data may be actual data that have been taken from previous operations or artificial data created for this purpose.

DEBUG: to detect, locate, and remove errors from a programming routine or malfunctions from a computer.

DIAGRAM: (1) a schematic representation of a sequence of subroutines designed to solve a problem. (2) A coarser and less symbolic representation than a flowchart, frequently including descriptions in English words. (3) A schematic or logical drawing showing the electrical circuit or logical arrangements within a computer.

DICTIONARY: a list of code names used in a routine or system and their intended meaning in that routine or system.

DOCUMENTATION: the group of techniques necessary for the orderly presentation, organization, and communication of recorded specialized knowledge in order to maintain a complete record of reasons for changes in variables.

ELEMENT, DATA: a specific item of information appearing in a set of data; e.g., in the following set of data, each item is a data element: the quantity of a supply item issued, a unit rate, an amount, and the balance of stock items on hand.

ENGLISH, RULY: a form of English in which every word has one and only one conceptual meaning and each concept has one and only one word to describe it. This is a hypothetical language, based on English, which complies uniformly to a definite set of rules, without exceptions.

EVALUATION, PERFORMANCE: the analysis in terms of initial objectives and estimates, usually made on site, of accomplishments using an automatic data processing system, to provide information on operating experience and to identify corrective actions required, if any.

FLOWCHART: a graphic representation for the definition, analysis, or solution of a problem in which symbols are used to represent operations, data flow, and equipment.

FLOWCHART, SYSTEMS: a schematic representation of the flow of information through the components of a processing system.

FLOWLINE: a line representing a connecting path between symbols on a flowchart.

FORMAT: (1) the predetermined arrangement of characters, fields, lines, page numbers, and punctuation marks, usually on a single sheet or in a file. This refers to input, output, and files. (2) The arrangement of code characters within a group, such as a word or message.

GENERATOR, REPORT: a technique for producing complete data processing reports, given only a description of the desired content and format of the output reports and certain information concerning the input file.

HEURISTIC: pertaining to exploratory methods of problem solving in which solutions are discovered by evaluation of the progress made toward the final result.

INFORMATION: the essential significance drawn from a collection of facts or other data.

INPUT: (1) the data to be processed. (2) The state or sequence of states occurring on a specified input channel. (3) The device or collective set of devices used for bringing data into another device. (4) A channel for impressing a state on a device or logic element. (5) The process of transferring data from an external storage to an internal storage.

INQUIRY: a request for information from storage, e.g., a request for a bibliography.

INTELLIGENCE, ARTIFICIAL: the capability of a device to perform functions that are normally associated with human intelligence, such as reasoning, learning, self-improvement.

INTERFACE: a common boundary between automatic data processing systems or parts of a single system. In communications and data systems, it may involve code, format, speed, or other changes as required.

LABEL: one or more characters used to identify an item of data.

LANGUAGE: a system for representing and communicating information or data between people, or between people and machines. Such a system consists of a carefully defined set of characters and rules for combining them into larger units, such as words or expressions, and rules for word arrangements or usage to achieve specific meanings.

LETTER: in an alphabet, a character used in the representation of sounds of a spoken language.

LINEAR FILE: a file which is stored in a continuous medium such as magnetic tape, perforated tape, etc.

LOGIC: (1) the science dealing with the criteria or formal principles of reasoning and thought. (2) The systematic scheme which defines the interactions of signals in the design of an automatic data processing system. (3) The basic principles and applications of truth tables and interconnections between logical elements required for arithmetic computation in an automatic data processing system.

LOGIC, FORMAL: the discipline that investigates the structure of propositions and of deductive reasoning by methods that abstract from the content of the propositions under consideration and deal only with their logical form.

LOGIC, SYMBOLIC: the discipline that treats formal logic by means of a formalized artificial language or symbolic calculus whose purpose is to avoid the ambiguities and logical inadequacies of natural languages. Advantages of the symbolic method are greater exactness of formulation and power to deal with more complex material.

MACHINE READABLE: information in a form which can be read by a specific machine.

MAN/MACHINE INTERFACE: that which may be considered the connection between man and the computer; the interface may be the equipment which permits this communication or the communication itself.

MAP: to transform information from one form to another.

MATHEMATICAL MODEL: a set of mathematical expressions that describes symbolically the operation of a process, device, or concept.

METHOD, MONTE CARLO: a trial-and-error method of repeated calculations to discover the best solution of a problem. Often used when a great number of variables are present, with interrelationships so complex as to forestall straightforward analytic handling.

MISTAKE: a human failing, e.g., faulty arithmetic, use of incorrect formulas, or incorrect instructions. Mistakes are sometimes called gross errors to distinguish from rounding and truncation errors. Thus, computers malfunction and humans make mistakes. Computers do not make mistakes and humans do not malfunction, in the strict sense of the words.

MNEMONIC: pertaining to assisting or intending to assist human memory; thus a mnemonic term, usually an abbreviation, is one that is easy to remember, e.g., mpy for multiply and acc for accumulator.

OPERATIONS RESEARCH: the use of analytic methods adopted from mathematics for solving operational problems. The objective is to provide management with a more logical basis for making sound predictions and decisions. Among the common scientific techniques used in operations research are the following: linear programming, probability theory, information theory, game theory, Monte Carlo method, and queuing theory.

PROCESS: a generic term which may include compute, assemble, compile, interpret, generate, etc.

REAL TIME: (1) pertaining to the actual time during which a physical process transpires. (2) Pertaining to the performance of a computation during the actual time that the related physical process transpires in order that results of the computations can be used in guiding the physical process.

RECOGNITION, CHARACTER: the technology of using a machine to sense and encode into a machine language characters which are written or printed to be read by human beings.

REDUNDANCE: in the transmission of information, redundance is the fraction of the gross information content of a message which can be eliminated without loss of essential information.

ROUTINE: a set of coded instructions arranged in proper sequence to direct the computer to perform a desired operation or sequence of operations. A subdivision of a program consisting of two or more instructions that are functionally related; therefore, a program.

RUN: the performance of one program on a computer; thus the performance of one routine, or several routines linked so that they form an automatic operating unit, during which manual manipulations by the computer operator are zero, or at least minimal.

SCAN: to examine sequentially part by part.

SEARCH: to match successfully the index terms of a store with a question in order to find documents or data which are described by the set of index terms equivalent to the question.

SEEK: to look for data according to information given regarding that data; occasionally used interchangeably and erroneously for search, scan, and screen.

SET, CHARACTER: an agreed set of representations, called characters, from which selections are made to denote and distinguish data. Each character differs from all others, and the total number of characters in a given set is fixed; e.g., a set may include the numerals 0 to 9, the letters *A* to *Z*, punctuation marks, and blank or space.

SIMULATE: to represent the functioning of a system or process by a symbolic (usually mathematical) analogous representation of it.

SIMULATION: (1) the representation of physical systems and phenomena by computers, models, or other equipment, e.g., an imitative type of data processing in which an automatic computer is used as a model of some entity, for example, a chemical process. Information enters the computer to represent the factors entering the real process, the computer produces information that represents the results of the process, and the processing done by the computer represents the process itself. (2) In computer programming, the technique of setting up a routine for one computer to make it operate as nearly as possible like some other computer.

SIMULATOR: (1) a computer or model which represents a system or phenomenon and which mirrors or maps the effects of various changes in the original, enabling the original to be studied, analyzed, and understood by means of the behavior of the model. (2) A program or routine corresponding to a mathematical model or representing a physical model. (3) A routine which is executed by one computer but which imitates the operations of another computer.

SURROGATE: a substitute for a document, such as an abstract, a bibliographic citation, or an accession number.

SYMBOL: a representation of something by reason of relationship, association, or convention.

SYSTEM: an organized collection of parts united by regulated interaction.

SYSTEM, INFORMATION RETRIEVAL: a system for locating and selecting, on demand, certain documents or other graphic records relevant to a given information requirement from a file of such material. Examples of information retrieval systems are classification, indexing, and machine searching systems.

TEXT: that part of the message which contains the information to be conveyed.

THEORY, GAME: a mathematical process of selecting an optimum strategy in the face of an opponent who has a strategy of his own.

THEORY, INFORMATION: a branch of probability theory that is concerned with the properties of transmitted messages. The bits of data comprising the message are subject to certain probabilities of transmission failure, distortion, and noise.

THEORY, PROBABILITY: a measure of likelihood of occurrence of a chance event, used to predict behavior of a group, not a single item in the group.

THESAURUS: a list of vocabulary terms which have been authorized for use in an information retrieval system, together with both a description of the hierarchic and semantic relationships between the terms and a definition of the terms to the extent required.

TRANSLITERATE: to represent the characters or words of one language by corresponding characters or words of another language.

TRUTH TABLE: a table that describes a logic function by listing all possible combinations of input values and indicating all the logically true output values.

VALIDITY: correctness; especially the degree of the closeness by which reiterated results approach the correct result.

VERIFY: to check a transcribing operation, by a compare.

VOCABULARY: a list of operating codes or instructions available to the programmer for writing the program for a given problem for a specific computer.

CHAPTER 7
IDENTIFICATION AND DEFINITION

The foremost objective of the identification and definition phase is to produce a definitive statement of the problem to be solved, adequate both as the basis for a decision to proceed and as the guideline to subsequent work. A system diagram of the typical elements and relationships in identification and definition is presented in Figure 7-1.

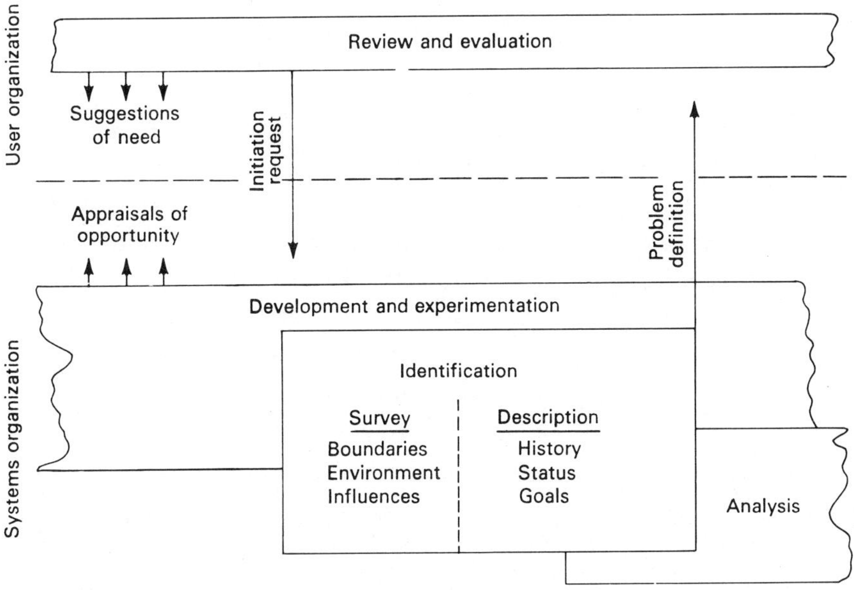

Figure 7-1.

It is probably not quite true that a good definition constitutes half the job, but misunderstandings about the real problem are still common. A brief but careful effort to establish mutual understanding is well advised.

The intensity of the need for a careful beginning is closely related to the scope of the problem. All systems projects need planning and specification. Minor tasks, simple mechanization efforts, and short duration modifications can be developed by intuition and encompassed by a mental plan. For example, the application of a simple sequential processing number to each paycheck, back order, or invoice will have a profoundly beneficial effect on control and audit processes but need not involve redesign of the entire technical processing system. Major efforts, substantial automation projects, and long-term developments defy effective comprehension, and the solutions may develop slower than the careers of the analysts. For example, success in establishing a worldwide identity number for each published item has eluded several generations of librarians and is not yet assured.[1] In all cases there is sound reason to study the problem and its setting, to establish authority and responsibility for further effort, and to document the objectives and resources.

NEED AND OPPORTUNITY

The recognition of the need for systems development and of the opportunity for profitable application of new technology is not closed to all but a few systems professionals. Useful ideas originate from dissatisfied patrons, innovative library personnel, and from eager suppliers. Each of these sources should be used to supplement the regular *development* and *experimentation* efforts.

A continuing effort in operational *review and evaluation* is a necessary part of the work of a competent and alert library staff. The

[1] A standards committee, working with American publishers through R. R. Bowker Company, with the support of the American Book Publishers' Council, has begun to implement a standard book number code. The International Standards Organization (ISO) TC-46 Committee has identified this system of coding as a priority item for consideration as an international standard. British book publishers, in cooperation with the American Book Publishers' Council, have already instituted the procedure for developing such a book numbering code in the United Kingdom.

scope of activities should include operation and statistical appraisals, patron surveys, and periodic staff discussions to evaluate goals, methods, and results. The work of other libraries provides a ready basis for comparison and is available for the price of a visit or a review of the professional journals.

There should be a clear distinction between the efforts which reflect operational *needs* and those which evaluate, identify, and interpret *opportunities* for use of new technology. The same persons may participate in both functions, but the productivity of useful ideas will be enhanced by a user/analyst dialogue. Good ideas can be encouraged, and some alluring, but impractical, devices and approaches can be avoided or quickly and firmly rejected after experimental trial.

The generation of ideas will initially proceed at a faster pace if the serious consideration of their worth is deferred, although a formal "brainstorming" approach may not be suited to the temperament of the staff. If it is used, the evaluation process should be carefully constrained to seek a balance between the extremes that stifle creativity or that divert too much effort into trivial changes.

There is value in "service consciousness" and "cost consciousness." An unambiguous measure of either service or cost is difficult to obtain and may be the reason for a persistent tendency to avoid an honest consideration of the worth of an idea apart from its cost.[2] The best systems project is one that maximizes the value received for the resources spent—essentially an investment viewpoint with full weight accorded to the subjective and intangible human and social implications.

INITIATION REQUEST

It is desirable that a simple and direct means be provided to initiate consideration of a systems project. The requirements that are imposed on the initiator must be minimal, or the idea will be lost in procedural detail.

[2] An especially effective technique to relieve the user of his uncertainty about technology is to ask for an estimate of the value of a solution assuming, for the moment, that the needed solution was immediately available without either development or operational cost. A separate estimate of cost can then be compared with the indicated value as a guide to net worth.

Whether the idea originates from a revealed need for improved methods or a discovered opportunity to introduce a new technology, there is a clear advantage to a formal, but simple, documentation of the idea in the form of a project or work initiation request.

The request should specify contact data about the originator, a description of the proposal, and the need or the opportunity that is recognized. Estimates of the costs and benefits are of little validity but should not be deprecated; they are best deferred until the problem and solution are better defined.

A prompt response that does no more than acknowledge receipt of the request is sufficient to start the process and to restrict the investment in time and effort to an acceptable and controllable level.

PROBLEM IDENTIFICATION

The identification effort is expected to assure that both the user and the analyst are thinking about and working on the same problem. Some classical misunderstandings have occurred when suggestions for minor improvements have been mistaken as requests for major redesign and serious proposals for substantial service improvements were treated as trivial ideas. The initial study effort should be strictly limited to that which is essential to the definition statement. There will be ample opportunity for consideration of details when a clear confirmation of mutual agreement is established.

The first task is to survey the problem boundaries, the environmental setting, and the influences, if any, which are imposed externally. Following the survey, it is possible to place the problem in historical perspective and describe the current status and major goals.

SURVEY

The problem survey begins with a view that there is a problem and that the problem can be distinguished from its surroundings and from other problems. In system terms the *boundaries* are drawn to enclose everything that might be changed and to reveal everything essential that is inherent in the environment or assumed to be unchangeable.

The boundaries of a system are arbitrary but need to be drawn with increasing care and precision until they become both definite and understandable. Narrow boundaries will constrain the possible solution alternatives, and broad boundaries will tax the capabilities and confidence of both the user and the system designers. Either extreme is to be avoided; good strategy is to start with a very broad definition and then reduce it to manageable proportions. It is usually easier to reduce the scale if it proves unwieldy than to extend the boundaries and resurvey to obtain the missing data.

The *environmental* setting of a problem is primarily a matter of assumption and viewpoint. There is no one correct way to express the setting of a problem, but it is important to assure that both the user and the analyst have compatible views. The usual concerns are to clarify whether a quick fix or major redesign is intended and if a single application or prototype of many future installations is desired.

The external *influences* that will control the allowable solutions should be systematically reviewed to determine which, if any, are critical. This review does not consider the tangible demands placed on the system—they are treated explicitly as the system boundaries—but rather the political, social, and human influences that make real but intangible demands on the library, the staff, and the patrons.

DESCRIPTION

The problem survey will provide the data needed to place the problem in perspective with *historical* developments, any *prior attempts* at solution, the current *practices,* and the apparent *reasons* for concern.

There are few libraries that face truly unique problems. A diligent survey of the literature will usually reveal that the problem has been recognized by others and, even if it has not been solved, will suggest which solutions have been tried. The current efforts of librarians throughout the world are not yet promptly and fully reported, and the literature should be systematically supplemented by participation in professional societies and associations. The applicability of work in other institutions is not always obvious, but other libraries with similar goals and other users of computers are good sources of ideas and offer interesting examples of technology in application.

The characteristics used to measure success in a library are clearly different from those used by industrial and commercial companies, universities, and equipment manufacturers. The differences should be considered when evaluating ideas, processes, and equipment to assure that the library concerns are properly and adequately reflected in the evaluation.

PROBLEM DEFINITION

The problem definition statement summarizes what is known or assumed about the problem and suggests whether further effort is justified.

The definition should provide a restatement of the problem, the assignment of authority and responsibility for further effort, and an estimate of the resources needed to complete the next phase of work.

It should be obvious that the user and the analyst will need to work closely together to complete such a definition. There are numerous opportunities for misunderstanding and confusion about concepts and terminology; prompt clarification of the idea is essential.

The typical definition will rarely, if ever, involve more than a few weeks' work. Each of the elements should be considered briefly and, if significant, treated in the definition.

There must be a regular and continuing flow of new ideas if the library is to continue to serve its patrons and to exploit the available technology. The percentage that is worth pursuing to completion will be small; the identification and definition phase can facilitate the processing and maintain an environment that is conducive to continued improvements.

SUGGESTED READING LIST

Bellomy, Fred L.: "Management Planning for Library Systems Development," *Journal of Library Automation,* 2(4): 187–217, December 1969.

Carlson, William H.: *What University Librarians are Thinking, Saying, and Doing About Automation,* Oregon State System of Higher Education, Corvallis, Ore., 1967. ED 026 073.

Eshelman, William R. "Put Out More Flags for Z39," *Datamation,* **16**: 59, February 1970.

Flood, Merrill M.: "The Systems Approach to Library Planning," in *The Intellectual Foundations of Library Education: the Twenty-ninth Annual Conference of the Graduate Library School, July 6–8, 1964,* University of Chicago, 1965, pp. 38–50.

Leimkuhler, Ferdinand F.: "System Analysis in University Libraries," *College and Research Libraries,* **27**: 13–18, January 1966.

Moore, Edythe: "Systems Analysis: An Overview," *Special Libraries,* **58**: 87–90, February 1967.

Morse, Philip M.: *Library Effectiveness: A Systems Approach,* M.I.T., Cambridge, Mass., 1968, 207 pp.

Orlicky, Joseph: *The Successful Computer System: Its Planning, Development, and Management in a Business Enterprise,* McGraw-Hill, New York, 1969, 283 pp.

Schultheiss, Louis A.: *System Analysis and Planning: Data Processing in Public and University Libraries,* Drexel Information Science Series, v. 3, Spartan Books, Washington, 1966, pp. 92–102.

Stone, C. Walter: "The Library Function Redefined," *Library Trends,* **16**: 181–196, October 1967.

Swanson, Don. R.: "Library Goals and the Role of Automation," *Special Libraries,* **53**: 466–471, October 1962.

CHAPTER 8
ANALYSIS AND SPECIFICATION

A system specification is a commitment to a particular goal and a particular approach to that goal. The analytic efforts should be clearly directed to the selection of the best approach, with the details left to later consideration during the design and development effort. Nevertheless, as indicated in Figure 8-1, there are many topics to be considered in an analysis.

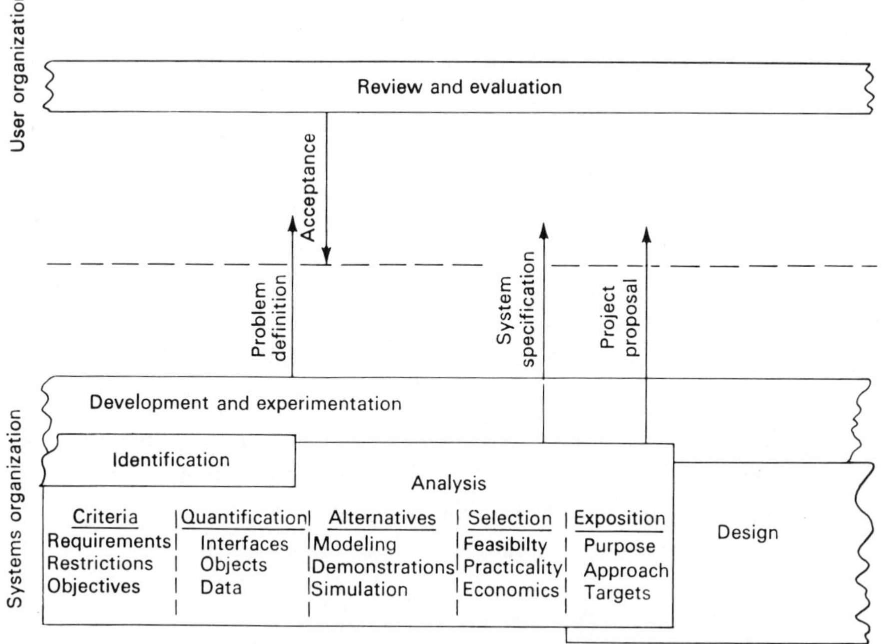

Figure 8-1.

The *specification* will reflect a set of assumptions about the future operational environment, the sophistication of the staff, the complexity and intricacy of the processing, the expected demands of the patrons, and the pace of development that will balance service objectives with financial resources. It is improbable that all those elements will be treated with equal validity and clarity, but it is important that the exposition of such key propositions be attempted; there is no subsequent time in the system history when the freedom to change major directions is so great and the cost so small. Basic errors in concept, objectives beyond the capability of the staff, and schemes that involve several simultaneous advances in technology will almost inevitably lead to demands of time and effort beyond even conservative estimates and produce results below expectations.

The analytic process is initiated during the problem identification and definition phase with preliminary consideration of the criteria and delineation of the problem boundaries.

The analysis phase begins with acceptance of the problem definition and continues with the primary goal of producing a system specification. The secondary goal is to prepare or obtain a system proposal for the work that is to be performed. The analysis phase encompasses five distinct steps although, in practice, the order may be altered and several steps may be underway together.

Depending on the circumstances it may be possible or even desirable to omit or curtail the effort for one or more of the steps. The tendency has been to omit too much in the early stages of a project and to make too many hidden assumptions. Unfortunately, it is also possible to study a problem to exhaustion and to lose sight of the goal in an impressive mass of detail. The ideal is to assure that each step and each phase provide all that is essential to subsequent work and nothing that is premature or redundant. The attainment of that ideal is not impossible, but it does require a variety of skills, balanced competence among the skills, and a systematic approach. Perhaps the most difficult task is to avoid commitments to the techniques or devices to be used before the purposes are established.

ESTABLISHING CRITERIA

The evaluation criteria must recognize *requirements, restrictions,* and *objectives*. These criteria, involving both tangible and intangible values, must be sufficient to guide the selection process to a choice of one or a few alternatives.

It is logically impossible to optimize simultaneously two or more related criteria. Improvement of one will be obtained only by degradation of another. The practical solution is to establish threshold and ceiling values for all but one of the criteria and stipulate that a solution must fulfill the minimum requirements and must not violate the imposed restrictions. If a solution is impossible under such constraints, the allowable range must be extended. A unique solution is then obtained, or the remaining alternatives are subject to a selection process to optimize the objective criterion.

The criteria for selection of a used car offer a ready example. The requirements may demand that the vehicle pass the state inspection; the restrictions may prohibit any alternative in excess of $1,000; and the objective may be operating economy. In this case, the trade-off would be based perhaps on direct operation and ownership costs and impressions of likely repair costs.

The establishment and application of such boundary constraints are equivalent to a partial preselection. They are clearly advantageous when the cost of developing the alternatives is high, when many persons are concerned with the choice, and when delay in attaining the final selection represents a real cost.

The tangible criteria typically focus upon economic costs and returns but may encompass processing rates, response times, and even quantitative measures of service fulfillment. The intangible criteria contemplate the historical and traditional values that are to be retained as well as the factors of risk and delay and the questions of the pace of progress that can be sustained and will be accepted by the staff and the patrons.

There is no clear answer to the dilemma that arises when the best near-term solution is different from and even contrary to the directions of the long-term solution. The final recourse must be a responsible decision that contemplates both the risks and the returns in the perspective of the goals and objectives.

QUANTIFICATION

The quantification effort is supplementary to the preliminary consideration of the system problem. Unless a very leisurely schedule is involved, it is desirable that the identification and the initial quantification work proceed together.

The demands and restrictions imposed from outside the system cannot be unilaterally changed and must, therefore, be discovered and measured as a precondition to the formulation of possible solutions.

The system boundaries delineate all the possible *interfaces* with organizations and activities not a part of the system. Each interface with an external element must be examined to determine if there is a flow either in or out of the system. Every flow must initially be presumed to be an inviolate requirement. A distinction can be drawn between requirements that are inherent in the environment and those that are material to the problem under analysis. Most routine administrative activities can be ignored for purposes of the analysis simply because the means to a solution are already well known and need not be reconsidered. The important interfaces are those that reveal what the system must accomplish if it is to be useful.

The usual measures will be in terms of the identification of accumulations and flows of physical *objects* and logical *data.* It is important to determine whether the physical embodiment is essential or merely convenient. The principal advantage of a data system is that data representations of physical objects can be stored more compactly, handled more easily, and manipulated much faster than the objects themselves. If the data are not recognized as distinct from the physical embodiment, the whole process will be severely restricted.

FORMULATING ALTERNATIVES

The formulation of alternative approaches to a solution is a routine, and perhaps trivial, matter if the solution boundaries have been drawn so small as to eliminate virtually all freedom of action. If the boundaries are too broad, there may not be any known approach to a solution. If a feasible solution cannot be devised to solve the problem as a single system, it is necessary to partition the problem into separate systems that individually have solutions and collectively solve the original problem.

A *model* is an abstraction that emphasizes the elements thought to be important and ignores all unessential detail. A road map, a floor plan, and a flow diagram are common models and, for their purposes, just as effective as more complex and more expensive representations and much more convenient to study and manipulate.

A model can serve either as an aid to formulating an alternative solution or as a means of exposition of the solution. The more complex and intricate models are usually developed in formulations where statistical, mathematical, and physical theories guide the analysis process. The simpler models for exposition are no less important, and many good ideas are lost in excess technical detail that does not speak to the interests of the reader.

When abstract models are ineffectual or inconclusive, the solution can be expressed in an operative *demonstration.* The demonstration need not prove the points that are already well accepted, but must address the features that are in contention.

A *simulation* of the solution is yet another form of model. Some complex systems cannot adequately be expressed in abstract forms and cannot be demonstrated to be valid on a small scale. If the number and importance of the interacting elements warrant it, the only possible means to confirm a solution is to simulate the operation in a model and infer the system properties from the results.

SELECTION

The selection process, which applies the evaluation criteria to the *feasible* alternatives, must consider both *practicality* and *economics.* Whatever the technical merits of an approach, the most critical test of its success or failure is the degree of acceptance by those who must use it from day to day. There can and must be some effort to overcome resistance to change and to instill a positive attitude toward improvement; rapid progress is possible if carefully planned.

The data processing requirements and materials handling requirements of a library automation system can be performed by either human or machine processors. Some of the tasks are clearly associated with unique human capabilities and are difficult or infeasible of accomplishment by a machine. A computer does not comprehend meaning and cannot make a subjective judgment. Humans are limited in strength and speed and do become bored and fatigued. A good system design must, therefore, allocate carefully the possible tasks and processors.

Accommodation of variability is an important human advantage. Each variant to be handled by a computer must be explicitly recognized and precisely planned. The unexpected must be rejected or reserved for human processing.

Speed is a machine strength and a human weakness. The only exception occurs when human cognitive abilities provide an entirely new approach that avoids a long sequence of logical operations.

A computer-based process is notably consistent—right or wrong. Since the allowed variability is low and the speed high, the practical result is either a highly productive success or a critical failure.

Economic analysis must address the facts of income and expense and also the more difficult question of intangible benefits. The argument that a mechanized or automated system is better should be tempered by the recognition that many present systems can be substantially improved without the necessity for machines.

An effective approach to a comparison of costs with economic worth is to begin with goals for scope, service, and response and to define what is desired. The system solution can then address the objectives without precommitment to either manual or machine processing. The system plan will permit estimation of the data processing needs and allocate them between people and machines. The evaluation will consider both the objective needs and the economics of scale that arise when many tasks can be recognized to have logically identical components and can be performed with common facilities.

EXPOSITION

The decision to proceed with a major automation project involving a significant fraction of available resources and a long-term commitment is not easily taken. A competent system specification is essential whether the work is to be done internally or by an outside contract.

The proposals to fulfill the system specification are comparable in concept to the problem definition in response to a project request. Each must undertake to confirm that the *purposes* are clearly understood, the *approach* is sound, and the *targets* are clear.

Consultation, design, programming, and installation services procured on contract are especially effective and beneficial only if the services are well defined and clearly understood by both parties and if the contractor is fully qualified and competent. Thus, the proposal request should seek to establish evidence of competence, experience, and personnel rapport rather than a specific solution to the design problem.

The library cannot yet enjoy the fruits of prior successes. The system elements that are unqualified successes are not very prevalent and the logical patterning of library operations has not yet proceeded to the point that meaningful standard systems are available. For the next few years the choice of a systems consultant will be a critical but uncertain process.

SUGGESTED READING LIST

Baker, Norman R., and Richard E. Nance: *The Use of Simulation in Studying Information Storage and Retrieval Systems,* library operations research project, Purdue University, Lafayette, Ind., Nov. 22, 1967, 18 pp. PB 176 507.

Becker, Joseph: "Systems Analysis—Prelude to Library Data Processing," *ALA Bulletin,* 59: 293–296, April 1965.

Bolles, Shirley, W.: "The Use of Flow Charts in the Analysis of Library Operations," *Special Libraries,* 58: 95–98, February 1967.

Burkhalter, Barton R.: *Case Studies in Systems Analysis in a University Library,* Scarecrow Press, Metuchen, N.J., 1968, 186 pp.

Computer Usage Company: *Specifications for an Automated Library System,* prepared for the University of California, Santa Cruz, Palo Alto, 1965, 122 pp.

Hare, Van Court: *Systems Analysis: a Diagnostic Approach,* Harcourt, Brace & World, New York, *c* 1967, 544 pp.

Leimkuhler, Ferdinand F.: "Operations Research in the Purdue Libraries," in Theodora Andrews (ed.), *Meeting on Automation in the Library, When, Where, and How, Purdue University, 1964, Papers,* Lafayette, Ind., 1965, pp. 82–89.

Simms, Daniel M.: "What is a Systems Analyst?" *Special Libraries,* 59: 718–721, November 1968.

CHAPTER 9 DESIGN AND DEVELOPMENT

The design process is intended to assure that the system accommodates all the inputs and generates all the outputs within the constraints that are imposed from outside the system and in accordance with the established evaluation criteria. The designer must go far enough to assure that the internal structure is self-consistent and that it is adequate to the demands and the conditions imposed on the system.

If the system specification is well done, it will provide a complete guide to the design without preempting any of the designer's prerogatives or restricting his freedom to fulfill the specifications to the best advantage. In like fashion, the designer must attempt to provide a completed design without invading the domain of implementation.

There is a constructive analogy to the process of product design. The research and development laboratory, the market analyst, and the business planner attempt to recognize a need and demonstrate feasibility of a product concept that might be produced and sold at a profit. The design engineer strives to interpret the product concept in such a way as to provide desirable performance features and to leave the manufacturing engineer freedom to choose the best production methods. There is a regular feedback of data and a recycling of the design for both products and data systems. All processes benefit if each function tries to avoid precommitment of subsequent functions.

DESIGN FOR EFFICIENCY

Since a system specification expresses *what* is to be accomplished rather than *how* it is to be done, the first concern in system design is to consider the logical structure of the solution rather than the detailed content.

It is relatively easy to provide a system that is specific to the content of the data to be processed. Most systems include a few instances of explicit content dependence simply because the designer is unable to recognize or accommodate common patterns. The generality and flexibility of a system are restricted in direct relation to the extent of the specific content control.

The ready justification for explicit rather than general procedures is increased efficiency. It is true, in general, that generality, flexibility, and ease of modification imply a less efficient process. However, unless efficiency is sought for its own sake, the best solution is defined in terms of the overall cost incurred in fulfilling the system demands.

Since about 1960 the costs associated with data processing equipment have been less than the costs associated with personnel to plan and operate the systems. The trend toward less expensive data manipulation and more expensive personnel is continuing. Since the commercial computer era began in the early 1950s, the cost of performing a typical mix of jobs has been reduced by half every thirty to thirty-six months. The unit cost of creating computer instructions has decreased, but the number of instructions needed for more complex tasks has grown so rapidly that personnel-related costs are now clearly greater than equipment costs and still rising.

There is little reason to expect any reversal of the trend. The ratio may well stabilize, but under present conditions, and for the foreseeable future, it is better to exercise tighter control of personnel costs even at the expense of equipment efficiency. Any further increases in the personnel/equipment ratio will favor increased use of logic devices whenever it is possible to reduce personnel effort.

DESIGN FOR MECHANIZATION

The design of a process to make effective use of a mechanized device to replace or supplement manual processing must anticipate both the characteristics of the device and the relationship with the people. Devices that perform simple physical processes in ways reminiscent of human actions are not difficult to comprehend and integrate. The typewriter, the cart, and the telephone each provide a specific form of extension of human capabilities.

More complex devices introduce processing methods that differ markedly from those used by humans. The distinction is not drawn in terms of capability to write neater or lift heavier or move faster, but in the substitution of new techniques that are difficult or impossible for humans to use. Microfilm is thus different from magnetic tape, especially in terms of the capability for reserve or emergency procedures when the device fails or is overloaded. The introduction of the more complex devices thus portends the first irremediable displacement of human efforts.

DESIGN FOR AUTOMATION

Growth beyond mechanization introduces active physical elements (hardware) and internal instruction sequences (software). In many respects the hardware is not different from that used in both simple and complex devices. When processing data, there are only a few basic processes to be accomplished; the variety arises from combinations of the basic elements as controlled by the software.

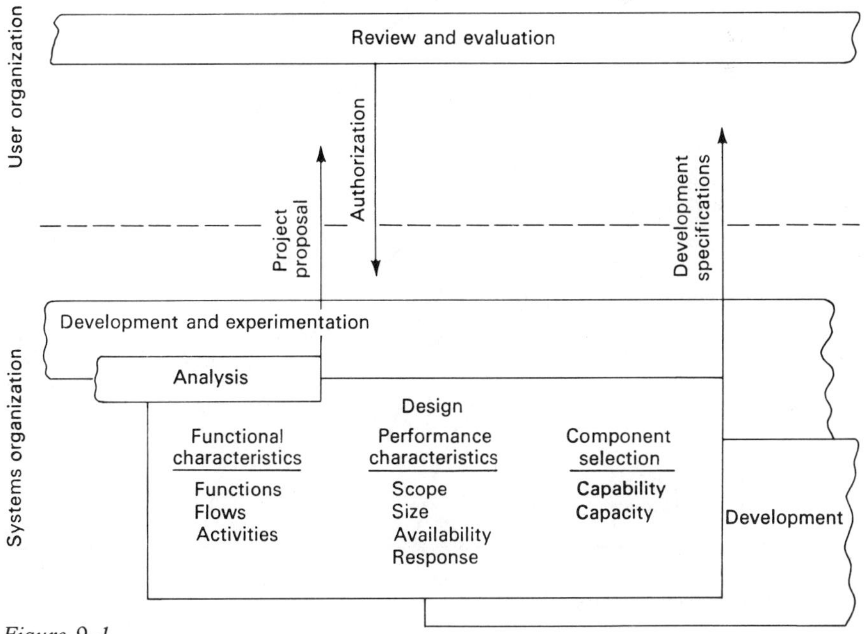

Figure 9–1.

The design process diagrammed in Figure 9-1 includes the whole span of activities that finally indicate a plan whereby machines are able to relieve people of burdensome and tedious tasks and to extend their capability to perform cognitive tasks. For either mechanization or automation the central problem is to link the rigor and precision of the logic device to the innovative and adaptable human mode. In relative terms, as suggested in Figure 9-2, the machine instruction set provides a complete but primitive capability, whereas the human demands are complex and sophisticated. Measured by the capability and demands for selection and for manipulation, the human is far removed from the capability of the computer.

The demand horizon reflects a variety of problems. The least complex demand is for *descriptive* data about past activities. A consistent and accurate record is relatively easy to obtain and vital to all the more complex data demands.

Comparative data in the form of goals, standards, and budgets provide the basis for evaluation and control. *Predictive* data suggest

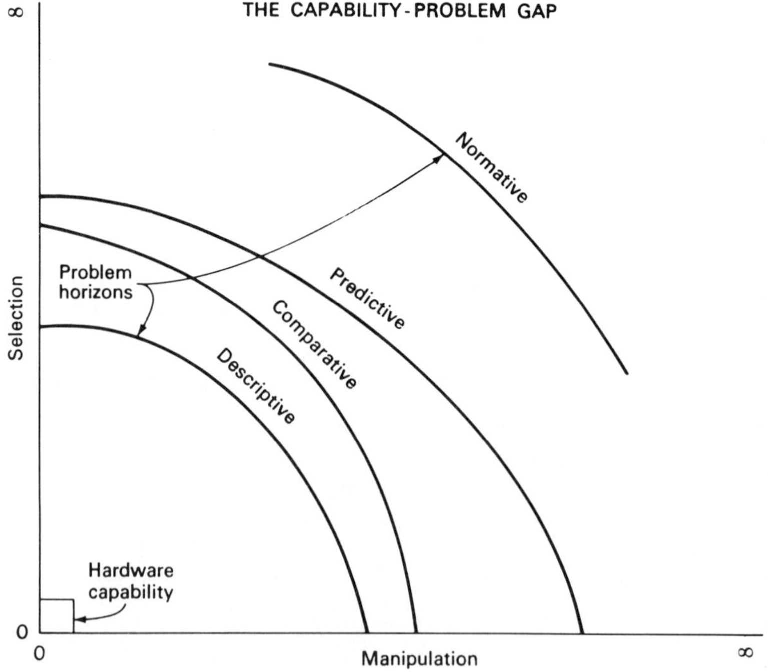

Figure 9–2.

what will occur in future periods if the environmental conditions remain the same and if the events are not redirected by administrative and managerial decisions. *Normative* data suggest what could be attainable if the decisions were optimal.

Communications involve massive selection problems but little manipulation—it is intended that the desired one telephone in millions receive in recognizable form the same voice signal as was transmitted. Scientific computation involves extensive data manipulation, but is usually based on carefully controlled and preselected data. The storage and retrieval systems lie in the middle area, with substantial problems of both selection and manipulation. When the retrieval goal is to obtain a reference list of objects that have high probability of containing pertinent data, the emphasis is on selection more than manipulation. This is the regimen of most present library storage and retrieval efforts. Carried one step further, the data about the selected entities are manipulated to yield implications. Figure 9-3 shows the province of business data processing and, in the future, the increasing concern of the library.

Net pay is an implication drawn from the authorized salary and deductions, just as a reference list is implied from coordinate matching

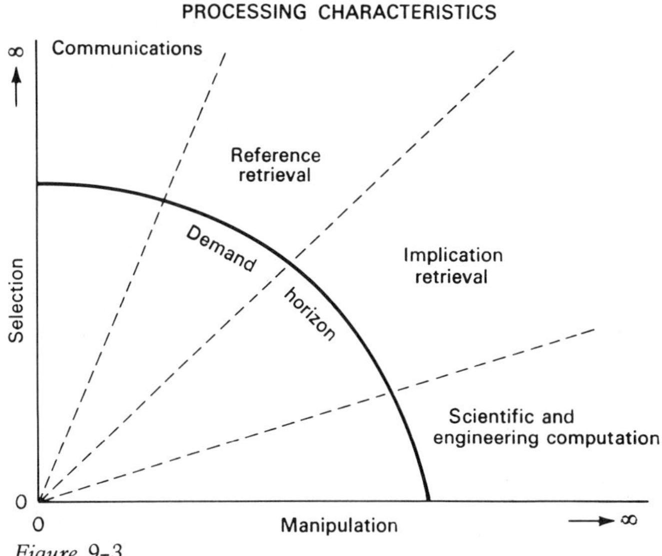

Figure 9-3.

of the description of the item and the description of the query. The scale and importance of the problem can be expected to increase as a natural consequence of the growing number of reference items.

SYSTEMS CHARACTERISTICS

A system is characterized by the *functions* it performs and the intensity of the performance. A library system involves both a physical system of books and other objects and a data system concerning the objects. There are seven system functions, one of which occurs twice, as indicated in Figure 9-4. A *flow* of any kind across the functional field leads to the notion of an *activity.* The principal activities in a data system are commonly aggregated into the seven major groups shown in Figure 9-5.

The first critical partitioning of the functional field reflects the distinction between objects and data. By convention, the data flows are shown in the top partition. The distinction between data and objects is simple and direct. The only restriction that may be imposed on data is the requirement that the information content be preserved.

In Figure 9-6 the procedural distinction between items and queries is recognized by a further flow separation at the identification function and a parallel set of paths through description, transformation, and accumulation. The flows recombine in the search manipulation, which matches the description set of the query to the description sets of all corresponding items.

The second critical partitioning recognizes the important consequences of a change from processing individual entities to processing a set of entities. The individual set boundary is crossed first when the entity descriptions are subjected to a transformation into a controlled vocabulary. The set processes are later terminated and individual entities delivered as output.

The flow paths and partitioning boundaries mark the regions in which recognizably different concepts and philosophies are employed. They also provide a convenient basis for dividing the whole systems problem into related but separate areas of focus that can be addressed in sequence if a complete integrated design project is not feasible.

SYSTEM FUNCTIONS

Detect existence	Acquire	Establish uniqueness	Describe	Transform (encode)	Accumulate	Manipulate	Transform (decode)	Present
Establish awareness of entity nominally of interest to the system	Obtain and accept entity	Distinguish entity from all others	Establish corres-pondence between character-istics of entity and character-istics significant to the system	Convert from one form to another to facilitate processing	Amass into a set	Compare descriptions and recover individuals from the set	Convert from one form to another to facilitate presentation	Exhibit or deliver entities

Figure 9–4.

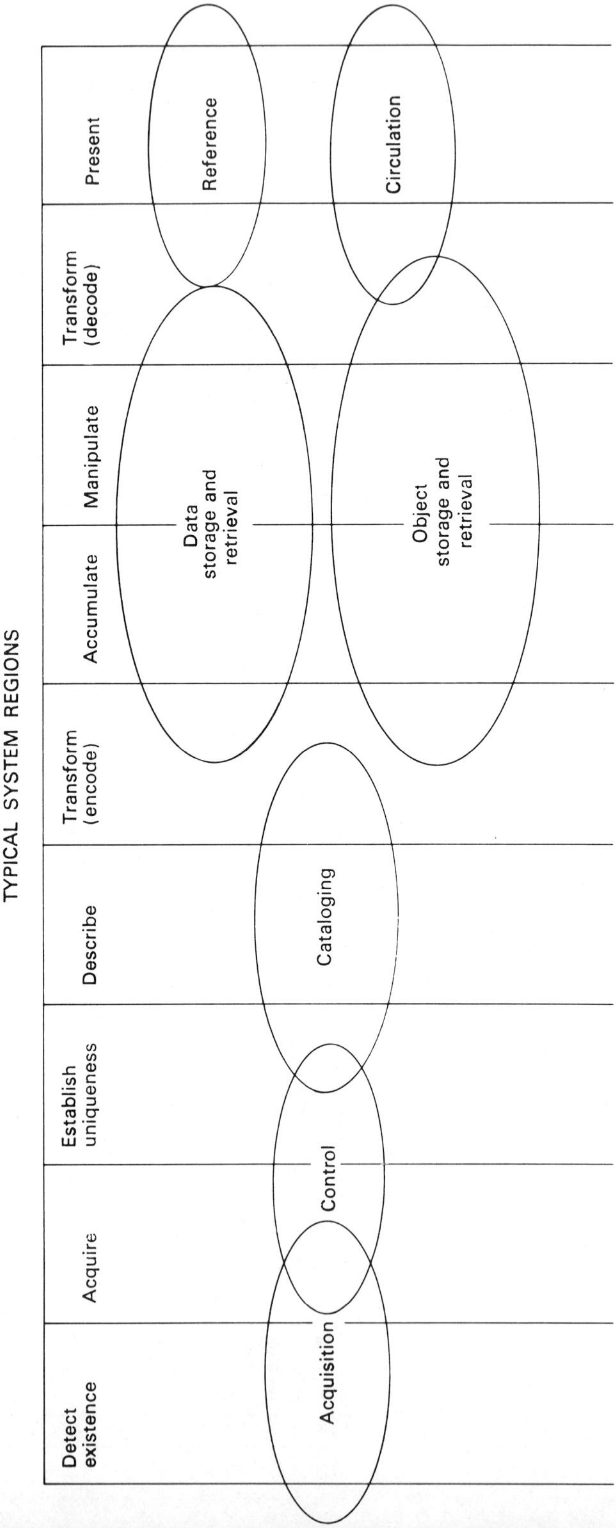

TYPICAL SYSTEM REGIONS

Detect existence	Acquire	Establish uniqueness	Describe	Transform (encode)	Accumulate	Manipulate	Transform (decode)	Present

Data storage and retrieval

Reference

Acquisition

Control

Cataloging

Object storage and retrieval

Circulation

Figure 9–5.

GENERAL SYSTEM FLOWS
Detect existence
Acquire
Establish uniqueness
Describe
Transform (encode)
Accumulate
Manipulate
Transform (decode)
Present
Data
Objects
Entities
Queries
Items
Answers
Location report
Reference list
Objects
Material
Individual
Set
Individual

Figure 9–6.

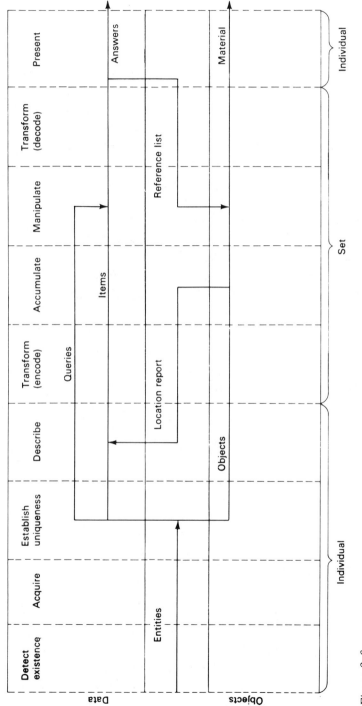

PERFORMANCE CHARACTERISTICS

The *scope* of a system is characterized by the range of functions it spans as well as the variety of entities allowed by the system. It is perhaps feasible to consider a library as a single system, but there is no particular advantage to be gained—the technology does not offer a single approach to a total solution, and it is significantly easier to treat the library as several major systems. Well-defined interfaces assure that one system can be designed in a manner compatible with others but otherwise independent.

In like fashion, our highways, automobiles, and garages could be considered as integral parts of a transportation system. The advantages may be significant but are not so impelling as to overcome the practical difficulty of such an approach.

The entire information system is not usually treated as a single system project because the logical demands of the different functions and different flows are not amenable to the same solution. Five major systems are delineated in Figure 9-5 by the partitions that separate the data and object processing into receipt, storage, and retrieval functions. Each of these systems may be further subdivided and, in some cases, combined to provide a system of suitable scope to match the objectives, policies, and resources of the institution.

Whatever the scope of the system, the design expresses the functions to be performed without regard for organizational assignments or current practices. The *size* of each system is defined by its interfaces with other systems and its internal logic. The interfaces, both input and output, provide the data flow paths and must consider all external inputs and outputs. The internal logic links the system interfaces and assures that some feasible solution that can provide the desired degree of *availability* of service and speed of *response* exists for each link.

The functional system plan is not a final result, and continued changes in detail are to be expected. The necessity for any major change in the overall plan suggests the need for a reconsideration of the basic design goals and approach.

The process of partitioning a system usually leads to a less than optimum solution but offers the advantage of reducing the whole problem to a set of simpler problems that are known to be solvable. Without at least one feasible solution to every subsystem, the project cannot continue with confidence. It is not essential that all the subsystem solutions be elegant or efficient; there will be continuing opportunities to improve upon the basic scheme during system design and even to replace modules of the completed system.

Each interface must be carefully defined in terms of the contiguous members and the identity and traffic rates of all elements that cross the demarcation line. Past and present flow rates should be obtained and future rates projected with consideration of any probable major influences on the interface. A high degree of accuracy is desirable in, but not imperative to, a design that offers a substantial reserve margin of capacity.

EQUIPMENT SELECTION AND INSTALLATION

The selection of equipment should be one of the last decisions rather than one of the first in an automation program. The objective and environmental constraints should be first reflected in a system plan. The development of the system leads naturally to considerations of data processing requirements—both manual and machine. The data processing plan then expresses the type and magnitude of data processing demands and thus the specifications of *capability* and *capacity* to be fulfilled by the equipment.

The most difficult equipment problem for the library is that the files are large and data retrieval is an inherently complex process best performed by a very capable computer. Since such devices are typically large, expensive, and very fast, they offer sufficient capacity to complete the day's work in a few minutes. If time sharing fulfills its promise of providing great capability in brief periods, it will serve well the library's needs. For the moment the practical reality is that computing capability is not offered in the form ideal for library use.

Whatever the initial plan, it is desirable if not imperative to consider how the capacity is to be increased to meet the growing demands. The third-generation computer, based on integrated circuits rather than vacuum tubes (first generation) or transistors (second generation), offers a reasonable opportunity to increase processing speed, memory size, storage capacity, and communications transfer capacity in modular units. It is no longer necessary to change the complete equipment set in order to advance to the next higher level.

DEVELOPMENT

The development efforts diagrammed in Figure 9-7 link the system design to the available capabilities of personnel and logic devices. The final products of development are instructions to guide the manual processes and programs to guide the logic devices; both are essential for all normal activities and for alternative trouble and error routines. The programs are necessarily more precise than the instructions, but the machines need not be trained to perform the intended tasks.

The level of detail to be provided depends on the capability level that is available. Manuals for an experienced staff need not repeat the details already familiar to the personnel; programs will reflect the

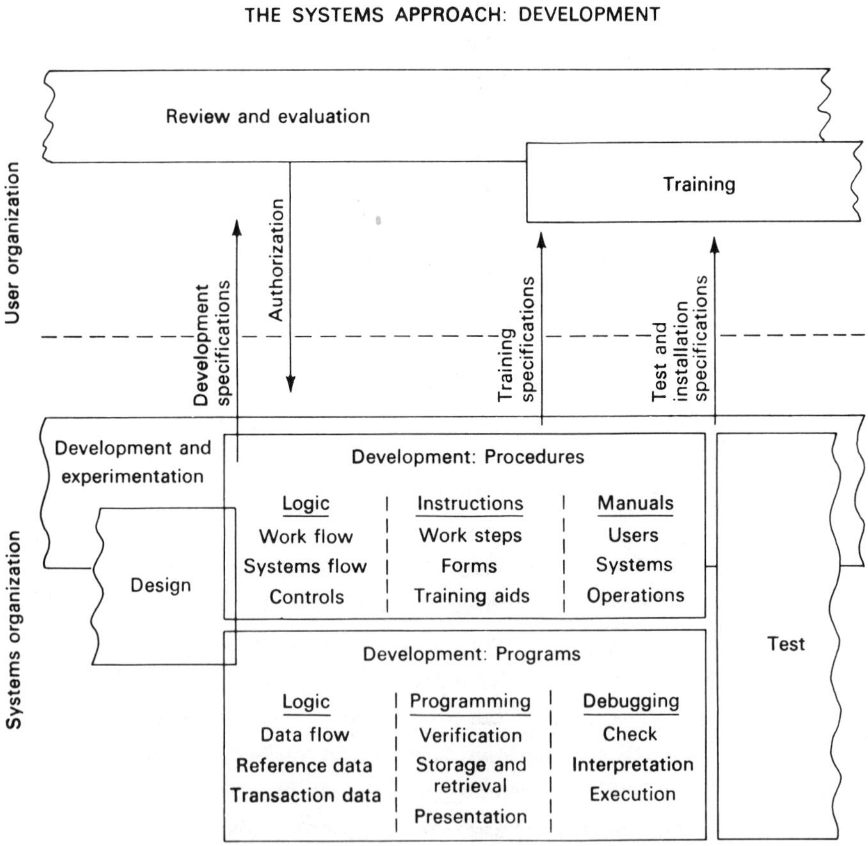

THE SYSTEMS APPROACH: DEVELOPMENT

Figure 9-7.

degree to which higher-level logic is available in the programming languages and usage for the equipment.

The common foundation reflected in the design is developed into separate but closely related plans for the processes to be performed. The logic for manual processing of both objects and data is expressed in programs which must be carefully tested to assure that the statement sequence is complete and error-free.

DEVELOPMENT OF MANUAL PROCEDURES

The solution selected during system design is developed into a complete logic plan in the development phase. The general *system flow* is detailed by subsystem, and each subsystem is arranged into specific work steps and *data flows.*

Data *controls* are defined to guide both the editing and verification processes of input and output as well as the data processing jobs. Data codes are devised to provide the desired capability of error detection and correction.

Each manual *work step* is covered by written instructions that show the relationship to other work steps, the use of computer processes, and the internal procedures, *forms,* and controls.

Training aids are prepared to guide the needed recruiting and training.

MANUALS

The successful use, operation, and maintenance of a data system requires careful exposition of the conceptual, design, and implementation strategy and specific instruction to all those concerned with the details of the system.

Whatever the preferences for interest and understanding, it remains true that the several groups which become involved with a computer-based data system do not use the same vocabulary and do not want or need the same data.

The most important instruction manual must be addressed to all those who have regular contact with the system either as contributors to it or as recipients of its products and services. The *users' manual* may well appear as many independent parts since the material should be carefully keyed to momentary interests and needs. A brief system outline may be appropriate, but the expressions of concepts and technology must be severely edited. The essential emphasis is on what is required and what is offered, with little or no concern for how the internal functions are performed.

The *operations manual* is similar in some respects, but necessarily more technical. The level of detail may properly vary with the experience and training of the staff, but, in general, there must be explicit guidance on what is to be done under normal circumstances and how to recognize and resolve common problems.

A meaningful choice must be made between presentation style suitable for training or for continued reference. Some aspects of both concerns may be presented, but the final result must be readily usable when questions or troubles arise. If a handbook style is not used, a thoroughgoing index must be provided.

The most complete and most technical presentation is the *systems manual* that provides a complete record of the objectives, the approach, and the solution. It should be anticipated that new techniques and new devices will continue to appear and that further improvements will be possible and desirable. A well-documented systems manual will assure that the basic design remains usable so long as the basic purposes of the library persist.

PERSONNEL SELECTION AND TRAINING

The most critical resource in an automated library is the operational staff. A variety of disciplines and a wide range of education and experience are essential. The smaller the installation, the more it is necessary for one person to provide for several functions. Whether one or many are involved, the full range of skills must be represented and maintained.

System analysts perform the tasks of problem definition, system specification, and system design. In larger departments the analytic efforts may justify the service of an analyst skilled in operations research, mathematical statistics, or management sciences. The usual educational background is a bachelor's degree in science or mathematics or a graduate degree in business administration or library science. Good analysts are in short supply and command premium salaries; careful systems planning and prompt resolution of policy and strategy questions are essential. The most common area of wasted effort is excessive detail that can best be left for implementation phases.

Programmers provide detail logic, prepare the instructions to control the logic devices, and debug and test the programs. In the larger computer centers a separate programming team concentrates on the hardware-oriented software with little more than a consulting interest in applications. The usual educational level has been rising in the past few years, and a college degree is now typical. A large center will need a few programmers with advanced degrees in information and computer science.

The peak demands that occur in starting a new system suggest that a service or consulting contract might provide better skills than could be acquired and maintained on a regular basis. Competent assistance is available, but cannot be obtained blindly; exceptional care is needed to assure a sucessful system.

The most obvious source of continued training is offered by equipment manufacturers. Many independent firms offer special courses, and most professional associations provide good forums for discussion. There is no easy solution to the problem of keeping current in a fast-paced technology, and there is a definite limit to the value of general ideas. Specific, planned training as a regular part of the job is still the best means to maintenance of skills and diffusion of new ideas.

INSTRUCTIONS AND DOCUMENTATION FOR MACHINE PROCESSING

The instructions for machine processing include all the software needed to direct the machine operations. If only one or two applications constitute the complete workload for the computer, the regular applications programs may be indistinguishable from hardware-oriented and logic-oriented software. The clear separation and appearance of data-oriented software that marks the mature installation should be anticipated and the foundation laid for systems programs to support a variety of applications.

During the programming process the general flowcharts provided during the design phase will be detailed as the programmer exercises his choice among the many techniques that are available. If the designer has gone beyond the bounds of design and encroached upon the freedom of the programmer, it will be necessary to revise the programming specifications. The clear separation between design and implementation is often obscured by the practice of assigning both tasks to the same analyst. It is feasible to use an integrated design and programming staff, but extra care must be exercised to assure sound professional results and usable documentation.

The ideal design would be valid under successive implementations, and such design is greatly to be desired. Obviously, the design cannot include great detail and must be carefully documented if it is to serve such a purpose.

The processes selected for machine implementation encompass only part of the whole system. The development decisions provide for the matching of system demands and technological capabilities and for the merging of manual and machine resources into a practical and economical solution. The detailed *data flows* must provide for the use of previously accumulated *reference data* as well as the prompt and controlled handling of *transaction data.* The very substantial cost involved in the generation of new data makes it imperative that redundant collection processes be minimized and that repetitive accesses to the available data be made convenient and reliable.

PROGRAMMING

Programming is the process of preparing a sequence of instructions to direct the operation of a computer. In the simplest form the effort is quite routine but nonetheless demanding of precision and rigor. For major projects the work is a significant challenge to ingenuity. From the earliest coding to the most complex logical analysis, good programmers are in short supply. Sound systems design and a well-defined methodology are essential to success and high productivity.

The programming logic provides, in essence, for the *acceptance* of data record about some entity or some event, the *manipulation* of a data record in conjunction with previously accumulated files, and the creation of *output* data and reports.

DEBUGGING

The requirement for a complete and precise exposition of every logic step in a process is an unusual requirement for any human activity. The problem of producing error-free instructions appeared with the first computers and since then has changed but not diminished. Developments in programming languages have reduced the level of detail in the programming process, but the growing size and complexity of systems have more than compensated for the gains.

Logical "bugs" arise whenever a logical structure is incomplete, inconsistent, or incorrect; data content is unanticipated, misinterpreted, or missing; or the system requirements are illogical or invalid. It is intended that the process function without error and produce the desired results. The inevitable defects must be removed, and the "debugging" process is more a matter of art than science.

The preferred strategy is to conduct a careful desk *check* of the program to assure that the work is complete and that the known data paths lead to correct results.

The next step is to *interpret* the program using other programs—assemblers, compilers, translators—that convert the statements to a more primitive form suitable for the computer and test it for conformity with the rules of the language.

The final step in debugging an isolated program is to arrange a test that determines whether sample data is processed as intended. Execution of individual programs is an essential step toward final *execution* of the entire set of programs that compose a system. The attainment of an operative single program does not assure success of the system, but failure does confirm the necessity for further effort at the elemental level.

SUGGESTED READING LIST

Franks, E.: "Development and Management of a Computer-centered Data Base," *Proceedings of the Symposium (10–11 June, 1963), Part 7: LUCID,* System Development Corp., Santa Monica, Calif., 1963. TM-1456/007/00. AD 662 957.

Furth, Stephen: "Data Processing Systems for Library Services," *Hawaii Library Association Journal,* 23: 21–25, June 1967.

Griffin, Hillis L.: "Estimating Data Processing Costs in Libraries," *College and Research Libraries,* 25: 400–403, September 1964.

Gull, Cloyd Dake: "Guidelines to Mechanizing Information Systems," in L. H. Hattery and E. M. McCormick (eds.), *Information Retrieval Systems, Information Retrieval Management,* Data Processing, Inc., Detroit, Mich., 1962, pp. 101–110.

Laden, H. N., and T. R. Gildersleeve: *System Design for Computer Applications,* Wiley, New York, 1963. SBN-471-51135-8.

Swenson, Sally: "Flow Chart of Library Searching Techniques," *Special Libraries,* 56: 239–242, April 1965.

CHAPTER 10
INSTALLATION AND OPERATION

The completion of a design and even the proof that a prototype is operational are not guarantees of success. A product fails if it cannot win market acceptance. A data system fails if it does not accommodate the intended input, provide an acceptable operational environment for the people, and produce the desired output. Product introduction and system installation problems are to be expected, and some degree of early dissatisfaction will be tolerated if it is not long continued.

A good design will become a successful system if it is properly tested and adjusted, if the installation is carefully planned and controlled, if the problems are promptly corrected, and if good communications are maintained with all affected persons.

TEST

When the several components of a system are completed, checked, and debugged, it is necessary to bring them together, as diagrammed in Figure 10-1, into an integrated whole; it is virtually certain that the total array will not function as designed.

All data systems are dominated by people, and the smooth operation of a major system is based on a great number of habitual actions. The impact of change can be reduced and adverse reactions minimized if the whole plan is clearly expressed but the actual changes introduced sequentially rather than simultaneously. In time, the chain of activities may be shortened, but for now and several years to come, people will provide the basis for continuity, and their experience will be essential to the work flow. The development of that experience should be started with the introduction of modified procedures as soon as the necessary personnel are trained.

Early introduction of some of the manual procedures offers the further advantage of generating current data that can be used in the final system tests.

INTEGRATED AND PARALLEL TESTS

Except in the simplest systems, the number of possible variations in input, processing, and output are nearly countless. It is difficult if not impossible to devise a test for every possibility, and it may not be meaningful to conduct a test on the basis of actual data. The range of variability is uncontrolled, and the assurance of general validity is not greatly increased by successful processing of an arbitrary sample.

The best strategy is to devise specific data *conditions* that exercise the extreme ranges of the logic—in brief, the likely as well as unlikely data patterns to be found in actual use.

The basic system tests examine the ability of the whole system to function as intended. The trained personnel, tested procedures, and debugged programs must be brought together, first in *functional groups,* then all together.

THE SYSTEMS APPROACH: INSTALLATION

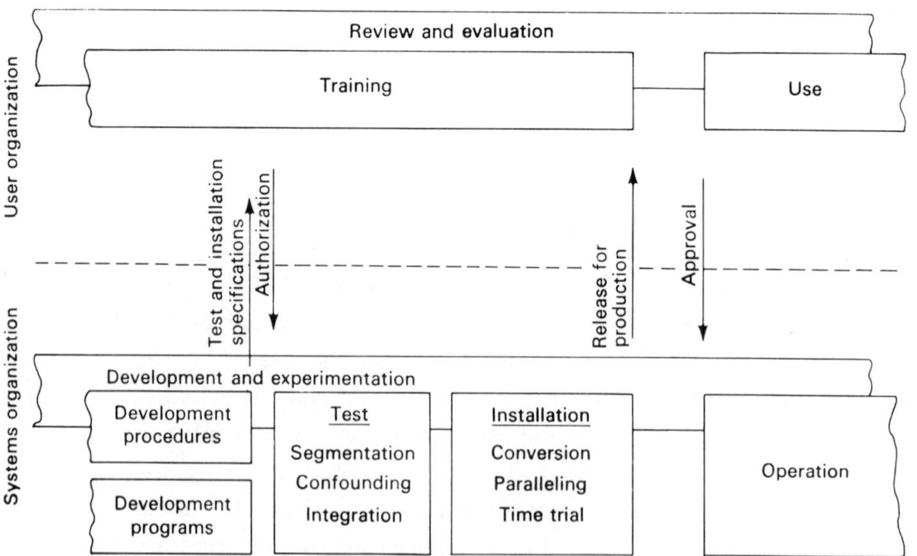

Figure 10-1.

The problems that occur and the errors that are revealed must be corrected and the system adjusted. If the interfaces were carefully defined and have been preserved, the effects of a defect will not propagate throughout the system and can be readily isolated and corrected.

When the basic tests are concluded, a period of *parallel* testing should be conducted, if there is an existing system with valid operational results. The parallel tests are intended to assure that all necessary inputs are accepted, that all desired output is obtained, and that the results are accurate.

The tests should not be long continued and will not be if well planned and carefully conducted. The burden of double operations is heavy, and one system or the other will be neglected. The tests will be inconclusive if the criteria for success were not predefined or if an attitude of doubt is conveyed to those using the system.

The key to a successful computer installation is a listing of every major task that must be done before the computer is in full operation. Facilities, utilities, air conditioning, personnel, supplies, and data must all be considered. Since the logical interrelationships among the tasks are critical, a network-flow diagram or precedence chart is a common means of showing all the tasks, all the relationships, and when each event must be completed. Without careful control a costly lag between availability and service is almost inevitable.

SYSTEM INTRODUCTION

The installation of a new data system, even with an existing computer center, offers numerous possibilities for confusion and misunderstanding. The *communication* channels need to be opened early and used often. Each person affected by the system should be given a written explanation of the system and the reasons for it, training as needed, and the opportunity to suggest problems and improvements.

The data processing requirements of a system may be fulfilled in several different ways depending on the magnitude of the operation and the intended future course of development. In all cases the economic factors will tend to dominate the decision, but there is a possible trade-off between present and future costs.

The small installation in the first *stages* of development has need for only a few minutes processing each day. Despite the small size, the problems involve about the same logical complexity as for a large system, and the response time allowed is about the same. Thus the small installation must either avoid the more complex tasks or arrange for brief use of a large facility.

The most typical pattern of operation growth starts by concentrating on the conceptual design using manual or rudimentary mechanization. The first installation is likely to be a very limited capability for mechanization of some of the more basic operations, especially those that involve many repetitive but simple operations. Most of the economic benefits stem from systems improvements, whereas service benefits are attained through application of advanced data processing capability.

The use of a remote computing facility with direct terminal devices remains an appealing opportunity but has not yet attained either the range of capability or the level of reliability needed to make it an appealing alternative. It is expected the next five to ten years will see fulfillment of the possibility for a common access to data over the communication network and support of the smallest library with devices that make accessible the contents of the largest.

INSTALLATION APPROVAL

The moment of truth for a data system comes when all the participants must certify that the system is ready for regular use. Whether the installation is total or incremental, each part of the installation deserves the careful judgment of the analyst, designer, implementer, operator, and user that the specifications have been fulfilled and all is in readiness. Any exceptions to the specifications and any details not yet completed should be precisely noted with an indication of the intent to cancel them or a plan to introduce them later. Upon certification, the period of regular operation and maintenance, as diagrammed in Figure 10-2, begins.

OPERATIONAL CONTROL

The obvious requirement of providing service to the staff and the users of the library must not be allowed to obscure the need for evaluation and managerial *guidance.* Operations can be conducted without regard for systematic recording of the types and levels of activities, but the opportunity for statistical analysis should not be neglected.

Input transactions should be identified, counted, and placed under rigorous *control.* If the objects being processed do not provide a constant means of identity, a processing control code should be applied as the first operation and maintained throughout the handling, at least until supplanted by a permanent identifier.

The things people ask for or want to do that are not accommodated in the system should be noted. An *analysis* of such data will reveal evidence of changing patterns and needs to guide the evolution of the system.

Production statistics should reflect the life of each job as well as the state of the whole process. It is not feasible to record everything and not useful to analyze everything, but if any record is made, it should be in a form that can be used for other purposes. There are perhaps few significant events or transactions that are not observed

THE SYSTEMS APPROACH: OPERATION AND MAINTENANCE

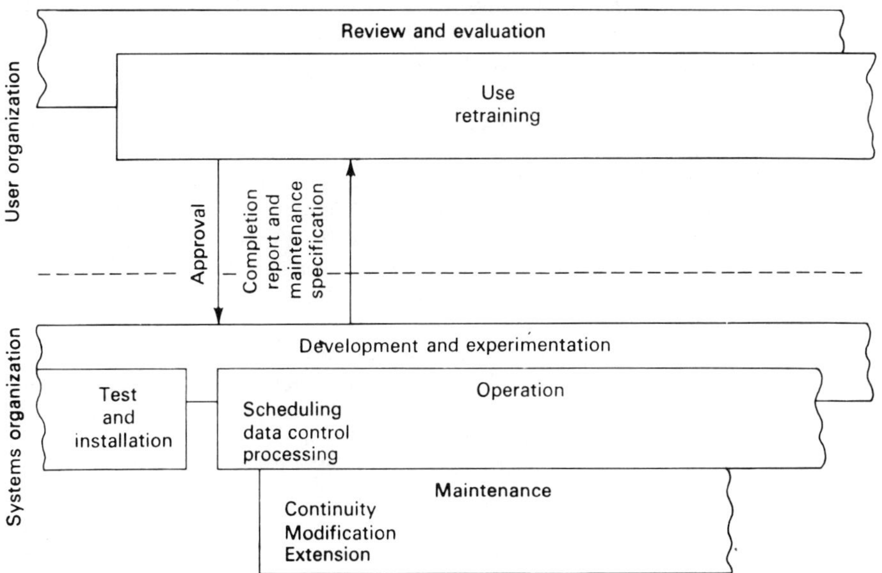

Figure 10–2.

and recorded, but many whose records are inaccessible and unusable for any other purpose.

MAINTENANCE CONTROL

An operational system must be responsive to new requirements. *Continuity,* which provides a basis for analysis of trends, must be tempered by the need for *modification* to accommodate changing circumstances and *extension* to accommodate new demands and services.

SUGGESTED READING LIST

Chapin, Richard E., and Dale H. Pretzer: "Comparative Costs of Converting Shelf List Records to Machine Readable Form," *Journal of Library Automation,* **1**: 66–74, March 1968.

De Gennaro, Richard: "A Strategy for the Conversion of Research Library Catalogs to Machine Readable Form," *College and Research Libraries,* **28**: 253-257, July 1967.

Jolliffe, John: "Tactics of Converting a Catalogue to Machine-readable Form," *Journal of Documentation,* **24**: 149–158, September 1968.

Lipetz, Ben-Ami: "Labor Costs, Conversion Costs and Compatibility in Document Control Systems," *American Documentation,* **14**: 117–122, April 1963.

Locke, William N.: "Computer Costs for Large Libraries," *Datamation,* **16**: 69–74, February 1970.

Parker, Ralph H.: "Not a Shared System: An Account of a Computer Operation Designed Specifically—and Solely—for Library Use at the University of Missouri," *Library Journal,* **92**: 3967–3970, Nov. 1, 1967.

Rauseo, M. J.: "Training Implications of Automated Personnel System," *American Documentation,* **18**: 248–249, October 1967.

Rogers, Frank B.: "Costs of Operating an Information Retrieval Service," *Drexel Library Quarterly,* **4**: 271–278, October 1968.

Saracevic, Tefko, et al.: *An Inquiry into Testing of Information Retrieval Systems,* Comparative Systems Laboratory Final Report, 3 parts, Center for Documentation and Communication Research, Case Western Reserve University, Cleveland, Ohio, 1968, 611 pp. PB 179 290. PB 180 951. PB 180 952.

PART III
TECHNOLOGY FOR LIBRARY AUTOMATION

The mid-twentieth century has brought the high speed of electronics, the compact storage of magnetics, and the precise rigor of arithmetic and logic together in computer, communication, and information technology.

The impact of technological opportunities is muted by the very nature of library economics and the inherent complexity of the storage and retrieval function.

There have been some predictions of collapse of the processing systems under a deluge of new materials and some utopian expectations about the potential for radical improvement of service. A collapse in processing is unlikely even with respect to the physical handling of materials. With insufficient stack space the holdings must be vigorously purged, the input rate reduced, or some vacant warehouse located; all other processes adjust rather automatically to minimize the effect of an overload. Insufficient cataloging effort reduces the retrievability of the material and thereby the demand for circulation. Slow processing makes current acquisitions and recent circulation returns unavailable. Crowded shelves impede retrieval and reshelving. The whole process becomes slower and less accurate but continues with degraded service.

Technology offers the hardware and software and the conceptual foundation from which to build an automated library.

Hardware has been changing with great rapidity for several decades under the impetus of the technological advances begun in the 1940s. Electronics, especially the digital computer, introduced radically new devices and then made them obsolescent in less than ten years. There is continuing expectation that the rapid pace of development will be sustained in the near future.[1]

[1] A survey of 174 participants from eleven countries in FILE 68, an international seminar on file organization held in Denmark in November, 1968, indicated: (1) Oral input to computers is expected about 1976–1983; (2) cards and paper tape will be replaced in the period 1977–1989; (3) computer prices will be decreased by a factor of 100 by 1983–1997. *Forecast 1968-2000 of Computer Developments and Applications,* Parsons and Williams, Copenhagen, Denmark, 1969.

The state-of-the-art practices in industry and government have progressed to a third generation of computers based on integrated circuits and have begun to probe intensive computer/communications linkages that may lead to a fourth generation of equipment in the mid-1970s. Except for a few pioneers, libraries are typically limited to punch-card processing, and many have few processing aids beyond those developed in the 1950s.

Software, the instruction sequences that control the equipment operations, assumes greater importance as equipment becomes capable of new functions and increased speed of operation. There is a basic similarity between software for computers and the instructions that guide manual processing. The essential difference is that experienced and dedicated personnel can adapt to new requirements whereas computers are restricted to the processes that have been specifically provided in programs.

The conceptual foundation for automation is relatively stable, but not unchanging. It will appear to change as research and experience reveal the most practical and most economical of the feasible ideas. Successful application will continue to highlight the logical propositions that are sound and useful.

The library process, a complex intermix of physical, logical, and cognitive operations, is presumed to be susceptible to improvement.

Virtually all design efforts assume that any given process can be improved. Careful analysis of operational systems and diligent experimentation with new ideas, equipment, and processes will provide possible alternative solutions. Further effort and time will serve to eliminate the infeasible, the impractical, and the uneconomical approaches and yield one or a few worthwhile choices. The final choice, if a choice remains, will be based on whatever criteria are thought to be of greatest importance—service to patrons, completeness of coverage, ease of use, reliability, prestige, or cost.

The purpose of mechanization efforts is to adapt some device to the performance of existing tasks; a new focus is required and a new realm of operations is possible when the objective is automation rather than mechanization.

The most repetitive manual processes can be replaced by mechanization. In virtually every case, there are both increased capability and changing cost patterns. A few processes will offer clear economic benefits; beyond that point the mechanization efforts begin to interact with many elements, and the overall merit is difficult to access. It is accepted that a few mechanized processes are good despite the uncertainty about the cost effects. The typewriter is perhaps the best example of a device that has become such a normal part of daily operations that its significance to mechanization or automation is forgotten. There is a place for mechanization in the library and a variety of benefits to be gained by such a course. There is a much more significant opportunity to fulfill the objectives of service by exploiting information technology in the broader approach implied by automation.

The intent of automation is to accomplish the same final purpose by designing the process to make optimum use of both human skills and mechanized aids. Automation, in any meaningful sense, is infeasible when the scope of the task is restricted to small segments of a process. There is no effective opportunity to modify, combine, or even eliminate tasks and major processes if all the present tasks are defined as essential. It is not necessary to consider every problem as a part of a single system or to plan a total system before any one part can be properly implemented. It is desirable to formulate a concept that embraces the essential aspects of an operation and to draw the system boundaries by a process of restricting a general approach rather than expanding a particular view of a single problem area.

What can and should be done depends on the view of the library's purpose. If access to books and other materials is the goal, the system must reflect the reality of the inevitable problem of dealing with many physical objects. If access to knowledge is paramount, the objects and data about them become means to that end and can be used or modified or supplanted as appropriate.

The storage and retrieval function implies that the accumulated material will be substantially greater in quantity than either the amount received or the amount issued in a unit time. Any technological change that is to have a substantial impact on the totality of the library function must encompass the whole accumulation and not just the current receipts and issues.

Mechanization efforts constrained to existing technical processes have limited impact. Automation, in addressing the basic logic of the entire storage and retrieval function, is prepared to encompass the whole process.

The devices to support mechanization and automation in the library are developing rapidly, but the full spectrum of needed capabilities is not yet available.

The data processing requirements of the library are similar in many respects to those of other institutions. The degree of similarity does not justify a direct copy of industrial practice for the library without consideration of the differences. In many respects the library is a more favorable environment than industry for the use of mechanical and electronic data processing, and routine adaptation of industrial practices has failed to recognize and exploit the favorable library characteristics. The consequence has been to involve the library in the same paper flood that characterizes industrial systems.

A clear recognition that the principal elements in the library environment are recurring—in sharp contrast to the fate of manufactured products—is the beginning of the insight needed to provide concepts suited to the library. Basic equipment provides that part of the requirements of an automated library directly concerned with data manipulation. Another part is needed to improve the processes which involve direct interaction of people with the devices and the data. The means to identify objects automatically, to interpret queries expressed in the language of normal use rather than the system language, and to display the results of an interrogation are not yet adequate for normal operations. Some of the needed equipment may be perfected elsewhere and made available to the library. It is not likely that all the requirements will be so fulfilled in a reasonable time; specific expression of library needs and specific designs to satisfy them are essential.

The software needed to make the available devices responsive to known demands is relatively complex and expensive.

Personnel costs for the analysis, design, and implementation of computer-based systems are comparable to equipment costs.

Salaries and fringe benefits are rising faster than equipment rentals. The productivity of analysts and programmers is rising, but the capability and capacity of the hardware is rising much faster, and it is certain that personnel costs will become increasingly more important.

The often repeated promises that general logic and programs will make computers easy to use and very inexpensive are still heard, but their fulfillment is unlikely in the next three to five years or the next decade. The introduction of processing aids to the library has not been marked by a sense of either great urgency or great excitement, except for those directly involved in technical processing activities.

The development of data processing concepts for the library has not matched the very fast pace of development of information technology.

The scope and importance of the data-handling activities that exist in every library were not recognized until a few years ago. Early computer developments were keyed to mathematical computations, and the symbol manipulating capability was not clearly defined or generally accepted until the 1960s.

In such an environment the goal was to substitute computer processes for human processes, in brief, to mechanize the operations. Since every computer process must be exactly and completely described in a program, it is obvious that the most successful applications were those that involved repetitive steps that were thoroughly understood. The obscure tasks performed in making judgments about complex choices did not appear to be either repetitive or well understood and were usually excluded.

Until about 1960 the capability of computers, calculators, and other earlier mechanical devices was severely limited. Many different functions could be performed, but not all the functions that people were performing and only one at a time. Unless applications were carefully chosen to correspond to the available capability, they were unlikely to succeed. Since neither the capability nor the requirements were clearly understood, the failures as well as the successes were obscured in an aura of mystery.

In the 1960s the computers attained sufficient size and capability to remove the former restrictions. It became feasible to design general approaches with the confidence that the equipment was able to support them. With an intensive concentration on instructions that guided the computer operations, it became obvious that, for the first time, whatever logical processes were clearly understood could be expressed to the computer and could be performed. Then, as now, the limiting factor was the understanding of what needed to be done to accomplish the desired goals.

The growing awareness that the computer could process data rather than simply perform computations on numbers led to many efforts to establish a consistent and useful vocabulary for information technology and to perfect concepts and techniques for data management systems.

Objects as the physical carriers of knowledge are less convenient than data as the logical carriers of knowledge.

For the foreseeable future, objects in many forms, and in multiple copies, will be the prevailing concern for most libraries; full digital and image storage will not soon match the convenience and low cost of the existing book forms.

An information system is marked by the separation of data about an object from the object itself. The degree of purity of the separation is measured by the extent to which the representation is freed of all physical restrictions. Theater tickets, paper currency, and books reflect information systems of low purity. The use of the seat, the exercise of economic power, and the understanding of the idea are represented in objects easier to transport and exchange, but invested with a form and substance that must be preserved lest the claim be lost.

When the first-order representations are found to be burdensome to deal with because of their number, size, or location, the information system is purified by even greater reliance on data. Reservations, credit cards, and catalog cards provide another step away from the reality they represent, but a step closer to convenience for the user.

This process is continued until, in concept, pure data is attained, free of any restrictions on its representation, storage, or transformation. Of course, the data is never free of physical embodiment; there are always pulses, holes, magnetic spots, or patterns. The goal is to remove all restrictions on the manipulation of the symbols except one—the information content must be preserved. There are no limitations on the entities that are involved or on the type, number, or value of the objects and no requirement that the manipulation be computer based. If the number of entities is very large, the required precision of manipulation very high, or the time allowed for response very brief, a more complete understanding of the process and the use of powerful data manipulation aids become imperative.

Many examples of information systems are apparent. Wherever it is inconvenient, costly, or impossible to manipulate physical objects, man resorts to manipulation of data. Einstein's equations provided a means to manipulate the universe—surely a strong case for preferring data manipulation. Claim checks, tickets, and maps all provide very impure data that substitute for physical entities. The variety of the data representations indicate the power and generality of the information systems concept. The loss of a sweepstakes ticket, a torn bill, and a forgotten unlisted phone number mark the seriousness of any failure to provide sufficiently complete and accurate data to represent the claim to physical objects and their use.

The centrality of the importance of knowledge about the object rather than the object itself is reflected in the close affinity of data processing and the library.

The logical attributes of data representations are well suited to the primary concerns of a library. When treated as data, the contents of a library become accessible to many users at the same time, even at different places.

The process of transfer of knowledge, to which the library contributes, spans most of human experience and many daily functions. The process of acculturation by which we perpetuate social, ethical, and political values is strongly dependent upon our ability to communicate what we have experienced, what we infer, and what we believe. A variety of methods serve these ends. Every possible human means of perception is tuned to those around us and those who left their record for our review.

Of the few basic patterns that are discernible in the knowledge transfer process, the most notable is the apparent distinction between transfer initiated by the originator and transfer originated by the recipient. The dissemination process covers the spectrum from the involuntary imposition of knowledge applicable in infancy to the fully voluntary seeking after knowledge.

The educational process is characterized by a shift from the imposed teaching of required topics through an increasing dedication to elective and optional subjects to the free choice and self-imposed discipline of adult education.

In this context it is apparent that the library serves the recipient far more than it does the contributor of knowledge. From the recipient's first contact with the library in kindergarten to the time when the focus of concern is with specified data rather than physical buildings and physical objects, the pattern is one of increasing emphasis on initiative and innovation by the recipient and a concomitant development by the library of capability-in-being-ready to serve, but not precommitted to either limited content or inflexible procedures.

The workings of any library can be extended, improved, and refined, but the basic goal is not the efficiency of a particular method, but rather the efficacy of the function. The institution is but the means to the end. If the end rather than the means is to be served, the underlying purpose must be identified and understood.

The available techniques for recording and appraising user demands do not offer any immediate prospects for substantial change of current practices. It is feasible to record interest profiles; it will be necessary to recognize that each person has many separate interests, some which are poorly articulated and others which are not consciously known.

Libraries can view their holdings as nationwide or worldwide if it is accepted practice to share the available data rather than insist on individual processing. In particular, there will be a sharper distinction between access to a physical object which can be shared over a limited geographic area and the data about it which can be shared without limit around the world. There will no longer be a necessity for hundreds or thousands of libraries to process objects individually; the basic data will be provided in conjunction with the contribution of the item itself and thereafter be used in common, supplemented, and refined as interests demand. The goal of the discovery and selection process will be to establish access to all entities of interest rather than to acquire the objects.

Effective control of technical processes and effective custody of physical objects are dependent upon consistent and unambiguous identification. Each entity must be placed under rigorous identity control at the point of its first processing and thereafter retained under control at all times.

A universal publisher's code is obviously needed but is clearly not in immediate prospect since those who would establish the code are handicapped by the deficiencies in identification and location control. A clear recognition of the need, agreement on the logical requirements for control, development of suitable labeling and reading equipment, and vigorous leadership on behalf of the libraries are all needed before uniform coding can be realized.

The description process provides for the representation of the item as data and the means to substitute data manipulation for object manipulation. If all future interest in the item were known, the description could simply provide the terms needed for future queries. The practical alternative is to express the description in the terms that are pertinent in the present context and to allow additional terms of description to be added whenever they are recognized as pertinent.

The close interaction among the selection, identification, and description processes is apparent. Whatever is chosen and identified is described, stored, and retrieved as a whole and not as any of its possible parts. A more precise search can be provided by partitioning the item and treating each part as a separate entity. This approach to the articles in a journal, the chapters in a book, and the maps in an atlas is constrained far more by the practical processing problems than by any lack of desire for precise service.

Greater precision can be expected where the capability for processing and the capacity for description of smaller entities are attained.

It will be necessary to establish the basis for effective retrieval in the recognition of the logical similarity between data about items to be stored for future reference and queries to be processed against the stored items. The potential advantages of a uniform logical design are especially appealing for the library since they provide a design concept that can be implemented in stages to accommodate a growing collection, to support increasing search precision, to foster shared operations, and to exploit both computers and communications.

A library will not sharply increase the demand for service by reducing service charges or eliminate the demand by charging more for services rendered. To a greater degree than other service functions, the library offers a service whose perceived value is not closely related to the individual items.

Thus the library displays a stability and continuity that favors long-term planning and budgeting. Except in relatively minor processes an immediate response to new capability is neither easy to implement nor easy to finance.

GLOSSARY

ACCESS: to communicate with a store in a data system for the purpose of either using or storing data in it.

ACCUMULATOR: a register in which the result of an arithmetic or logic operation is stored.

ADDRESS: an identification for a register, location in storage, or other data source or destination; the identification may be a name, label, or number.

ALGOL: *ALGO*rithmic *L*anguage. A data processing language utilizing algebraic symbols to express problem-solving formulas for machine solution.

ANALOG: the representation of numerical quantities by means of physical variables; e.g., translation, rotation, voltage, or resistance.

ANALOG COMPUTER: a computer which represents variables by physical analogies (as contrasted with a digital computer); i.e., an analog computer measures, and a digital computer counts.

ANALOG DATA: data represented in continuous form, as contrasted with digital (discontinuous) form. Analog data is usually represented by means of a physical variable such as voltage, resistance, rotation, etc. Some familiar analog devices: speedometer, thermometer, thermostat, batch scale.

ASSEMBLE: to prepare a machine language program from a symbolic language program by substituting absolute operation codes and addresses for symbolic operation codes and addresses.

ASSEMBLY SYSTEM: an automatic programming software system which includes a programming language and a number of machine language programs. These programs aid the programmer by performing different programming functions such as checkout, updating, etc.

ASR: *A*utomatic *S*end-*R*eceive set. A combination teletypewriter transmitter and receiver with transmission capability from either keyboard or paper tape. Most often used in a half-duplex circuit.

ASYNCHRONOUS: pertaining to a lack of time coincidence in a set of repeated events where this term is applied to a computer to indicate that the execution of one operation is dependent on a signal that the previous operation is completed.

AUXILIARY (PERIPHERAL) EQUIPMENT: equipment not actively involved during the processing of data, such as input/output equipment and auxiliary storage utilizing punch cards, magnetic tapes, discs, or drums.

BAUD: a technical term, originally used to express the capabilities of a telegraph transmission facility in terms of "modulation rate per unit of time." For practical purposes, it is now used interchangeably with "bits per second" as the unit of measure of data flow. It was derived from the name Baudot, after whom the Baudot code was named.

BAUDOT CODE: the standard five-channel teletypewriter code consisting of a start impulse and five character impulses, all of equal length, and a stop impulse whose length is 1.42 times the start impulse. Also known as the 7.42 unit code. The Baudot code has been used by the telegraph industry for about 100 years.

BINARY: (1) pertaining to a characteristic or property involving a selection, choice, or condition in which there are two possibilities. (2) Pertaining to the number representation system with a base of two.

BINARY CODED DECIMAL (BCD): a type of notation in which each decimal digit is identified by a group of binary ones and zeros.

BIONICS: the functions, characteristics, and phenomena of living systems and the relating of these to the development of hardware systems.

BITS: (1) the abbreviation for binary digit. (2) A basic unit of information.

BLANK: (1) a regimented place of storage where data may be stored, e.g., a location in a storage medium. Synonymous with *space.* (2) A character used to indicate an output space on a printer in which nothing is printed. (3) A condition of "no information at all" in a given column of a punch card or in a given location in a perforated tape. In the case of tape, the feed hole is perforated, but no intelligence is perforated into the same vertical column. In some cases, however, processing equipment may be programmed to recognize a blank and perform certain functions, just as with any other function code.

BRANCH: (1) a sequence of instructions executed as a result of a decision instruction. (2) To depart from the usual sequence of executing instructions in a computer; synonymous with jump or transfer.

BUFFER: a temporary storage device used to compensate for a difference in the speed of data flow or the occurrence of events when data is being moved from one device to another.

BYTE: a generic term to indicate an easily manipulated portion of consecutive binary digits, e.g., an 8-bit byte.

CABLE: an assembly of insulated pairs of voice conductors in a common protective sheath so arranged as to permit the conductors to be identified. The number of fine-gauge conductors in telephone cables may run into thousands.

CABLE, COAXIAL: a cable consisting of one conductor, usually a small copper tube or wire, within and insulated from another conductor of larger diameter, usually copper tubing or copper braid.

CALCULATOR: (1) a device capable of performing arithmetic. (2) A calculator as in (1), which requires frequent manual intervention. (3) Generally and historically, a device for carrying out logical and arithmetical digital operations of any kind.

CARD, EDGE NOTCHED: a card of any size provided with a series of holes on one or more edges for use in coding information for a simple mechanical search technique. Each hole position may be coded to represent an item of information by notching away the edge of the card into the hole. Cards containing desired information may then be mechanically selected from a deck by inserting a long needle in a hole position and lifting the deck to allow the notched cards to fall from the needle. Unwanted cards remain in the deck.

CARD, EIGHTY (80) COLUMN: a punch card with eighty vertical columns representing eighty characters. Each column is divided into two sections, one with character positions labeled zero (0) through nine (9), and the other labeled eleven (11) and twelve (12). The eleven (11) and twelve (12) positions are also referred to as the X and Y zone punches, respectively.

CARD, PUNCH: a heavy stiff paper of constant size and shape, suitable for punching in a pattern that has meaning, and for being handled mechanically. The punched holes are sensed electrically by wire brushes, mechanically by metal fingers, or photoelectrically by photocells.

CARD VERIFYING: a means of checking the accuracy of key punching. A duplication check. A second operator verifies the original punching by depressing the keys of a verifier while reading the same source data. The machine compares the key depressed with the hole already punched in the card.

CATHODE-RAY TUBE (CRT): a vacuum tube used as a storage or a visual display device.

CENTRAL PROCESSING UNIT (CPU): the unit of a computing system that contains the circuits that calculate and perform logic decisions based on a man-made program of operating instructions.

CHAIN: (1) any series of items linked together. (2) Pertaining to a routine consisting of segments which are run through the computer in tandem, only one being within the computer at any one time and each using the output from the previous program as its input.

CHARACTER: (1) one symbol of a set of elementary symbols such as those corresponding to the keys on a typewriter. The symbols usually include the decimal digits 0 through 9, the letters *A* through *Z*, punctuation marks, operation symbols, and any other single symbols which a computer may read, store, or write. (2) The electrical, magnetic, or mechanical profile used to represent a character in a computer, and its various storage and peripheral devices. A character may be represented by a group of other elementary marks, such as bits or pulses.

CLEAR: to put a storage or memory device into a state denoting zero or blank.

CLOCK: (1) a device that generates periodic signals used for synchronization. (2) A device that measures and indicates time. (3) Equipment providing a time base used in a transmission system to control the timing of certain functions such as the duration of signal elements, the sampling, etc.

COBOL: *CO*mmon *B*usiness Oriented *L*anguage. A data processing language that resembles business English.

CODE: (1) a set of rules that are used to convert data, e.g., the set or correspondence in the American Standard Code for Information Interchange. (2) A set of representations.

CODE, DICTIONARY: an alphabetical arrangement of English words and terms, associated with their code representations.

CODING: the ordered list, in computer code or pseudocode, of the successive computer instructions representing successive computer operations for solving a specific problem.

COLLATOR: a device designed to compare data from two decks of punch cards and to sequence-check them, merge them, and/or select cards from them based on this data.

COMMAND: an instruction in machine language.

COMPARE: to examine the representation of a quantity to discover its relationship to zero, or to examine two quantities, usually for the purpose of discovering identity or relative magnitude.

COMPILE: to prepare a machine language program from a computer program written in another programming language by performing the usual functions of an assembler and also by making use of the overall logical structure of the program or generating more than one machine instruction for each symbolic statement or both.

COMPILER: a special machine language routine used to perform the compiling operations. A compiler usually contains its own library of closed routines.

COMMENT: an expression which explains or identifies a particular step in a routine, but which has no effect on the operation of the computer in performing the instructions for the routine.

COMPUTER: (1) a device capable of solving problems by accepting data, performing prescribed operations on the data, and supplying the results of these operations. Various types of computers are calculator, digital computer, and analog computer. (2) In information processing, usually, an automatic stored program computer.

COMPUTER, ANALOG: a computer which represents variables by physical analogies, thus any computer which solves problems by translating physical conditions such as flow, temperature, pressure, angular position, or voltage into related mechanical or electrical quantities and uses mechanical or electrical equivalent circuits as an analog for the physical phenomenon being investigated. In general it is a computer which uses an analog for each variable and produces analogs as output. Thus an analog computer measures continuously, whereas a digital computer counts discretely.

COMPUTER, DIGITAL: a computer that solves problems by operating on discrete data representing variables, by performing arithmetic and logical processes on these data.

COMPUTER, GENERAL-PURPOSE: a computer that is designed to solve a wide class of problems.

CONJUNCTION: the logical operation which makes use of the AND operator or logical product. The conjunction of two variables, or expressions, may be written as $A \bullet B$, $A \wedge B$, $A \cap B$, or just plain AB. These may also be described as an intersection when using Venn diagrams.

CONNECTIVES, LOGICAL: the operators or words, such as AND, OR, OR ELSE, IF THEN, NEITHER NOR, and EXCEPT, which make new statements from given statements and which have the property that the truth or falsity of the new statements can be calculated from the truth or falsity of the given statements and the logical meaning of the operator.

CONSOLE: the unit of equipment used for communication between the operator or service engineer and the computer.

CONTROL: in a digital computer, those parts that effect the retrieval of instructions in proper sequence, the interpretation of each instruction, and the application of the proper signals to the arithmetic unit and other parts in accordance with this interpretation.

CONTROL, NUMERICAL: descriptive of systems in which digital computers are used for the control of operations, particularly of automatic machines; e.g., drilling or boring machines, wherein the operation control is applied at discrete points in the operation or process.

CONTROL, PROCESS: descriptive of systems in which computers, most frequently analog computers, are used for the automatic regulation of operations or processes. Typical are operations in the production of chemicals wherein the operation control is applied continuously and adjustments to regulate the operation are directed by the computer to keep the value of a controlled variable constant.

CONVERSION: (1) the process of changing information from one form of representation to another; such as, from the language of one type of machine to that of another or from magnetic tape to the printed page. Synonymous with *data conversion.* (2) The process of changing from one data processing method to another or from one type of equipment to another, e.g., conversion from punch-card equipment to magnetic-tape equipment.

CORE, MAGNETIC: a configuration of magnetic material that is, or is intended to be, placed in a rigid special relationship to current-carrying conductors and whose magnetic properties are essential to its use. For example, it may be used to concentrate an induced magnetic field as in a transformer, induction coil, or armature, to retain a magnetic polarization for the purpose of storing data, or for its nonlinear properties as in a logic element. It may be made of such material as iron, iron oxide, or ferrite in such shapes as wires, tapes, toroids, or thin film.

DECIMAL: (1) pertaining to a characteristic or property involving a selection, choice, or condition in which there are ten possibilities. (2) Pertaining to the number representation system with a radix of 10.

DECISION, LOGICAL: the choice or ability to choose between alternatives. Basically this amounts to an ability to answer yes or no with respect to certain fundamental questions involving equality and relative magnitude; e.g., in an inventory application, it is necessary to determine whether or not there has been an issue of a given stock item.

DECK: a collection of cards, commonly a complete set of cards which have been punched for a definite service or purpose.

DECODING: (1) performing the internal operations by which a computer determines the meaning of the operation code of an instruction; also sometimes applied to addresses. In interpretive routines and some subroutines, an operation by which a computer determines the meaning of parameters in the routine. (2) Translating a secretive language into the clear.

DEVICE, STORAGE: a device into which data can be inserted, in which it can be retained, and from which it can be retrieved.

DIAGNOSTIC ROUTINE: a programming routine designed to locate and explain errors in a computer routine or hardware components.

DICTIONARY, AUTOMATIC: the component of a language translating machine which will provide a word-for-word substitution from one language to another. In automatic searching systems, the automatic dictionary is the component which substitutes codes for words or phrases during the encoding operation.

DIGIT: a character used to represent one of the integers smaller than the radix, e.g., in decimal notation, one of the characters 0 to 9.

DIGITAL COMPUTER: a computer which processes information represented by combination or discrete or discontinuous data as compared with analog computer for continuous data.

DIGITAL DATA: data represented in discrete (discontinuous) form, as contrasted with analog data represented in continuous form. Digital data is usually represented by means of coded characters, e.g., numbers, signs, symbols, etc. Some common digital devices: mileage gauge, adding machine, abacus, cash register.

DIRECTORY: a file with the layout for each field of the record which it describes; thus a directory describes the layout of a record within a file.

DISC STORAGE: a method of storing information in code, magnetically, in quickly accessible segments on flat rotating discs.

DRUM STORAGE: a method of storing information in code, magnetically, on the surface of a rotating cylinder.

DUMP: (1) to copy the contents of all or part of a storage, usually from an internal storage into an external storage. (2) The process in (1). (3) The data resulting from the process in (1). Synonomous with *memory dump, core dump, memory printout,* and *storage dump.*

DUPLEX, FULL: method of operation of a communication circuit where each end can simultaneously transmit and receive. When used on a radio circuit, duplex operation requires two frequencies.

DUPLEX, HALF: method of operation which permits one direction, electrical communications between stations. Technical arrangements may permit operation in either direction but not simultaneously. Therefore, this term is qualified by one of the following suffixes: S/O for send only; R/O for receive only: S/R for send or receive.

EAM: *E*lectrical *A*ccounting *M*achines. Pertaining to data processing equipment that is predominantly electromechanical, such as key punches, mechanical sorters, collators, and tabulators.

ELECTRICAL COMMUNICATIONS: in electrical communications, some material with relatively low electrical resistance (as copper wire) is provided as a link between sending and receiving points. The sender uses a translating device (i.e., telephone) which is capable of producing a detectable electrical configuration in response to the sender's emitting pattern.

ELECTROMAGNETIC COMMUNICATIONS: the electromagnetic wave conductor is space itself. The electromagnetic frequencies available today for communications fall into two categories: frequencies which form "wireless" communications (such as visual light of fairly high frequency); and frequencies man uses for wireless communications (such as radio, shortwave and microwave transmitting, or relatively lower frequencies). In communicating by radio, shortwave, and microwave frequencies, translators similar in principle to those used in electrical communications are needed, though the equipment requirement increases.

ENCODE: to apply the rules of a code.

ENCODER: a device capable of translating from one method of expression to another method of expression, e.g., translating a message, "Add the contents of *A* to the contents of *B*," into a series of binary digits.

EQUIPMENT, AUTOMATIC DATA PROCESSING: (1) a machine, or group of interconnected machines, consisting of input, storage, computing, control, and output devices which uses electronic circuitry in the main computing element to perform arithmetic and/or logical operations automatically by means of internally stored or externally controlled programmed instructions. (2) The data processing equipment which directly supports or services the central computer operation.

EQUIPMENT, OFF-LINE: the peripheral equipment or devices not in direct communication with the central processing unit of a computer.

EQUIPMENT, ON-LINE: descriptive of a system and of the peripheral equipment or devices in a system in which the operation of such equipment is under control of the central processing unit, and in which information reflecting current activity is introduced into the data processing system as soon as it occurs. Thus, directly on-line with the main flow of transaction processing.

EQUIPMENT, PERIPHERAL: the auxiliary machines which may be placed under the control of the central computer. Examples of these are card readers, card punches, magnetic-tape feeds, and high-speed printers. Peripheral equipment may be used on-line or off-line depending upon computer design, job requirements, and economics.

EQUIPMENT, TABULATING: the machines and equipment using punch cards.

ERROR: (1) the general term referring to any deviation of a computed or measured quantity from the theoretically correct or true value. (2) The part of the error due to a particular identifiable cause, e.g., a truncation error. Contrasted with *mistake*. In a restricted sense, that deviation due to unavoidable random disturbances or to the use of finite approximations to what is defined by an infinite series. (3) The amount by which the computed or measured quantity differs from the theoretically correct or true value.

EXECUTION OF AN INSTRUCTION: the set of elementary steps carried out by the computer to produce the result specified by the operation code of the instruction.

EXTRACT: (1) to copy from a set of items all those items which meet a specified criterion. (2) To remove only a given set of digits or characters occupying certain specified locations in a computer word, such as to extract the 8, 9, and 10 binary digits of a 44-bit word, as specified by the filter. (3) To derive a new computer word from part of another word, usually by masking.

FACSIMILE (FAX): transmission of pictures, maps, diagrams, etc., by wire. The image is scanned at the transmitter and reconstructed at the receiving station.

FETCH: to obtain a quantity of data from a place of storage.

FIELD: a specified area of a record used for a particular category of data, e.g., a group of card columns used to represent a wage rate, or a set of bit locations in a computer word used to express the address of the operand.

FILE: a collection of related records; e.g., in inventory control, one line of an invoice forms an item, a complete invoice forms a record, and the complete set of such records forms a file.

FILE MAINTENANCE: the processing of data in a file to keep it up to date.

FLIP-FLOP: (1) a bistable device; i.e., a device capable of assuming two stable states. (2) A bistable device which may assume a given stable state depending upon the pulse of history of one or more input points and having one or more output points. The device is capable of storing a bit of information.

FORM FEEDING OR FORM FEEDOUT: the rapid, accurate positioning of document forms on a teleprinter or business machine.

FORTRAN: *FOR*mula *TRAN*slation. Any of several specific procedure-oriented programming languages.

FRAME, MAIN: (1) the central processor of the computer system. It contains the main storage, arithmetic unit, and special register groups. Synonymous with central processing unit (CPU). (2) All that portion of a computer exclusive of the input, output, peripheral, and, in some instances, storage units.

FULL-DUPLEX OPERATION: full-duplex, or duplex, operation refers to communication between two points in both directions simultaneously.

GENERATOR, PROGRAM: a program which permits a computer to write other programs, automatically. Generators are of two types: (1) the character-controlled generator, which operates like a compiler in that it takes entries from a library tape, but unlike a simple compiler in that it examines control characters associated with each entry and alters instructions found in the library according to the directions contained in the control characters; (2) The pure generator, which is a program that writes another program. When associated with an assembler, a pure generator is usually a section of program which is called into storage by the assembler from a library tape and which then writes one or more entries in another program. Most assemblers are also compilers and generators. In this case the entire system is usually referred to as an assembly system.

GENERATOR, RANDOM NUMBER: a special machine routine or hardware designed to produce a random number or series of random numbers according to specified limitations.

HALF-DUPLEX OPERATION: half-duplex or single telegraph operation refers to communication on a circuit in only one direction at a time, with or without a break feature. The break feature enables the receiving station to interrupt the sending station.

HANDSHAKING: in a synchronous transmission scheme, the term is used to describe the process by which predetermined configurations of characters are exchanged by the receiving and transmitting equipment to establish synchronization.

HARD COPY: a printed copy of machine output, e.g., printed reports, listings, documents.

HARDWARE: the mechanical, magnetic, electrical, and electronic devices of a computer.

HEAD: a device that reads, records, or erases information in a storage medium; e.g., a small electromagnet used to read, write, or erase information on a magnetic drum or tape, or the set of perforating, reading, or marking devices and block assembly used for punching, reading, or printing on paper tape.

HEADER: the first part of a message, which contains all necessary information for directing the message to the destination(s).

HOLLERITH: a widely used system of encoding alphanumeric information onto cards, hence Hollerith cards is synonymous with punch cards. Such cards were first used in 1890 for the United States census and were named after Herman Hollerith, their originator.

HOUSEKEEPING: (1) pertaining to administrative or overhead operations or functions which are necessary in order to maintain control of a situation; e.g., for a computer program, housekeeping involves the setting up of constants and variables to be used in the program. (2) A general term used to describe coding which reserves, restores, and clears memory areas.

IDLE TIME: the time that a computer is available for use but is not in operation.

INDEX: (1) an ordered reference list of the contents of a file or document, together with keys or reference notations for identification or location of those contents. (2) A symbol or a number used to identify a particular quantity in an array of similar quantities; e.g., the terms of an array represented by $X(1)$, $X(2)$, . . . $X(100)$ have the indexes 1, 2, . . . 100, respectively. (3) Pertaining to an index register.

INPUT-OUTPUT: a general term for the equipment used to communicate with a computer and the data involved in the communication.

INSTRUCTION: a statement that specifies an operation and the values or locations of all operands.

INTERLEAVE: to insert segments of one program into another program so that, during processing delays in one program, processing can continue on segments of another program; a technique used in multiprogramming.

INTERPRETER: (1) a program that translates and executes each source language expression before translating and executing the next one. (2) A device that prints on a punch card the data already punched in the card.

INTERRUPT: to temporarily disrupt the normal operation of a routine by a special signal from the computer. Usually the normal operation can be resumed from that point at a later time.

I/O: an abbreviation for input/output.

ITEM: (1) a set of one or more fields containing related information. (2) A unit of correlated information relating to a single person or object. (3) The contents of a single message.

ITERATE: to repeat, automatically, under program control, the same series of processing steps until a predetermined stop or branch condition is reached; to loop.

ITERATIVE: describing a procedure or process which repeatedly executes a series of operations until some condition is satisfied. An iterative procedure can be implemented by a loop in a routine.

KEYBOARD: a device for the encoding of data by key depression which causes the generation of the selected code elements.

KEY PUNCH: a keyboard-operated device that punches holes in a card to represent data.

KEY-VERIFY: to use the punch card machine known as a verify, which has a keyboard, to make sure that the information supposed to be punched in a punch card has actually been properly punched. The machine signals when the punched hole and the depressed key disagree.

KSR: *K*eyboard *S*end-*R*eceive set. A combination transmitter and receiver with transmission capability from keyboard only.

LANGUAGE, ALGORITHMIC: an arithmetic language by which numerical procedures may be precisely presented to a computer in a standard form. The language is intended not only as a means of directly presenting any numerical procedure to any suitable computer for which a compiler exists, but also as a means of communicating numerical procedures among individuals. The language itself is the result of international cooperation to obtain a standardized algorithmic language. The International Algebraic Language is the forerunner of ALGOL.

LANGUAGE, COMMON BUSINESS ORIENTED: a specific language by which business data processing procedures may be precisely described in a standard form. The language is intended not only as a means for directly presenting any business program to any suitable computer, for which a compiler exists, but also as a means of communicating such procedures among individuals. Synonymous with COBOL.

LANGUAGE, MACHINE-ORIENTED: (1) a language designed for interpretation and use by a machine without translation. (2) A system for expressing information which is intelligible to a specific machine; e.g., a computer or class of computers. Such a language may include instructions which define and direct machine operations, and information to be recorded by or acted upon by these machines.

LANGUAGE, PROBLEM-ORIENTED: (1) a language designed for convenience of program specification in a general problem area rather than for easy conversion to machine instruction code. The components of such a language may bear little resemblance to machine instructions. (2) A machine independent language where one needs only to state the problem, not the how of solution.

LIBRARY: (1) a collection of information available to a computer, usually on magnetic tapes. (2) A file of magnetic tapes.

LOAD: (1) to put data into a register or storage. (2) To put a magnetic tape onto a tape drive, or to put cards into a card reader.

LOG: a record of everything pertinent to a machine run, including identification of the machine run, record of alteration switch settings, identification of input and output tapes, copy of manual key-ins, identification of all stops, and a record of action taken on all stops.

LOOP: (1) a sequence of instructions that is repeated until a terminal condition prevails. (2) A communications circuit between two private subscribers or between a subscriber and the local switching center.

MACHINE ACCOUNTING: (1) a keyboard machine that prepares accounting records. (2) A machine that reads data from external storage media, such as cards or tapes, and automatically produces accounting records or tabulations, usually on continuous forms.

MACHINE, DATA PROCESSING: a general name for a machine which can store and process numeric and alphabetic information.

MACHINE, ELECTRICAL ACCOUNTING: the set of conventional punch-card equipment including sorters, collators, and tabulators.

MACHINE LANGUAGE: a code used directly to operate a computer.

MACRO INSTRUCTION: a single instruction that causes the computer to execute a predetermined sequence of machine instructions.

MAGNETIC CORE: a small doughnut-shaped ferrite designed and constructed for on or off magnetization and used to store information in the computer.

MAGNETIC INK: ink containing particles of magnetic substance which can be detected and read by automatic devices, e.g., the digits printed on some bank checks for magnetic-ink character recognition.

MAGNETIC-INK CHARACTER RECOGNITION (MICR): a method of storing information in characters printed with ink containing particles of magnetic material. The information can be detected or read at high speed by automatic devices.

MAGNETIC TAPE: a continuous flexible recording medium whose base material is impregnated or coated with a magnetic-sensitive material ready to accept data in the form of magnetically polarized spots.

MAGNETIC THIN-FILM: a logic or storage element coated with an extremely thin layer of magnetic material, usually less than one micron thick (about four hundred-thousandths of an inch).

MARK: a sign or symbol used to signify or indicate an event in time or space, e.g., an end of word or message mark, a file mark, a drum mark, and an end of tape mark.

MARK-SENSE: to mark a position on a card or paper form with a pencil. The marks are then interpreted electrically for machine processing.

MATCH: a data processing operation similar to a merge except that, instead of producing a sequence of items made up from the input, sequences are matched against each other on the basis of some key.

MATRIX: (1) an array of quantities in a prescribed form; in mathematics, usually capable of being subject to a mathematical operation by means of an operator or another matrix according to prescribed rules. (2) An array of coupled circuit elements; e.g., diodes, wires, magnetic cores, and relays which are capable of performing a specific function.

MEDIUM: the material or configuration thereof on which data is recorded, e.g., paper tape, cards, magnetic tape, etc.

MEMORY BANK: a term for any device capable of retaining information. Also a term to indicate the total of such devices.

MEMORY: the high-speed magnetic .core internal storage unit contained within the central processor.

MERGE: to combine items into one sequenced file from two or more similarly sequenced files without changing the order of the items.

MESSAGE: (1) a group of words, variable in length, transported as a unit. (2) A transported item of information.

MESSAGE (COMMUNICATIONS): a transmitted series of words or symbols intended to convey information. As used in message switching, a message consists of header, text, and an end of message.

MESSAGE SWITCHING: a system in which data transmissions between stations on different circuits within a network are accomplished by routing the data through a central point.

MICR: *M*agnetic *I*nk *C*haracter *R*ecognition. A check-encoding system employed by banks for the purpose of automating check handling. Checks are imprinted using magnetic ink) with characters of a type face and dimensions specified by the American Banking Association. There are fourteen characters—ten numbers (0-9) and four special symbols—which are used to provide amount, identifying, and control information.

MICROSECOND: one millionth of a second.

MILLISECOND: one thousandth of a second.

MODE: (1) a computer system of data representation, e.g., the binary mode. (2) A selected mode of computer operation. (3) A method of card reading and punching. There are two: *(a)* the normal mode, which reads and punches the Hollerith code—i.e., it interprets each column as a 6-bit alphanumeric character; and *(b)* the transcription mode, which interprets each punch as a binary one and each nonpunch as a binary zero.

MODEM: contraction of modular-demodulator. A device to convert one form of signal to another form for equipment compatibility.

MODULATION: the process by which some characteristic of one wave is varied in accordance with another wave. This technique is used to make business machine signals compatible with communications facilities.

MODULATION, AMPLITUDE (AM): the form of modulation in which the amplitude of the carrier is varied in accordance with the amplitude of the original signal.

MODULE: (1) an interchangeable plug-in item containing components. (2) An incremental block of storage or other building block for expanding the computer capacity.

MULTIPLEX: the process of transferring data from several storage devices operating at relatively low transfer rates to one storage device operating at a high transfer rate in such a manner that the high-speed device is not obliged to wait for the low-speed devices.

MULTIPROCESSOR: a machine with multiple arithmetic and logic units for simultaneous use.

MULTIPROGRAMMING: the interleaved or simultaneous execution of two or more programs by a single computer.

NANOSECOND: one billionth of a second.

NETWORK: the interconnection of a number of points by communications facilities.

NULL: (1) an absence of information, as contrasted with zero or blank for the presence of no information. (2) Zero. (3) Pertaining to no deflection from a center or end position.

NUMBER, BINARY: a number, usually consisting of more than one figure, representing a sum, in which the individual quantity represented by each figure is based on a radix of two. The figures used are 0 and 1.

NUMBER, DECIMAL: a number, usually of more than one figure, representing a sum, in which the quantity represented by each figure is based on the radix of ten. The figures used are 0 through 9.

NUMBER, HEXADECIMAL: a number, usually of more than one figure, representing a sum, in which the quantity represented by each figure is based on a radix of sixteen.

NUMBER, OCTAL: a number of one or more figures, representing a sum, in which the quantity represented by each figure is based on a radix of eight. The figures used are 0 through 7.

OFF-LINE: pertaining to peripheral equipment or devices not in direct communication with the central processing unit of a computer.

ON-LINE: an on-line system may be defined as one in which the input data enter the computer directly from their point of origin and/or output data are transmitted directly to where they are used. The intermediate stages such as punching data into cards, or paper tape, writing magnetic tape, or off-line printing are largely avoided.

OPERATING SYSTEM: an integrated collection of computer instructions that handle selection, movement, and processing of programs and data needed to solve problems.

OPERATION: (1) a defined action; namely, the act of obtaining a result from one or more operands in accordance with a rule that completely specifies the result for any permissible combination of operands. (2) The set of such acts specified by such a rule or the rule itself. (3) The act specified by a single computer instruction. (4) A program step undertaken or executed by a computer, e.g., addition, multiplication, extraction, comparison, shift, or transfer. The operation is usually specified by the operation part of an instruction. (5) The event or specific action performed by a logic element.

OPERATOR, MACHINE: the person who manipulates the computer controls, places information media into the input devices, removes the output, and performs other related functions.

OPTICAL READER: a device used for machine recognition of characters by identification of their shapes.

OPTIMIZE: to rearrange the instructions or data in storage so that a minimum number of time-consuming jumps or transfers are required in the running of a program.

ORDER: (1) a defined successive arrangement of elements or events. This term is losing favor as a synonym for instructions, due to ambiguity. (2) To sequence or arrange in a series. (3) The weight or significance assigned to a digit position in a number.

OUTPUT: (1) that data that has been processed. (2) The state or sequence of states occurring on a specified output channel. (3) The device or collective set of devices used for taking data out of a device. (4) A channel for expressing a state on a device or logic element. (5) The process of transferring data from an internal storage to an external storage.

OVERFLOW: (1) the condition which arises when the result of an arithmetic operation exceeds the capacity of the storage space allotted in a digital computer. (2) The digit arising from this condition if a mechanical or programmed indicator is included; otherwise, the digit may be lost.

OVERLAY: a technique for bringing routines into high-speed storage from some other form of storage during processing, so that several routines will occupy the same storage locations at different times. Overlay is used when the total storage requirements for instructions exceed the available main storage.

PAPER TAPE: a continuous flexible recording medium made of paper; perforations are then made for the recording of information.

PAPER-TAPE READER: a device which senses and translates the holes in perforated tape.

PARALLEL: (1) pertaining to the simultaneity of two or more processes. (2) Pertaining to the simultaneity of two or more similar or identical processes. (3) Pertaining to the simultaneous processing of the individual parts of a whole, such as the bits of a character and the characters of a word, using separate facilities for the various parts.

PARAMETER: (1) a quantity in a subroutine whose value specifies or partly specifies the process to be performed. It may be given different values when the subroutine is used in different main routines or in different parts of one main routine, but it usually remains unchanged throughout any one such use. Related to *program parameter.* (2) A quantity used in a generator to specify machine configuration, to designate subroutines to be included, or otherwise to describe the desired routine to be generated. (3) A constant or a variable in mathematics which remains constant during some calculation. (4) A definable characteristic of an item, device, or system.

PERIPHERAL EQUIPMENT: equipment which is not under direct control of the central processing unit; also referred to as auxiliary equipment.

PERMUTATION: any of the total number of changes in position or form that are possible in a group.

POLL: a flexible, systematic method, centrally controlled, for permitting stations on a multipoint circuit to transmit without contending for the line.

PRECISION: (1) the degree of exactness with which a quantity is stated. (2) The degree of discrimination or amount of detail; e.g., a three-decimal digit quantity discriminates among 1,000 possible quantities. A result may have more precision than it has accuracy; e.g., the true value of pi to six significant digits is 3.14159; the value 3.14162 is precise to six figures, given to six figures, but is accurate only to about five.

PRE-EDIT: to edit the input data previous to the computation.

PRINTER: a device which prints results from a computer on paper.

PRINTER, LINE: a device capable of printing one line of characters across a page; i.e., 100 or more characters simultaneously as continuous paper advances line by line in one direction past type bars or a type cylinder that contains all characters in all positions.

PRINTER, WIRE: a high-speed printer that prints characterlike configurations of dots through the proper selection of wire ends from a matrix of wire ends, rather than conventional characters through the selection of type faces.

PRINTOUT: (1) dynamic printout: a printout of data which occurs during the machine run as one of the sequential operations. (2) Static printout: a printout of data which is not part of the sequential operations and occurs after the machine run.

PROCESSING, BATCH: a technique by which items to be processed must be coded and collected into groups prior to processing.

PROCESSING, REAL TIME: the processing of information or data in a sufficiently rapid manner that the results of the processing are available in time to influence the process being monitored or controlled.

PROCESSOR: the program or equipment to process, e.g., a compiler, translator, generator.

PROGRAM: (1) the plan and operating instructions needed to produce results from a computer. (2) To plan the method of attack for a defined problem.

PROGRAMMER: a person who prepares problem-solving procedures and flowcharts and who may also write and debug routines.

PROGRAM, OBJECT: the program which is the output of an automatic coding system. Often the object program is a machine language program ready for execution, but it may well be in an intermediate language.

PROGRAM, SOURCE: a computer program written in a language designed for ease of expression of a class of problems or procedures, by humans, e.g., symbolic or algebraic. A generator, assembler translator, or compiler routine is used to perform the mechanics of translating the source program into an object program in machine language.

RADIX: the quantity of characters for use in each of the digital positions of a numbering system. In the more common numbering systems the characters are some or all of the Arabic numerals as follows:

System Name	*Characters*	*Radix*
Binary	(0, 1)	2
Octal	(0, 1, 2, 3, 4, 5, 6, 7)	8
Decimal	(0, 1, 2, 3, 4, 5, 6, 7, 8, 9)	10

Unless otherwise indicated, the radix of any number is assumed to be 10. For positive identification of a radix 10 number, the radix is written in parentheses as a subscript to the expressed number; i.e., $126_{(10)}$. The radix of any nondecimal number is expressed in similar fashion; e.g., $11_{(2)}$ and $5_{(8)}$.

RANDOM ACCESS: random-access files are storage media holding a large amount of information in such a way that any item may be read or written at random with a short access time, i.e., usually less than one second. Examples of random-access files are disc storages, drums, and magnetic tape or strip files.

RANGE: (1) the set of values that a quantity or function may assume. (2) The difference between the highest and lowest value that a quantity or function may assume.

READER, CARD: (1) a mechanism that senses information punched into cards. (2) An input device consisting of a mechanical punch-card reader and related electronic circuitry which transcribes data from punch cards to working storage or magnetic tape.

RECORD, UNIT: (1) a separate record that is similar in form and content to other records, e.g., a summary of a particular employee's earnings to date. (2) Sometimes refers to a piece of auxiliary equipment, e.g., a card reader or printer.

RECURSIVE: pertaining to a process which is inherently repetitive. The result of each repetition is usually dependent upon the result of the previous repetition.

REGISTER: a high-speed device used in a central processing unit for temporary storage of small amounts of data or intermittent results during processing.

RESTART: to go back to a specific planned point in a routine, usually in the case of machine malfunction, for the purpose of rerunning the portion of the routine in which the error occurred. The length of time between restart points in a given routine should be a function of the mean free error time of the machine itself.

SCREEN: (1) the surface in an electrostatic cathode-ray storage tube where electrostatic charges are stored, and by means of which information is displayed or stored temporarily. (2) To make a preliminary selection from a set of entities, selection criteria being based on a given set of rules or conditions.

SEARCH, BINARY: a search in which a set of items is divided into two parts, where one part is rejected and the process is repeated on the accepted part until those items with the desired property are found.

SEMICONDUCTOR: a solid with an electrical conductivity that lies between the high conductivity of metals and the low conductivity of insulators.

SENSE: (1) to examine, particularly relative to a criterion. (2) To determine the present arrangement of some element of hardware, especially a manually set switch. (3) To read punched holes or other marks.

SEQUENCE: (1) to put a set of symbols into an arbitrarily defined order; i.e., to select *A* if *A* is greater than or equal to *B*, or select *B* if *A* is less than *B*. (2) An arbitrarily defined order of a set of symbols, i.e., an orderly progression of items of information or of operations in accordance with some rule.

SEQUENTIAL ACCESS: access of locations in a store through a prescribed sequence. Pure sequential access would involve reading only one bit or code element at a time. In some systems, the sequence is a sequence of codes within which there is parallel access to individual code elements, e.g., bits on an eight-channel tape.

SERIAL: (1) pertaining to the time-sequencing of two or more processes. (2) Pertaining to the time-sequencing or two or more similar or identical processes, using the same facilities for the successive process. (3) Pertaining to the time-sequential processing of the individual parts of a whole, such as the bits of a character, the characters of a word, etc.

SET: (1) a collection. (2) To place a storage device into a specified state, usually other than that denoting zero or blank. (3) To place a binary cell into the "one" state.

SHARED TIME: carrying out two or more functions during the same time period by allocating small divisions of the total time to each function in turn.

SHOP, CLOSED: the operation of a computer facility where programming service to the user is the responsibility of a group of specialists, thereby effectively separating the phase of task formulation from that of computer implementation. The programmers are not allowed in the computer room to run or oversee the running of their programs.

SHOP, OPEN: the operation of a computer facility where computer programming, coding, and operating can be performed by any qualified employee of the organization, not necessarily by the personnel of the computing center itself, and where the programmer may assist in or oversee the running of his program on the computer.

SIGN: (1) in arithmetic, a symbol which distinguishes negative quantities from positive ones. (2) An indication of whether a quantity is greater than zero or less than zero. The signs often are the marks + and −, respectively, but other arbitrarily selected symbols may be used. Examples: 0 and 1, or 0 and 9, when used as codes at a predetermined location, can be interpreted by a person or machine.

SIGNAL: the event, phenomenon, or electrical quantity which conveys information from one point to another.

SOFTWARE: the totality of programs and routines used to extend the capabilities of computers, such as compilers, assemblers, narrators, routines, and subroutines.

SOLID STATE: the electronic components that convey or control electrons within solid materials, e.g., transistors, germanium diodes, and magnetic cores. Thus, vacuum and gas tubes are not included.

SORT: to arrange items of information according to rules dependent upon a key or field contained in the items or records; e.g., to digital sort is to sort first the keys on the least significant digit and to resort on each higher-order digit until the items are sorted on the most significant digit.

SORT, MERGE: to produce a single sequence of items, ordered according to some rule, from two or more previously unordered sequences, without changing the items in size, structure, or total number; although more than one pass may be required for a complete sort, items are selected during each pass on the basis of the entire key.

SORTER: a machine which puts items of information into a particular order; e.g., it will determine whether *A* is greater than, equal to, or less than *B* and sort or order.

SOURCE LANGUAGE: a language nearest to the user's usual business or professional language, which enables him to instruct a computer more easily. FORTRAN, COBOL, ALGOL, BASIC, PL/L are a few examples.

STORAGE: (1) pertaining to a device into which data can be entered and from which it can be retrieved at a later time. (2) Loosely, any device that can store data.

STORAGE, MAGNETIC: a storage device that utilizes the magnetic properties of materials to store data, e.g., magnetic cores, tapes, and films.

STORAGE, MAGNETIC CORE: a storage device in which binary data is represented by the direction of magnetization in each unit of an array of magnetic material, usually in the shape of toroidal rings, but also in other forms such as wraps or bobbins.

STORAGE, MAGNETIC DISC: a storage device or system consisting of magnetically coated discs, on the surface of which information is stored in the form of magnetic spots arranged to represent binary data. These data are arranged in circular tracks around the discs and are accessible to reading and writing heads on an arm which can be moved mechanically to the desired disc and then to the desired track on that disc. Data from a given track are read or written sequentially as the disc rotates.

STORAGE, MAGNETIC TAPE: a storage device in which data are stored in the form of magnetic spots on metal or coated plastic tape. Binary data are stored as small magnetized spots arranged in column form across the width of the tape. A read-write head is usually associated with each row of magnetized spots so that one column can be read or written at a time as the tape traverses the head.

STORAGE, RANDOM-ACCESS: a storage technique in which the time required to obtain information is independent of the location of the information most recently obtained. This strict definition must be qualified by the observation that we usually mean relatively random. Thus, magnetic drums are relatively nonrandom access when compared to magnetic stores for main storage, but are relatively random access when compared to magnetic tapes for file storage.

STORAGE, SERIAL: a storage technique in which time is one of the factors used to locate any given bit, character, word, or groups of words appearing one after the other in time sequence, and in which access time includes a variable latency or waiting time of from zero to many word times. A storage is said to be serial by word when the individual bits composing a word appear serially in time; or a storage is serial by character when the characters representing coded decimal or other nonbinary numbers appear serially in time; e.g., magnetic drums are usually serial by word but may be serial by bit, or parallel by bit, or serial by character and parallel by bit.

STORE: (1) to transfer an element of information to a device from which the unaltered information can be obtained at a later time. (2) To retain data in a device from which it can be obtained at a later time. (3) The British term for storage. (4) To put in storage.

STORE-AND-FORWARD SWITCHING CENTER: a message switching center in which the message is accepted from the sender whenever he offers it, held in a physical store, and forwarded to the receiver whenever he is able to accept it.

STORED PROGRAM COMPUTER: a digital computer that stores instructions in main core and can be programmed to alter its own instructions as though they were data and can subsequently execute these altered instructions.

SUBROUTINE: (1) the set of instructions necessary to direct the computer to carry out a well-defined mathematical or logical operation. (2) A subunit of a routine. A subroutine is often written in relative or symbolic coding even when the routine to which it belongs is not. (3) A portion of a routine that causes a computer to carry out a well-defined mathematical or logical operation. (4) A routine which is arranged so that control may be transferred to it from a master routine and so that, at the conclusion of the subroutine, control reverts to the master routine. Such a subroutine is usually called a closed subroutine. (5) A single routine may simultaneously be both a subroutine with respect to another routine and a master routine with respect to a third. Usually control is transferred to a single subroutine from more than one place in the master routine; the reason for using the subroutine is to avoid having to repeat the same sequence of instructions in different places in the master routine.

SUM, LOGICAL: a result, similar to an arithmetic sum, obtained in the process of ordinary addition, except that the rules are such that a result of one is obtained when either one or both input variables is a one, and an output of zero is obtained when the input variables are both zero.

SWITCHING, CIRCUIT OR LINE: a switching technique where the connection is made between the calling party and the called party prior to the start of a communication.

SWITCHING, MESSAGE: the technique of receiving a message, storing it until the proper outgoing circuit is available, and then retransmitting it.

SYSTEM, NUMBER: (1) a systematic method of representing numerical quantities in which any quantity is represented as the sequence of coefficients of the successive powers of a particular base with an appropriate point. Each succeeding coefficient from right to left is associated with and usually multiplies the next higher power of the base. The first coefficient to the left of the point is associated with the zero power of the base. For example, in decimal notation 371.426 represents $(3 \times 10^2) + (7 \times 10^1) + (1 \times 10^0) + (4 \times 10^{-1}) + (2 \times 10^{-2}) + (6 \times 10^{-3})$. (2) The following are names of the number systems with bases 2 through 20: 2, binary; 3, ternary; 4, quaternary; 5, quinary; 6, senary; 7, septenary; 8, octal or octonary; 9, novenary; 10, decimal; 11, undecimal; 12, duodecimal; 13, terdenary; 14, quaterdenary; 15, quindenary; 16, sexadecimal, or hexadecimal; 17, septendecimal; 18, octodenary; 19, novemdenary; 20, vicenary. Also 32, duosexadecimal or duotricinary; and 60, sexagenary. The binary, octal, decimal, and hexadecimal systems are widely used in computers.

SYSTEMS, OPERATING: an integrated collection of service routines for supervising the sequencing of programs by a computer. Operating systems may perform debugging, input-output, accounting, compilation, and storage assignment tasks.

TABLE: a collection of data, each item being uniquely identified either by some label or by its relative position.

TAG: a specific identifier such as a label, index, etc.

TAPE, MAGNETIC: (1) a tape with a magnetic surface on which data can be stored by selective polarization of portions of the surface. (2) A tape of magnetic surface used as the constituent in some forms of magnetic cores.

TAPE, PAPER: a strip of paper capable of storing or recording information. Storage may be in the form of punched holes, partially punched holes, carbonization or chemical change of impregnated material, or imprinting. Some paper tapes, such as punched paper tapes, can be read by the input device of a computer or a transmitting device sensing the pattern of holes which represent coded information.

TELECOMMUNICATION: any transmission or reception of signals, writing sounds, or intelligence of any nature by wire, radio, visual, or electromagnetic systems. Often used interchangeably with "communication."

TELEPRINTER: descriptive name for telegraphic terminals.

TWX (TELETYPE-WRITER EXCHANGE SERVICE): a switched network providing interconnection for American Telephone & Telegraph teletypewriter subscribers. In effect, therefore, a private telegraph service; a large company often uses this type of service if the volume of messages between offices, etc., is heavy.

TELEX (TEX): name used by Western Union to designate an automatic teleprinter exchange service provided in the United States and Canada.

TERMINAL: (1) a point in a system or communications network at which data can enter or leave. (2) A general term referring to the equipment at the end of a telegraph circuit; modems and associated equipment.

TERMINAL UNIT: a device, such as a key-driven or visual display terminal, which can be connected to a computer over a communications circuit and which may be used for either input or output from a location either near or far from the computer.

TIME SHARE: to interleave the use of a computer to serve many problem-solvers during the same time span.

TOKEN: a distinguishable unit in a sequence of characters.

TRANSDUCER: a device which converts energy from one form to another, as a hi-fi pickup cartridge converts mechanical to electrical energy.

TRANSLATOR: a routine for changing information from one representation or language to another.

TRANSMISSION: the electrical transfer of a signal, message, or other form of intelligence from one location to another.

TUBE, CATHODE-RAY: (1) an electronic vacuum tube containing a screen on which information may be stored by means of a multigrid modulated beam of electrons from the thermionic emitter storage effected by means of charged or uncharged spots. (2) A storage tube. (3) An oscilloscope tube. (4) A picture tube.

UNIT RECORD EQUIPMENT: electromechanical machines used to process data recorded on punch cards. Often used as input/output devices connected to an electronic stored-program computer.

UPDATE: (1) to put into a master file changes required by current information or transactions. (2) To modify an instruction so that the address numbers it contains are increased by a stated amount each time the instruction is performed. (3) During the checkout period, the updating run deletes and adds programs, corrections, test data, etc., to the master program file.

WORD: an ordered set of characters which occupies one storage location and is treated by the computer circuits as a unit and transferred as such. Ordinarily a word is treated by the control unit as an instruction and by the arithmetic unit as a quantity. Word lengths may be fixed or variable depending on the particular computer.

WRITE: (1) to transfer information, usually from main storage, to an output device. (2) To record data in a register, location, or other storage device or medium.

CHAPTER 11
HARDWARE

Libraries have readily accepted mechanical aids for virtually every function that seemed to offer possibilities of better performance, lower cost, or less clerical effort.

The easiest and most obvious way to mechanize an operation has been to obtain one of the machines that others use. The hard reality of a machine provides ready evidence of progress, a better conservation piece than abstract logic, and a possible first step.

The second step, and those that follow, provide the real test of a mechanization program and the foundation for automation. When the walking is done and it is time to run, the approach must start with needs and lead to a selection of human and automatic capabilities rather than start with a machine and lead to an application to keep it busy.

It is now rather clear that a deeper view of what we desire to accomplish is more instructive than any examination of specific devices. What is intended will persist; the machines of today will be obsolescent in less than a decade.[1]

An array of noisy, busy machines is no longer a valid representation of the state of the art in mechanization and is not at all applicable to automation equipment for data processing. Even more, when the objective is automation, a data processing device that involves a mechanical operation can only be at the periphery of the process. The needs for speed and compactness have forced the main-line processes toward electronic functions and eliminated virtually all of the busy-looking machines.

[1] The availability of good basic presentations of data processing concepts and equipment is limited because of the very rapid obsolescence of the devices. A recommended recent publication that is consistent with the current state of the art is *More About Computers,* International Business Machines Corporation, Armonk, N.Y., 1969.

Present computers are typically classified as third-generation equipment. The first generation of digital computers, based on vacuum tubes, was introduced commercially in the early 1950s. They were, by current standards, bulky, slow, hot, and unreliable, but they represented a great advance to those who needed to perform many computations.

The second generation, based on transistors, provided processors that were notably smaller and faster. In the few years around 1960 the older computers were quickly displaced, though still in operative condition, because they were much too expensive to retain. For the first time it was clear that computing power more than adequate to many problems was readily available. Hardware ceased to be the absolute limitation on advances, and software emerged as an acute problem.

By 1965 the change to the third generation, using integrated circuits, was well under way. Memories were an order of magnitude larger; speeds, an order of magnitude faster; and reliable random storage for hundreds of millions of characters became a reality. With the third-generation equipment the dream of an integrated data system became technically feasible, and the combination of the computer and telecommunications became economically attractive.

Hardware and software capabilities are essentially adequate to current demands, but the demands are poorly satisfied because of limitations in the abilities to relate the devices to the needs. It is relatively easy to design a computer-based system to replicate physical processes and remarkably difficult to design a replacement for cognitive and judgmental processes.

The successes in mechanization of manual movements and the failures in automation of mental processes both indicate that mere perpetuation of manual processes is not an effective means to exploit the full capabilities of computers and telecommunications. If automation is more than mechanization, there must be a clearer appreciation of what hardware can do and a diligent effort to assure that those capabilities respond to, rather than define, system needs.

FUNCTIONS

The whole spectrum of devices can be understood by considering the five functions that can be and are performed by data processing hardware: *conversion* from one form of representation to another, *storage* for varying periods of time, *communication* by movement of data, logical and arithmetic *processing,* and finally, *display* in human-sensible form.

The wide array of machines offers various combinations of these functions in a range of sizes and speeds. Most equipment performs several functions with emphasis on but one or two. The devices directly usable at the human/machine interface provide the widest range of functional versatility but are typically scaled to human speeds and capabilities. The devices least concerned with human contact feature the fastest and most specialized uses.

CONVERSION

The first function of data processing hardware is to convert data from one form to another and especially to forms that can serve at the human/machine interface.

Machines can be provided to detect discrete events (digital data), to measure continuous processes (analog data), and to capture patterns (image data). Machine detection of discrete events and recognition of occurrence are the most common digital processes; a wide variety of analog measurements are used in process control in chemical and metalworking industries, most commonly by converting the analog signals to digital form. Photographs, drawings, and microforms are extensively used, both alone and in combination with digital and analog data as locator aids.

There are only a few practical combinations of human-actuated–machine-sensed processes. Man has no effective capacity to provide input to a machine sensor except by touch and speech. Many variations on the use of the sense of touch are now common. Keystroking, button pushing, switch throwing, pointing, and preformation have been very successful and are widely used. Mechanical auditory sensors that can provide conversion to any other data forms are still relatively slow and unreliable, so the predominant interface is by human touch, as in using a keyboard or drawing a symbol. Machine sensing of a single key from the whole keyboard array thus accounts for virtually all the input.

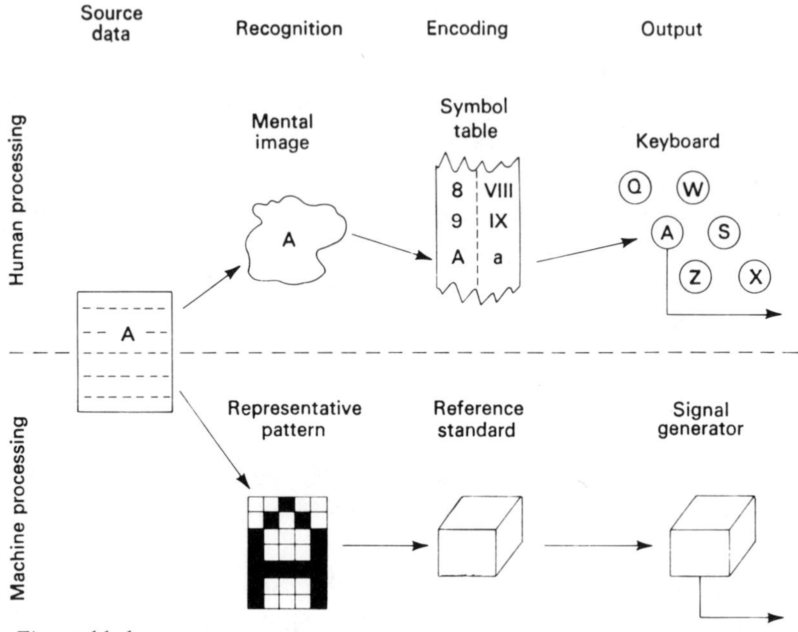

Figure 11-1.

The more complex conversion processes, as sketched in Figure 11-1, begin with a recognition stage where the source data are used to construct a mental image or are traced by some device to create a representative pattern. The image or pattern is then standardized and issued in some suitable machinable form. Human processing is still far more capable than that of any device in pattern recognition, and a dual (manual then machine) conversion is usually needed to make effective use of both types of capability.

Symbol recognition by automatic devices follows a similar logic in that the recognized pattern must be matched to a table of standard patterns. If the recognized pattern is not in the input list, it is comparable to human recognition of a symbol not in the language or not included on the keyboard. In either instance, there must be a choice or guess as to the correct selection or an indication of an error.

Conventional typing includes machine sensing of the selected key, but in most cases the recognition is used only to drive the symbol imprinting device. In a few instances, a machinable record in the form of a magnetic- or paper-tape record of the typed sequence is produced as a by-product of the printing. To a limited degree, the typed page is machinable if in a form suitable for optical character recognition (OCR).

Magnetic codes incorporated into recognizable numerals provide a unique dual record, and magnetic-ink character recognition (MICR). has become a widely accepted practice in banking.

A few devices are available to detect discrete selections based on the touching of specified areas of a surface. The analogy to a keystroke is obvious. The light pen used as an active pointer to regions of an electronic display is yet another variation of the keyboard principle.

A substantially complete array of devices is available for conversion from one simple machine-sensible form to another. Switch and shaft positions, holes, magnetic orientation, electromagnetic emanations, and electric pulses are all used, although there is a clearly recognizable preference for conversion to electronic signals whenever possible.

Manual data conversion is a high-cost process. The cost is well justified if the process is necessary, that is, if included are one or more processes not well structured and therefore not well suited to automation. Conversion processes based on physical representations, as in punch cards, are relatively expensive because of the handling problems introduced by the card itself. Typical operations involve a few thousand cards per minute in devices that cost a few hundred dollars per month and require the attention of a trained operator. The range of cost is thus from several hundred to a few thousand dollars per billion bytes of data (gigabyte).

Magnetic representation offers operations rates that are higher by a factor of 100. The machine cost is substantially higher, but operator attention is much lower and total costs are about equal to those involved in card processing. Unit costs, therefore, range from a few dollars to a few tens of dollars per gigabyte.

When the machine process is exclusively electronic, the unit costs are further reduced and will rarely exceed one dollar per gigabyte.

In contrast, manual conversion is very expensive. The preparation of machinable data by keystroking is perhaps the best example of conversion from the conceptual form that people can handle to some machine-sensible form. At standard rates of 8,000 to 12,000 keystrokes per hour, the cost exceeds $600,000 per gigabyte.

Apart from any consideration of purpose or method, it is clear that manual data conversion should be reduced to a minimum. When data are once captured, they should be retained thereafter in machinable form.

STORAGE

Effective automation is closely related to the degree to which data storage can be in machinable form. Data stored for human reference are almost exclusively in the form of optical symbols or audio records. Other forms, for example, Braille symbols, represent only a very small fraction of the total. For machine processing, storage may be in mechanical, electronic, or magnetic form depending on the desired capacity of storage and speed of access.

As in the conversion function, machine-accessible storage can be in digital, analog, or image form. For the present, these three forms are not readily interchangeable and only partially compatible. In consequence, image storage is extensively used in conjunction with a parallel digital system but rarely tied directly to digital search processes. With few exceptions, the usual means of storage for search and retrieval is digital.

Many other media have been proposed and tried, and radical changes in storage technology may become practical in the next decade. Lasers and holographs suggest many intriguing possibilities but offer no immediate hope of extensive practical application. The ideas extend to concepts far removed from past experience. One suggestion is to transmit the data in a signal bounced off a distant planet. Such a scheme would use the vacuum of deep space as the storage medium and yet assure that any portion of the data could be recovered in, at most, the few minutes needed for the signal to reach the planet and return.

Mechanical storage as holes, notches, raised or depressed areas in cards and tape, and switch settings is lowest in capacity, slowest of access, and well suited to common human and machine interpretation, but rather expensive because of the low density of recording.

The standard punch card is surely the most common mechanical storage medium. At eighty characters per card and a handling speed of a few thousand cards per minute, the maximum access rate is a few hundred thousand characters per minute (CPM) or a few thousand characters per second (CPS). Storage density is about 10^6 characters per cubic foot.

Electronic or electrical storage is usually limited to storage during transportation. The pulses are essentially the same either on a local basis within a machine or on a long-distance basis in a telecommunication network. The prevailing hesitancy to exploit the communications on a regular basis can be expected to disappear very quickly when the technology is better appreciated.

Magnetic storage in memory cores, tape, disc, drum, or strips is by far the most common means of storage of large quantities of digital data. Recording densities of thousands of bits per inch are common, with access speeds that provide up to several hundred thousand characters per second.

The physical arrangement of the storage area controls the effective access delay. Tape in the form of reels of up to 2,400 feet requires several minutes to unwind. Disc or drum surfaces offer random access to any of the recorded data in one hundred milliseconds or less. Tape-strip storage is comparatively slow since the selected strip must be located, removed from its container, and wrapped on a drum for reading or recording. Access time is about one second or less, but the storage capacity is very great, and the cost is lower than for disc storage.

A variety of other storage techniques, including optical recording, are under development. It is expected that continued advances will be made in storage density, access speed, and transfer rates. Existing techniques are likely to persist without radical change for several years, but supplementary techniques should be available within the decade.

The economics of data storage relate both to the storage capacity and the retrieval response. In general, the cost increases with increases in the speed of response and with enhanced capability to manipulate the data. There is no doubt that the data content of books and related library materials is very economic storage. It is not ideal, and extra costs are commonly incurred to increase the storage density by use of microforms, to increase the speed of access by use of containers and conveyors, and to provide for multiple use by provision of extra copies and throwaway reproductions.

The data about the contents must be relatively quick and easy of access and therefore incur a much higher storage cost. Punch cards, printed materials, and microforms offer a wide range of storage density, but the access capability is dominated by the continuing need for physical handling. Microforms hold some promise of providing both human-sensible and machine-sensible forms and of providing automatic handling to reduce the access time by one or two orders of magnitude.

In the realm of machine-sensible storage there is a sharp inverse relationship between storage density and speed. Computer memories are too small and expensive for file storage. Magnetic tape is too slow to support direct interaction with the data and is further handicapped by the necessity for manual handling.

There is a reasonable prospect that discs may provide a suitable interim capability for storage. There are clear prospects for an increase in storage density of one to two orders of magnitude with some related increase in access speed. Magnetics or other recording techniques will provide a feasible solution to the library storage problem in the next five to ten years only if many libraries exploit telecommunications capability to provide access to a common file of index and processing data. In the more distant future, new storage techniques may provide a truly vast storage capacity at low cost and with fast access, but the need for shared work and cooperative use is the only reasonable hope for an economical solution. The cost of generating cataloging data is too great to be repeated hundreds or thousands of times, however cheaply it may be stored.

COMMUNICATION

The movement of data from one location to another is a much simpler and more logical process than is apparent from most discussions of computer and communications networks. The short-distance moves have been virtually ignored, whereas long-distance moves have been invested with an aura of mystery and magic that almost matches the mystery and magic accorded the computer.

There are many involved technical aspects of communication, but the basic process is usually as obvious as moving the storage device. Cards, tapes, and discs are all common and effective carriers in movements that do not require great speed. With the recent introduction of removable disc packs, the stationary storage elements are essentially reduced to memory cores and drums.

The basic means to fast movement is by an electrical pulse along a wire, and there is far more similarity than difference between internal signal movements and external telecommunications. The principal technical difficulty is in the devices that interface the internal signals, all of which are under precise and rigorous control by a single master clock, to the external signals which are controlled by different clocks and involve significant transmission delays.

Suitable solutions to the synchronization problem are now available, and routine use of the telephone network is clearly underway. The standard voice-grade telephone line is well suited to use by the library; it is readily available, well accepted, and can be reliable and economical. Transmission rates are sufficient to drive line printers at several hundred lines per minute using standard devices. Substantially greater capacity is available, but few libraries have a sustained need for more service than can be handled by a single voice-grade line. It is expected that the capability of the lines and devices will increase at least as rapidly as the application demands. Thus, the library can expect to have access to sufficient communication service as soon as the needs for such service are identified.

The transport cost decreases as more compact storage media and faster movement are provided. Both characteristics serve to remove the data from human-sensible form and the human scale of speed. If a workcart with 10,000 cards can be pushed at a speed of 5 miles per hour, the cost is some $1,000 per gigabyte mile. The significance of electronic representation and telecommunications is apparent in that transport using voice-grade telephone lines at 2,400 band offers a cost of about $10 per gigabyte mile.

PROCESSING

The power of a computer is derived from: (1) great speed, (2) the generality of the primitive operations, (3) the programs—software—that specify the sequence of use of the operations, and (4) the interconnection of a variety of input, storage, and output devices that makes it possible to keep the processing unit busy.

The processing speed of a modern general-purpose digital computer is measured in very small fractions of a second. Just a decade ago an operation that required hundredths or thousandths of a second was considered to be very fast. In the intervening years the vocabulary of small time increments has become widely known as the clock rates and processing speeds have increased from milliseconds (thousandths) to microseconds (millionths) to nanoseconds (billionths). In 1960 a cycle increment of less than ten microseconds meant a fast computer; now the threshold is at tens or hundreds of nanoseconds and the increase is not yet at an end.

Processing speed is closely related to the reduction in size of the active components. Sharp reductions in size have brought corresponding decreases in heat dissipation demands and permitted yet closer packing. The ultimate will be reached when sizes reach molecular scale, but that requires decreases of a thousand times or more and presents a challenge to the hardware designers that will be unfulfilled for many years.

The basic processing capabilities of a data processing device reside in a very few primitive operations. Electromechanical devices,[2] from desk calculators to small computers, are limited to a few operations, but even medium- to large-scale computers need only about one hundred operations. The operations repertoire includes a variety of control functions to start and stop related devices, several move commands to read data between memory locations and various processing elements, and, finally, a few logical and arithmetic functions.

The economics of computation and logical processing are simple and clear. Large central processors are more capable and less expensive than smaller computers and can be expected to continue to offer

[2] The most common designation for the card-handling devices is electric accounting machines (EAM), a tribute to concentrated applications in business.

reductions in costs per computation by as much as one-half every three to four years.

The actual cost of processing depends on many factors of which the most important are loading and efficiency. The expected low unit costs are obtained only if the full capacity is used for productive purposes. The gross capacity for performing computations and logical operations is defined by the amount of data handled in one computer cycle and the time required for a cycle. The basic cost of the equipment and its operation then provides the data for the theoretical minimum cost. The cost advantage of larger processors indicates that it is now economic to transport data by means of a telecommunications network in order to avoid the cost of a smaller computer. The communications horizon is not infinite but appears to recede by about one thousand miles for each doubling of capacity.

There are substantial costs for the support of complex operating systems and some compensating advantages in dealing with a computer of a scale larger than the size of a single program. These two opposing characters suggest a statistical probability of a good balance between the capacity and the load.

DISPLAY

Display capabilities are the most important of hardware functions in the sense that the effort in data gathering and storage is intended to lead to ultimate use. Apart from the occasional need to prepare extensive reports, the critical demands are for prompt display of a small fraction of the stored data. The oft-repeated complaint that computers imply a literal flood of printed output is well founded in fact and practice. The very nature of data processing in batches means that processing of many or all records of a file in the same manner is greatly improved. It is also true that access to one or a few records is severely inhibited. It is practical but inconvenient to find one record in a stack of printed output. A more critical problem is that of assuring up-to-date data.

A display is a presentation of data in human-sensible form. Visual display in printed form accounts for most of the output. Audible output is now available for presentation of certain well-structured output such as a report of the available balance in a bank account.

"Soft" displays on a cathode-ray tube (CRT) are now becoming commonplace, and there is an exciting possibility that such devices can be used for immediate and direct access to one or a few records. Such a capability is especially significant when correct treatment of current transactions requires reference to prior data, as when a cataloger needs reference to the data about a book that was previously generated in the acquisition, funding, and classification processes.

The value of the output has typically an inverse relationship to response delay. There is increasing evidence that the relationship changes sharply at some point and introduces a radically different mode of interaction, as shown in Figure 11-2. This is directly akin to the change in the mode of communication that occurs with the switch from increasingly fast correspondence to telephone or face-to-face conversation. There is a radical change in both the content and manner of communication and a corresponding increase in satisfaction with the process. Such direct interaction—in effect, a conversation with the data—is not a complete solution to library search, but will eliminate the vast gap in space and time that now separates the librarian from the library of data.

VALUE AND COST OF FAST RESPONSE

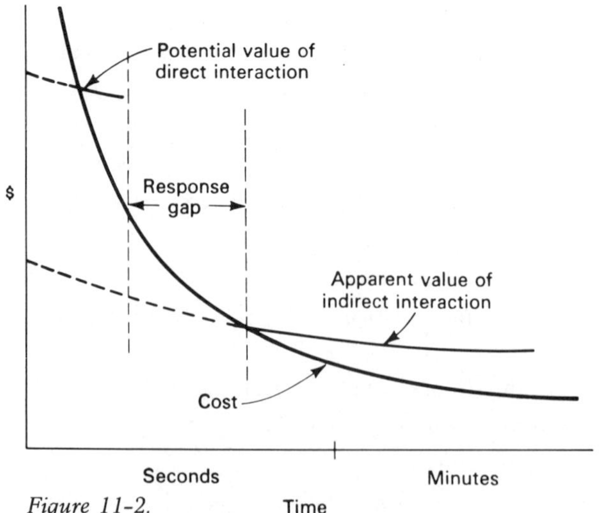

Figure 11-2.

The economics of display are perhaps more complex than those of any other process. It is increasingly clear that use of data is an interaction between man and data in which the final result is dependent upon the process itself.

It is cheaper to print a page of output than to generate a display. It is, conversely, cheaper to generate one display than to print thousands of pages of output, especially when the data are dynamic and the needs are scattered in time and space.

In net terms these developments will substantially change the balance of workload from that which mechanization implied to that which automation demands—the more optimum use of both human and machine capabilities.

SUGGESTED READING LIST

Abrahamson, Ed.: "Mini-computers for Large Scale Process Control? A Mini-computer System Is Described Whose Goals Are Decentralization and Simplification," *Datamation,* **16**: 123-130, February 1970.

Bauer, Walter F.: "Computer Communications Systems—Patterns and Prospects," *Computer Communications Symposium, University of California at Los Angeles, 20-22 March, 1967,* Prentice-Hall, Englewood Cliffs, N.J., 1967 pp. 13-37.

Berul, Lawrence: "Survey of Equipment Developments in the Information Storage and Retrieval Field," *F.I.D./I.F.I.P. Conference, June 14-17, 1967,* Auerbach Corp., Philadelphia, 1967.

Borko, Harold, and H. P. Burnbaugh: "Interactive Displays for Document Retrieval," *Information Display,* **3**: 47-90, September-October 1966.

Dennis, Jack B.: "A Position Paper on Computing and Communications," *Communications of the ACM,* **11**: 370-377, May 1968.

Gentle, Edgar C., Jr.: *Data Communications in Business, an Introduction,* American Telephone and Telegraph Company, New York, *c* 1965. 163 pp. Paperback.

Gull, Cloyd Dake: "The Hardware of Data Processing," *Library Resources and Technical Services,* **9**: 6-18, 1965.

Manning, Josephine: "Facsimile Transmission—Problems and Potential," *Library Journal,* **93**: 4102-4104, Nov. 1, 1968.

Nett, Roger, and Stanley A. Hetzler: *An Introduction to Electronic Data Processing,* Free Press, New York, 1959, 287 pp.

Schieber, William D., and Ralph M. Shoffner: *Telefacsimile in Libraries: A Report on Experiment in Facsimile Transmission and an Analysis of Implications for Interlibrary Loan Systems,* Institute of Library Research, University of California, Berkeley, 1968, 139 pp. ED 019 106.

CHAPTER 12
SOFTWARE

Software is, technically, the sequence of instructions that directs the execution of a corresponding sequence of operations. The operations may be either human or machine, but the designation as software is not usually applied except in reference to control of hardware operations. The responsiveness of the operation is related to the variety of primitive operations that are provided and the complexity of the instruction sequence. In a device of utter simplicity, such as a light switch, there is no stored sequence of instructions. The conversion of the intention to machinable form—flipping the switch—is the whole

SIMPLE LIST SEQUENCE

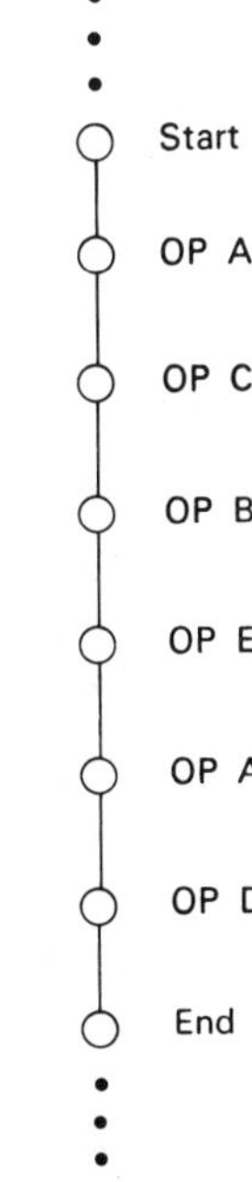

Figure 12–1.

sequence. In more complex arrangements there are instruction sequences of thousands of operations.

The simplest instruction sequence is a list of operations to be performed only once. The same primitive operations may appear many times in the list. The checklist used in aircraft landings and takeoffs is typical of the simple list diagrammed in Figure 12-1.

The introduction of a branching choice provides increased variety.

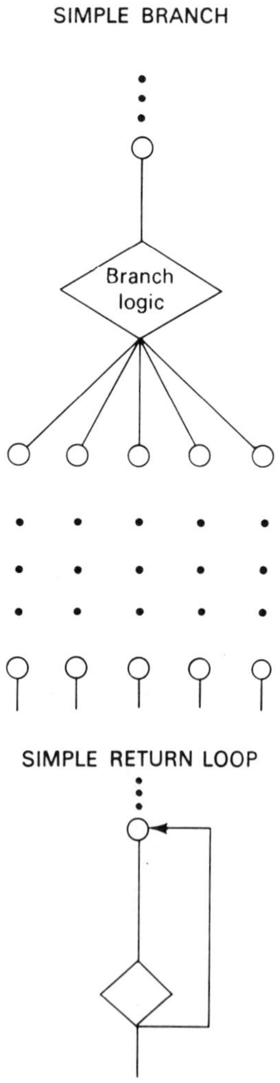

Figure 12-2.

As shown in Figure 12-2, the branch leads to one of many lists. The use of return loops is the most powerful means of providing a very long effective sequence since it can control the reexecution of a sequence of operations thousands or millions of times. To direct operations for a processing run of one hour in a computer that performs an operation in one microsecond requires an effective list of 3.6 billion instructions. Without the means to use portions of the

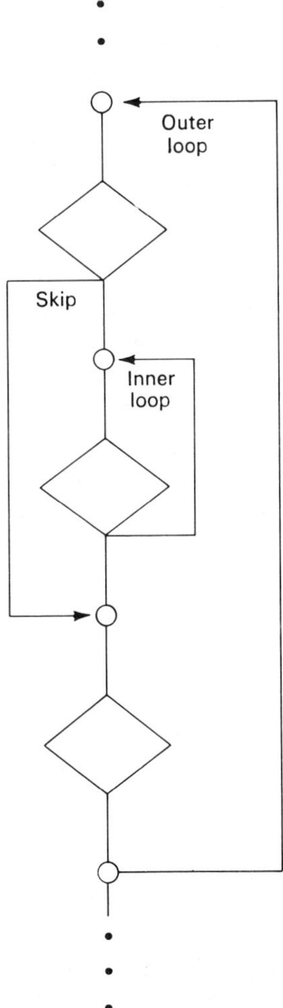

Figure 12–3.

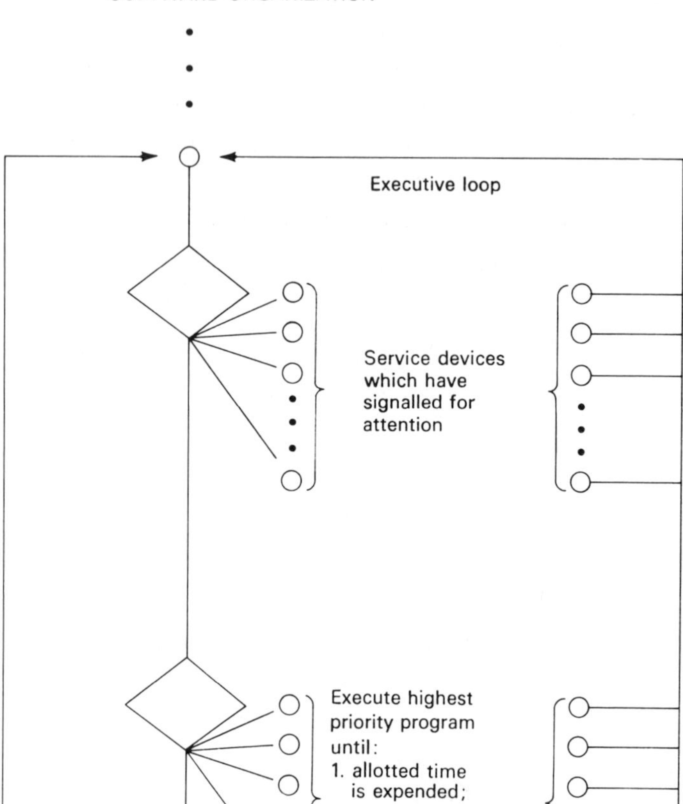

Figure 12-4.

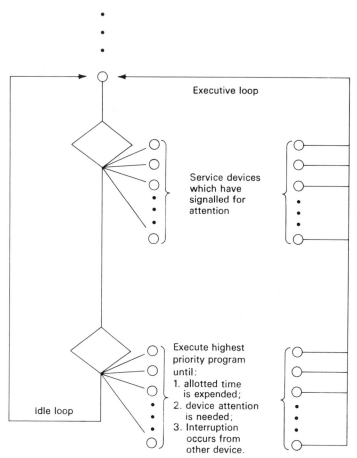

sequence repeatedly, such a list would be impossible to develop and impractical to maintain.

Arranging alternative branches and loops within loops, as indicated in Figure 12-3, provides a complex network of instructions that can control the full repertoire of operations for long periods of time.

The software organization for a major computer, as outlined in Figure 12-4, would include an executive loop that controls service to any device that has signaled for attention, branches to the application programs in priority order, and, if no device or program is ready, cycles repeatedly through an idle loop.

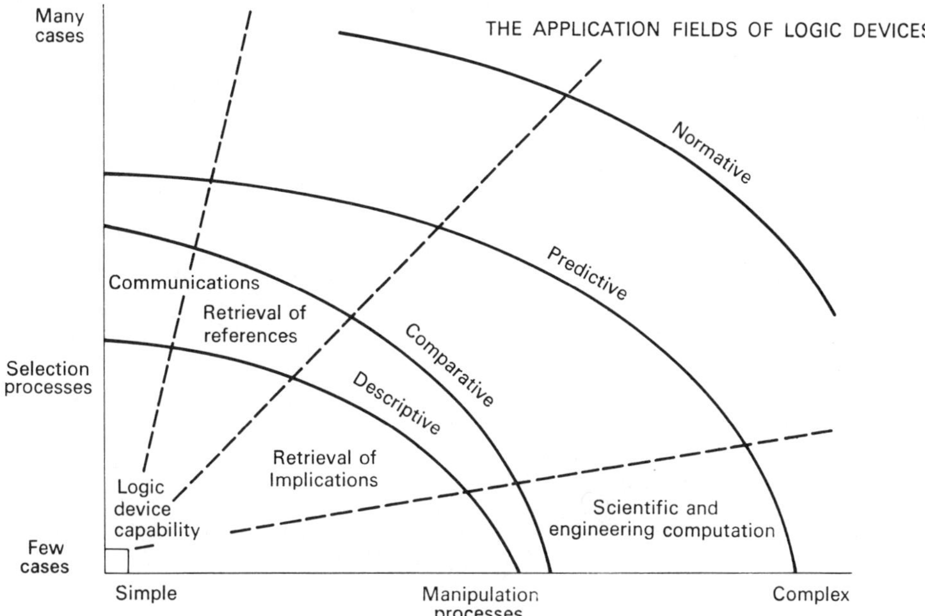

Figure 12-5.

A less technical view of software recognizes that it is the human/machine interface that is paramount and that software is the means whereby people can obtain effective control over the sequence of operations that a machine can perform. In this view the purpose of software is to eliminate the gap between what people want done and what machines can do. Thus the application fields of logic devices as diagrammed in Figure 12-5 reflect the combination of demand and processing characteristics presented in Chapter 9.

The gap between what people want and what machines can do is narrowed, as shown in Figure 12-6, by the system design efforts that convert a vague problem idea into a precise, well-defined specification. It is inevitable that this process will yield a version of the problem which is simpler than the real problem. Further, the specification will usually reflect an unconscious preference for either selection or manipulation and, therefore, move the problem toward one of the axes—not directly toward the origin.

Machine-oriented software extends the equipment operations by providing control and sequencing logic to handle the job stream and to

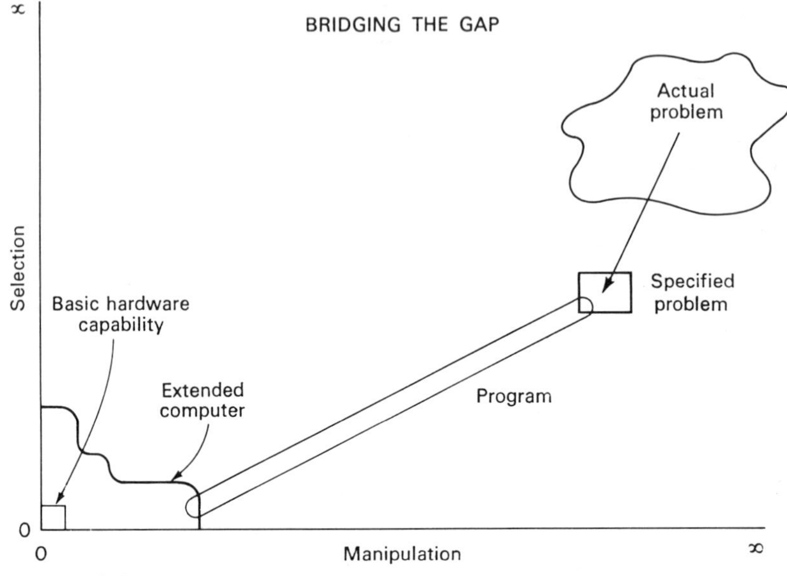

Figure 12-6.

allocate the equipment components to the job needs. The remainder of the gap is bridged by general utility programs that are either logic-oriented or data-oriented and by specific application-oriented programs.

MACHINE-ORIENTED SOFTWARE

The language for instructing a computer in the simple recurring processes common to every application is dominated by the hardware design. The most fundamental processes are the executive or supervisory routines (operating system) that control the allocation of the hardware resources to the tasks to be done. In a small computer there is little or no capability to work on two or more tasks together and, therefore, little need or opportunity for automatic control. Job assignment is controlled by the operator, and the operating system never appears. In more complex arrangements a dozen or more tasks may be active together since the central processor can handle the data much faster than the attached input, storage, and output devices.

Operating systems for control of such computer and communication networks must have a variety of capabilities and must function with high reliability.

APPLICATION-ORIENTED SOFTWARE

The ultimate product of the programming process and the culmination of the hardware/software relationship is the sequence of instructions that specifies the execution of a corresponding sequence of primitive operations. This "object" code is obtained by use of a program which assembles, compiles, or interprets the "source" code prepared in a manual operation. The programmer's source language is one or a combination of the three available levels of programming language.

The lowest level of program code is machine language. It provides an instruction sequence directly usable by the equipment but requires completion of every detail by the programmer. Although machine-language coding was the original means to specify instruction sequences, it is a burden to the programmer and is now used only in rare circumstances in the process of designing the computer itself.

The second level of programming is characterized by the use of codes from which to assemble the machine-language codes on a one-for-one basis. Assembly languages are tedious to use but provide substantial clues to guide the programmer; the classical example is the use of the letter *A* to signify the process of addition. Assembly language is still widely used in some applications and is unsurpassed in providing the means whereby the skilled programmer can exploit the ultimate logical capabilities of the equipment. Assembly coding, in application programming, is a powerful and efficient tool, but one that uses programming time very poorly. A sound balance of the elements of total cost will usually dictate that most of the programming be done in a higher-level language, with only a small part of the most exacting logic expressed in assembly code.

Compiler languages in which a single statement is "compiled" into several assembly or machine-level statements are the common higher-level language of the 1960s. A wide variety of languages, each focused on a particular view of the processing requirements is now available. FORTRAN and ALGOL, the most successful for scientific and engineering applications, have found little application in libraries. COBOL, the language of business data processing, is widely used for the same types of functions represented in library control and administrative processes and is reasonably well suited to the many file-handling processes inherent in technical processing.

The problem-oriented languages have been postulated as the next-higher-level language. There are good theoretical reasons for assuming that a language that addresses what is to be accomplished without specification of how to do it will be useful and acceptable. Procedure-free logic is not yet a substantial factor in other disciplines and is not likely to be a powerful influence in the library in the near future.

It may be that advances in logic-oriented and data-oriented software will so change the character of application programming that the emphasis on an all-encompassing language will be of minimal importance.

LOGIC-ORIENTED SOFTWARE

There is a gap between hardware-oriented and application-oriented software that can be substantially narrowed by the use of common utility programs to relieve the programmer of a part of the burden of detail. Such utilities have been available since the first days of commercial computer usage but until recently were considered as a part of the hardware-oriented software. Two distinct classes of utility programs are now apparent. One includes the assembler and compiler logic that is used to interpret and process the programmer's source statements. The other includes a wide variety of useful processes such as sorting routines, mathematical and logical functions, and housekeeping logic.

DATA-ORIENTED SOFTWARE

Data-oriented software did not exist in any recognizable way until very recently. Application programs that encompassed the whole spectrum of processes from input to output did not leave any obvious opportunities for meaningful common use of data or for access to data structures designed for other specific purposes.

The essence of data management logic lies in a clear distinction between the particular processes that are concerned with content to be stored in the data base and the general processes that generate the data superstructure and then use it to access the data content. Data management logic makes it possible for the application design to focus on the users' needs with the assumption that all the data content is accessible and that the ease of access is directly responsive to changing needs.

A data inventory is the best way to establish the magnitude of the task of data management. The inventory must provide an identification of all data files and an estimate of their size but must avoid multiple counting of data held in duplicate files. The classical file survey does not provide an accurate measure since redundancies and omissions are not recognizable in any systematic way. The data inventory is focused on data entities, relationships, and events rather than the details of file content because it is a tool for management planning rather than programming control. It is obtained by a study of the data environment rather than of the files held by the different organizational units.

The first step in conducting the inventory is to identify the physical and conceptual *entities* that are of interest to the library. The physical entities obviously include books and other holdings, employees, equipment, facilities, patrons, and donors. The conceptual entities include fund accounts, organizational codes, classification structures, and authority lists. It is certain that the more important entities will be identified first, and thus, if a few are momentarily forgotten, the error will not be great and will in due time be corrected.

The *relationships* that do exist or might exist can then be discovered by the simple process of inquiring whether there are reflexive relationships among entities of the same type or hierarchic or associative relationships between pairs of entities. This examination will reveal the obvious links between and among the holdings and the classification and authority lists as well as the less obvious pairings that link the technical and business processes.

The *events* that bring together several entities in a temporary relationship are the most complex. They are similar to the simpler relationships except that events imply the existence of specific data about transactions, such as the date of occurrence or the amount or value of a purchase or fine.

When the entities, relationships, and events have been listed, the next step is to estimate the amount of data associated with each of them and the number of members in each set. It is necessary to consider both the data to be retained in file and the rate of data flow that must be processed. Call numbers, for example, will be stored in the file as a part of the descriptive data about the book and also used in search and reference.

The summation of the data estimates will provide a total measure of the minimum probable file and the recurring flow rates. The actual files and rates will be greater than the minimum to the degree that duplicate records or files are established. The comparison of the minimum to the current actual sizes will indicate the severity of the redundancy problem and suggest the potential value of an automated data system that provides common access to a single nonredundant data base.

SUGGESTED READING LIST

Blier, Robert E.: *Treating Hierarchical Data Structures in the SDC Time-shared Data Management System (TDMS)*, System Development Corporation, Santa Monica, Calif., 1967. SP-2750.

Borowski, C.: "An Experimental System for Automatic Identification of Personal Names and Personal Titles in Newspaper Texts," *American Documentation*, 18: 131–138, July 1967.

Bregzis, Ritvars: "Query Language for the Reactive Catalogue," in Albert B. Tonik (ed.), *Proceedings National Colloquium on Information Retrieval, Fourth, Philadelphia, May 3–4, 1967*, International Information Inc., Philadelphia, 1967, pp. 77–90; discussion, pp. 90–91.

Climensen, W. Douglas: "File Organization and Search Techniques," *Annual Review of Information Science and Technology*, vol. 1, Interscience-Wiley, New York, 1966, pp. 107–135.

Meadow, C. T.: *Analysis of Information Systems: A Programmer's Introduction to Information Retrieval,* Wiley, New York, 1967, 301 pp.

Minker, J., and J. Sable: "File Organization and Data Management," *Annual Review of Information Science and Technology,* vol. 2, Interscience-Wiley, New York, 1967, pp. 123–160.

Moyne, J. A.: "Information Retrieval and Natural Language," *Proceedings of the American Society for Information Science, 32nd Annual Meeting, San Francisco, California, October 1-4, 1969;* 6: 259–263, Greenwood, Westport, Conn., 1969.

CHAPTER 13
CONCEPTS

There is a need for a data system and an opportunity to provide a useful service when two preliminary conditions have been fulfilled:

1. There is, in fact or in prospect, a physical system and environment.
2. There is a management system which seeks either to influence and control some activities of the physical system within the environment or to understand its functioning.

Data make it possible for the management system to influence the physical system and the environment. The importance of the data depends upon the significance of the management influences and the degree to which direct control is possible or convenient.

If the physical system is a car and the management system is a driver, the management influence is vital, and direct control is both possible and convenient. There is little need for more than the human data system of the driver, although computer-controlled braking systems may become a practical reality. If the vehicle is a space rocket, the control requirements are too numerous and too exacting for direct human control, and an elaborate automatic data system is essential.

If the physical system is the universe, the direct control opportunities are severely limited, and the data system includes a sophisticated mathematical model that can be manipulated to predict physical relationships. The test of such predictions is the proof of success or failure of the understanding of the physical system.

If the physical system is a library, it may well be possible to fulfill the management requirements with a manual data system. When either the size or the managerial concepts grow, it becomes necessary to provide supplemental data manipulation capabilities. In either case, there is potential advantage in considering the data system processes as guides to continuing planning and control. These data processes are readily apparent in the system functions discussed in Chapter 9 and outlined in Figures 9-3 and 9-4.

The first process is *discovery* of the existence of entities that may be of concern. The basic definition of concern arises from the established physical and management systems. In a library there are a host of discovery aids that suggest new contributors, new materials, new services, and new recipients.

The second process is *identification* of each entity to assure that it is uniquely distinguished from all others. It is important that unique identification, once established, is not lost and that each physical entity be associated with its identity data.

The third process is *description* of the entity to provide a data description distinct from any physical object. The unique identification assures that later additions to the description will not be lost and that the object and the data can be logically associated even though physically separated.

The fourth process is *transformation* of both the objects and the data. The objects may be labeled, transformed in size, gathered into unit loads, converted to Braille, or otherwise changed to facilitate processing, storage, and handling, and to assist the recipient. The data may be encoded, converted to machinable form, communicated, translated, and displayed. As with objects, the transformation can serve both the library and the recipient.

The fifth process is *accumulation* of the objects and the data in anticipation of future demands. There is no necessary presumption that all the objects or the data are physically together. In particular, the data may be reproduced for use in many locations.

The sixth process is *manipulation* of the objects and the data. In general it is expected that the data, being easier, faster, and cheaper to process, will be manipulated first to establish the identity of individual entities or groups of entities. The identification that links the data to the object is then used to obtain the object. Of course, there is no necessity for the object in many cases; the data provides all that is needed.

Finally, the seventh process is *delivery* of the data and the objects to the recipient.

These processes can be traced through every data system. A library reflects several data systems linked together to serve administrative needs as well as the major activities of acquisition, cataloging, and reference, and control of resources and processes.

THE LIBRARY IN PERSPECTIVE

The stock-in-trade of a library need not be limited, in concept or in fact, to the books, journals, maps, photographs, and recordings that are now accepted as typical library contents. The library process is applicable to all these, but the process is better appreciated in terms of what it excludes and the degree to which the exclusion is functional rather than traditional.

Many institutions with librarylike features are well known by other names, but there is an echo of their activities in every library.

To a retailer, value depends upon consumption; consumable materials are preferably indistinguishable. When style, color, or other characteristics are introduced, the apparent variety is increased, average usage rates decline, and inventory levels, obsolete stock, and spoilage become crucial problems. In contrast, the library concentrates on materials whose value is derived from use, not consumption. Extensive variety is advantageous, and duplication is minimized, if not eliminated. The contrast is strong, but not absolute; multiple copies facilitate service, reduce transportation, and speed response; throw-away copies are sometimes the most convenient and economical method of providing the requested material.

A museum prefers one-of-a-kind originals or truly representative examples. The emphasis on physical objects restricts the presentation of ideas and concepts except as they may be evidenced in artifacts. The library offers replicates, copies, images, and interpretations and commonly maintains a variety of means for reproduction of selected material; still the attitude of a museum, if not the name, persists in the rare book and historical document collections.

Financial institutions concentrate upon materials of appreciable intrinsic value and upon legal claims to economic value; intellectual content is not a major concern. To a library, the intellectual content is dominant, and economic values are derived from it. There is a continuing effort to foster scholarly endeavor, to derive new knowledge by synthesis and implication, and to interpret old knowledge in new contexts. Nevertheless, the library is a part of the economic structure. In its business operations it partakes of the features of other economic endeavors and is never far removed from economic life and activity.

Manufacturers live with the threat of obsolescence and a continuing decline in the value of the retained materials. Rarely is the value of a manufactured object enhanced by the passage of time. Changing events and new viewpoints constantly refresh and reinvigorate the value of a portion of the library material; in some instances true perspective and significant interrelations appear only in the context of decades or centuries of patient accumulation and searching examination. Styles and tastes do change, however, and excess copies and unwanted items must be purged if the holdings are to be responsive to changing demands.

Newspaper, newsmagazine, journal, and book publishers concentrate on volume demands and strive to eliminate the return flow. The offerings are chosen to reflect current tastes and fashions, but the initiative rests with the contributor rather than the recipient, especially for short-lived materials such as newspapers. The desire to respond to recipient demands makes it necessary for the library to perform far more processing than a newsstand and effectively limits the ability to deal in short-lived material. The library encourages circulation and reuse, but communication is too often a one-way flow that provides little if any feedback; what one user learns is rarely available to the next.

The communications industry is increasingly message-oriented and less and less concerned with physical lines and connections. The dominant concern is with structural forms; the goal is to make all content functionally identical. This goal is nearly attained with voice messages in the worldwide telephone network; the voice signal is changed in many ways during the transmission, but is finally reproduced with recognizable fidelity. There remains a notable discontinuity between the processing methods applied to voice and data messages that may well persist for another decade. The library is increasingly concerned with the need to preserve content, but rapid communication can provide the equivalent of access to a nearly infinite collection that is physically dispersed.

Through many media, the contributor speaks to the recipient. Without care the great volume of communication traffic that can be generated becomes overwhelming. Most speech is gone after a few seconds, most broadcasts after a few hours, most newspapers after a few days, and most publications after a few years. If messages do not find a recipient promptly, they are unrecoverable except by a retrieval process that depends far more on the recipient than on the contributor.

In this context it is apparent that the library function is critically dependent upon the capacity for storage of many entities over long periods of time and the capability to retrieve selected entities upon demand. There are still greater opportunities for service by reducing the input delay and enhancing the output selectivity. These features are indicative of the reasons for the subjective evaluation that data processing, computers, and communications are important to the library.

THE LIBRARY AND OBJECT HANDLING

Diverse physical objects in great number cannot quickly and reliably be processed, stored, and retrieved. Only if they are represented as data can the speed of movement be increased from meters per minute to kilometers per second. Only if the retrieval index is recorded as data can the density of storage be increased from books per cubic foot to thousands of characters per cubic centimeter. Data about objects, but not the objects themselves, could be accumulated from around the world and placed in accessible storage within hours of its generation and searched for any desired content.

It is indeed rare that current events are seen in historical context or ideas recognized for all their implications. The interpretive value of the entities that are observed, the relationships detected among them, and the events that transpired emerge later. Man needs time to reflect, to learn of other happenings in other places, and to hypothesize and test. This process is inherently dominated by the recipient rather than the contributor. It is facilitated by access to a vast collection from which many tiny elements can be extracted, examined, and combined into new patterns and combinations.

The concept of such a collection introduces new and profound problems. The sources of library materials and the demands for library services are widely dispersed. It is difficult, if not infeasible, to create a single physical collection and to provide meaningful access to it. The alternative is to maintain a pattern of physical dispersal and to provide logical access to data about all the holdings. In current practice, and to a greater extent in the future, a library provides the services of an object-handling system for a small part of the total collection as well as a data-handling system with access to the total holdings. These two tasks of a library are clearly distinct but mutually compatible and indispensable. In combination they reflect the reality that a library is an information system—generating, collecting, storing, manipulating, and delivering both data and objects.

One of the most compelling realities of present libraries is the sheer number, size, and weight of the objects they handle. Ancient libraries frequently accumulated a million or more items, and present holdings are only tens of millions. The limitation to a tenfold increase indicates the continuing restriction inherent in the physical materials.

The physical characteristics of library materials are not always ideal for purposes of receipt, storage, or retrieval. Individual items offer few possibilities for modification. Long-term improvement can be expected in the instances in which libraries can agree upon objective standards and can provide effective means to express their desires. Whenever possible the library must champion the cause of meaningful standardization and otherwise devise ways to minimize or obviate the problems. Until such concerted action is attained, the primary defense must be the hope that human scale and human capabilities will be a natural choice of those who create the materials. Extremes in weight, size, shape, and texture contribute little that the library can count as valuable and introduce great complexity and inefficiency in library processes.

ACCOMMODATION OF INDIVIDUAL CHARACTERISTICS

The problems of materials handling arise from specific individual characteristics that prove to be inconvenient. Since there is no inherent natural form in which to embody knowledge, there is a possibility that every characteristic could be constrained or modified in such a way as to minimize or eliminate the object-handling problems. The basic scale of library operations is bound to human proportions, and, for the most part, those who produce library materials are inevitably conditioned to the same dimensions.

Deviations from the dimensions that are quickly, accurately, and reliably manipulated have a greater impact upon the library than upon the producer. The typical production lot of several thousand copies provides a substantial number of standardized units for the manufacturer's processing. Each library deals with only one or a few copies and what was standard to the publisher becomes diversity to the library. Of course, the library has occasion to perform maintenance and preservation of materials and can introduce some changes at that time. Extensive change in size or shape is not usually feasible, and the value of standard bindings and uniform colors is limited.

Weights from a few ounces to a few pounds are readily handled. Within the acceptable range the weight is not critical since the time and cost of a manual operation is strongly related to each piece, but not to the weight. It is a common practice to limit weight by dividing large objects into several volumes or by using thinner paper and smaller type. If such segmentation is inconvenient for the user, as in the case of an unabridged dictionary, the solution is to provide special handling devices and to retain the massive document in a fixed location.

Shape is closely related to the degree to which the technology of preparation dominates the form of the object. Recordings, slides, photographs, and film cannot be freely reshaped, but these and the more common books, journals, and maps are constrained to convenient dimensions.

Handling and storage operations and our three-dimensional world favor a rigid rectilinear outline, suitable for dense volumetric storage. Thin objects are easily damaged and readily misplaced. The library exerts a standardizing force on shape both in a positive sense by suggesting preferred dimensions and in a negative, if inadvertent, sense by making the unusual shapes less readily accessible.

The substance of an item is frequently unsuited to the library since most of the output is intended for users who have far less concern for durability and longevity. Archival quality materials, environment control, and aggressive preservation programs are essential to compensate for deterioration, fading, and desiccation. Dust jackets and protective covers are now commonplace for books in active circulation.

The practice of issuing single-use copies of documents that would be difficult to replace is an effective substitute, especially if only small portions of the documents are needed.

ACCOMMODATION OF COLLECTIVE CHARACTERISTICS

It is perhaps inevitable that the means to attainment of favorable group characteristics are found in modification of individual characteristics far beyond normal human ranges. Thus, the most common and most successful response to overwhelming mass is to reduce size below the limits of normal human capability.

Materials that are too light, too small, or too frail for normal handling can be collected together and repackaged for both protection and control. Variation in size can be minimized by classification based at least partially on size if compensating means are provided to accommodate the demand for browsing. Microforms and ultramicroforms offer a means to minimize the problems of weight and multiple access to frequently requested materials.

The processes involved in handling a large collection of objects favor average demands, and they work in opposition to the most critical service requests. For example, books in active circulation are more likely to be demanded than those that have never been used. Thus, when a call occurs, it is the popular book that is likely to be in circulation or in process or on its way back to the shelf and therefore unavailable for hours or even days. Of course, the extreme case of this phenomenon is apparent in the fact that the book that is always available is the one that is never requested.

The delays incurred by the necessity to move the object over a finite distance and by the contention for service during peak demands cannot be eliminated unless the physical objects are eliminated. The best that can be done is to assure that exact location of the object is reliably known and that the positioning is as well suited to demand patterns as is possible.

AUTOMATION OF PHYSICAL PROCESSES

The desirability of automation of the physical handling processes will not be eliminated by complete automation of the data-handling system unless it proceeds to the point of eliminating all object storage. Such a development is unlikely for many years and may not even be desirable.

It is reasonable to assume that improvements in data storage efficiency and decreases in image reproduction costs will make it practicable to eliminate many objects from the shelves and provide access to their contents by display of the retrieved data.

Standardization of physical size and shape will increasingly be provided by the introduction of unit loads or containerization, in which many pieces of different size and shape are placed in a package of uniform dimensions that can be handled, stored, and returned under automatic control by mechanical devices.

The final level of automation will be based on the process characteristics, especially the statistical pattern of usage and storage. It is apparent that the probability of reference is not the same for all objects. In virtually all storage and retrieval operations there is a distinctive pattern of demands that can be exploited in system design. If demand were uniformly distributed over all objects, it would correspond to line *A* in Figure 13-1. In practice the usual pattern follows

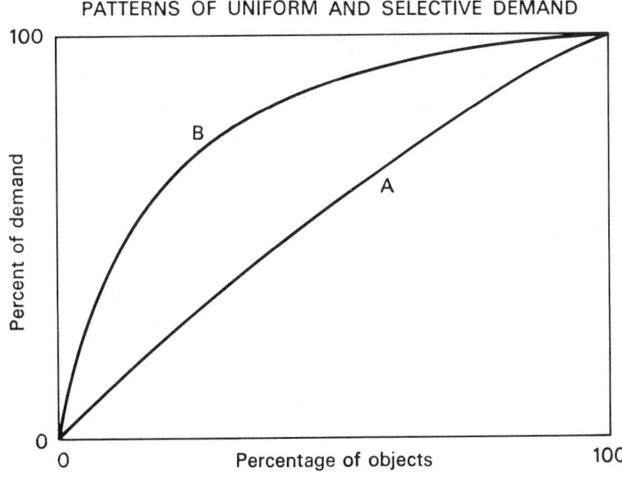

Figure 13–1.

line *B,* and a small percentage of the objects account for virtually all the demand.[1]

In a library this pattern suggests that the average distance of movement can be reduced if the objects are stored in accordance with the observed patterns of usage. Thus, the most popular fraction of the collection would be located nearest to the reference center. Of course, this shelving pattern would sharply reduce the value of shelf browsing and would necessitate a high order of location control.

Each operation in the object-handling process involves some concern for data about the process and its results. As the system is developed from individual, to collective, to process control and finally is automated, there is increasing need for a data-handling capability to complement the object-handling process and to maintain the basis for control of the system.

THE LIBRARY AS A DATA-HANDLING SYSTEM

When a library is viewed as an object-handling system, the conceptual basis for the design is immediate and obvious. The forms chosen by the contributors and desired by the requesters are the beginning and the end. The objects can be replicated, preserved, separated, bound, enlarged, or reduced using a variety of well-known processes. In each instance, the criteria for evaluation of the fidelity of the process are clear and direct. There are well-defined conventions and reasonably accurate guides to operational requirements, productivity, and cost.

The library as a data-handling system is, by comparison, poorly understood. The problem begins with the fact that the system deals with representations of something and not with the thing itself, as indicated in Figure 13-2. It is not only the book as an object that the data system contemplates. The concern is also with the knowledge represented by the content of the book, the form of its embodiment, and the processes it experiences.

We can conceive of a pure quantum of knowledge but cannot convey it directly from one mind to another. It must be repackaged

[1] *Annual Report of the Librarian of Congress, 1966,* Washington, 1967. In this year the Library of Congress circulated only 6,907,000 of its 54,289,000 objects.

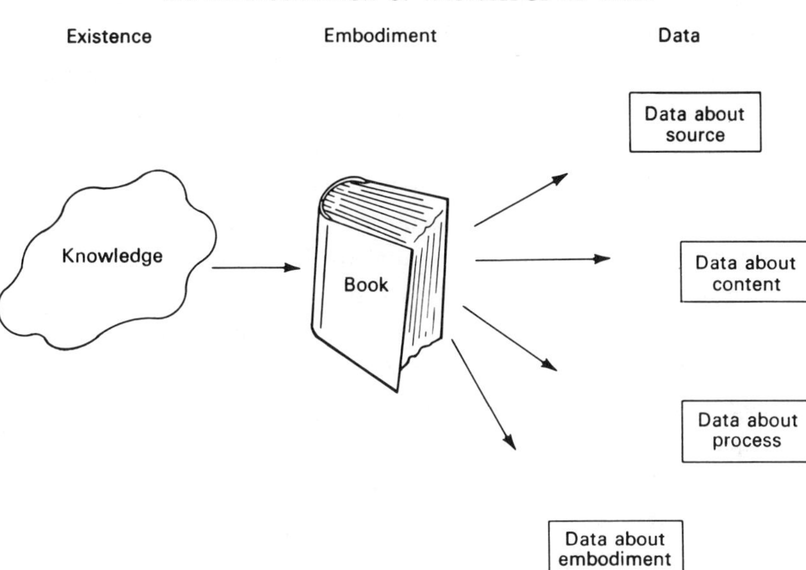

Figure 13-2.

for transfer, storage, and retrieval. The process of repackaging varies with the quantity and the importance of the knowledge and also with the characteristics of the offerer and the recipient. Oral transfer, embellished by gesture and emphasis, stands as the most successful means for direct interchange. The capability of the human mind for retrieval, storage, and synthesis is superb for that relatively small body of knowledge that can be retained in an active state.

The long-term preservation offered by written symbols introduces real difficulties in language and interpretation but greatly extends the limits imposed by the memory span, experience, and consistency of the storyteller. The introduction of physical records incorporating many small quanta of knowledge in a cohesive pattern represents the first library; the clay tablet, memorial stone, scroll, and book are exemplary of complete microlibraries. The accommodation of thousands or millions of entities over centuries of time and the integration of many facets of knowledge accent the scope but do not change the essential character of the transfer function.

The original documentation of the knowledge is the first important step in data representation. The knowledge represented in the document will be obscured if, at any stage, the distinction between the knowledge and its representation is not retained. In the Holy Bible and other documents that have received the fullest dedication of human concern, we have evidence that the word can be preserved through many translations if each document is viewed as a representation of value rather than the value itself.

When a library acquires an object, a systematic process of identification and description is essential to data control and ultimately to reliable access to the entity it reflects. Every step must be clearly defined and carefully linked to the overall logical design.

Automation can begin with the imposition of an absolute identity control on every object that enters the system and may reach effective maturity with the provision of means for automatic recognition of each piece by means of a machine-readable label in order to link the object to the data about it.

Identity arises from existence but does not constitute the basis of existence. Whatever is, is, even without identification. Identification, in common usage, implies the ability to distinguish a selected entity from all others. A person or any other entity can be identified by description. To assure unambiguous identity, a great many elements must be used, and each must be verifiable. It is sufficient to attain unique identification by profuse description, but there is no necessity for the identification to describe the entity in any way. The difficulty of consistent and unique identification, which is imperative to the continued functioning of a variety of information systems, is the reason for the selection of serial numbers as a common identifier for both persons and things. The true nature of identifiers that do not describe is perhaps best illustrated by those who object to the use of an identity number and insist that their name is the only proper identifier. Of course, a name is an arbitrary identifier with no more intrinsic merit than a number, except possibly pronounceability, and even less assurance of uniqueness.

In the library this proposition allows a collection, a series, a book, a chapter, a page, a paragraph, or even a sentence, and all the attributes related to them, to be accorded recognition, jointly and severally. The rationale of identification provides a structure to accommodate any desired content if only the requirements for consistency and uniqueness are fulfilled.

The freedom to choose any desired composition to be treated as an entity is restricted by the condition that other observers at other times and places will, with high probability, recognize the same entity.

A unique identity link assures that the specific object or objects represented by the data can be recognized when they are recovered. Searches conducted on the basis of descriptive attributes do not necessarily yield single identities and imply that retrieval of any member of the described set is acceptable. In like manner, the data manipulation may lead to some integral part of a physical unit or even to a set whose members are described by the desired properties. Thus any copy of a desired book, a single volume of a series, or a single chapter or article, or any one of many different translations may satisfy a request.

It is naïve to assume that an identity number is the correct answer to all questions of identity of library entities. Where identification symbols can be used, they offer a convenient basis for identity control, and there are many opportunities for such use that have not yet been exploited. Physical containment, as when classification work documents are placed in the book and moved together; sequence control, as in the placement according to a shelving symbol; and descriptive recognition all can be used to supplant the control offered by an identity label.

SYMBOLS

The apparent simplicity of number systems and alphabets hides a remarkable capability to convey complex and abstract ideas. These symbols and the more complicated pictographic images are the building blocks for all visual communication beyond interpretation of gestures.

The power of symbolic writing depends upon the establishment of a well-defined interpretation for each symbol and group of symbols. The symbol set need not be extensive to convey intricate data; digital computers employ bistable devices representing only two symbols, conventionally 0 and 1, for everything they do. Richer symbol sets involve a more complex interpretation base but employ fewer symbols to convey any given idea.

The symbol sets that employ combinations of symbols are formed from a group of basic elements that can be integrated into patterns.

This combinational property may well mean that all possible symbols have never been drawn, but could be interpreted on the basis of the constituent elements. The pictographic languages are relatively difficult to learn and use but are well suited to a rapidly evolving culture and are quite difficult to mechanize.

The languages that employ individual symbols do not all have meager symbol sets. The numeric sets are quite small, with two, eight, ten, and sixteen elements being the most common. These notations correspond to the binary, octal, decimal, and hexadecimal number systems that find common usage in computational devices. The easy generality associated with symbols is well exemplified in hexadecimal notation in which the values for ten through fifteen are symbolized as

MULTIPLICATION IN HEXADECIMAL

	0	1	2	3	4	5	6	7	8	9	A	B	C	D	E	F
0	00	00	00	00	00	00	00	00	00	00	00	00	00	00	00	00
1	00	01	02	03	04	05	06	07	08	09	0A	0B	0C	0D	0E	0F
2	00	02	04	06	08	0A	0C	0E	10	12	14	16	18	1A	1C	1E
3	00	03	06	09	0C	0F	12	15	18	1B	1E	21	24	27	2A	2D
4	00	04	08	0C	10	14	18	1C	20	24	28	2C	30	34	38	3C
5	00	05	0A	0F	14	19	1E	23	28	2D	32	37	3C	41	46	4B
6	00	06	0C	12	18	1E	24	2A	30	36	3C	42	48	4E	54	5A
7	00	07	0E	15	1C	23	2A	31	38	3F	46	4D	54	5B	62	69
8	00	08	10	18	20	28	30	38	40	48	50	58	60	68	70	78
9	00	09	12	1B	24	2D	36	3F	48	51	5A	63	6C	75	7E	87
A	00	0A	14	1E	28	32	3C	46	50	5A	64	6E	78	82	8C	96
B	00	0B	16	21	2C	37	42	4D	58	63	6E	79	84	8F	9A	A5
C	00	0C	18	24	30	3C	48	54	60	6C	78	84	90	9C	A8	B4
D	00	0D	1A	27	34	41	4E	5B	68	75	82	8F	9C	A9	B6	C3
E	00	0E	1C	2A	38	46	54	62	70	7E	8C	9A	A8	B6	C4	D2
F	00	0F	1E	2D	3C	4B	5A	69	78	87	96	A5	B4	C3	D2	E1

For example: B $\times$ D = 8F

$$(11) \times (13) = (8 \times 16) + (1 \times 15)$$

$$(143) = (143)$$

Figure 13-3.

A, B, C, D, E, and *F.* The initial shock may be great, but computation with letters is routine and even easy, as shown in Figure 13-3.

Alphabetic sets usually include a few dozen symbols with the Roman alphabet the most common in the Western Hemisphere. The ten numerals, twenty-six letters, and dozen special symbols provide the regular basis for hundreds of languages. The Cyrillic alphabets contain a few more symbols but are used in a similar manner.

CODING

The theories and practices in coding are concerned with the systematic assignment of symbols. The symbol set is itself an example of a simple code. In more common usage, coding provides the means by which several symbols are used to signify one of many thousands or millions of cases.

The capacity of a code depends upon the variety of different symbols available and the number of symbols used to represent each case. If there are only two different symbols, as in a binary number system, and three symbols are allowed, the code can distinguish no more than eight cases: 000,001,010,011,100,101,110, and 111. The two-symbol set is the most basic code language and the natural language of any device that can only recognize two states. The electronic (on-off) and magnetic (north-south) basis of virtually all digital computers is thus naturally related to binary digits.

The mathematical rule governing a code is expressed as $N = S^n$ where N is the number of cases that can be distinguished, S is the variety of symbols available, and n is the number of symbols used. For example, the three-position binary code offers $2^3 = 8$ cases. A three-position letter code will accommodate 26^3 or 17,576 cases. The efficiency of a code measures the degree to which every possible pattern is used. There are 17,576 three-letter codes, but only a few three-letter words in the English language since many combinations are not considered to be words.

Any inefficiency in assignment of the code will tend to increase the number of symbols to be handled. In general, inefficient codes provide redundant data that make it possible to interpret the intended meaning even when a portion of the data has been lost or garbled.

This aspect of tolerance of imperfect communications is a powerful advantage of mature languages and probably accounts for the human preference for narrative rather than numeric conversation.

It has been estimated that the English language provides such a high order of redundancy that each letter is used at an efficiency of about 20 percent.

Using the binary digit (bit) as our unit of measure, the information content[2] of a two-symbol set is defined as a $\log_2 26 = 4.8$ bits. Thus, our usage provides an average of only one bit of information rather than the theoretical maximum for each letter used. If it is true that a typical idea can be represented by an average of four 5-letter words, then a typical idea contains twenty bits of information. Twenty questions, each allowing a yes-no answer, should provide a fair game!

In a fundamental sense the very process of representing an entity as data is coding. Names, "dog tag" numbers, and serial numbers are code representations. There is a recurring problem of confusion between inanimate objects and data about them and even some difficulty with persons and data about them. The violent emotional reaction to all-number telephone dialing and to extensive use of identity numbers reflects the attitude that names are somehow better than numbers. Both names and numbers are, in fact, codes and are little different except that the number set employs fewer types of symbols.

SUMMARY

There is a persuasive link between physical objects and coded data about them. When ideas first became too numerous to remember and reproduce orally, writing provided a means to preserve the idea in physical form. The word made manifest was easier to obtain whenever desired than the contents of the storyteller's memory. A particular solution to each problem and question requires substantial time and effort. In a world of impatient people with limited resources there is obvious merit in classes of solutions that offer a measure of generality

[2] Claude E. Shannon and Warren Weaver, *The Mathematical Theory of Communication,* University of Illinois Press, Urbana, 1949.

and flexibility. The most typical class solution is a *structure* which accommodates many variations in *content.*

The first requirement for manipulating many similar elements without loss or confusion is to establish unique *identification.* Any means to uniqueness is suitable, but efficiency, convenience, and accuracy strongly favor certain techniques and approaches.

The means to human communication are *symbols* that can be perceived by the senses. Understanding depends on knowing the *code* of meaning represented by the symbols. For example, foreign language symbols may be identical or similar to those of a native language, but the significance is lost if the code is not known.

Since humans and logical devices do not manipulate symbols in the same manner, the preferred symbol set is not identical. The highly encoded symbols that permit efficient processing are not convenient to human use, and *mapping* from one symbol set to another is desirable.

The broad spectrum of data processing begins with the concept that a regular *data flow* exists even if it is broken into fixed segments by working days, arbitrary calendars, and accounting periods.

This flow must be carefully regulated to assure that the accumulated data are consistent and valid. Without such *data control* the integrity of the system as well as the meaning of the symbols is uncertain.

A *data base* is simply the accumulated body of data. If carefully arranged, the means to convenient data access can be provided by erecting a *superstructure* on the data base.

A thesaurus provides one means to directory search and in dynamic form provides vocabulary control on a par with cataloging control. Except in the simplest cases the directory search capability must be supplemented by a means to coordinate search to bridge the transfer gap between a contributor to knowledge and a perspective recipient of it.

The library offers many aspects more favorable to the use of data automation systems than most industries but lacks the driving force of profit seeking to provide the incentive and reward for innovation. In large measure, the material sources, fund sources, personnel, holdings, and patrons change only slowly. There are continued additions, losses, and deletions, but most of the elements recur.

The inputs from the encoding / key-punch / verify / card-handling process that has been borrowed from industrial and commercial applications are not well suited to the library. They serve to separate the users of data from the data and are, therefore, strongly resisted. Card catalogs imply encouragement to direct access and, therefore, persist even when they become unwieldy and out of date.

The library needs to reconsider what it is trying to accomplish and then to explore how the goals can be served. There must be minimal concern for human data processing, but great concern for human convenience. There must be clear recognition of the hardware that serves the needed functions and less concern for the functions that suit the equipment.

SUGGESTED READING LIST

Batten, W. E.: "We Know the Enemy, Do We Know Our Friends?: The Sociological Place of Information and the Problems Obstructing Its Progress," *Library Journal,* **93**: 945–947, Mar. 1, 1968.

Crowley, Thomas H.: *Understanding Computers,* McGraw-Hill, New York, *c* 1967, 142 pp. Paperback.

Cuadra, Carlos A., et al.: *Technology and Libraries,* National Advisory Commission on Libraries, Washington, 1967, 165 pp. ED 022-481.

Culbertson, Don S.: "New Library Science: A Man-Machine Partnership," *PNLA Quarterly,* **29**: 25–31, October 1964.

Dubester, Henry J.: "The Librarian and the Machine," *Institute on Information Storage and Retrieval, 1st, University of Minnesota, 1962: Information Retrieval Today,* University of Minnesota, Minneapolis, 1966, pp. 167–176.

Gull, Cloyd Dake: "Implications for the Storage and Retrieval of Knowledge," in L. E. Asheim (ed.), *Future of the Book,* pp. 53–63. Also appeared in *Library Quarterly,* **25**: 333–343, October 1955.

Hayes, Robert M.: "Automation and the Library of Congress: Three Views: Information Scientist," *Library Quarterly,* **34**: 229–232, July 1964.

Kent, Allen, ed.: *Library Planning for Automation,* Spartan, Washington, 1965, 193 pp.

———: *Textbook on Mechanized Information Retrieval,* Interscience-Wiley, New York, *c* 1962, 268 pp.

Kilgour, Frederick G.: "Systems Concepts and Libraries," *College and Research Libraries,* **28**: 167–170, May 1967.

Markuson, Barbara Evans: "An Overview of Library Systems and Automation," *Datamation,* **16**: 60–68, February 1970.

Morse, Philip M.: "The Prospect for Mechanization," *College and Research Libraries,* **25**: 115–119, March 1964.

Orlichy, Joseph: *The Successful Computer System: Its Planning, Development, and Management in a Business Enterprise,* McGraw-Hill, New York, 1969, 283 pp.

Simpson, D. J.: "Before the Machines Come," *ASLIB Proceedings,* **20**: 21–33, January 1968.

PART IV
THE PROSPECTS FOR LIBRARY AUTOMATION

The economic and social forces that have disturbed the serenity of the library are more likely to intensify rather than abate. The drive to know and understand is generating an ever growing body of material to be held and retrieved upon demand and is extending the demand to every country and subject. The quest for meaningful employment is raising salaries and accenting the sterility of tasks that are repetitive or boring and of working environments that frustrate the desire to accomplish an intended purpose with high reliability and consistent success.

There will continue to be an impelling need to improve library services and reduce operating costs and a continuing hope that automation will satisfy a part of that need.

Every aspect of human life that is or appears to be related to the rapid developments in science and technology is expected to match the technological pace. The library is thus expected to provide more complete services, with greater precision and reliability, and to do so with little or no delay. Each demonstration of the ability to fulfill those expectations will encourage increased demands, and each failure will be met with increasing dissatisfaction.

There is little reason to expect that library patrons will be willing to accept increased costs through taxation or service fees unless there is obvious and continued improvement in services and a clear demonstration that inefficient and redundant procedures are being eliminated.

In such an environment the possible solutions are to change the allocation of the applied resources or to improve their productivity. It is possible to accommodate a fixed budget and stable productivity by sacrificing some activities in order to sustain and improve others, and there may even be some value in reconsidering what library features are still worth perpetuating. It is clearly the hope that productivity can be enhanced, whatever the total availability of resources.

That hope must center on the selective mix of human skills and machine capabilities, for there is little near-term prospect for radical improvement in the ability or willingness of people to perform library processes.

The prospect for attainment of some of the technological advances that have been anticipated for many years is very favorable in the next decade. Major advances in design concepts can be expected in the next two to three years as the library is recognized to present some unique problems and opportunities at the human/machine interface. Subsequent developments in special hardware and data manipulation logic will follow in the next three-to-ten-year period.

The technological and economic constraints that have appeared as hardware and operational deficiencies are, in part, the result of misapplication of borrowed devices and concepts.

The library provides a much more stable environment than the industrial and commercial world. The same suppliers, the same materials, and the same patrons offer sharp contrast to changing products, job-shop manufacture, and mobile customers. For the library the punch card was a reasonable solution only because it was available. It will be unfortunate if a punch-card philosophy serves to obscure the logical functions that should be served. There need not be a paperwork and card-handling problem in the library, and these offending elements will disappear as the true goal is better understood and alternate techniques become more capable and less expensive.

The conceptual constraints and the attitudes that perpetuate unsuitable devices and concepts can be expected to change with a continuing influx of personnel familiar with the essential functions of the library and confident enough to adapt data systems concepts and data processing techniques to library needs rather than to modify the needs to suit available devices. The desire to provide effective and economic service and the economics of labor costs will be the impelling forces that encourage a better mix of human and machine capabilities.

The essential library function and attainable technological offerings will come to focus as people are given direct access to data and the means to direct control of the data-handling processes.

The subsequent changes will occur with the development of capability for dynamic vocabulary control and adaptive file organization. These topics are clearly more technical in nature but, in fact, are dependent upon direct interaction.

The practical effect of direct interaction will be to emphasize that cognitive and judgmental processes are reserved to humans. There will be a reduction in the efforts to reduce human thought processes to precise logic and thence to computer programs.

The dynamic vocabulary and adaptive file will provide the capability for mass data manipulation that humans are unable to do with sufficient accuracy and speed and unwilling to do with sufficient interest and reliability.

Library automation will not be feasible, practical, and economical for every library or even for every function in the 1970s.

The mass of materials, the attitude and training of library personnel, the variety of sizes and shapes and the very low probability of demand for most library items virtually guarantee that book forms and manual operations will be the prevailing characteristics for at least another decade. There will probably be some fine examples of automation of physical processes, especially in large new libraries. High labor costs and new concepts in containerization and handling controls will provide new alternatives to a few fortunate libraries. There is no foreseeable prospect for the margin of advantage needed to justify substantial changes to existing structures.

There may be the beginning of an accelerated move to nonbook forms, but a complete change would not be likely even if there were some ideal costless alternatives. Remote generation of materials on demand would require massive communication capacity. If the new telecommunications additions in the next decade provided capacity equal to that of the existing system and were somehow provided without cost, the net effect would be to reduce communications cost by half and that is not sufficient to provide an economic alternative to local stacks and holdings.

For these reasons, the automation efforts are expected to be focused on the technical and control processes that now absorb a substantial fraction of the library budget and are susceptible to effective joint man/machine efforts. Automation of the most difficult processes, notably cataloging and retrieval, may be possible, but it is far more likely that the cataloger and reference librarian will be aided, not supplanted.

CHAPTER 14 LIBRARY AUTOMATION IN THE 1970s

The elements necessary for effective library automation are now available, with a few critical qualifications:

1. The understanding and appreciation of the logical concepts of the library and of systems and data processing have not been available to a sufficient number of librarians.
2. The equipment has not been adequate to library needs, and attempts to borrow industrial applications have introduced massive card-handling and paperwork problems.
3. The library has not been clearly recognized as presenting unique technological problems and opportunities.

PERSONNEL AND AUTOMATION

It is abundantly clear that elegant technology cannot be exploited and complex systems cannot be sustained by hostile, fearful, or untrained personnel. There is always some resistance to change, perhaps derived from a preference for operational reality over potential reality, but change is possible, and stagnation is not acceptable. There is resistance to foreign ideas, perhaps because fully accepted ideas—whatever the source—are no longer foreign; but new concepts are essential to change.

Extrapolation of past experience does not reflect the change in attitude and behavior that occurs when response time approaches the human reaction time. For example, faster and faster mail delivery will

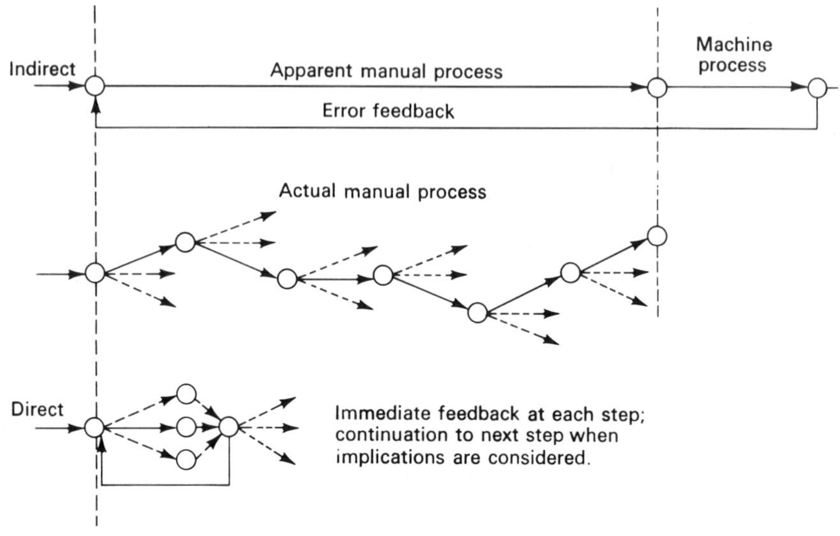

Figure 14-1.

provide some added value, but the whole mode of communication changes when written messages are supplanted by telephone conversation and again when the impersonal character of the telephone is supplanted by direct conversation.

The essential characteristics of present man/machine interaction are represented in Figure 14-1. The manual processes include a series of steps, each subject to error and each dependent, to some degree, on the steps already taken and the data already in the system. Since it has not been practical to provide immediate examination of the steps for logical errors or to provide immediate access to existing data, the manual processes are well advanced before machine processing is started. Of course, some of the steps have been mechanized, but the essential nature of the results has not changed.

When the tests of logic finally begin, there is a strong possibility that some errors occurred in early steps, thereby invalidating all subsequent steps. The process of data preparation, input, editing, error reporting, evaluation, and correction is rather extensive and a notable burden to the library. Even if the steps were correct, there is the real possibility that the judgments would have been different if access to existing data had been provided.

The efforts to solve this problem by assigning all the functions to the computer have not been either notably successful or operationally satisfying.

The solution is to provide a means for direct user control of the data and the system. Each operation involving the generation, change, or use of data will be under direct manual control, with the computer providing access to existing data, accepting new data for addition to the files, and giving computational support. People must continue to do the thinking, to exercise the judgment, to recognize the new combination, and to grasp the new opportunities.

The special equipment that is needed for library automation will relieve the librarian of a series of repetitive routine tasks rather than the much more challenging cognitive and judgmental duties. There is still some hope that the computer will generate catalog data and perform searches not understandable by the human mind, and such marvels may yet come to be; but the technical feasibility is not yet proven, and the economics are distinctly unfavorable.

What are needed and what can probably be provided in the next decade are better devices to serve the interface between human and machine activities.

The most obvious need is for some careful reconsideration of what is to be accomplished. If the understanding of the problem never goes deeper than the assumption that punch cards must be processed, there is little reason for hope of improvement. Punch cards are not inherent in the library and should not be assumed as a part of any library system. Punch cards, and all other paraphernalia of data processing, should be recognized as evidences of *how* data processing has been done and not as evidence of *what* is being accomplished. Only when the design process begins with *what* and proceeds to *how* can a conclusion on devices and techniques have merit—and even then the method should be considered as transitory, for the means to better processing are ever changing.

The devices needed to serve real library needs, as distinct from devices that can be used in the library, are not yet identified. There are a few obvious candidates, and automated circulation will be discussed here in terms of the potential of a direct-reading device which can read information from a label on a book or other piece of library material directly into the computer-based data system.

The book card has always been a piece of the book. Traditionally the card has been signed by the reader and filed away by date-due and call number order as the only record of the whereabouts of the book. When the book is returned, the book card is pulled from the file and returned to the book. This last process is called "slipping." This movement of the book card is prone to errors. Misfiling of the book card and, more particularly, mis-slipping of the book, are inevitable. Data collection systems improved this situation by keeping the book card and book together at all times, except during charging. In this system, the card is run through the machine along with the reader's ID card to generate two transaction cards, one of which goes to the computer and the other to book servicing as a date-due card and a discharging card for the computer. With a direct-reading device the book card can be eliminated. This would prevent the mixing and/or loss of book cards and avoid the necessity for handling transaction cards.

If the book card can be eliminated, it means that the book card is not essential to the library function but is only an artifact of past processing methods.

Librarians need and have sought an alternative to the fine system. The more affluent readers choose to view a library fine as a charge, and the less affluent readers resent the penalty. The librarian, trying to get the book back for other readers, is caught in the middle. Traditionally, the circulation department types overdue notices to the delinquent readers on the basis of the leftover book cards. The introduction of the computer has made possible computer printout of overdue notices with speed and accuracy. A direct-reading device might eliminate the need for fines. An on-line check of the overdue "blacklist" would stop the issue of a pass at the circulation station. Without the pass, the reader cannot take his book past the exit control point. Refusal of borrowing privileges until previous overdue books are returned would encourage better borrowing habits. For those readers who view the fine as a charge and who do not mind paying, the system offers a control. An added advantage to any circulation system where it is felt necessary to collect fines is the ability to levy charges and control collections in the business office.

The circulation librarian is always haunted by the thought of the reader with an overdue notice who claims that the book was returned. The standard answer is, "Please go home and look again." The direct-reading device setup for book return would produce a receipt when the book is actually returned. The receipt can now be the patron's proof and the librarian's assurance that the system has accepted the book. One of the old manual systems did, in effect, give a receipt when the borrower's card had the loan date, call number, and date returned stamped and written for each book.

There are other possibilities for devices that address the unique aspects of the library function. Some will become available from applications that recognize similar needs and solve them with devices of great flexibility. There appear to be favorable prospects for development of suitable access terminals, and even the direct-reading device may appear in response to recognized needs in inventory control. For the library, the essential problem is to identify what is needed to permit implementation of a full automation program.

TECHNOLOGY AND AUTOMATION

The characteristics that distinguish the library from other institutions are not trivial or unimportant. The application of technology, conceived and perfected in other environments, must be responsive to and reflect the characteristics that make the library distinct. Conversely, the needs of the library must be related to the concepts and terminology of the available technology if the needs/opportunity match is to be completed. When the available technology is inadequate, there should be a deliberate and firm decision to wait until a reasonable match is possible. The experience of the past decade suggests that substantial changes must be introduced in three separate but related concepts: data management, dynamic vocabulary control, and direct interaction.

DATA MANAGEMENT

Theory and practice in file organization and search strategy in mechanized systems over the past decade have produced many techniques applicable to automated data systems. The organization of the data in the repository has a major impact on the convenience and satisfaction of the users and the utility and efficiency of the devices and logic of the system. It is of the greatest importance that the design and implementation provide a sound system foundation and versatile application programs that can readily accommodate the data content that appears and can readily be adapted to changing demands and preferences. Only in this way is it possible to assure that the system does not require major correction and reworking as it grows and evolves.

The flow of data from the description process through transformation and into storage is one of the most important system processes. If the data records are designed in terms of a physical embodiment, it is inevitable that the design will restrict system response to changing conditions and, in due time, become obsolete.

When entities are treated individually, there is no recourse to the generality and flexibility of treating items in sets. Objects are relatively difficult to collect into sets, but the advantages of set manipulation are so great that unitized loads, pallets, piggyback freight, containerization, and unit trains are bold concepts and powerful economic forces in transportation.

Data are relatively easy to accumulate and manipulate as the rapid growth and extension of both the computer and the communications network attest. Under such conditions it is inevitable that an accumulation of data will be encouraged by those who perceive that data about objects can be manipulated easier and faster than the objects themselves and can yield equal or better results. Inferences are best drawn from data about different things or about the same thing at different times. Of these, it is not unlikely that the common demands will encompass a combination of different things at different times. This aggregation of data has been given many designations, but one of the most insightful is the recent designation of *data base*.

The suggestive value of this name derives from the implied continuation of a concept of a *data superstructure* that is built upon the base. Logically, the superstructure is the means whereby the strength and stability in the foundation data can be brought to support a variety of uses. With a broad and unified base, many different uses can be served and many higher-order uses erected from the simple beginnings.

The establishment of a data base and the erection of a data superstructure by which to make effective use of the data must proceed in the same manner as in building construction. The base must be laid first, with due consideration for the shape and extent of the intended edifice.

Given a sound foundation, a variety of structures can be erected, and to a significant degree, portions of the superstructure can be later modified and extended. In a data system it is essential that the access superstructure be erected upon the base and adapted to the actual data content. The attempts to anticipate data content and thereby use the superstructure in creating the base have been of limited success and yield a structure of restricted flexibility.

The development of the data superstructure can proceed directly and logically from a data base. In concept each entity is represented in the data base in a manner convenient for access when the principal identification term is known and feasible for access when any of the identity or description terms are specified.

The data base provides a structure to accommodate any data content which fulfills the validation requirements. The guiding purpose is not to facilitate later use in search and output but to accommodate all input and to facilitate maintenance and updating of the data. A consistent data structure will assure that all needs for search and output can be met.

The data superstructure is generated from the actual data contained in the data base to establish access paths for selected types of requests. The structure may be extended whenever a new access capability is desired and reorganized as needed without invalidating, and even without changing, the data base. The presentation capabilities are limited only by the actual data content. New output demands require a new formatting procedure but not a reorganization of the data base.

Computer-based storage of data offers a compact store with the potentiality for very rapid access. Data storage is a supplement to, not a substitute for, the object. The description provides data about the entity; it is not a complete replication of the entity. Thus, the data storage is primarily intended to support the search and retrieval process. If the search demands can be expressed in terms of the identity of the objects wanted or in terms of just a few descriptive characteristics, conventional shelving procedures and card catalogs provide a viable solution, even for very large libraries.

There must be many characteristics that are difficult to accommodate in a manual system before an automated system is needed. In general, large collections, rapid response, and complex search specifications favor the use of automated systems. The difficulty of fulfilling such conditions in a manual system may imply that automation is the only feasible solution and as such is acceptable despite its cost.

The file generation and search process can be recognized as a problem in two dimensions. All the item identities are defined by one dimension and all the possible terms of description are defined by the other. Thus, the full description of an item is a thin slice covering not one term, but the whole vocabulary. The usage of a term is another thin slice covering one descriptive term and every item.

Just a few years ago when data-handling capabilities were severely limited, it was not convenient to deal with more than one thin slice at a time. The techniques provided either a term-on-item file or the opposite (inverted) slice, an item-on-term file.

It is now apparent that neither organization is optimal or even adequate. A combination of both access paths in a more complex matrix organization is needed to manipulate the data along both dimensions.

The search process requires the comparison of the terms of the query description to the stored item description. Three sequential steps are involved, any one of which may yield a negative result or provide a final answer.

The first step is to match the query terms to the established term vocabulary. The basic vocabulary process is comparable to that involved in adding a new item to the file but somewhat simpler since a new entry need not be added to the file. In either instance the term may prove to be different from all previously recorded terms and therefore a candidate for addition to the vocabulary. New input terms need to be resolved promptly in order that the complete description may be stored for access. New query terms, however, do not inhibit the search. If the term is logically essential to the query, its absence from the vocabulary is conclusive evidence that no items are responsive to the search. If the term is conditional, it can be evaluated, immediately, and the search continued to other terms.

Next, the search strategy should include the use of any simple search specifications that can be fulfilled by linear or directory searches. Such preliminary manipulation will reduce the size of the candidate set by eliminating unsuitable items or groups. The discriminating power of a simple search is severely limited, however, and a coordinate search will be needed in manipulating files for which an acceptable answer set involves discrimination to less than about 1 percent of the items.

The final step, if needed, involves a "coordinate match" whereby all the items located by the directory search on individual terms are evaluated for the entire search specification. Of course, the search process can be implemented in a variety of ways, but all valid procedures must accomplish one or more of the basic search steps. A coordination search requires the retrieval of those items whose descriptions fulfill the requirements of a complex search specification.

The final consequence of the search through the data superstructure is a list of addresses of records that fulfill the search specifications. Retrieval of the associated records, computation based on their contents, and use of the output formatting procedures will then provide the basis for the retrieval of the physical object if the reference lists does not itself suffice.

When data is retrieved from the base it should be freed of the code used for internal efficiency and returned to a form well suited to human use. The efficiencies and economics of coding should not be imposed upon the users beyond the point of convenience to them.

The sequential exploration process that provides an estimate of the probable number of references and a few sample abstracts, then the complete reference list, then selected abstracts, and finally the chosen objects implies a strong interaction process that is not readily attainable but is a clear indication of the desirable direction of future developments.

DYNAMIC VOCABULARY CONTROL

Ideas, not things, should be on library shelves; knowledge, not symbols, is the goal of an intellectual search. The practical approximation of a solution to that ideal is to provide access to physical objects that contain the knowledge by the use of logical data that describe the understanding of it.

The representation of the entity in data is a practical as well as logical necessity. The recognition of the separateness of objects and data provides the basis for manipulation of data in lieu of manipulation of objects. That basis becomes meaningless if the object and data do not refer to the same entity; it is unavailing if the object and data cannot both be freely and independently processed yet reliably reassociated whenever desired.

The ability to communicate is critically dependent upon the degree to which different persons or the same person at different times observes the same attributes and provides a consistent evaluation of them. The obvious inability of different people to generate identical descriptions of an object or even of the same person to be consistent over a long period of time explains much of the preference for precise means to identification, even means based on completely arbitrary identity procedures. Despite the differences, whatever attributes are recognized and evaluated, either qualitatively or quantitatively, can be recorded as data, for data are what human beings use to symbolize their perception of existence.

The entire vocabulary of the library becomes an integral part of the data system when the design is not restricted to an attempt to mechanize existing methods.

Every term, every code, and all recurring errors are the stock-in-trade when describing items for retention and queries for search. Errors in spelling and differences in usage are normal and inevitable; it must be the intent to correct the errors and resolve the differences in the manner that best serves the needs and preferences of people, not devices.

When the descriptive process is viewed as the means to represent entities as data, it is apparent that the process must be applied in a consistent manner to every element of the vocabulary. In so doing, the variations among people and over time are reflected in a manner that bridges the barrier between different persons and resolves the slow drift of language and meanings.

When informal vocabulary was clearly recognized to be inadequate, the obvious solution was to record the word lists in use and encourage the use of the established vocabulary. This same logic is still valid if the static character and slow response of published lists are replaced by dynamic and responsive access to the vocabulary.

The conventional term list or thesaurus imposes a control on the human side of the man/system interface and attempts to assure that all input seen by the system conforms to a single standard. This approach requires that future usage be anticipated and that the desired transformation from the normal vocabulary to the control vocabulary be provided. Apart from the difficulty of anticipating future usage and otherwise updating the thesaurus to reflect new additions, the input control is not precise. Even with diligent effort, a complete and correct description cannot be obtained. Careful editing and error correction procedures are needed to produce even marginally usable data.

There is a meaningful and commendable inclination for people to use what is already available if it is accessible and convenient. It is desirable to allow a contributor or requester to employ the vocabulary he knows and normally uses since the purpose of the discourse is to express, as data, the entities of interest. Obviously, the most competent expression cannot be produced under artificial restraints. The accommodation of variations in usage and meaning will be easy and direct if the entire vocabulary of the system is accessible and means are provided to resolve any mismatch that is detected. Of course, if neither the system nor the user detects any discrepancy, the vocabulary control has passed a critical pragmatic test.

The initial selection of the terms of description for an item or a query is the consequence of a complex blend of vocabulary and experience. Human perception of an entity is not consistent, and all the variations that are introduced must be removed if the linkages between the contributor of an entity and all potential recipients are to be completed. There is a slow but persistent language drift that changes the meanings of terms, creates new modes of expression and new areas of discourse, and finally diffuses terminology and usage across technological and geographic boundaries.

The variations introduced by one person over a lifetime are minor in comparison to the mismatch that occurs between descriptions offered by different persons. The greatest opportunity for enhanced transfer of knowledge thus occurs in the very circumstances that create the greatest vocabulary mismatch—the delayed interdisciplinary transfer from one individual as contributor to another as recipient.

There is no essential difference in the scope or depth of the problem if the descriptions are automatically generated. The strategy used by the automatic process and the objects from which the descriptions are obtained faithfully reflect human vocabulary practices.

The control of vocabulary and the bridge between the vocabularies of the contributor and the recipient can be provided at any point in the processing. Convenience to the contributors and the recipients implies application within the system; efficiency in processing suggests that all internal system processing be conducted in the context of rigorous control and uniform vocabulary practices. Thus, the logical conclusion is that the vocabulary as it is known to the library patron must be acceptable to the system.

Since the purpose of the vocabulary is to provide a common link between the contributors and the users of knowledge, any term which does not aid in discriminating among the items is useless. A term applied to every item and a term not used at all are equally poor, and, as the usage approaches either extreme condition, the value declines.

OPTIMAL VOCABULARY CONTROL STRATEGY

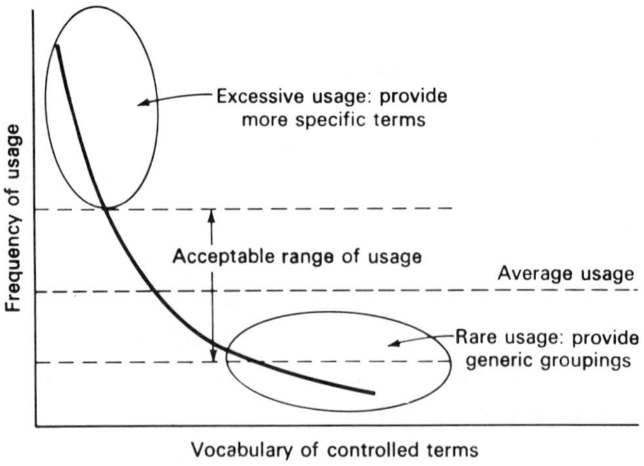

Excessive usage: provide more specific terms

Frequency of usage

Acceptable range of usage

Average usage

Rare usage: provide generic groupings

Vocabulary of controlled terms

Figure 14-2.

As shown in Figure 14-2, the vocabulary control process must strive to obtain a vocabulary which finds equal frequency of use of each entry.

The optimal condition of perfectly equal usage is not practically attainable, but something can be done about extreme cases. A term too often used can be noted for those preparing item description with the suggestion that a more specific entry be chosen and also reported to those preparing query specifications with the suggestion that it be avoided or combined with other more discriminating terms. A term too seldom used can be grouped with other rare terms of comparable meaning to form a generic term of appreciable use.

DIRECT INTERACTION

It is apparent that in the modern library as well as in industry, commerce, and government there is no shortage of data, but there is a critical deficiency in the techniques and practices for access to the data. There is little of significant importance that is not observed and recorded, but much that cannot later be located or retrieved because of the restricted access capabilities.

For now, the attainable level of automation can be characterized by continued isolation of the user from the system and the data it contains and by response times in hours and days rather than seconds or minutes. In each step of the information system process, the equipment, the concepts, and the pace of development are keyed to current technology, except in the few libraries that can participate in research efforts to advance the frontiers of technology.

Existing library data systems may be compared to an attempt to drive an automobile from the back seat by detailed instructions to a chauffeur. The communication linkages are too coarse to be used with great precision, and the effort is so great that an inordinate amount of thought and attention is expended in the process. There is all too little left to consider long-range goals or to evaluate current results.

A new regime of operation occurs when the conversation becomes face to face or when the driver moves to the front seat, and a corresponding change will occur when the librarian is provided with a truly responsive data system.

Typical approaches to mechanization tend to obscure rather than reveal the essential logical simplicity of data files.

Three distinct levels of file organization can be recognized:

1. The first level consists of groups of records about distinguishable physical and conceptual *entities*. These entities include employees, patrons, donors, publishers, facilities, and equipment, as well as books and other library materials.
   Entity files are very common but rarely recognized as having a reason for existence apart from specific use. Thus, the typical practice is to organize a file to serve a few related uses and to accept that the same data may be duplicated in other files for other applications. An equally poor solution is to equate the entity files with a data base and fail to distinguish the other levels of file structure.
2. The second level consists of *relationships* between and among entities. These records would contain, for example, data relating employees to organizational elements, books to authors and classifications, and patrons to interests. It is very common for such data to be included in the entity file without any recognition that the data are not descriptive of the entity and without the means to reflect the nature of the relationship.
3. At the third level the records describe *transaction events* involving two or more of the entities. This circulation is represented as a temporary association of a patron, a book, an established loan period, and a date.
   By nature of the entities and transactions, the entity files reflect the body of data being maintained, while the transactions reflect the day-to-day data flow.

The library is an especially good place to recognize and exploit these logical levels of data since, more than most other institutions, it deals with the same entities, relationships, and events on a recurring basis. The inherent stability of the objects offers a favorable environment for direct access as well as for sharing the process and the access with other libraries.

Operational control, whether applied to a steel mill or moon-rocket engine, must include a means to detect what is occurring, to evaluate selected parameters, to determine a suitable response, and to direct the accomplishment of that response all in less time than is required for the process to change beyond the control limits.

Thus, the important aspect of "real time" is the inherent characteristics of the system either to remain stable or to tend toward excessive variability. An appropriate response within the stable interval implies real-time control even if the interval is hours, days, or even years in duration.

If the response cannot be reliably provided within the stable interval, the system is segmented into smaller and smaller subsystems until the needed response becomes so simple that it can be produced quickly and reliably. The segmentation strategy is as apparent in the specialization of tasks in mass production as it is in cataloging. In each instance the task span is quite narrow—except that the cataloger is deeply concerned with the whole process even when it cannot be done except by mixing it with similar tasks on other items, so that the net productive time of a few minutes or hours is spread over many days or weeks.

The most significant opportunity for effective exploitation of data system technology is in the prospect of a new regime of direct interaction of the librarian with the data in all the library processes.

There is no inherent value in speed for speed's sake, but there are clear possibilities for exploiting fast response capabilities.

The increased value that results from faster response will be accompanied by increased costs for supporting the faster operation. At some point the added cost will exceed the added value if there is no change in the pattern. But there is good reason to expect a sharp increase in value and ample evidence that it will occur in the library in the near future.

SUGGESTED READING LIST

Aines, Andrew A.: "The Promise of National Information System," *Library Trends,* **16**: 410–418, January 1968.

Batten, W. E.: "Future of Information Work," *ASLIB Proceedings,* **19**: 163–172, June 1967.

Becker, Joseph: "Information Network Prospects in the United States," *Library Trends,* **17**: 306–317, January 1969.

Bregzis, Ritvars: "Library Networks of the Future," *Drexel Library Quarterly,* **4**: 261–270, October 1968.

Clapp, Verner W.: *The Future of the Research Library,* University of Illinois, Urbana, 1964.

Dunkin, Paul S.: "Peek into Paradise," *Library Resources and Technical Services,* **9**: 143–148, 1965.

Gorchels, Clarence: "Of New Libraries and Futuristic Libraries," *College and Research Libraries,* **4**: 267–268, 1964.

Griffin, Marjorie: "Automation in Libraries: A Projection," *Canadian Libraries,* **23**: 360–367, March 1967.

Gull, Cloyd Dake: "Automation, Documentation, Current Systems and Trends in the U.S.A.," *Revue Internationale de la Documentation,* **29**: 57–62, May 1962.

"Libraries of the Future," panel with discussion, *Law Library Journal,* **60**: 379–397, November 1967.

Licklider, J. C. R.: *Libraries of the Future,* M.I.T., Cambridge, Mass., 1965, 219 pp.

Lowry, W. K.: "New Concepts in Library Service," *Bell Laboratory Record,* **42** (1): 2–7, January 1964.

Management 2000: Dedication of the AFMR Manager Learning Center and Donald W. Mitchell Memorial Library, Hamilton, New York, August, 1967, panel discussion, "The State of Information Retrieval and Data Processing in the Year 2000 and Its Implications for Management," American Foundation for Management Research, *c* 1968, pp. 48–97.

Minder, Thomas L.: *The Regional Library Center in the Mid-1970s: A Concept Paper,* School of Library and Information Sciences, University of Pittsburgh, Pittsburgh, 1968, 34 pp.

Shera, Jesse H.: "What Is Past Is Prologue: Beyond 1984," *ALA Bulletin,* **61** 35–47, January 1967.

Taylor, Robert S.: "Toward the Design of a College Library for the Seventies," *Wilson Library Bulletin,* **43**: 44–51, September 1968.

Vickery, B. C.: "The Future of Libraries," *Library Association Record,* **68**: 252–260, July 1966.

BIBLIOGRAPHY

1. Abrahamson, Ed.: "Mini-computers for Large Scale Process Control? A·Mini-computer System Is Described Whose Goals Are Decentralization and Simplification," *Datamation,* **16**:123–130, Feb. 1970.
2. Adams, C. J.: "Automated Libraries for Northwest Indiana: A Five-year Plan," *Focus,* **20**:53–56, Nov. 1966.
3. Adams, J. Robert: "Systems Study of the Circulation Department of the University of Chicago Library," unpublished master's thesis, Graduate Library School, University of Chicago, Aug. 1968, 129 pp.
4. Adams, Scott: "Library Communications System," *Library Trends,* **5**:206–215, Oct. 1956.
5. Adams, Scott: "The Scientific Revolution and the Research Library," *Library Resources and Technical Services,* **9**:133–142, Spring 1956.
6. Adkinson, Burton W.: "Scientific Information and the U.S. Federal Government," *Revue de la Documentation,* **28**:4, Nov. 1961.
7. Agenbroad, James E., et al.: *Catalog Data File Creation for the New England Regional Library Technical Processing Center, NELINET* (New England Library Information Network), Inforonics, Inc., Cambridge, Mass., June 1968, 64 pp. ED 026 077.
8. Agenbroad, James E., et al.: *New England Library Information Network, Progress Report, July 1, 1967–March 30, 1968,* 2 vols., Inforonics, Inc., Cambridge, Mass., Apr. 5, 1968.
9. Agenbroad, James E., et al.: *Systems Design and Pilot Operation of a Regional Center for Technical Processing for the Libraries of the New England State Universities, NELINET* (New England Library Information Network), Progress Report, July 1, 1967–Mar. 30, 1968, Inforonics, Inc., Cambridge, Mass., Apr. 5, 1968, vol. I, text, 41 pp. ED 026 078; vol. II, appendices, 169 pp. ED 026 079.
10. Ahn, Herbert K.: "Computer Assisted Library Mechanization (CALM): Acquisition (ACQ)," *CALMACQ Project Notebook,* University of California, Irvine, 1967.
11. Aines, Andrew A.: "The Promise of a National Information System," *Library Trends,* **16**:410–418, Jan. 1968.
12. Aitchison, J., and C. Cleverdon: *A Report on a Test of the Index of Metallurgical Literature of Western Reserve University,* Cranfield, Bedford, England, 1963.
13. *ALA Filing Rules,* 2d ed., abr., American Library Association, Chicago, *c* 1968, 94 pp.
14. Alanen, Sally, David E. Sparks, and Frederick G. Kilgour: "A Computer-monitored Library Technical Processing System," *Proceedings of the American Documentation Institute,* **3**:419–426, Adrianne Press, 1966.
15. American Council of Learned Societies, Committee on Research Libraries: *On Research Libraries, Statement and Recommendations,* submitted to National Advisory Commission on Libraries, Nov. 1967, M.I.T., Cambridge, Mass., *c* 1969, 104 pp.
16. American Society for Information Science: *Proceedings of the American Society for Information Science Annual Meeting, Columbus, Ohio, Oct. 20–24,*

1968, Information Transfer, vol. 5, Greenwood, New York, *c* 1968, 362 pp.

17. American Society for Information Science: *Proceedings of the American Society for Information Science, 32nd Annual meeting, San Francisco, California, October 1-4, 1969,* Cooperative Information Societies, vol. 6, Greenwood, Westport, Conn., *c* 1969, 532 pp.
18. American Society of Planning Officials: *National Planning Conference, Houston, Texas, April, 1967: Threshold of Planning Information Systems,* Chicago, 1967, 108 pp.
19. Amey, Gerald X.: "Channel Hierarchies for Matching Information Sources to Users' Needs," *Proceedings of the American Society for Information Science, Annual Meeting, Columbus, Ohio, Oct. 20-24, 1968,* vol. 5, Greenwood, New York, 1968, pp. 11-14.
20. Andrews, Theodora, ed.: *Meeting on Automation in the Library—When, Where, and How, Purdue University, 1964, Papers,* Purdue University, Lafayette, Ind.
21. Angell, Richard S.: "On the Future of the Library of Congress Classification," *Proceedings of the Second International Study Conference on Classification for Information Retrieval, Elsinore, Denmark, 14-18 September, 1964,* Munksgaard, Copenhagen, 1965, pp. 101-112; discussion, pp. 118-119.
22. *Annual Review of Information Science and Technology,* vol. I, Interscience-Wiley, New York, 1966. For annual state-of-the-art reviews.
23. Armitage, J. E., M. F. Lynch, and J. H. Petrie: "Computer Generation of Articulated Subject Indexes," *Proceedings of the American Society for Information Science, 32nd Annual Meeting, San Francisco, California, October 1-4, 1969,* 6:253-257, Greenwood, Westport, Conn., 1969.
24. Artandi, Susan: "Automatic Book Indexing by Computer," *American Documentation,* **15**:250-257, Oct. 1964.
25. Artandi, Susan: "Book Indexing by Computer," doctoral thesis, Graduate School of Library Service, Rutgers University, New Brunswick, N.J., 1963, 200 pp.
26. Artandi, Susan: *An Introduction to Computers in Information Science,* Scarecrow Press, Metuchen, N.J., 1968, 145 pp.
27. Artandi, Susan: "Investigation of Systems for the Intellectual Organization of Information," *Proceedings of the Second International Study Conference on Classification for Information Retrieval, Elsinore, Denmark, 14-18 September, 1964,* Munksgaard, Copenhagen, pp. 339-421; discussion, pp. 422-427.
28. Artandi, Susan: Keeping up with Mechanization," *Library Journal,* **90**:4715-4717, Nov. 1, 1965.
29. Artandi, Susan: "Measure of Indexing," *Library Resources and Technical Services,* 8:229-235, Summer 1964.
30. Artandi, Susan: "Mechanical Indexing of Proper Nouns," *Journal of Documentation,* **19**:187-196, Dec. 1963.
31. Artandi, Susan: "A Selective Bibliographic Survey of Automatic Indexing Methods," *Special Libraries*, **54**:630-634, Dec. 1963.
32. Artandi, Susan: "SYNTOL: A New System for the Organization of Information," *Congress of International Federation for Documentation (FID), Washington, D.C., 10-15 October, 1965, Abstracts,* p. 60.

33. Artandi, Susan: "Thesaurus Controls Automatic Book Indexing by Computer," *Automation and Scientific Communication, Part I: Proceedings of the 26th Annual Meeting of the American Documentation Institute, Chicago, October 6–11, 1963,* Washington, 1963, pp. 1–2.

34. Artandi, Susan and T. C. Hines: "Roles and Links, or Forward to Cutter," *American Documentation,* **14**:74–77, Jan. 1963.

35. Association of Special Libraries and Information Bureaus (ASLIB) Library: ASLIB Library Coordinate Indexing: *ASLIB Library Bibliography No. I,* London, ASLIB, 1962, 18 pp.

36. Association of Special Libraries and Information Bureaus (ASLIB) Library: "Conference on Coordinate Indexing," *ASLIB Proceedings,* vol. 15, no. 6, June 1963, London, ASLIB, 1963.

37. Association of Special Libraries and Information Bureaus (ASLIB) Library: "Computer Applications for Public Libraries," *ASLIB Proceedings,* vol. 18, no. 9, Sept. 1966, London, ASLIB, 1966.

38. Atherton, Jay: "Mechanization of the Manuscript Catalogue at the Public Archives of Canada," *American Archivist,* **30**:303–309, Apr. 1967.

39. Atherton, Pauline A.: "Development of Machine-generated Tools," *The Present and Future Prospects of Reference/Information Service, Proceedings of the Conference held at the School of Library Service, Columbia University,* American Library Association, Chicago, 1967. pp. 121–133.

40. Atherton, Pauline A.: *File Organization: Principles and Practices for Processing and Maintaining the Collection: Information Handling: First Principles,* Spartan, Washington, D.C., 1963.

41. Atherton, Pauline A.: "Indexing Requirements of Physicists," *Proceedings of Conference on the Literature of Nuclear Science, Its Management and Use, September 11–13, 1962.* U.S. Atomic Energy Commission, Division of Technical Information Extension, Oak Ridge, Tenn., Dec. 1962, pp. 215–22. TID-7647.

42. Atherton, Pauline A.: *Three Experiments with Citation Indexing and Bibliographic Coupling of Physics Literature,* American Institute of Physics, New York, 1962.

43. Atherton, Pauline A., and John Wyman: "Searching MARC Project Tapes Using IBM/Documentation Processing System," *Proceedings of the American Society for Information Science, 32nd Annual Meeting: San Francisco, California, October 1–4, 1969,* **6**:83–93, Greenwood, Westport, Conn., 1969.

44. Auld, Lawrence: "Automated Book Order and Circulation Control Procedures at the Oakland University Library," *Journal of Library Automation,* **1** (2): 93–109, June 1968.

45. Auld, Lawrence: *Automation Report,* Kresge Library, Oakland University, Rochester, Mich., 1966, 8 pp. plus appendices.

46. Ausherman, Mariam R., William D. Wittekind, and Robert T. Dirett: "PIL (Processing Information List): A Control Procedure for Technical Services Management," *Medical Libraries Association Bulletin,* 55:394–398, 1967.

47. Austin, C. J. "Transmission of Bibliographic Information: Brasenose Conference on Automation of Libraries," *Proceedings of the Anglo-American Conference on the Mechanization of Library Services, Oxford, England, 1966,* Mansell, London, 1967, pp. 143–149.

48. *Author Catalog,* Florida Atlantic University Library, Boca Raton, Fla., 1964, 463 pp.

49. *Author Catalog,* 2d ed., Florida Atlantic University Library, Boca Raton, Fla., 1966, 636 pp.

50. *Automated Literature Processing Handling and Analysis Systems—First Generation,* ATLIS Report, no. 17, Hayes International Corp., Huntsville, Ala., 1967, 500 pp. RSIC-549. AD 658 081.

51. Avram, Henriette D.: *The MARC Pilot Project: Final Report on a Project Sponsored by the Council on Library Resources, Inc.,* Library of Congress, Washington, 1968, 183 pp.

52. Avram, Henriette D.: "MARC: The First Two Years," *Library Resources and Technical Services,* **12**:245–250, Summer 1968.

53. Avram, Henriette D.: "The Philosophy Behind the Proposed Format for a Library of Congress Machine-readable Record," in *Institute on Information Storage and Retrieval,* University of Minnesota, Minneapolis, 1965, pp. 155–174.

54. Avram, Henriette D., Kay D. Guiles, and T. Meade Guthrie: "Fields of Information on Library of Congress Catalog Cards: Analysis of a Random Sample, 1950–1964," *Library Quarterly,* **37**:180–192, Apr. 1967.

55. Avram, Henriette D., and B. E. Markuson: "Library Automation and Project MARC: An Experiment in the Distribution of Machine-readable Cataloging Data: Brasenose Conference on the Automation of Libraries," *Proceedings of the Anglo-American Conference on the Mechanization of Library Services, Oxford, England, 1966,* Mansell, London, 1967, pp. 97–126.

56. Avram, Henriette D., and Julius R. Droz: "MARC II and COBOL," *Journal of Library Automation,* **1**:261–272, Dec. 1968.

57. Avram, Henriette D., John F. Knapp, and Lucia J. Rather: *The MARC II Format: A Communications Format for Bibliographic Data,* Library of Congress, Information Systems Office, Washington, Jan. 1968, 181 pp. ED 024 413.

58. Ayers, F. H., Janice A. German, and C. F. Cayless: "Some Applications of Mechanization in a Large Special Library," *Journal of Documentation,* **23**: 34–44, Mar. 1967.

59. Bagley, D. E.: *Computers in Libraries: A Selected Bibliography,* Hatfield College of Technology Library, Hatfield, England, 1966, 15 pp. Available from Hertfordshire County Council Technical Library and Information Service (HERTIS).

60. Bagshaw, M. G.: "Enter Computer: Book-ordering Practices and Procedure of the Toronto Public Library," *Top News,* **23**:39–42, Nov. 1966.

61. Baker, Norman R., and Richard E. Nance: *The Use of Simulation in Studying Information Storage and Retrieval Systems,* Library Operations Research Project, Purdue University, Lafayette, Ind., Nov. 22, 1967, 18 pp. PB 176 507.

62. Baker, Walter S., and Alexander G. Hoshovsky: "The Storage and Retrieval of Visuals," *Graphic Science,* **10**:22–27, Mar. 1968.

63. BALANCE (Bay Area Libraries Associated Network for Cooperative Exchange): *A Report on Computerized Procedures,* Bay Area Library Working Committee, San Jose, Calif., 1966, 78 pp.

64. Balfour, Frederick M.: "Conversion of Bibliographic Information to Machine-

readable Form Using On-line Computer Terminals, *Journal of Library Automation,* **1**:217–226, Dec. 1968.

65. Balfour, Frederick M.: *Producing Library Indexes from Machine-readable Sources: A Study of Alternative Methods and Costs,* Technical Information Dissemination Bureau, State University of New York, Buffalo, 1968, 8 pp.
66. Balz, Charles F., and Richard H. Stanwood, eds.: *Literature on Information Retrieval and Machine Translation,* 2d ed., Federal Systems Division, Gaithersburg, Md., International Business Machines Corporation, Jan. 1966, 168 pp. 953-0300-1.
67. Balz, Charles F., and Richard H. Stanwood: "MERGE: A Current Awareness and Retrospective Searching System for Technical Documents," in Benjamin F. Cheydleru (ed.), *Colloquium on Technical Preconditions for Retrieval Center Operations, Proceedings,* Spartan, Washington, 1965, pp. 61–62.
68. Bardwell, John D.: *New England Land-grant Network: A Preliminary Report,* Educational Facilities Laboratories, New York, June 1968, 94 pp.
69. Bartlett, K. A.: "Transmission Control in a Local Data Network," *Congress of the International Federation for Information Processing (IFIP), 4th, Edinburgh, 5–10 August, 1968, Proceedings,* North-Holland Publishing, Amsterdam, 1968.
70. Baruch, Jordan J.: "The Generalized Medical Information Facility," in *Proceedings of the Congress of the International Federation for Information Processing (IFIP), 4th, Edinburgh, 5–10 August, 1968,* North-Holland Publishing, Amsterdam, 1968, pp. 155–162.
71. Bass, David W.: "LAPL (Los Angeles Public Library) and the Data Service Bureau," *Wilson Library Bulletin,* **41**:405–408, Dec. 1966.
72. Bassette, E. P.: *An Annotated Guide to Automated Library Systems,* 3M Company, Microfilm Products Division, St. Paul, Minn., 1968, 15 pp. Available from 3M Company.
73. Bateman, Betty B., and Eugene H. Farris: "Operating a Multi-library System Using Long-distance Communications to an On-line Computer," *Proceedings of the American Society for Information Science: Annual Meeting, Columbus, Ohio, October 20–24, 1968,* vol. 5, pp. 152–155.
74. Batten, W. E.: "Future of Information Work," *ASLIB Proceedings,* **19**: 163–172, June 1967.
75. Batten, W. E.: "We Know the Enemy, Do We Know Our Friends?: The Sociological Place of Information and the Problems Obstructing Its Progress," *Library Journal,* **93**:945–947, Mar. 1, 1968.
76. Batty, C. D., ed.: *Libraries and Machines Today,* North Midlands Branch, Library Association, Nottingham, 1967, 50 pp.
77. Batty, C. D.: *Library and the Machine,* selected papers and discussions from a study conference held at Nottingham, Apr. 19–22, 1966, on library applications of computers and data processing equipment, North Midlands Branch, Library Association, Nottingham, 1966, 58 pp.
78. Bauer, Charles K.: "Computerized Information Systems at the Lockheed-Georgia Company, a Division of Lockheed Aircraft Corporation," *Hawaii Library Association Journal,* **23**:36–41, June 1967.
79. Bauer, Walter F.: "Computer Communications Systems—Patterns and Prospects," *Computer Communications Symposium, University of California at*

Los Angeles, 20-22 March, 1967, Prentice-Hall, Englewood Cliffs, N.J., 1967, pp. 13-37.

80. Bayly, R.: "Project MARC and the ICL 1900 Series," *Program: News of Computers in British Libraries,* 2:95-98, Oct. 1968.
81. Bearman, H., and K. Gordon: "Library Computerization in West Sussex," *Program,* 2:53-58, July 1968.
82. Becker, Joseph: "Automatic Preparation of Book Catalogs," *ALA Bulletin,* 58:714-718, Sept. 1964.
83. Becker, Joseph: "Automating the Serial Record," *ALA Bulletin,* 58:557-558, June 1964.
84. Becker, Joseph: *Automation Activities at the Biblioteca Nationale Centrale, Firenze,* Bethesda, Md., Oct. 15, 1968, 55 pp.
85. Becker, Joseph: "Circulation and the Computer," *ALA Bulletin,* 58:1007-1010, Dec. 1964.
86. Becker, Joseph: "Development of Storage and Retrieval Systems," in *Conference on the Present Status and Future Prospects of Reference/Information Service, 1966, Columbia University,* ALA, Chicago, 1967, pp. 151-156.
87. Becker, Joseph: "Documentation and Electronic Data Processing," *American Documentation,* 19:311-316, July 1968.
88. Becker, Joseph: "IBM Circulation Control," *Drexel Library Quarterly,* 1: 20-32, Jan. 1965.
89. Becker, Joseph: "Information Network Prospects in the United States," *Library Trends,* 17:306-317, Jan. 1969.
90. Becker, Joseph: "New Technology of Interest to Librarians," *Drexel Library Quarterly,* 4:310-316, Oct. 1968.
91. Becker, Joseph: "System Analysis—Prelude to Library Data Processing," *ALA Bulletin,* 59:293-296, Apr. 1965.
92. Becker, Joseph: "Tomorrow's Library Services Today," *News Notes of California Libraries,* 63:422-440, Fall 1968.
93. Becker, Joseph: "Using Computers in a New University Library," *ALA Bulletin,* 59:823-826, Oct. 1965.
94. Becker, Joseph, and Robert M. Hayes: *A Proposed Library Network for Washington State,* working paper, Washington State Library, Pullman, Wash., Sept. 1967, 50 pp. ED 027 055.
95. Becker, Joseph, and Wallace D. Olsen: "Information Networks," *Annual Review of Information Science and Technology,* vol. 3, Encyclopaedia Britannica, Chicago, *c* 1968, pp. 289-327.
96. Bellomy, F. L.: "The Systems Approach Solves Library Problems," *ALA Bulletin,* 62:1121-1125, Oct. 1968.
97. Bellomy, F. L.: "Management Planning for Library Systems Development," *Journal of Library Automation,* 2 (4):187-217, Dec. 1969.
98. Benenfeld, Alan R.: *Generation and Encoding of the Project Intrex Augmented Catalog Data Base,* Electronic Systems Laboratory, M.I.T., Cambridge, Massachusetts, 1968, 61 pp. AD 677 418.
99. Benkin, James: "Automated Procedures at Purdue University Library: Accounting Procedures, in Theodora Andrews (ed.), *Meeting on Automation in the Library—When, Where and How, Purdue University, 1964, Papers,* Purdue University, Lafayette, Ind., 1965, pp. 36-38.

100. Benson, Joseph, Forrest Carhart, Jr., and Richard M. Dougherty: "Library Technology," *Law Library Journal,* 61:409–420.

101. Bentley, Jane F.: "General Systems-Serials-Holding Records," *Automation in libraries; First ATLIS Workshop, November, 1966,* Redstone Scientific Information Center, Redstone Arsenal, Ala., 1967, pp. 97–102. AD 654 766.

102. Bering, Edgar A., Jr.: "The Neurological Information Network of the National Institute of Neurological Diseases and Blindness," *Bulletin of the Medical Library Association,* 55:135–140, Apr. 1967.

103. Berul, Lawrence: *Application of Computers to the Information Products and Services Business: A State-of-the-art Review,* presented to Information Industry Association, Mar. 21, 1969, Auerbach Corp., Philadelphia, 1969, 19 pp.

104. Berul, Lawrence: *Information Storage and Retrieval, a State-of-the-art Report,* Auerbach Corp., Philadelphia, 1964, 235 pp. AD 630 089.

105. Berul, Lawrence: *Survey of Equipment Developments in the Information Storage and Retrieval Field,* presented to the F.I.D./I.F.I.P. Conference, June 14–17, 1967, Auerback Corp., Philadelphia, 1967.

106. Bidwell, Charles M., and Dominick Auricchio: *A Prototype System for a Computer-based Statewide Film Library Network: A Model for Operation,* Center for Instructional Communications, Syracuse University, Syracuse, 1968, 31 pp.

107. Bidwell, Charles M., and Muriel L. Day: *Statewide Film Library Network: User's Manual,* Center for Instructional Communications, Syracuse University, Syracuse, N.Y., 1968, 53 pp.

108. Billington, Jack: "Circulation Control Systems," *C.A.C.U.L. Workshop on Library Automation, University of British Columbia, 1967,* Canadian Association of College and University Libraries, Ottawa, 1967, pp. 89–92.

109. Bishop, D. A., et al.: "Development of the IBM Magnetic Tape Selectric Composer," *IBM Journal Research & Development,* 12:380–398, Sept. 1968.

110. Bishop, David, Arnold L. Milner, and Fred W. Roper: "Publication Patterns of Scientific Serials," *American Documentation,* 16:113–121, Apr. 1965.

111. Black, Donald V.: "Creation of Computer Input in an Expanded Character Set," *Journal of Library Automation,* 1:110–120, June 1968.

112. Black, Donald V.: "Library Information System Time-sharing on a Large, General-purpose Computer," *Clinic on Library Applications of Data Processing, 6th, University of Illinois, Urbana, 5-8 May, 1968, Proceedings.*

113. Black, Donald V., and Donald M. Bethe: "Library Serials Control Using a General-purpose Data Management System," *Proceedings of the American Society for Information Science, 32nd Annual Meeting, San Francisco, California, October 1-4, 1969,* 6:5–11, Greenwood, Westport, Conn., 1969.

114. Black, Donald V., and Earl A. Farley: "Library Automation," *Annual Review of Information Science and Technology,* 1:273–303, Interscience-Wiley, New York, 1966.

115. Blackburn, Robert H.: "On Producing Catalogues in Book Form for Five Libraries at Once (Ontario New Universities Library Project)," in *Library Automation Projects: A Collection of Papers by Canadian Librarians,* Canadian Library Association, occasional paper no. 48, Ottawa, 1965, pp. 20–22.

116. Blau, Edmund J.: "An Automated Circulation System and Master File for a Medium-sized Scientific Library," *Proceedings of the American Society for Information Science, 32nd Annual Meeting, San Francisco, California, October 1-4, 1969,* 6:21-28, Greenwood, Westport, Conn., 1969.

117. Blier, Robert E.: *Treating Hierarchical Data Structures in the SDC Time-shared Data Management System (TDMS),* System Development Corporation, Santa Monica, Calif., 1967. SP-2750.

118. Blier, Robert E., and Alfred H. Vorhaus: *File Organization in the SDC Time-shared Data Management System (TDMS),* System Development Corporation, Santa Monica, Calif., 1968. SP-2907.

119. Blum, B. I.: "Approaches to Searching and Retrieval at a Data Analysis Center," *Proceedings of the American Society for Information Science, 32nd Annual Meeting, San Francisco, California, October 1-4, 1969,* 6:369-373, Greenwood, Westport, Conn., 1969.

120. Blumenthal, J. G.: "Preparation of CODEN for Periodical Titles for Computer Printing in Upper and Lower-case Letters," *Proceedings of the American Society for Information Science, 32nd Annual Meeting, San Francisco, California, October 1-4, 1969,* 6:107-112, Greenwood, Westport, Conn., 1969.

121. Bobrow, D. B., et al.: "Automated Language Processing," *Annual Review of Information Science and Technology,* vol. 2, Interscience-Wiley, New York, 1967, pp. 161-186.

122. Bolles, Shirley, W.: "The Use of Flow Charts in the Analysis of Library Operations," *Special Libraries,* 58:95-98, Feb. 1967.

123. Bolt, Beranek, and Newman, Inc.: *Toward the Library of the 21st Century: A Report on Progress Made in a Program of Research Sponsored by the Council on Library Resources,* Cambridge, Mass., 1964, 41 pp.

124. Bolvin, Boyd M.: "Libraries of the Future—A Multimedia Presentation," *News Notes of California Libraries,* 63:395-404, Fall 1968.

125. Borko, Harold, ed.: *Automated Language Processing,* Wiley, New York, 1967, 386 pp.

126. Borko, Harold: "Design of Information Systems and Services, *Annual Review of Information Science and Technology,* vol. 2, Interscience-Wiley, New York, 1967, pp. 35-61.

127. Borko, Harold: "Information Science: What Is It?", *American Documentation.* 19:3-5, Jan. 1968.

128. Borko, Harold: "National and International Information Networks in Science and Technology," *AFIPS Conference Proceedings, 1968 Fall Joint Computer Conference,* vol. 33, part 2, Thompson, Washington, pp. 1469-1472.

129. Borko, Harold: "Research in Computer Based Classification Systems," *Proceedings of the Second International Study Conference on Classification Research, Elsinore, Denmark, 14-18 September, 1964,* Munksgaard, Copenhagen, 1965, pp. 220-257.

130. Borko, Harold, and H. P. Burnbaugh: "Interactive Displays for Document Retrieval," *Information Display,* 3:47-90, Sept.-Oct. 1966.

131. Borkowski, C.: "An Experimental System for Automatic Identification of Personal Names and Personal Titles in Newspaper Texts," *American Documentation,* 18:131-138, July 1967.

132. Bossmeyer, Christine, Bernhard Adams, Harro Heim, and Gunther Pflug: *Die automatisierte Buchausleihe Erfahrungen in der Universitatsbibliothek Bochum,* Bochum, 1967, 165 pp.

133. Boyd, A. H.: "Computer Processing of Library of Congress Book Numbers," *Program,* **1**:1-7, Jan. 1967.

134. Boylan, Merle N., et al.: *Automated Acquisition, Cataloging, and Circulation in a Large Research Library,* Lawrence Radiation Laboratory, Livermore, Calif., 1968, 94 pp.

135. Bradley, Albert P.: "The NASA Manned Spacecraft Center Library Practical Mechanization of Library Functions on a Daily Basis," *Special Libraries,* **41**: 692-697, Dec. 1966.

136. Brandhorst, W. T., and T. F. Eckert: *Guide to the Processing, Storage, and Retrieval of Bibliographic Information at the NASA Scientific and Technical Information Facility,* Documentation, Inc., College Park, Md., 1966. NASA-CR-62033.

137. "Brasenose Conference on the Automation of Libraries, Oxford, England, 1966," in John Harrison and Peter Laslett (eds.), *Proceedings of the Anglo-American Conference on the Mechanization of Library Services,* under the Chairmanship of Sir Frank Francis and sponsored by the Old Dominion Foundation of New York, Mansell, London and Chicago, 1967, 172 pp.

138. Bregzis, Ritvars: "Library Networks of the Future," *Drexel Library Quarterly,* **4**:261-270, Oct. 1968.

139. Bregzis, Ritvars: "The Ontario New Universities Library Project—an Automated Bibliographic Data Control System," *College and Research Libraries,* **26**:495-508, Nov. 1965.

140. Bregzis, Ritvars: "The ONULP Bibliographic Control System: An Evaluation," *Clinic on Library Applications of Data Processing, University of Illinois, 3rd, 1965, Proceedings,* Illinois Union Bookstore, Champaign, Ill., 1966, pp. 112-140.

141. Bregzis, Ritvars: "Query Language for the Reactive Catalogue," in Albert B. Tonik (ed.), *National Colloquium on Information Retrieval, 4th, Philadelphia, 3-4 May, 1967. Proceedings,* International Information, Philadelphia, 1967, pp. 77-90, discussion, pp. 90-91.

142. Brenner, E. H., and D. P. Helander: "Petroleum Literature and Patent Retrieval," *Special Libraries,* **60**:146-152, Mar. 1969.

143. Briggs, Louis I., and Darinka Z. Briggs: "Information Systems Design and Operation at a Geological Educational Research Center, *Proceedings of the American Society for Information Science, 32nd Annual Meeting, San Francisco, California, October 1-4, 1969,* **6**:375-385, Greenwood, Westport, Conn., *c* 1969.

144. Brodman, Estelle: "Printed Catalogs: Retrospect and Prospect," *Special Libraries,* **59**:783-788, Dec. 1968.

145. Brodman, Estelle, and Geraldine S. Cohen: "Communications to the Editor: Changes in Acquisitions-cataloging Methods at Washington University School of Medicine Library," *Medical Library Association Bulletin,* **54**: 259-260, July 1966.

146. Bromberg, E. I., et al.: "Bonneville Power Administration Selective Dissemination of Information Program," *Special Libraries,* 58:569-575, Oct. 1967.

147. Brookes, B. C.: "Scientific Information and the Computer," *Library Association Record,* **69**:191–197, June 1967.

148. Brooks, Frederick P., James K. Ferrell, and Thomas M. Gallie: "Organizational, Financial, and Political Aspects of a Three-university Computing Center," *Congress of the International Federation for Information Processing* (IFIP), *4th, Edinburgh, 5–10 August, 1968, Proceedings,* North-Holland Publishing, Amsterdam, 1968.

149. Brown, Curtis: "Experience with a Magnetic Tape Selectric Composer (MT/SC) in the Preparation of a Monthly Abstract Bulletin," *Proceedings of the American Society for Information Science, 32nd Annual Meeting, San Francisco, California, October 1–4, 1969,* **6**:69–73, Greenwood, Westport, Conn., 1969.

150. Brown, Curtis: "Mechanized Information Retrieval for the Paper Chemistry," *Indian Pulp & Paper,* **23**:73–83, July 1968.

151. Brown, G. W., J. G. Miller, T. A. Keenan: *EDUNET Report of the Summer Study on Information Networks Conducted by the Interuniversity Communications Council (EDUCOM),* Wiley, New York, 1967, 440 pp.

152. Brown, Margaret C.: "A Book Catalog at Work (Free Library of Philadelphia)," *Library Resources and Technical Services,* **8**:349–358, 1964.

153. Brown, Norman A., and Paula M. Strain: "Use of an Automated Shelflist," *Sci-Tech News,* **21**:36–37, Summer 1967.

154. Brown, Peter: "Some Approaches to the Concept of a National Catalog," in N. S. M. Cox and M. W. Grose (eds.), *Organization and Handling of Bibliographic Records by Computer,* Oriel Press, Newcastle upon Tyne, England; Archon, Hamden, Conn., 1967, pp. 130–134.

155. Brown, S. C.: "A Bibliographic Search by Computer," *Physics Today,* **19**: 59, 1966.

156. Brown, W. L.: "A Computer-controlled Charging System at Essendon Public Library," *Australian Library Journal,* **16**:231–239, Dec. 1967.

157. Bryan, Harrison: "American Automation in Action," *Library Journal,* **92**: 189–196, Jan. 15, 1967.

158. "Bryn Mawr, Haverford, and Swarthmore Establish Joint Computer Center," *Communications of the ACM,* **11**:793, Nov. 1968.

159. Buchanan, J. R.: "Analysis and Automated Handling of Technical Information at the Nuclear Safety Information Center," *American Documentation,* **18**:235–241, Oct. 1967.

160. Buchanan, J. R., and E. M. Kidd: "Development of a Computer System with Console Capability for the Nuclear Safety Information Center," *Proceedings of the American Society for Information Science, 32nd Annual Meeting, San Francisco, California, October 1–4, 1969,* **6**:151–158, Greenwood, Westport, Conn., 1969.

161. Buckland, Lawrence F.: *The Recording of Library of Congress Bibliographical Data in Machine Form: A Report Prepared for the Council on Library Resources, Inc.,* rev., Council on Library Resources, Inc., Washington, 1965, 54 pp.

162. Buhl, Norman A., and Myra S. Feldman: *Computer Programs for Ordering, Listing, and Circulating Books,* Savannah River Lab., E. I. Du Pont de Nemours and Co., Savannah, Ga., Sept. 1967, 50 pp. DP 1113.

163. Bundy, Mary Lee: "Automation as Innovation," *Drexel Library Quarterly,* **4**:317–328, Oct. 1968.

164. Bunge, Charles A.: "Charting the Reference Query," *Reference Quarterly,* 8(4):245–250, Summer 1969.

165. Burgess, Thomas K., and L. Ames: *LOLA: Library On-line Acquisitions Sub-system,* Washington State University Systems Office, Pullman, 1968, 73 pp. PB 179 892.

166. Burke, Frank G.: "The Application of Automated Techniques in the Management and Control of Source Materials," *American Archivist,* **30**:255–278, Apr. 1967.

167. Burke, Frank G.: "Automated Techniques in the Manuscript Division," *Library of Congress Information Bulletin,* **25**:389–390, July 14, 1966.

168. Burke, Frank G.: "Report on a Survey of Automation Activities in Archives and Manuscript Repositories in the U.S. and Canada," *American Archivist,* **31**:208–210, Apr. 1968.

169. Burkhalter, Barton R.: *Case Studies in Systems Analysis in a University Library,* Scarecrow Press, Metuchen, N.J., 1968, 186 pp.

170. Burton, Hilary D., and Theodore B. Yerke: "Famulus: A Computer-based System for Augmenting Personal Documentation Efforts," *Proceedings of the American Society for Information Science, 32nd Annual Meeting, San Francisco, California, October 1–4, 1969,* **6**:53–56, Greenwood, Westport, Conn., 1969.

171. Butler, Robert W., and Paula Z. Schofield: *Simultaneous Production of Catalog Cards and Computer Input,* Department of the Army, Fort Detrick, Frederick, Md., 1967, 46 pp. AD 647 111.

172. Cain, Alexander M.: "Steps Towards a Computer-based Library Network: A Survey of Three Medical Libraries," *Bulletin of the Medical Library Association,* 55:279–289, July 1967.

173. Cain, Alexander M., and Irwin H. Pizer: "The SUNY Biomedical Communication Network: Implementation of an On-line, Real time, User-oriented System," *Proceedings of the 30th Annual Meeting of the American Documentation Institute,* New York, Oct. 1967, pp. 258–262.

174. Caless, T. W., and D. B. Kirk: "Application of the UDC to Machine Searching," *Journal of Documentation,* **23**:208–215, Sept. 1967.

175. Cammack, Floyd M.: "Remote-control Circulation (University of Hawaii)," *College and Research Libraries,* **26**:213–218, May 1965.

176. Cammack, Floyd, and Donald Mann: "Institutional Implications of an Automated Circulation Study (Oakland University)," *College and Research Libraries,* **28**:129–132, Mar. 1967.

177. Campbell, G. R.: "Automated Systems in British Columbia," *British Columbia Libraries Quarterly,* **30**:4–8, Apr. 1967.

178. Campbell, Rita R.: "Automation and Information Retrieval in Archives—The Broad Concepts," *American Archivist,* **30**:279–286, Apr. 1967.

179. Canadian Association of College and University Libraries: "Automation in Libraries," *C.A.C.U.L. Workshop on Library Automation, University of British Columbia,* C.A.C.U.L., Ottawa, 1967, 154 pp.

180. Carlson, William H.: *What University Librarians Are Thinking, Saying, and*

Doing about Automation, State System of Higher Education, Corvallis, Ore., 1967, 14 pp. ED 026 073.

181. Carmon, James L.: "Education through Remote Terminals—The University of Georgia Computer Network," *Computers and Automation,* **17**:18-20, Mar. 1968.

182. Carter, Kenneth: "Dorset County Library: Computers and Cataloguing," *Program,* **2**:59-67, July 1968.

183. Carter, Launor F., et al.: *National Document-handling Systems for Science and Technology,* Wiley, New York, 1967, 344 pp.

184. Carter, Launor F.: "What Are the Major National Issues in the Development of Library Networks?," *News Notes of California Libraries,* **63**:405-417, Fall 1968.

185. Cartwright, Kelley L., and R. M. Shoffner: *Catalogs in Book Form: a Research Study of Their Implications for the California State Library and the California Union Catalog, with a Design for Their Implementation,* Institute of Library Research, University of California, Berkeley, Calif., 1967, 69 pp.

186. Cason, Cleo S.: "General Systems—Supervisors View of Implementing ALPHA I," *Automation in Libraries: First ATLIS Workshop, Nov. 15-17, 1966,* Redstone Scientific Information Center, Redstone Arsenal, Ala., 1967, pp. 103-109, AD 654 766.

187. *Centralized Processing for the State of Florida,* report to the Florida State Library, Arthur D. Little, Inc., Boston, 1968, 68 pp. ED 022 505.

188. Chamis, Alice Yanosko.: "The Application of Computers at the B. F. Goodrich Research Center Library," *Special Libraries,* **59**:24-29, Jan. 1968.

189. Chapin, Richard E.: "Administrative and Economic Considerations for Library Automation," *Clinic on Library Applications of Data Processing: University of Illinois: 5th, 1967, Proceedings,* Graduate School of Library Science, University of Illinois, Urbana, Ill., 1967, pp. 55-69.

190. Chapin, Richard E., and Dale H. Pretzer: "Comparative Costs of Converting Shelf List Records to Machine Readable Form," *Journal of Library Automation,* **1**:66-74, Mar. 1968.

191. Chapman, Edward A., and Paul L. St. Pierre: *Systems Analysis and Design as Related to Library Operations,* Rensselaer Libraries, Rensselaer Polytechnic Institute, Troy, N.Y., 1966, 78 pp.

192. Chappell, D. L.: "Automatic Circulation Procedures at Utah State University," *The LARC Reports,* **1**(10):1-18, July 1968.

193. Chasen, Lawrence I.: *The Development of Random Access Information Retrieval in the GE/MSD Library: And User Interactions,* Missile and Space Division, General Electric Co., Philadelphia, May, 1967, 21 pp. AD 663 286.

194. Cheek, Robert C.: "TOPS: The Westinghouse Teletype Order Processing and Inventory Control System," *The Computer: Tool for Management,* Business Press, Elmhurst, Ill., 1968, pp. 78-90.

195. Chen, Ching-Chih, and E. Robert Kingham: "Subject Reference Lists Introduced by Computer," *Journal of Library Automation,* **1**:178-197, Sept. 1968.

196. Cherry, Colin: *On Human Communication: A Review, a Survey, and a Criticism,* 2d ed., M.I.T., Cambridge, Mass., *c* 1966, 337 pp.

197. Childers, Thomas, et al.: *Book Catalog and Card Catalog—A Cost and*

Service Study, Baltimore County Public Library, Towson, Md., 1967, 55 pp. ED 019 099.

198. Clapp, Verner W.: "Closing the Circuit: Automation and Data Processing for Libraries," *Library Journal,* **91**:1165–1171, Mar. 1966.

199. Clapp, Verner W.: *The Future of the Research Library,* University of Illinois Press, Urbana, Ill., 1964, 114 pp.

200. Clapp, Verner W.: "Mechanization and Automation in American Libraries," *Libri,* **14**:369–375. 1964.

201. Clark, James P.: "General Systems—Book Circulation," *Automation in Libraries: First ATLIS Workshop, November 15–17, 1966,* Redstone Scientific Information Center, Redstone Arsenal, Ala., 1967, pp. 71–79. AD 654 766.

202. Cleverdon, Cyril, ed.: *Cranfield Research Project: Report on the Testing and Analyses of an Investigation into the Comparative Efficiency of Indexing Systems,* Cranfield, Bedford, England, 1962.

203. Cleverdon, Cyril, et al.: "Uncovering Some Facts of Life in Information Retrieval," *Special Libraries,* 55:86–91, Feb. 1964.

204. Climensen, W. Douglas: "File Organization and Search Techniques," *Annual Review of Information Science and Technology,* **1**:107–135, Interscience-Wiley, New York, 1966.

205. Clyde, Eric: "Progress in the automation of serials at the National Science Library." *C.A.C.U.L. Workshop on Library Automation, University of British Columbia, 1967,* Canadian Association of College and University Libraries, Ottawa, 1967, pp. 64–75.

206. Coblans, Herbert: "The Mechanization of Documentation—A Tentative Balance Sheet," in Anthony De Reuck and Julie Knight (eds.), *Communication in Science: Documentation and Automation,* Little, Brown, Boston, 1968, pp. 78–83.

207. Coblans, Herbert: "Use of Mechanized Methods in Documentation Work," *ASLIB,* London, 1966, 89 pp.

208. Coenenberg, Richard: "Synergizing Reference Service in the San Francisco Bay Region," *ALA Bulletin,* **62**:1379–1384, Dec. 1968.

209. Comité pour l'automation des services de la bibliothèque: *Rapport,* Université Laval, Quebec, 1966, 46 pp.

210. Committee on Library Work and Documentation, Sub-committee on Machine Input Records: *ANSI Standard for a Format for Bibliographic Information Interchange on Magnetic Tape,* American National Standards Institute, New York, 1969. ANS Z39.Z-1969.

211. Committee on Scientific and Technical Information, Federal Council for Science and Technology: *Guidelines for the Development of Information Retrieval Thesauri,* 1st ed., Washington, 1967, 9 pp.

212. *Conference on Libraries and Automation, Airlie Foundation, 1963, Proceedings,* Library of Congress, Washington, 1964, 268 pp.

213. *Conference on Machine-readable Catalog Copy, 2nd, Library of Congress, 1965, Proceedings,* Council on Library Resources, Inc., Washington, 1965, 35 pp.

214. *Conference on Machine-readable Catalog Copy, 3rd, Library of Congress, 1966, Proceedings (Discussion of the MARC Pilot Project),* Library of Congress, Washington, 1966, 30 pp.

215. *Conference on Machine-readable Catalog Copy, 4th, Library of Congress, 1967, Proceedings,* Library of Congress, Washington, 1968, 13 pp. PB 179 826.

216. Cooney, Leo J.: "On-line Applications—ALPHA-2 and NAPALM," *Automation in Libraries: First ATLIS Workshop, November, 1966,* Redstone Scientific Information Center, Redstone Arsenal, Ala., 1967, pp. 149–156. AD 654 766.

217. Cooper, Marianne: "Current Information Dissemination—Ideas and Practices," *Journal of Chemical Documentation,* 8:207–218, Nov. 1968.

218. Cooper, W. S.: "Expected Search Length: A Single Measure of Retrieval Effectiveness Based on the Weak Ordering Action of Retrieval Systems," *American Documentation,* **19**:30–41, Jan. 1968.

219. Corbett, L.: "Chemical Titles: SDI (Selective Dissemination of Information) Trial at AWRE (Atomic Weapons Research Establishment)," *Journal of Documentation,* **23**:150–151, June 1967.

220. Corbin, John Boyd: "Automatic Data Processing in the Texas State Library," *Texas Library Journal,* **41**:12–14, 1965.

221. Costello, John C., Jr.: "Coordinate Indexing," *Systems for the Intellectual Organization of Information,* vol. VII, Rutgers, New Brunswick, N.J., 1966, 218 pp.

222. Courain, Margaret E., and Arlene C. Peterson: "1,250,000 Pages of Biological Information to Microstorage for Retrieval in a Pharmaceutical Information System," *Proceedings of the American Society for Information Science, 32nd Annual Meeting, San Francisco, California, October 1–4, 1969,* **6**:353–357, Greenwood, Westport, Conn., 1969.

223. Courtright, Benjamin: "Automated Circulation Systems," in *Practical Problems of Library Automation,* Special Libraries Association, Washington, D.C., 1967, pp. 39–45.

224. Covill, George W.: "Librarian + Systems Analyst = Teamwork?" *Special Libraries,* 58:99–101, Feb. 1967.

225. Coward, Richard E.: "BNB and Computers," *Library Association Record,* **70**:198–202, Aug. 1968.

226. Coward, Richard E.: "MARC International," *Journal of Library Automation,* **2**(4):181–186, Dec. 1969.

227. Coward, Richard E.: *MARC Record Service Proposals,* Council of the British National Bibliography, Ltd., London, July 1968.

228. Coward, Richard E.: "A New Look in National Bibliographies: Some Implications of the Use of Computers with Special Reference to the Deutsche Bibliographie," *Library Association Record,* **69**:310–313, Sept. 1967.

229. Coward, Richard E.: "The United Kingdom MARC Record Service," in N. S. M. Cox and M. W. Grose (eds.), *Organization and Handling of Bibliographic Records by Computer,* Oriel, Newcastle upon Tyne, England, Hamden, Conn., 1967, pp. 107–117.

230. Cowburn, L. M., and B. J. Enright: "Computerized UDC Subject Index in the City University Library, *Program,* **1**:1–5, Jan. 1968.

231. Cox, Carl R.: "The Mechanization of Acquisition and Circulation Procedures at the University of Maryland Library," *IBM Library Mechanization Sym-*

posium, Endicott, N.Y., 1964, Proceedings, International Business Machines Corp., White Plains, N.Y., 1965, pp. 205-236.

232. Cox, Carl R.: "Mechanized Acquisitions Procedures at the University of Maryland," *College and Research Libraries,* **26**:232-236, May 1965.

233. Cox, Nigel S. M., J. D. Dews, and J. L. Dolby: *The Computer and the Library: The Role of the Computer in the Organization and Handling of Information in Libraries,* Archon, Hamden, Conn., *c* 1966, 95 pp.

234. Cox, Nigel S. M., and Michael W. Grose: *Organization and Handling of Bibliographic Records by Computer,* Archon, Hamden, Conn., 1967, 192 pp.

235. Cravens, David W.: *Information Systems for Technology Transfer,* Aerospace Research Applications Center, Indiana University, Bloomington, Ind. 1966.

236. Creager, William A., and David E. Sparks: *A Serials Data Program for Science and Technology: Final Report to the National Science Foundation,* Information Dynamics, Reading, Mass., 1965. 190 pp. NSF-C-413.

237. Crismond, Linda F., and Sylvia B. Fatzer: "Automated Serials Check-in and Binding Procedures at the San Francisco Public Library," *Proceedings of the American Society for Information Science, 32nd Annual Meeting, San Francisco, California, October 1-4, 1969,* **6**:13-20, Greenwood, Westport, Conn., 1969.

238. Crowley, Thomas H.: *Understanding Computers,* McGraw-Hill, New York, *c* 1967, 142 pp.

239. Croxton, F. E.: "General Systems-ALPHA in General," *Automation in Libraries: First ATLIS Workshop, November, 1966,* Redstone Scientific Information Center, Redstone Arsenal, Ala., 1967, pp. 5-14. AD 654 766.

240. Cuadra, Carlos A., et al.: *Technology and Libraries,* National Advisory Commission on Libraries, Washington, 1967, 165 pp. ED 022 481.

241. Cuadra, Carlos A., and Jules Mersel: "Libraries and Technological Forces Affecting Them," *Conference on the Library in Society—Towards the Year 2000,* School of Library Science, University of Southern California at Los Angeles, 1968, preprint, 25 pp.

242. Culbertson, Don S.: "Computerized Serial Records," *Library Resources and Technical Services,* **9**:53-58, 1965.

243. Culbertson, Don S.: "The Costs of Data Processing in University Libraries: In Book Acquisitions and Cataloging," *College and Research Libraries,* **24**: 487-489, Nov. 1963.

244. Culbertson, Don S.: "Data Processing for Technical Procedures at the University of Illinois Library," *Institute on Information Storage and Retrieval, 1st, University of Minnesota, 1962: Information Retrieval Today,* University of Minnesota, Minneapolis, 1966, pp. 99-107.

245. Culbertson, Don S.: "New Library Science: A Man-Machine Partnership," *PNLA Quarterly,* **29**:25-31, Oct. 1964.

246. Culbertson, Don S., et al.: *An Investigation into the Application of Data Processing to Library Filing Rules,* University of Illinois, Chicago, 1962, 27 pp. PB 164-441.

247. Cummings, Martin M.: "The Biomedical Communications Problem," in *Ciba Foundation Symposium on Communication in Science: Documentation and Automation,* Little, Brown, Boston, 1967, pp. 110-122.

248. Cummings, Martin M.: "Plans for the Development of a Medical Library Network," *Bulletin of the Cleveland Medical Library Association,* **15**:68–79, Apr. 1968.

249. Cummings, Martin M.: "The Role of the National Library of Medicine in the National Biomedical Library Network," *Annals of the New York Academy of Sciences,* **142**:503–512, Mar. 31, 1967.

250. Cummings, Martin M., and Ralph A. Simmons: "Automation in Medical Libraries," *Conference on the Use of Computers in Medical Education, University of Oklahoma Medical Center, Oklahoma City, 3–5 April, 1968, Proceedings,* Oklahoma City, 1968, pp. 74–92.

251. Cunningham, Jay L., and Theodore E. Leach: "Bibliographic Dimensions of the MARC Pilot Project," *American Documentation Institute: Levels of Interaction between Man and Information,* Thompson, Washington, 1967, pp. 278–281.

252. Curley, Walter W.: "The Data Processing Program in Operation at the Suffolk Co-Operative Library System, Patchogue, N.Y.," *Clinic on Library Applications of Data Processing, University of Illinois, 3rd, 1965, Proceedings,* Illinois Union Bookstore, Champaign, Ill., 1966, pp. 15–42.

253. Curran, Ann T.: "The Mechanization of the Serial Records for the Moving and Merging of the Boston Medical and Harvard Medical Serials," *Library Resources and Technical Services,* **10**:362–372, 1966.

254. Curran, Ann T., and Henriette D. Avram: *The Identification of Data Elements in Bibliographic Records,* final report of the Special Project on Data Elements for the Subcommittee on Machine Input Records (SC-2) of the Sectional Committee on Library Work and Documentation (Z-39) of the United States of America Standards Institute, May 1967, 126 pp. AD 666 447.

255. "Current Australian Projects in Library Automation," *Australian Library Journal,* **16** (Supplement no. 8):41–44, Aug. 1967.

256. Dahlberg, I.: "Verwicklung einer medernen Universitatsbibliothek," *Verband Bibl Landes Nordrhein-Westfalen Mitt.,* **15**:86–105, July 15, 1965. Automation of library processes at Florida Atlantic University.

257. Daily, Jay E.: "Automation and Authority vs. Autonomy," *Library Journal,* 92:3606–3609, Oct. 15, 1967.

258. Dammers, H. E.: "Integrated Information Processing and the Case for a National Network," *Information Storage and Retrieval,* **4**:113–131, June 1968. Presented at the First Cranfield International Conference on Mechanized Information Storage and Retrieval Systems, College of Aeronautics, Cranfield, England, Aug. 1967, pp. 29–31.

259. Darby, R. L.: "Information Analysis Centers as a Source for Information and Data," *Special Libraries,* 59:91–97, Feb. 1968.

260. Darling, L.: "MEDLARS: A Regional Search Center," *Institute on Information Retrieval, 1965, University of Minnesota, Information Retrieval with Special Reference to the Biomedical Sciences,* Nolte Center for Continuing Education, University of Minnesota, Minneapolis, 1966, pp. 49–60.

261. Data Processing Division: *Record Compaction Techniques,* International Business Machines Corp., White Plains, N.Y., n.d. E20-8252.

262. Davies, D. W.: "Communication Networks to Serve Rapid-response Computers," *Congress of the International Federation for Information Processing*

(IFIP), 4th, Edinburgh, 5–10 August, 1968, Proceedings, North-Holland Publishing, Amsterdam, 1968.

263. Davies, D. W.: "The Principles of a Data Communication Network for Computers and Remote Peripherals," *Congress of the International Federation for Information Processing (IFIP), 4th, Edinburgh, 5–10 August, 1968, Proceedings,* North-Holland Publishing, Amsterdam, 1968.

264. Davis, Richard J.: "Information Transfer in a Universal Health Information Bank by Use of the Social Security Number," *American Society for Information Science Annual Meeting, Columbus, Ohio, 20–24 October, 1968, Proceedings,* vol. 5, Greenwood, New York, 1968, pp. 249–253.

265. Dechief, Helene: "Automation of Serials at the Canadian National Railways," *C.A.C.U.L. Workshop on Library Automation, University of British Columbia, 1967,* Canadian Association of College and University Libraries, Ottawa, 1967, pp. 49–63.

266. De Gennaro, Richard: "Automation in the Harvard College Library," *Harvard Library Bulletin,* **16**:217–236, July 1968.

267. De Gennaro, Richard: "A Computer Produced Shelf List," *College and Research Libraries,* **26**:311–315, 353, July 1965.

268. De Gennaro, Richard: "The Development and Administration of Automated Systems in Academic Libraries," *Journal of Library Automation,* **1**: 75–91, Mar. 1968.

269. De Gennaro, Richard: "A Strategy for the Conversion of Research Library Catalogs to Machine Readable Form," *College and Research Libraries,* **28**: 253–257, July 1967.

270. De Jarnett, L. R.: "Library Circulation Control Using IBM 357's at Southern Illinois University," *IBM Library Mechanization Symposium, Endicott, N.Y., 1964, Proceedings,* International Business Machines Corp., White Plains, N.Y., 1965, pp. 77–94.

271. De Lucia, A.: The Human-readable/Machine-readable (HRMR) Mass Memory as the File Processor for a Network of Documentation/Analysis Centers," *Proceedings of the American Society for Information Science, 32nd Annual Meeting, San Francisco, California, October 1–4, 1969,* **6**:339–343, Greenwood, Westport, Conn., 1969.

272. Dennis, Jack B.: "A Position Paper on Computing and Communications," *Communications of the ACM,* **11**:370–377, May 1968.

273. De Varennes, R.: "Computerized Serials Record at Laval University: A Progress Report," *Canadian Libraries,* **24**:122–123, Sept. 1967.

274. *Development of a Computer Processing Center for the New England State University Libraries:* Final Report, Inforonics, Inc., Cambridge, Mass., 1967, 61 pp. ED 028 799.

275. Dews, J. David: "Computers and Libraries," *Program,* **1**:25–34, July 1967.

276. Dillon, Howard W.: *Program for the Utilization of Automatic Data Processing Equipment,* Ohio State University, Columbus, 1965, 7 pp.

277. *Directory of Computerized Information in Science and Technology,* Science Associates/International, New York, 1968.

278. Divett, Robert T.: "There's Nothing Like Pushing a Button," *Bulletin of the Medical Library Association,* 55:324–328, July 1967.

279. Dixon, Paul: *Cost Analysis and Administration of Information Retrieval*

Systems, presented to the American Management Association, May 1968, Auerbach Corp., Philadelphia, 1968, 31 pp.

280. Dobb, T. C.: "Simon Fraser's Automated Acquisitions System," *C.A.C.U.L. Workshop on Library Automation, University of British Columbia, 1967,* Canadian Association of College and University Libraries, Ottawa, 1967. pp. 25–36.

281. *DOD User Study—Phase I: Final Technical Report,* Auerbach Corp., Philadelphia, 1965, 171 pp. 1151-TR-3. AD 615 501.

282. *DOD User-needs Study—Phase I: Final Technical Report,* Auerbach Corp., Philadelphia, 1965, 255 pp. 1151-TR-3. AD 615 502.

283. Dolby, J. L.: *An Algorithm for Noisy Matches in Catalog Searching,* prepared for the Institute of Library Research of the University of California at Berkeley, R & D Consultants Co., Los Altos, Calif., 1968.

284. Dolby, J. L.: *Computerized Library Catalogs: Their Growth, Cost, and Utility,* M.I.T., Cambridge, Mass., 1969, 164 pp.

285. Dolby, J. L.: *An Evaluation of the Utility and Cost of Computerized Library Catalogs,* final report, R & D Consultants Co., Los Altos, Calif., 1968, 214 pp. ED 022 517.

286. Dolby, J. L., and V. J. Forsyth: "An Analysis of Cost Factors in Maintaining and Updating Card Catalogs," *Journal of Library Automation,* **2**(4):218–241, Dec. 1969.

287. Dolby, J. L., and H. L. Resnikoff: "On the Structure of Written English Words," *Language,* **40**:167–196, 1964.

288. Dolby, J. L., H. L. Resnikoff, and J. W. Tukey. A Ruly Code for Serials. *Proceedings of the American Society for Information Science, 32nd Annual Meeting, San Francisco, California, October 1-4, 1969,* **6**:113–124, Greenwood, Westport, Conn., 1969.

289. Dougherty, Richard M.: "Manpower Utilization in Technical Services," *Library Resources and Technical Services,* **12**:77–82, Winter 1968.

290. Dougherty, Richard M., et al.: *Policies and Programs Designed to Improve Cooperation and Coordination among Technical Service Operating Units,* Graduate School of Library Science, University of Illinois, Urbana, 1967, 45 pp.

291. Dougherty, Richard M., and James G. Stephens: *Investigation concerning the Modification of the University of Illinois Computerized Serials Book Catalog to Achieve an Operative System at the University of Colorado Libraries,* University of Colorado Libraries, Boulder, Apr. 1968, 65 pp. NSF-GN-641. PB-178 216.

292. Doyle, Stephen E.: "Integration of Computer Research Facilities with Telecommunication Systems: Some Legal Problems," *Law and Computer Technology,* **1**:2–4, Apr. 1968.

293. Drew, D. L., et al.: "An On-line Technical Library Reference Retrieval System," *American Documentation,* **17**:3–7, Jan. 1966. A description of CONVERSE at Lockheed.

294. Dubester, Henry J.: "The Librarian and the Machine," *Institute on Information Storage and Retrieval, 1st, University of Minnesota, 1962: Information Retrieval Today,* University of Minnesota, Minneapolis, 1966, pp. 167–176.

295. Dueker, Kenneth J.: "A Look at State and Local Information Systems Efforts," *National Conference of the Association for Computing Machinery,*

23rd, Las Vegas, Nevada, 27-29 August, 1968, Proceedings, Brandon Systems Press, Princeton, N.J., 1968, pp. 133-142.

296. Dunkin, Paul S.: "1964: Peek into Paradise," *Library Resources and Technical Services,* 9:143-148, 1965.

297. Dunlap, Connie R.: "Automated Acquisitions Procedures at the University of Michigan Library," *Library Resources and Technical Services,* **11**:192-202, Spring 1967.

298. Easton, William W.: "Automating the Illinois State University Map Library," *Special Libraries Association Geography and Map Division Bulletin,* **67**:3-9, Mar. 1967.

299. *EDP Systems Development Services, Report of the Survey of Data Processing Feasibility,* Prince Georges County Memorial Library System, Hyattsville, Md., 1965, 48 pp.

300. Educational Facilities Laboratories: *The Impact of Technology on the Library Building,* New York, 1967, 12 pp. ED 018 147.

301. Elias, Arthur W., ed. *Third Technical Information Center Administration Conference, Philadelphia, Pa., 29 August-1 September, 1966, Proceedings,* Spartan, New York, 1967.

302. Eller, James L., and Robert L. Panek: "Thesaurus Development for a Decentralized Information Network," *American Documentation,* **19**:213-220, July 1968.

303. Enright, B. J.: "An Experimental Periodicals Checking List," *Program,* **1**: 4-11, Oct. 1967.

304. Eshelman, William R.: "Put out More Flags for Z 39," *Datamation,* **16**:59, Feb. 1970.

305. *An Evaluation of the New York State Library's NYSILL Pilot Program,* Nelson Associates, Inc., New York, Mar. 1968, 15 pp.

306. Evans, A. J., and R. A. Wall: "Library Mechanization Projects at Loughborough University of Technology, *Program,* **1**:1-4, July 1967.

307. Eyman, Eleanor G., et al.: "Periodicals Automation at Miami-Dade Junior College," *Library Resources and Technical Services,* **10**:341-361, 1966.

308. Fasana, Paul J.: "Automating Cataloging Functions in Conventional Libraries," *Library Resources and Technical Services,* 7:350-363, 1963.

309. Felter, Jacqueline W.: "The Union Catalog of Medical Periodicals of New York," *Institute on Information Storage and Retrieval, 2d, University of Minnesota, 1965, Information Retrieval with Special Reference to the Biomedical Sciences,* Minneapolis, 1966, pp. 117-131.

310. Felter, Jacqueline W., and Djoeng S. Tjoeng: "A Computer System for a Union Catalog: Theme and Variations," *Medical Library Association Bulletin,* University of Minnesota Library School, Minneapolis, **53**:163-177, Apr. 1965.

311. Fenn, L. R.: "ICI Union Catalogue," *Program,* **2**:47-52, July 1968.

312. Ferris, H. Donald: "Automated Procedures at Purdue University Library: Order Department," *Meeting on Automation in the Library—When, Where, and How, Purdue University, 1964, Papers,* Purdue University, Lafayette, Ind., 1965, pp. 39-42.

313. *Fiction in the Greenwich Library,* The Greenwich Library, Greenwich, Conn., *c* 1969, 443 pp.

314. *Final Report on Phase I: Systems Design and Action Plan for the Pesticides*

Information Center, National Agricultural Library, Department of Agriculture, submitted by Datatrol Corp., a subsidiary of Control Data Corp., 1965, 90 pp.

315. Fischer, M.: "The KWIC Index Concept: A Retrospective View," *American Documentation,* **17**:57–70, Apr. 1966.
316. Fisher, Barbara: "The Archivist and the Computer," *PNLA Quarterly,* **32**: 8–12, Jan. 1968.
317. Fisher, Barbara, and Frank B. Evans: "Automation, Information and the Administration of Archives and Manuscript Collections: Bibliographic Review," *American Archivist,* **30**:333–348, Apr. 1967.
318. Flannery, Anne, and James D. Mack: "Mechanized Circulation System, Lehigh University Library," *Library Systems Analysis, Report No. 4,* Center for Information Sciences, Lehigh University, Bethlehem, Pa., 1966, 17 pp.
319. Flood, B.: "Analysis of Questions Addressed to a Medical Reference Retrieval System: Comparison of Question and System Terminologies," *American Documentation,* **18**:216–227, Oct. 1967.
320. Flood, Merrill M.: "The Systems Approach to Library Planning," *The Intellectual Foundations of Library Education: The Twenty-ninth Annual Conference of the Graduate Library School, July 6–8, 1964.* University of Chicago Press, Chicago, 1965, pp. 38–50.
321. Flora, Betty, and John Willhardt: "High School Library Data Processing," *Journal of Library Automation,* **2**(1):10–19, Mar. 1969.
322. Forget, Guy: "Library Catalogue Production at Laval University," *C.A.C.U.L. Workshop on Library Automation, University of British Columbia, 1967,* Canadian Association of College and University Libraries, Ottawa, 1967, pp. 109–112.
323. Forsythe, G. E.: "Computer Science and Education," *Congress of the International Federation for Information Processing (IFIP), 4th, Edinburgh, 5–10 August, 1968, Proceedings,* North-Holland Publishing, Amsterdam, 1968, pp. 92–106.
324. Franke, Richard D.: "Computerized Library Catalog," *Datamation,* **14**: 445–452.
325. "Franklin and Marshall College Plans 50-College Computer Network," *College Management,* Jan. 1967, p. 16.
326. Franks, E.: "Development and Management of a Computer-centered Data Base," *Proceedings of the Symposium (10–11 June, 1963),* LUCID, part 7, System Development Corporation, Santa Monica, Calif., 1963. TM-1456/-007/00. AD-662 957.
327. Freeman, David N., and Robert R. Pearson: "Efficiency vs. Responsiveness in a Multiple-services Computer Facility," *National Conference of the Association for Computing Machinery, 23rd, Las Vegas, Nevada, 27–29 August, 1968, Proceedings,* Brandon Systems Press, Princeton, N.J., 1968, pp. 25–34B.
328. Freeman, M. E.: "Science Information Exchange as a Source of Information," *Special Libraries,* 59:86–90, Feb. 1968.
329. Freeman, Robert R.: "Trends in Bibliographic Data Processing in the Context of Reclassification of Libraries," Jean M. Perrault (ed.), *Conference on Reclassification, University of Maryland, College Park, 4-6 April, 1968, Proceedings: Reclassification, Rationale, and Problems,* School of Library and

Information Services, University of Maryland, College Park, Md., 1968, pp. 164–178.

330. Freeman, Robert R., and P. Aherton: *AUDACIOUS—An Experiment with an On-line Interactive Reference Retrieval System Using the Universal Decimal Classification as the Index Language in the Field of Nuclear Science,* American Institute of Physics, New York, 1968. AIP/UDC-7.

331. *Functional and Software Considerations for Bibliographical Data Base Utilization,* Auerbach Corp. Report to the National Agricultural Library, Auerbach Corp., Philadelphia, May 1969. 1582-100-TR 4.

332. *Functional System Specifications for the National Library of Medicine,* prepared through the cooperative efforts of the Auerbach Corp. and the Task Force for New Computer Implementation, National Library of Medicine, Bethesda, Md., 1967, 193 pp.

333. Funk, Charles: "Automated Union Catalog of the Libraries in Connecticut," *The LARC Reports,* **1**(32):1–12, Dec. 1968.

334. Furth, Stephen: "Data Processing Systems for Library Services," *Hawaii Library Association Journal,* **23**:21–25, June 1967.

335. Fussler, Herman H. "Economics, Libraries and Project INTREX," in Carl E. J. Overhage and R. Joyce Harman (eds.), *Planning Conference on Information Transfer Experiments (INTREX), Woods Hole, Mass., 2 August–3 September, 1965,* M.I.T., Cambridge, Mass., 1965, pp. 163–164.

336. Fussler, Herman H.: "University of Chicago Library Automation Program," in Elizabeth E. Hamer, *Report of the Sixty-ninth Meeting of the Association of Research Libraries,* U.S. Library of Congress, Washington. Also in *Information Bulletin,* **26**:72–73, Jan. 26, 1967.

337. Fussler, Herman H., and Charles T. Payne: "Development of an Integrated, Computer-based, Bibliographic Data System for a Large University Library," *Annual Report, 1966/1967,* University of Chicago Library, Chicago, 1967, 66 pp. PB 179 426.

338. Gechman, Marvin C.: "Development of a Corporate-wide Technical Reports Processing System," *Proceedings of the American Society for Information Science, 32nd Annual Meeting, San Francisco, California, October 1–4, 1969,* **6**:361–367, Greenwood, Westport, Conn., 1969.

339. Geddes, Andrew: "Data Processing in a Cooperative System—Opportunities for Service (Nassau Library System)," in John Harvey (ed.), *Data Processing in Public and University Libraries,* Drexel Information Science Services, vol. 3, Spartan, Washington, 1966, pp. 25–35.

340. Geddes, Andrew: "Library Automation: An Essential of Service," *ALA Bulletin* **61**:624–646, June 1966.

341. Geller, William Spence: "Duplicate Catalogs in Regional and Public Library Systems (The Los Angeles County Public Library System)," *Library Quarterly,* **34**:57–67, Jan. 1964.

342. Gentle, Edgar C., Jr.: *Data Communications in Business: An Introduction,* American Telephone and Telegraph Company, New York, *c* 1965, 163 pp. Paperback.

343. Giering, R. H.: *Information Processing and the Data Spectrum,* Data Corporation (Eastern Division), Arlington, Va., 1967. DTN-68-2.

344. Gilchrist, Alan D. B.: "Further Comments on the Terminology of the Analysis of Library Systems, *ASLIB Proceedings,* **20**:408–412, Oct. 1968.

345. Giuliano, V. E., and P. E. Jones: *Study and Test of Methodology for Laboratory Evaluation of Message Retrieval Systems,* interim report prepared by Arthur D. Little, Inc., Air Force Systems Command, Hanscom Field, Bedford, Mass., 1966, 183 pp.

346. Glaser, E., D. Rosenblatt, and M. K. Wood: "The Design of a Federal Statistical Data Center," *American Statistician,* **21**:12–20, Feb. 1967.

347. Goffman, W., and V. A. Newill: "Methodology for Test and Evaluation of Information Retrieval Systems," *Information Storage and Retrieval,* **3**:19–25, Aug. 1966.

348. Gold, Michael M., and Lee L. Selwyn: "Real Time Computer Communications and the Public Interest," *AFIPS Conference Proceedings, 1968 Fall Joint Computer Conference,* vol. 33, part 2, Thompson, Washington, pp. 1473–1478.

349. Goldhor, Herbert: "New Technology; Promise and Reality," *Library Quarterly,* **33**:102–114, Jan. 1963.

350. Goldhor, Herbert, ed.: *Proceedings of the 1963 Clinic on Library Applications of Data Processing, University of Illinois Graduate School of Library Science,* Illinois Union Bookstore, Champaign, Ill., *c* 1964, 176 pp.

351. Goodman, Arnold F.: *Flow of Scientific and Technical Information: The Results of a Recent Major Investigation,* Douglas Aircraft Co., Huntington Beach, Calif., 1967, 59 pp. AD 657 558.

352. Goodman, Arnold F., et al.: DOD User-needs Study, Phase II: Flow of *Scientific and Technical Information within the Defense Industry,* Frequency Distributions and Correlation, vol. III A, Relationship and Comparison, vol. III B, North American Aviation, Inc., Anaheim, Calif., 1966, 538 pp. AD 649-284.

353. Goodman, Arnold F., et al.: *Final Report: DOD User-needs Study, Phase II: Flow of Scientific and Technical Information within the Defense Industry,* Overview, vol. I, North American Aviation, Anaheim, Calif., 1966, 68 pp. AD 647 111.

354. Goodman, Arnold F., et al.: *Final Report: DOD User-needs Study, Phase II: Flow of Scientific and Technical Information within the Defense Industry,* Technical Description, vol. II A, Technical Appendices, vol. II B, North American Aviation, Inc., Anaheim, Calif., 1966, 513 pp. AD 647 112.

355. Gorchels, Clarence: "Of New Libraries and Futuristic Libraries," *College and Research Libraries,* **4**:267–268, 1964.

356. Gordon, Galvy E.: "Columbus Conversion to Data Processing," *Wilson Library Bulletin,* **41**:414–417, Dec. 1966.

357. Gould, E. P., and J. W. Mosior: "TELPORT—Time-shared Information Systems," *Bell Laboratories Record,* **46**:197–202, June 1968.

358. "Government Adopts Standard Code for Information Interchange," *Scientific Information Notes,* **10**:8, April-May 1968.

359. Graduate Library School: *Requirements Study for Future Catalogs,* Progress Report, no. 2, University of Chicago, Chicago, Mar. 1968. NSF Grant GN-432.

360. Graziano, E. E.: "'Machine-Men' and Librarians, an Essay," *College and Research Libraries,* **28**:403–406, Nov. 1967.

361. Greenberger, Martin: "The Border-line between Communications and Data Processing," *Law and Computer Technology,* **1**:7–9, July 1968.

362. Greiner, William E.: "Data Processing Equipment and the Library," in Francis B. Jenkins (ed.), *Clinic in Library Applications of Data Processing, University of Illinois, 3rd, 1965, Proceedings,* Illinois Union Bookstore, Champaign, Ill., 1966, pp. 175-192.

363. Griffin, Hillis L.: "Automation of Technical Processes in Libraries," *Annual Review of Information Science and Technology,* vol. 3, Encyclopaedia Britannica, Chicago, 1968, pp. 241-262.

364. Griffin, Hillis L.: "Estimating Data Processing Costs in Libraries," *College and Research Libraries,* 25:400-403, Sept. 1964.

365. Griffin, Marjorie: "Automation in Libraries: A Projection," *Canadian Libraries,* 23:360-367, Mar. 1967.

366. Grimes, George H.: "The Regional Information System in Education: Its Background, Structure, Development, and Implementation," *Proceedings of the American Society for Information Science, 32nd Annual Meeting, San Francisco, California, October 1-4, 1969,* 6:387-398, Greenwood, Westport, Conn., 1969.

367. Grose, M. W.: "The Place of the Librarian in the Computer Age," *Library Association Record,* 70:195-197, Aug. 1968.

368. Grose, M. W., and B. Jones: "The Newcastle University Library Order System," in N. S. M. Cox, and M. W. Grose (eds.), *Organization and Handling of Bibliographic Records by Computer,* Oriel, Newcastle upon Tyne, England, Archon, Hamden, Conn., 1967, pp. 158-167.

369. Gruenberger, Fred: *Computers and Communications—Toward a Computer Utility,* Prentice-Hall, Englewood Cliffs, N.J., 1968, 219 pp.

370. Gull, Cloyd Dake: "Attitudes and Hopes Where Automation Is Concerned," *Meeting on Automation in the Library—When, Where, and How, Purdue University, 1964, Papers,* Purdue University, Lafayette, Ind., 1964, pp. 53-64.

371. Gull, Cloyd Dake: "Automation, Documentation, Current Systems and Trends in the USA," *Revue Internationale de la Documentation,* 29:57-62, May 1962.

372. Gull, Cloyd Dake: "Challenges of Teaching the Information Sciences," *Journal of Education for Librarianship,* 6:61-64, Summer 1965.

373. Gull, Cloyd Dake: "Convergence toward Common Standards in Machine-readable Cataloging, *Medical Library Association Bulletin,* 57:28-35, Jan. 1969.

374. Gull, Cloyd Dake: "Guidelines to Mechanizing Information Systems," in L. H. Hattery, and E. M. McCormick (eds.), *Information Retrieval Systems,* information retrieval management, Data Processing, Inc., Detroit, 1962, pp. 101-110.

375. Gull, Cloyd Dake: "The Hardware of Data Processing," *Library Resources and Technical Services,* 9:6-18, 1965.

376. Gull, Cloyd Dake: "How Will Electronic Information Systems Affect Cataloging Rules?" *Library Resources and Technical Services,* 5:135-139, 1961.

377. Gull, Cloyd Dake: "Impact of Electronics upon Cataloguing Rules: Working Paper No. 17," *International Conference on Cataloguing Principles, 1961, Paris, Report,* Organizing Committee, I.C.C.P., London, 1963, pp. 281-290.

378. Gull, Cloyd Dake: "Implications for the Storage and Retrieval of Knowledge,"

in L. E. Asheim (ed.), *Future of the Book,* pp. 53-63. Also *Library Quarterly,* 25:333-343, Oct. 1955.

379. Gull, Cloyd Dake: "Keeping Informed about Current Work," *American Documentation,* **18**:252-253, Oct. 1967.

380. Gull, Cloyd Dake: "Logical Flow Charts and Other New Techniques for the Administration of Libraries and Information Centers," *Library Resources and Technical Services,* **12**:47-66, Winter 1968.

381. Gull, Cloyd Dake: "Personnel Requirements for Automation in Libraries," in J. F. Harvey (ed.), *Data Processing in Public and University Libraries,* Spartan, Washington, 1966, pp. 125-141.

382. Gull, Cloyd Dake: "Possibility of a Subject Index for the National Union Catalog," *Southeastern Librarian,* **16**:20-26, Spring 1966.

383. Gull, Cloyd Dake: "Posting for the Interm System of Coordinate Indexing," *American Documentation,* **7**:9-21, Jan. 1956.

384. Gull, Cloyd Dake: "The Present State of Library Automation: A Study in Reluctant Leadership," *Clinic on Library Applications of Data Processing, University of Illinois, 3rd, 1965, Proceedings,* Illinois Union Bookstore, Champaign, Ill., 1966, pp. 1-14.

385. Gull, Cloyd Dake: "Structure of Indexing Authority Lists, *Library Resources and Technical Services,* **10**:507-511, Fall 1966.

386. Gull, Cloyd Dake: "Technological Advances in Medical Librarianship, a Symposium: Mechanization, Implications for the Medium-size Medical Library," *Medical Library Association Bulletin,* **23**:269-271, May 1967.

387. Haas, Warren J.: "Computer Simulations at the Columbia University Libraries," in Herbert Goldhor (ed.), *Clinic on Library Applications of Data Processing, University of Illinois, 2d, 1964, Proceedings,* Illinois Union Bookstore, Champaign, Ill., 1965, pp. 36-46.

388. Hage, Elizabeth B.: "An Administrator's Approach to Automation at the Prince George's County (Maryland) Memorial Library," *Clinic on Library Applications of Data Processing, University of Illinois, 1967, Proceedings,* Graduate School of Library Science, University of Illinois, Urbana, Ill., 1967, pp. 90-97.

389. Hage, Elizabeth B.: "Computer Potential in Maryland (Prince George's County Memorial Library)," *Wilson Library Bulletin,* **41**:401-403, Dec. 1966.

390. Hagler, Ronald: "The Place of the Book Catalog in the University Library," *PNLA Quarterly,* **28**:125-127, Jan. 1964.

391. Hake, Shirley: "Book Catalogs in the Public Library System (King County, Wash.)," *PNLA Quarterly,* **28**:132-133, 136, Jan. 1964.

392. Hale, M.: "Music Library Computerized," *Ontario Library Review,* **51**: 222-223, Dec. 1967.

393. Hamilton, Robert E.: "Illinois State Library Computer System," *Wilson Library Bulletin,* **42**:721-722, Mar. 1968.

394. Hamilton, Robert E.: "On-line Circulation System at the Illinois State Library," *The LARC Reports,* **1**(35):1-30, Dec. 1968.

395. Hammer, Donald P.: "Automated Operations in a University Library: A Summary," *College and Research Libraries,* **26**:19-29, 44, Jan. 1965.

396. Hammer, Donald P.: "Automated Procedures at Purdue University Library Serials Department, Including Binding," *Meeting on Automation in the*

Library, When, Where, and How, Purdue University, 1964, Papers, Purdue University, Lafayette, Ind., 1965, pp. 26–35.

397. Hammer, Donald P.: "Automated Serials Control in the Purdue University Libraries," *IBM Library Mechanization Symposium, Endicott, N.Y., 1964, Proceedings,* International Business Machines Corp., White Plains, N.Y., 1965, pp. 133–144.
398. Hammer, Donald P.: "Problems in the Conversion of Bibliographical Data, a Keypunching Experiment," *American Documentation,* **19**:12–17, Jan. 1968.
399. Hammer, Donald P.: "Reflections on the Development of an Automated Serials System," *Library Resources and Technical Services,* **9**:225–230, 1965.
400. Hammer, Donald P.: "Scheduling Conversion," in John Harvey (ed.), *Data Processing in Public and University Libraries,* Drexel Information Science Series, vol. 3, Spartan Books, Washington, 1966, pp. 103–123.
401. Hampel, Viktor, R. J. Howerton, and John A. Wade: *A Computerized Library and Evaluation System for Integral Neutron Experiments,* Lawrence Radiation Laboratory, Livermore, Calif., 1969. UCRL-71584 Rev. 1.
402. Hampel, Viktor, and John A. Wade: "'Master Control'—a Unifying Free-form Data Storage and Data Retrieval System for Dissimilar Bases (work performed under the auspices of the U.S. Atomic Energy Commission)," *Proceedings of the American Society for Information Science, 32nd Annual Meeting, San Francisco, California, October 1-4, 1969,* **6**:159–174, Greenwood, Westport, Conn., 1969.
403. Hanson, D. G.: "A Computer Program to Maintain a Subject Index on Magnetic Tape in Alphabetical and Classified Order. *Program,* **1**:6–12, Jan. 1968.
404. Hare, Van Court: Systems Analysis: A Diagnostic Approach, Harcourt, Brace & World, New York, *c* 1967, 544 pp.
405. Haring, Donald R.: "Computer-driven Display Facilities for an Experimental Computer-based Library, *AFIPS Conference Proceedings* **33**(1):255–265, Thompson, Washington, 1968.
406. Haring, Donald R.: "Display Console for an Experimental Computer-based Augmented Library Catalog, *Association for Computing Machinery Conference, 1968, Princeton, N.J., Proceedings,* Branden Systems Press, London, 1968, pp. 35–43.
407. Harris, Ira: "Reader Services Aspects of Book Catalogs," *Library Resources and Technical Services,* 8:391–398, 1964.
408. Harris, Michael H.: "The 357 Data Collection System for Circulation Control," *College and Research Libraries,* **26**:119–120, Mar. 1965.
409. Harris, Neville: "Pilot Projects Using Variable Length Library Records," *Program,* **1**:13–16, Jan. 1968.
410. Harris, Robert: "Circulation Control in the U.B.C. Library," *C.A.C.U.L. Workshop on Library Automation, University of British Columbia, 1967,* Canadian Association of College and University Libraries, Ottawa, 1967, pp. 93–96.
411. Harrison, David F.: "An Automated Music Programmer (MUSPROG)," *Journal of Library Automation,* **2**:1–9, Mar. 1969.
412. Harvey, J. F., ed.: *Data Processing in Public and University Libraries:*

Combined Proceedings of the Drexel Conference on Data Processing in Public Libraries, 1965, Spartan, Washington, 1966, 150 pp.

413. Hayes, Robert M.: "Automation and the Library of Congress: Three Views: Information Scientist," *Library Quarterly,* **34**:229–232, July 1964.

414. Hayes, Robert M.: "The Concept of an On-line, Total System," *Library Technology Reports,* American Library Association, Chicago, May, 1965, 13 pp.

415. Hayes, Robert M.: "The Development of a Methodology for System Design and Its Role in Library Education," *The Intellectual Foundations of Library Education: The Twenty-ninth Annual Conference of the Graduate Library School, July 6–8, 1964,* University of Chicago Press, Chicago, 1965, pp. 51–63.

416. Hayes, Robert M.: "Library-handling Books and the Contents," in R. W. Gerard (ed.), *Computers and Education,* McGraw-Hill, New York, 1967, pp. 119–150.

417. Hayes, Robert M.: "Library Systems Analysis," in John Harvey (ed.), *Data Processing in Public and University Libraries,* Drexel Information Science Series, vol. 3, Spartan Books, Washington, 1966, pp. 5–20.

418. Hayes, Robert M.: "The Meaning of Automation to the Library Profession," *PNLA Quarterly,* **27**:7–16, Oct. 1962.

419. Hayes, Robert M.: *Mechanized Information Services in the University Library—Introduction and Summary,* Institute of Library Research, University of California, Los Angeles, 1967, 15 pp.

420. Hayes, Robert M., Ralph M. Shoffner, and David C. Weber: "The Economics of Book Catalog Production," *Library Resources and Technical Services,* **10**:57–90, 1966.

421. Heiliger, Edward: "Application of Advanced Data Processing Techniques to University Library Procedures," *Special Libraries,* **53**:472–475, Oct. 1962.

422. Heiliger, Edward: "La Documentacion Cientifica en los Estados Unidos," *Seminario Latino Americano sobre Documentacion Cientifica, Lima, 3–8 Septiembre de 1962, Conferencia V,* Centro de Cooperacion Cientifica de la UNESCO para America Latina, Montevideo, Uruguay, 1962, pp. 1–13.

423. Heiliger, Edward M.: "Florida Atlantic University Library," *Clinic on Library Applications of Data Processing, University of Illinois, 3rd, 1965, Proceedings,* Illinois Union Book Store, Champaign, Ill., 1966, pp. 92–111.

424. Heiliger, Edward M.: "Florida Atlantic University: New Libraries on New Campuses," *College and Research Libraries,* **25**:181–185, May 1964.

425. Heiliger, Edward M.: "Staffing a Computer Based Library," *Library Journal,* **89**:2738–2739, July 1964.

426. Heiliger, Edward M.: "Use of a Computer at Florida Atlantic University Library for Mechanized Catalog Production," *IBM Library Mechanization Symposium, Endicott, N.Y., 1964, Proceedings,* International Business Machines Corp., White Plains, N.Y., 1965, pp. 165–186.

427. Henderson, James W., and Joseph Rosenthal, eds.: *Library Catalogs: Their Preservation and Maintenance by Photographic and Automated Techniques,* M.I.T., Cambridge, 1968, 267 pp.

428. Henderson, John D.: "The Book Catalogs of the Los Angeles County Public Library," *Clinic on Library Applications of Data Processing, University of*

Illinois, 1st, 1963, Proceedings, Illinois Union Bookstore, Champaign, Ill., 1964, pp. 18–32.

429. Henry, Otha, and Matt Roberts: "The Evolution of Automated Circulation Procedures in the Washington University Libraries," *The LARC Reports,* **1** (11):1–27, July 1968.

430. Herner, Saul: "System Design, Evaluation, and Costing," *Special Libraries,* 58:576–581, Oct. 1967.

431. Hersey, C. F., and W. Hammond: "Computer Usage in the Development of a Water Resources Thesaurus," *American Documentation,* **18**:209–215, Oct. 1967.

432. Hewitson, Theodore: "The Book Catalog of the Los Angeles County Public Library: Its Function and Use," *Library Resources and Technical Services,* **4**: 228–232, 1960.

433. Hickey, Doralyn J.: "Bridging the Gap between Cataloging and Information Retrieval," *Library Resources and Technical Services,* **11**:178–183, Spring 1967.

434. Highum, Clayton D.: "Cataloging for Document Retrieval at Florida Atlantic University," *College and Research Libraries,* **25**:197–199, May 1964.

435. Highum, Clayton D.: *Centralized Processing for Public Libraries in Illinois.* Illinois State Library Research Series, no. 10, Springfield, 1967, 115 pp. ED 018 226.

436. Hines, Theodore C.: "Computer Manipulation of Classification Notations," *Journal of Documentation* **23**:216–223, Sept. 1967.

437. Hines, Theodore C.: "Computers, Supervisors, Libraries," *ALA Bulletin,* **62**:153–157, Feb. 1968.

438. Hines, Theodore C., and Jessica L. Harris: *Computer Filing of Index, Bibliographic, and Catalog Entries,* Bro-Dart Foundation, Newark, N.J., 1966, 126 pp.

439. Hirst, Robert I.: "Adapting the IBM MT/ST (Magnetic Tape "Selectric" Typewriter) for Library Applications—A Manual for Planning," *Special Libraries,* 59:626–633, Oct. 1968.

440. Hoffer, J. R.: "Relationship of Natural and Social Sciences to Social Problems and the Contribution of the Information Scientist to Their Solutions," *American Documentation,* 18:228–234, Oct. 1967.

441. Holt, G. A., et al.: "The IBM Selectric Composer," *IBM Journal of Research & Development* **12**:2–91, Jan. 1968.

442. Holzbaur, Frederick W., and Eugene H. Farris: *Library Information Processing Using an On-line, Real-time Computer System,* International Business Machines Corp., Poughkeepsie, N.Y., 1966, 47 pp. TR 00. 1548.

443. Holzbauer, Herbert: *Mechanized Bibliography of Documentation and Information Sciences,* U.S. Department of the Interior, Jan. 1967, 166 pp. Also Supplement no. 1, Aug. 1967. 47 pp. AD 656 550.

444. Holzbauer, Herbert: "Trends in Announcement, Searching and Retrieval Services," *Special Libraries,* **49**:105, Feb. 1968.

445. Honnold Library: *Acquisitions Department and Computer Cataloging Instructions,* Honnold Library, Claremont, Calif., 1966, 40 pp.

446. Horty, J. F.: "Electronic Data Retrieval in Legal Research," *Law Library Journal,* **60**:387–397, Nov. 1967.

447. Horty, J. F.: "Retrieval of Statutory and Case Law," *1965 Computer Law Institute,* Washington, Dec. 1965.

448. Housman, Edward M.: "Survey of Current Systems for Selective Dissemination of Information (SDI)," *Proceedings of the American Society for Information Science, 32nd Annual Meeting, San Francisco, California, October 1-4, 1969,* 6:57-61, Greenwood, Westport, Conn., 1969.

449. Howerton, R. J., et al.: "ECSIL. A System for Storage, Retrieval and Display of Experimental Neutron Data," *An Integrated System for Production of Neutronics and Photonics Calculational Constants,* vol. 1, Lawrence Radiation Laboratory, Livermore, Calif., 1968. UCRL-50400.

450. Humphrey, James: "The Computer as Art Cataloguer," *Computers and the Humanities,* **1**:164-169, May 1967.

451. Hunt, C. J.: "Computer Production of Catalogues of Old Books," in N. S. M. Cox and M. W. Grose (eds.), *Organization and Handling of Bibliographic Records by Computer,* Archon, Hamden, Conn., 1967, pp. 137-149.

452. "IBM Computer in the Stocks," *Data Processor,* vol. 12, no. 3, July 1969.

453. *Implementation of BALANCE (Bay Areas Libraries Associated Network for Cooperative Exchange) Phases I and II: Book Catalog Production,* Santa Clara Valley Library System, Santa Clara, Calif., 1966, 52 pp.

454. *Implementing Centralized Processing for the Public Libraries of New York State,* report to the Board of Trustees of the Association of New York Libraries for Technical Services, Nelson Associates, Inc., New York, Nov. 1967, 35 pp. ED 023 431.

455. Information Science and Automation Division: *Library Automation, a State-of-the-art Review,* papers presented at the Preconference Institute on Library Automation held at San Francisco, Calif., June 22-24, 1967, American Library Association, 1969, 175 pp.

456. *Information Systems Operation: A Final Report on Improving Information Flow in a University Library,* prepared under contract with the University of Illinois, Defense Systems Department, General Electric Co., Washington, 1961, 113 pp.

457. *Information Systems Section,* resource data developed for the contract with the University of Illinois, Defense Systems Department, General Electric Co., Washington, 1961, 90 pp.

458. Institute of Library Research: *Developmental Program for a Center for Information Services,* University of California, Los Angeles, Dec. 15, 1967, 41 pp.

459. Institute of Library Research: *Preliminary Specifications (Hardware and Software) for a Center for Information Services,* University of California, Los Angeles, Dec. 15, 1967, 43 pp.

460. Intergovernmental Task Force on Information Systems: *The Dynamics of Information Flow: Recommendation to Improve the Flow of Information within and among Federal, State, and Local Governments,* Washington, Apr. 1968, 37 pp. PB-178 307.

461. International Business Machines Corporation, Federal Systems Division: *Report of a Pilot Project for Converting the Pre-1952 National Union Catalog to a Machine Readable Record,* a study sponsored by the Council on Library Resources, Inc., Rockville, Md., 1965, 52 pp., appendices.

462. *Intersystem Compatibility and Convertibility of Subject Vocabularies,* Auerbach Corp. Report to the National Agricultural Library, Auerbach Corp., Philadelphia, May 1969. 1582-100-TR5.

463. Interuniversity Communications Council: "Functioning Media Networks," *EDUCOM,* **3**:2–4, May 1968.

464. *INTREX: Semi-annual Activity Report, 15 March 1968 to 15 September, 1968,* M.I.T., Cambridge, Mass., 1968.

465. "Iowa Colleges Plan Regional Computer Network," *Communications of the ACM,* **11**:584, Aug. 1968.

466. Irwin, Manley R.: "Government Policy Implications in Data Management," *Datamation,* **14**:37–40, June 1968.

467. Irwin, Manley R.: "Time-shared Information Systems: Market Entry in Search of a Policy," *AFIPS Conference Proceedings, 1967 Fall Joint Computer Conference,* vol. 31, Thompson, Washington, 1967, pp. 513–520.

468. "ITT's Expanding Network Adds Time-sharing Service," *Datamation,* **14**: 100, 105, June 1968.

469. Jackson, Eugene B.: "The Use of Data Processing Equipment by Libraries and Information Centers—The Significant Results of the SLA-LTP Survey," *Special Libraries,* 58:317-327, June 1967.

470. Jackson, Ivan F.: An Approach to Library Automation Problems, *College and Research Libraries,* **28**:133–137, Mar. 1967.

471. Jacob, Mary Ellen: "Standard Format for Data Exchange," *Special Libraries,* 59:258–260, Apr. 1968.

472. Jahoda, Gerald: *Information Storage and Retrieval for Individual Researchers,* Wiley, New York, 1970.

473. Jahoda, Gerald, and Ferrol Ann Accola: "Library Records Prepared with the Aid of Data Processing Equipment," *College and Research Libraries,* **26**: 129–137, Mar. 1965.

474. Jahoda, Gerald, and M. Culnan: "Unanswered Science and Technology Reference Questions: With Suggestions for Improving the Bibliographic Apparatus, *American Documentation,* **19**:95–100, Jan. 1968.

475. Jenkins, Francis B., ed.: *Proceedings of the 1965 Clinic on Library Applications of Data Processing, University of Illinois Graduate School of Library Science,* Illinois Union Bookstore, Champaign, Ill., *c* 1966, 201 pp.

476. Jennings, Michael: "The CDS of Library Automation," *PNLA Quarterly,* **32**: 12–17, Jan. 1968.

477. Johns, Loeta: "P (acific) N (orthwest) B (ook) C (atalog) Past and Future," *PNLA Quarterly,* **28**:120–123, Jan. 1964.

478. Johnson, H. R.: "Computers and the Public Welfare: Law Enforcement, Social Services and Data Banks," in *Computer Communications Symposium, University of California at Los Angeles, 20–22 March, 1967, Computers and Communications—Toward a Computer Utility,* Prentice-Hall, Englewood Cliffs, N.J., 1967, pp. 173–190.

479. Johnson, Richard D.: "A Book Catalog at Stanford," *Journal of Library Automation,* **1**:13–50, Mar. 1968.

480. Johnson, Richard D.: "Book Catalog for the Undergraduate Library," *Stanford University Libraries Bulletin,* **27**:87–88, July 16, 1965.

481. Johnson, Ted: "Dial, Remote and Random," *ALA Bulletin,* **62**:1085-1088, Oct. 1968.

482. Joliffe, John: "Tactics of Converting a Catalogue to Machine-readable Form," *Journal of Documentation,* **24**:149-158, Sept. 1968.

483. Jones, H. W.: "Computerized Subscription and Periodicals Routing in an Aerospace Library," *Special Libraries,* 58:634-638, Nov. 1967.

484. Jones, Robert C.: "A Book Catalog for Libraries—Prepared by Camera and Computer (The Junior College District of St. Louis)," *Library Resources and Technical Services,* **9**:205-206, 1965.

485. Jordan, John R.: "A Framework for Comparing SDI (Selective Dissemination of Information) Systems," *American Documentation,* **19**:221-222, July 1968.

486. Jordan, John R.: "Let the Computer Select Your Reading List (KWOC Indexes)," *Datamation,* **16**:91-97, Feb. 1970.

487. Jordan, J. R., and W. J. Watkins: "KWOC Index as an Automatic By-product of SDI," *Proceedings of the American Society for Information Science, Annual Meeting, Columbus, Ohio, October 20-24, 1968,* vol. 5, Greenwood, New York, *c* 1968, pp. 211-215.

488. Kaltwasser, F. G.: "Elektronische Kataloge in Bibliotheken," *Verband Bibl Landes Nordrhein-Westfalen Mitt.,* **15**:67-85, July 15, 1965, Electronic catalogs in libraries.

489. Kanasy, J. Emery: "Circulation Control Systems," *C.A.C.U.L. Workshop on Library Automation, University of British Columbia, 1967,* Canadian Association of College and University Libraries, Ottawa, 1967, pp. 76-88.

490. Kaplan, Sidney J.: "The Advancing Communication Technology and Computer Communication Systems," *AFIPS Conference Proceedings, 1968 Spring Joint Computer Conference,* vol. 32, Thompson, Washington, 1968, pp. 119-133.

491. Kayton, I.: "Retrieving Case Law by Computer: Fact, Fiction, and Future," *George Washington Law Review,* **35**:1-49, Oct. 1966.

492. Kellogg, C. H.: *CONVERSE—A System for the On-line Description and Retrieval of Structural Data Using Natural Language,* System Development Corporation, Santa Monica, Calif., 1967. SP-2635/000/00.

493. Kemeny, J. G., and T. E. Kurtz: *The Dartmouth Time-sharing Computing System: Final Report,* Dartmouth College, Hanover, N.H., 1967.

494. Kennedy, James H., and Merle N. Boylan: *IBM 1401 Computer Produced and Maintained Printed Book Catalogs at the Lawrence Radiation Laboratory,* Lawrence Radiation Laboratory, Livermore, Calif., 1964, 25 pp. UCRL 7555.

495. Kennedy, John P.: "A Local MARC Project: The Georgia Tech Library," *Clinic on Library Applications of Data Processing, 6th, University of Illinois, Urbana, 5-8 May, 1968, Proceedings,* in press, preprint, 19 pp.

496. Kennedy, R. A.: "Bell Laboratories; Library Real-time Load System (BELLREL)," *Journal of Library Automation,* **1**:128-146, June 1968.

497. Kenney, Brigitte L., and Patricia M. Hutchins: "First Steps toward an Automated Serials System," *Reminder,* **25**:1-38, May 1968.

498. Kent, Allen, ed.: *Library Planning for Automation,* Spartan, Washington, 1965, 193 pp.

499. Kent, Allen: *Specialized Information Centers,* Spartan, Washington, 1965.

500. Kent, Allen: *Textbook on Mechanized Information Retrieval,* Interscience-Wiley, New York, *c* 1962, 268 pp.

501. Kershaw, George, and J. Eugene Davis: "Mechanization in Defense Libraries," *Datamation,* **14**:48–50, 53, Jan. 1968.

502. Kessler, M. M.: "Search Strategies of the M.I.T. Technical Information Program," *Institute on Information Retrieval, 1965, University of Minnesota,* information retrieval with special reference to the biomedical sciences, Nolte Center for Continuing Education, University of Minnesota, Minneapolis, 1966, pp. 23–27.

503. Kieffer, Paula: "The Baltimore County Public Library Book Catalog," *Library Resources and Technical Services,* **10**:133–141, 1966.

504. Kikuchl, T.: "Scientific and Technical Information in Japan," *American Documentation,* **18**:250–252, Oct. 1967.

505. Kilgour, Frederick G.: "Basic Systems Assumptions of the Columbia-Harvard-Yale Medical Libraries Computerization Project," *Institute on Information Retrieval, 1965, University of Minnesota,* information retrieval with special reference to the biomedical sciences, Nolte Center for Continuing Education, University of Minnesota, Minneapolis, 1966, pp. 145–154.

506. Kilgour, Frederick G.: "Comprehensive Modern Library Systems: Brasenose Conference on the Automation of Libraries, Oxford, England, 1966," *Proceedings of the Anglo-American Conference on the Mechanization of Library Services,* Mansell, London and Chicago, 1967, pp. 45–56.

507. Kilgour, Frederick G.: "Costs of Library Catalog Cards Produced by Computer," *Journal of Library Automation,* **1**:121–127, June 1968.

508. Kilgour, Frederick G.: "Development of Computerization of Catalogs in Medical and Scientific Libraries," *Clinic on Library Applications of Data Processing, University of Illinois, 2nd, 1964, Proceedings,* Illinois Union Bookstore, Champaign, Ill., 1965, pp. 25–35.

509. Kilgour, Frederick G.: "Implications for the Future of Reference/Information Service," *Conference on the Present Status and Future Prospects of Reference/Information Service, 1966, Columbia University: Present Status and Future Prospects of Reference/Information Service,* American Library Association, Chicago, 1967, pp. 172–183.

510. Kilgour, Frederick G.: "Initial System Design for the Ohio College Library Center: A Case History," *Clinic on Library Application of Data Processing, 6th, University of Illinois, Urbana, 5–8 May, 1968, Proceedings,* Graduate School of Library Science, University of Illinois, Urbana, in press, preprint, 21 pp.

511. Kilgour, Frederick G.: "Library Catalogue Production on Small Computers," *American Documentation,* **17**:124–131, July 1966.

512. Kilgour, Frederick G.: "Mechanization of Cataloging Procedures," *Medical Library Association Bulletin,* **53**:152–162, Apr. 1965.

513. Kilgour, Frederick G.: "Recorded Use of Books in the Yale Medical Library," *American Documentation,* **12**:266–269, Oct. 1961.

514. Kilgour, Frederick G.: "A Regional Network—Ohio College Library Center," *Datamation,* **16**:87–90, Feb. 1970.

515. Kilgour, Frederick G.: "Retrieval of Single Entries from a Computerized Library Catalog File," *Proceedings of the American Society for Information*

Science, Annual Meeting, Columbus, Ohio, October 20-24, 1968, 5:133-136, Greenwood, New York, 1968.

516. Kilgour, Frederick G.: "Systems Concepts and Libraries," *College and Research Libraries,* **28**:167-170, May 1967.

517. Kilgour, Frederick G.: "University Libraries and Computation," *Drexel Library Quarterly,* **4**:157-176, July 1968.

518. Kimber, Richard T.: *Automation in Libraries,* International Series of Monographs in Library and Information Science, vol. 10, Pergamon Press, Oxford, Eng., 140 pp.

519. Kimber, Richard T.: "Computer Applications in the Fields of Library Housekeeping and Information Processing," *Program,* **1**:5-25, July 1967.

520. Kimber, Richard T.: "Conversational Circulation," *LIBRI,* **17**(2):131-141, 1967.

521. Kimber, Richard T.: "The Cost of an On-line Circulation System," *Program,* **2**:81-94, Oct. 1968.

522. Kimber, Richard T.: "The MARC II Format," *Program,* **2**:34-40, Apr. 1968.

523. Kimber, Richard T.: "An Operational Computerized Circulation System with On-line Interrogation Capability," *Program,* **2**:75-80, Oct. 1968.

524. Kimber, Richard T.: "Studies at the Queen's University of Belfast on Real-time Computer Control of Book Circulation," *Journal of Documentation,* **22**: 116-122, June 1966.

525. King, Donald W.: "Design and Evaluation of Information Systems," *Annual Review of Information Science and Technology, 1968,* vol. 3, Encyclopaedia Britannica, Chicago, 1968, pp. 62-103.

526. King, Gilbert W.: "Automation and the Library of Congress: Three Views: Chairman of Survey Team," *Library Quarterly,* **34**:234-239, July 1964.

527. King, Gilbert W., et al.: *Automation and the Library of Congress,* U.S. Government Printing Office, 1963, 88 pp.

528. Kingery, Robert Ernest, and Maurice F. Tauber, eds.: *Book Catalogs,* Scarecrow Press, New York, 1963, 330 pp.

529. Knapp, John F.: "Design Considerations for the MARC Magnetic Tape Formats," *Library Resources and Technical Services,* **12**:275-285, Summer 1968.

530. Kochen, Manfred, ed.: *The Growth of Knowledge: Readings on Organization and Retrieval of Information,* Wiley, New York, 1967, 394 pp.

531. Kochen, Manfred: "Newer Techniques for Processing Bibliographic Information," *Drexel Library Quarterly,* **4**:233-258, July 1968.

532. Kochen, Manfred, ed.: *Some Problems in Information Science,* Scarecrow Press, New York, 1965, 309 pp.

533. Kochen, Manfred, and Renata Tagliacozzo: "Book-indexes as Building Blocks for a Cumulative Index," *American Documentation,* **18**:59-66, 1967.

534. Kochen, Manfred, and Renata Tagliacozzo: "A Study of Cross-referencing," *Journal of Documentation,* **24**:173-191, Sept. 1968.

535. Kottenstette, James P.: "Student Reading Characteristics: Comparing Skill-levels Demonstrated on Hardcopy and Microform Presentation," *Proceedings of the American Society for Information Science, 32nd Annual Meeting, San Francisco, California, October 1-4, 1969,* 6:345-349, Greenwood, Westport, Conn., 1969.

536. Kountz, John C.: "Computers Now: Public Libraries and a Happy Union," *ALA Bulletin,* **62**:683-687, June 1968.

537. Kountz, John C.: "Cost Comparison of Computer versus Manual Cataloging Maintenance," *Journal of Library Automation,* **1**:159-177, Sept. 1968.

538. Kountz, John C., and Robert E. Norton: "Biblios—A Modular Approach to Total Library ADP," *Proceedings of the American Society for Information Science, 32nd Annual Meeting, San Francisco, California, October 1-4, 1969,* **6**:39-50, Greenwood, Westport, Conn., 1969.

539. Kountz, John C., and Robert E. Norton: "Biblios—A Modular System for Library Automation," *Datamation,* Feb. 1970.

540. Kozlow, Robert D.: *Report on a Library Project Conducted on the Chicago Campus of the University of Illinois,* National Science Foundation, Washington, 1966, various paging. NSF Grants 77 and 302.

541. Kozumplik, William A.: "Time and Motion Study of Library Operations," *Special Libraries,* 58:585-588, Oct. 1967.

542. Kozumplik, William A., and R. T. Lange: "Computer-produced Microfilm Library Catalog," *American Documentation* **18**:67-80, Apr. 1967.

543. Kraft, Donald H.: *Total Systems Approach to Library Mechanization,* Texas State Library (Austin) Monograph no. 6, Texas Library and Historical Commission, Austin, 1966, pp. 7-12. Available on loan from LOCATE, Library of Congress, Washington, 20540.

544. Kretzmer, E. R.: "Modern Techniques for Data Communication over Telephone Channels," *Congress of the International Federation for Information Processing (IFIP), 4th, Edinburgh, 5-10 August, 1968, Proceedings,* North-Holland Publishing, Amsterdam, 1968.

545. Krikelas, James: "Library Applications of Data Processing: An Emunerative Bibliography, 1964-65," *Clinic on Library Applications of Data Processing, University of Illinois, 4th, 1966, Proceedings,* Illinois Union Bookstore, Champaign, Ill., 1966, pp. 211-218.

546. Krinos, John D.: "Conversion of Existing Library Catalogues to Computer Files," presented at the fifth National Colloquium on Information Retrieval, Philadelphia, May 4, 1968, Hamilton Standard, Farmington, Conn., Jan. 1968, 11 pp. SP 01U68.

547. Kurmey, William J.: "Management Implications of Mechanization, "*C.A.C.-U.L. Workshop on Library Automation, University of British Columbia, 1967,* Canadian Association of College and University Libraries, Ottawa, 1967, pp. 116-123.

548. Laden, H. N., and T. R. Gildersleeve: *System Design for Computer Applications,* Wiley, New York, 1963. SBN-471-51135-8.

549. Lamkin, Burton E.: "Systems Analysis in Top Management Communication," *Special Libraries,* 58:90-94, Feb. 1967.

550. Lancaster, F. W.: "On the Need for Role Indicators in Post-coordinate Retrieval Systems," *American Documentation,* **19**:42-46, Jan. 1968.

551. Landau, Herbert B.: "Design Criteria for a Multi-input Data Base for the National Agricultural Library," *Proceedings of the American Society for Information Science, 32nd Annual Meeting, San Francisco, California, October 1-4, 1969,* **6**:101-104, Greenwood, Westport, Conn., 1969.

552. Lane, David O.: "Automatic Catalog Card Production (Boston University)," *Library Resources and Technical Services,* **10**:383-386, 1966.

553. Laucus, Carol A., and Susan Russell: *Serials Automation Project at Baker Library: Preliminary Report.* Graduate School of Business Administration, Harvard University, Boston, 1966, 47 pp.

554. Lazerow, Samuel: "Progress in Serials Data Planning," *Library of Congress Information Bulletin,* 27:41–42, Jan. 25, 1968.

555. Lazerow, Samuel: "The U.S. National Libraries Task Force: An Instrument for National Library Cooperation," *Special Libraries,* 50:698–703, Nov. 1968.

556. Lazorick, Gerald J.: *Proposal for a Real-time Circulation System,* in collaboration with Hugh Atkinson and John Herling, University Libraries, State University of New York, Buffalo, 1966, 10 pp.

557. Lazorick, Gerald J.: *Proposal for Conversion of Shelf List Bibliographic Information to Machine Readable Form and Production of Book Indexes to Shelf List,* in collaboration with Hugh Atkinson and John Herling, University Libraries, State University of New York, Buffalo, 1966, 13 pp.

558. Lazorick, Gerald J., and Hugh C. Atkinson: *Gift and Exchange Department Automation Study,* State University of New York, Buffalo, 1965, 2 pp.

559. Lazorick, Gerald J., and John P. Herling: "A Real Time Library Circulation System without Prepunched Cards," *American Documentation Institute: Proceedings, Levels of Interaction between Man and Information,* Thompson, Washington; Academic Press, London, 1967, pp. 202–206.

560. Leach, Theodore Edward: "A Compendium of the MARC System," *Library Resources and Technical Services,* 12:250–275, Summer 1968.

561. Lebowitz, A. I.: "Mechanized System for Cataloging and Indexing Legislative Materials at the U.S. Atomic Energy Commission Headquarters Library," master's thesis, Catholic University of America, Washington, 1966, 63 pp.

562. Leffler, William L.: "A Statistical Method for Circulation Analysis," *College and Research Libraries,* 15:488–490, Nov. 1964.

563. Leimkuhler, Ferdinand F.: "Bradford Distribution (of References in a Collection of Pertinent Source Documents)," *Journal of Documentation,* 23: 197–207, Sept. 1967.

564. Leimkuhler, Ferdinand F.: "Mathematical Models for Library Systems Analysis," *Drexel Library Quarterly,* 4:185–196, July 1968.

565. Leimkuhler, Ferdinand F.: "Operations Research in the Purdue Libraries," *Meeting on Automation in the Library, When, Where, and How, Purdue University, 1964, Papers,* Purdue University, Lafayette, Ind., 1965, pp. 82–89.

566. Leimkuhler, Ferdinand F.: "System Analysis in University Libraries," *College and Research Libraries,* 27:13–18, Jan. 1966.

567. Leimkuhler, Ferdinand F., and Anthony F. Neville: "The Uncertain Future of the Library," *Wilson Library Bulletin,* 43:30–38, Sept. 1968.

568. Leiter, Joseph, and Cloyd Dake Gull: "The MEDLARS System in 1968," *American Society for Information Science, Annual Meeting, Columbus, Ohio, 20–24 October, 1968, Proceedings,* vol. 5, Greenwood, New York, 1968, pp. 255–262.

569. Leonard, Lawrence E., Joan M. Maier, and Richard M. Dougherty: *Colorado Academic Libraries Book Processing Center Study,* final report, Feb. 1, 1967–Apr. 30, 1968, on phases 1 and 2, Norlin Library, University of Colorado, Boulder, June 15, 1968, 397 pp. PB-178-421.

570. Leondar, Judith C., et al.: "Workshop Proceedings, Report Literature and Sources of Information," *Special Libraries,* 59:84-106, Feb. 1968.

571. Lesser, Richard C., and Anthony Ralston: "The Development of a Multi-campus Regional Computing Center," *Congress of the International Federation for Information Processing (IFIP), 4th, Edinburgh, 5-10 August, 1968. Proceedings,* North-Holland Publishing, Amsterdam, 1968.

572. Levy, F.: "Operational Study on Scientific Information Processing: General Economy of a Mechanized Documentation Chain," *UNESCO Bulletin of Libraries,* **21**:230-239, Sept. 1967.

573. Levy, Richard P., and Maxine R. Cammarn: "Information Systems Applications in Medicine," *Annual Review of Information Science and Technology,* vol. 3, Encyclopaedia Brittanica, Chicago, 1968.

574. Lewis, Anita: "General Systems—The Language Control Sub-system of ALPHA," *Automation in Libraries: First ATLIS Workshop, 15-17 November, 1966,* Redstone Scientific Information Center, Redstone Arsenal, Ala., 1967, pp. 29-48. AD 654 766.

575. Lewis, Peter R.: "The Present Range of Documentation Services in the Social Sciences," *ASLIB Proceedings,* **17**(2):40-49, Feb. 1965.

576. Libbey, M. A., and A. R. Blum: *A Study of Information Elements for the National Information System for Physics,* American Institute of Physics, New York, 1968, 62 pp. ED 025 273.

577. Liberman, E.: *Descriptors and Computer Codes Used in Naval Ordnance Laboratory Library Retrieval Program,* Naval Ordnance Lab., White Oak, Md., Dec. 1964, pp. 288. Noltr-64-20, AD-708404.

578. "Libraries of the Future," panel with discussion, *Law Library Journal,* **60**: 379-397, Nov. 1967.

579. *Libraries: System Requirements,* Cornell University, Ithaca, N.Y., 1965. 12 pp.

580. *Library and Information Science Abstracts* (formerly *Library Science Abstracts*), Library Association, London, 1969, 1-

581. Library Association of the City University of New York: *New Directions for the City University Libraries,* papers presented at an Institute sponsored by the Library Association of the City University of New York, Apr. 18, 1968, Kingsborough Community College Library, 1968, 72 pp.

582. *Library Automation Plan: Preliminary Statement,* University of Pittsburgh, Pittsburgh, Nov. 1966, 5 pp.

583. Library System Planning Committee: *Biomedical Library Computer Project for Serials,* University of California, Los Angeles, 1964, 6 pp.

584. *Library Technology and Architecture: Report of a Conference Held at the Harvard Graduate School of Education, February 9, 1967,* Graduate School of Education, Harvard University, Cambridge, Mass., 1968, 51 pp.

585. Licklider, J. C. R.: *Libraries of the Future,* M.I.T., Cambridge, Mass., 1965, 219 pp.

586. Lilje, Pauline, and W. David Panniman: "Initiation to Automation," *Special Libraries,* 57(10):697-700, Dec. 1966.

587. Linder, L. H.: "Comparative Costs of Document Indexing and Book Catalog-

ing," *Congress of International Federation for Documentation, FID, Washington, D.C., October 10–15, 1965, Abstracts,* 74 pp.

588. Line, Maurice B.: "Automation of Acquisition Records and Routine in the University Library, Newcastle upon Tyne," *Program,* no. 2, 4 pp, June 1966.

589. Lipetz, Ben-Ami, and Szetong T. Song: *How Many Cards per File Guide? Optimizing the Two-level File,* Research Dept., Yale University Library, New Haven, Conn., 1969.

590. Lipetz, Ben-Ami: "Influence of File Activity, File Size, and Probability of Successful Retrieval on Efficiency of File Structures," *Proceedings of the American Society for Information Science, 32nd Annual Meeting, San Francisco, California, Oct. 1–4, 1969,* **6**:175–179, Greenwood, Westport, Conn., 1969.

591. Lipetz, Ben-Ami: "Labor Costs, Conversion Costs and Compatibility in Document Control Systems," *American Documentation,* **14**:117–122, Apr. 1963.

592. Lipetz, Ben-Ami, D. E. Sparks, and P. E. Fasana: *Techniques for Machine Assisted Cataloging of Books,* Information Science Laboratory, ITEK Corp., Lexington, Mass., 1962.

593. Lipetz, Ben-Ami, and Peter Stangl: "User Clues in Initiating Searches in a Large Library Catalog," *Proceedings of the American Society for Information Science, Annual Meeting, Columbus, Ohio, October 20–24, 1968,* **5**:137–139, Greenwood, New York, 1968.

594. Lipetz, Ben-Ami, Peter Stangl, and Kathryn F. Taylor: "Performance of Ruecking's Word-compression Method When Applied to Machine Retrieval from a Library Catalog," *Journal of Library Automation,* **2**:266–270, Dec. 1969.

595. Little, John L., and Calvin N. Mooers: "Standards for User Procedures and Data Formats in Automated Information Systems and Networks," *AFIPS Conference Proceedings, 1968 Spring Joint Computer Conference,* vol. 32, Thompson, Washington, 1968, pp. 89–94.

596. Locke, William N.: "Computer Costs for Large Libraries," *Datamation,* **16**: 69–74, Feb. 1970.

597. Loeber, Thomas S.: "OSL (Oregon State Library) Master Book Catalog Distributed in September, or Mohammed and the Catalog," *PNLA Quarterly,* 35:5–7, Oct. 1967.

598. Logue, Paul: "Deep Indexing Technical Reports," *Journal of Chemical Documentation,* pp. 215–219, Oct. 1962.

599. Loman, D.: "Standardization in Documentation," *Journal of Documentation,* **21**(1):1–26, Mar. 1965.

600. Loukopoulas, Loukas: "Indexing Problems and Some of Their Solutions," *American Documentation,* **17**:17–25, 1966.

601. Lowry, W. K.: "New Concepts in Library Service," *Bell Laboratory Record,* **42**(1):2–7, Jan. 1964.

602. Lufkin, Richard C.: *Determination and Analysis of Some Parameters Affecting the Subject Indexing Process,* Electronic Systems Laboratory, Department of Electrical Engineering, M.I.T., Cambridge, Mass., 1968, 47 pp. ESL-364. M.I.T. Project DSR 70054.

603. Luhn, Hans Peter: "Automation and Scientific Communication," short

papers, *Proceedings of the 26th Annual Meeting of the American Documentation Institute,* New York, Oct. 1963.

604. Luhn, Hans Peter: *General Rules for Creating Machinable Records for Libraries and Special Reference Files,* IBM Corporation Advanced Systems Development Division, Yorktown Heights, N.Y., 1960.

605. Luhn, Hans Peter: "Indexing, Language, and Meaning," in M. Taube and H. Wooster (eds.), *Symposium in Information Storage and Retrieval, Theory, Systems, and Devices,* Columbia University Press, New York, 1958, pp. 208–218.

606. Luhn, Hans Peter: "Selective Dissemination of New Scientific Information with the Aid of Electronic Processing Equipment," *American Documentation,* **12**(2):131–138, Apr. 1961.

607. Lunham, Richard: "Marian the Technologist?" *SDC Magazine,* **11**:2–9, Nov. 1968.

608. Lundstedt, Sven: "Information Retrieval and Psychological Research," *Journal of Psychology,* **41**:81–86, Sept. 1965.

609. Lynch, M. F.: "Subject Indexes and Automatic Document Retrieval," *Journal of Documentation,* **22**:167–185, 1966.

References beginning with Mac and Mc are at the end of the M's.

610. Maegerlein, Robert C., Sr.: "A Simple-minded Documentation System (Internal Systems Information System—ISIS)," *Datamation,* **16**:131–132, Feb. 1970.

611. Maidment, W. R.: "Computer Methods in Public Libraries," *Program,* **2**:1–6, Apr. 1968.

612. Mallison, K.: "New Haven's Mechanized Processing: A Report," *CLA News & Views,* **9**:3–5, Mar. 1967.

613. *Management 2000: Dedication of the AFMR Manager Learning Center and Donald W. Mitchell Memorial Library, Hamilton, New York, August, 1967,* chapter, "The State of Information Retrieval and Data Processing in the Year 2000 and Its Implications for Management," *c* 1968, pp. 48–97.

614. Manning, Josephine: "Facsimile Transmission—Problems and Potential," *Library Journal,* **93**:4102–4104, Nov. 1968.

615. *MARC Project Participation,* Washington State Library, Olympia, Wash., 1966, 18 pp.

616. Markuson, Barbara Evans: "Aspects of Automation Viewed from the Library of Congress," *Clinic on Library Applications of Data Processing, University of Illinois, 5th, 1967, Proceedings,* Graduate School of Library Science, University of Illinois, Urbana, 1967, pp. 98–129.

617. Markuson, Barbara Evans: "Automation in Libraries and Information Centers," *Annual Review of Information Science and Technology,* vol. 2, Interscience-Wiley, New York, 1967, pp. 255–284.

618. Markuson, Barbara Evans: "Bibliography, Automation, and the Historian," *Bibliography and the Historian: The Conference at Belmont of the Joint Committee on Bibliographical Services to History, May, 1967,* CLIO, Santa Barbara, Calif., 1968, pp. 82–95.

619. Markuson, Barbara Evans, ed.: "Libraries and Automation," *Proceedings of the Conference on Libraries and Automation Held at Airlie Foundation, Warrenton, Virginia, May 26–30, 1963,* under the sponsorship of the Library

of Congress, National Science Foundation, and Council on Library Resources, Inc., Library of Congress, Washington, 1964, 268 pp.

620. Markuson, Barbara Evans: "The Library of Congress Automation Program: A Progress Report to the Stockholders," *ALA Bulletin,* **61**:647-655, June 1967.
621. Markuson, Barbara Evans: "An Overview of Library Systems and Automation," *Datamation,* **16**:60-68, Feb. 1970.
622. Markuson, Barbara Evans: "A System Development Study for the Library of Congress Automation Program," *Library Quarterly,* **36**:197-273, July 1966.
623. Markuson, Barbara Evans: "The United States Library of Congress Automation Survey," *UNESCO Bulletin for Libraries,* **19**:24-34, 1965.
624. Marron, Harvey: "ERIC—A National Network to Disseminate Educational Information," *Special Libraries,* **59**:775-782, Dec. 1968.
625. Marthaler, M. P., and A. K. McGurk: *Computerized IR and Catalogue Production within the ISIS (Integrated Scientific Information Service) System,* Central Library and Documentation Branch, International Labour Office, Geneva, 1967, 15 pp.
626. Martin, Frank, and Jack Banning: *Library Circulation Control at Michigan State University,* Michigan State University Library, East Lansing, Mich., 1966, 11 pp.
627. Martin, Lowell A.: "The Changes Ahead," *Library Journal,* **93**:711-716, Feb. 15, 1968.
628. *Masfile-I Pilot Project: Final Report,* Five Associated University Libraries, Syracuse, N.Y., 1969, 35 pp. ED 028 801.
629. Mather, Dan: "Data Processing in an Academic Library: Some Conclusions and Observations," *PNLA Quarterly,* **32**:4-21, Summer 1968.
630. Mathews, W. D.: "The TIP Retrieval System of MIT," in G. Schecter (ed.), *Information Retrieval: A Critical Review,* Thompson, Washington, 1967.
631. Matta, Seoud Makram: "The Card Catalog in a Large Research Library: Present Condition and Future Possibilities in the New York Public Library," doctoral thesis, Columbia University, New York, 1965, 248 pp.
632. Matthews, F. W., and D. L. Oulton: "A Simplified Computer-produced Book Catalogue," *American Documentation Institute: Levels of Interaction between Man and Information,* Thompson, Washington, 1967, pp. 191-196.
633. Meadow, C.. T.: *Analysis of Information Systems: A Programmer's Introduction to Information Retrieval,* Wiley, New York, 1967, 301 pp.
634. *Mechanization of Library Procedures, Project 1963,* Lockheed Georgia Co., Marietta, Ga., 1962.
635. *Mechanized Information Services in the University Library, Phase I: Planning,* vol. 1, parts 1-8, 340 pp., vol. 2, parts 9-13, 222 pp., Library Research Institute, University of California at Los Angeles, 1967. PB 178441 and PB 178442.
636. *Mechanized Library Procedures for the Advanced Systems Development Division Library, Los Gatos, California,* Technical Publications Department, International Business Machines Corp., White Plains, N.Y., 1967, 82 pp.
637. Meise, Norman R.: *Conceptual Design of an Automated National Library System,* Scarecrow Press, Metuchen, N.J., 1969, 243 pp.

638. Meise, Norman R.: *Increased Library Effectiveness via Automation,* paper presented at the Thirty-first National Meeting of the Operations Research Society of America, New York, June, 1967, United Aircraft Corporate Systems Center, Farmington, Conn., 1967, 16 pp.

639. Meister, D., and D. J. Sullivan: *Evaluation of User Reactions to a Prototype On-line Information Retrieval System,* Bunker-Ramo Corp., Canoga Park, Calif., Oct. 1967, 62 pp.

640. Melcher, D.: "Automation: Rosy Prospects and Cold Facts," *Library Journal,* **93**:1105–1109, March 15, 1968.

641. Melin, John S.: "Libraries and Data Processing: Where Do We Stand?" Graduate School of Library Science, Occasional Paper no. 72, University of Illinois, Urbana, 1964, 44 pp.

642. Meltzer, Morton F.: *Information Center: Management's Hidden Asset,* American Management Association, New York, 1967, 160 pp.

643. Miller, J. G.: "Design for a University Health Science Information Center," *Journal of Medical Education,* **42**:404–429, May 1967.

644. Mills, R. G.: Man-machine Communication and Problem Solving, *Annual Review of Information Science and Technology,* vol. 2, Interscience-Wiley, New York, 1967, pp. 223–254.

645. Minder, Thomas L.: *The Regional Library Center in the Mid-1970s: A Concept Paper,* School of Library and Information Sciences, University of Pittsburgh, Pittsburgh, 1968. 34 pp.

646. Minder, Thomas L., and Gerald J. Lazorick: "Automation of the Penn State University Acquisitions Department," *IBM Library Mechanization Symposium,* International Business Machines Corp., White Plains, N.Y. 1965, pp. 157–163.

647. Minker, J., and J. Sable: "File Organization and Data Management, *Annual Review of Information Science and Technology,* vol. 2, Interscience-Wiley, pp. 123–160.

648. *Modes of Bibliographic Data Base Interaction and Initial Screening of Alternate Modes,* Auerbach Corp. Report to the National Agricultural Library, Philadelphia, Mar. 1969. 1582-100-TR2.

649. Mohrhardt, Foster E.: "Emergent Library, Hybrid or Sport?" *Garden Journal of the New York Botanical Garden,* **16**:46–48, March 1966.

650. Mohrhardt, Foster E., ed.: "Science Abstracting Services, Commercial, Institutional and Personal," *Library Trends,* Jan. 1968.

651. Mohrhardt, Foster E., and Blanche L. Oliveri: "A National Network of Biological-Agricultural Libraries," *College and Research Libraries,* 28:9–16, Jan. 1967.

652. Mooers, Calvin N.: *Standards for User Procedures and Data Formats in Automated Information Systems and Networks,* in four parts, Zator Co., Cambridge, Mass., 1967. PB 177 553. PB 177 551. PB 177 552.

653. Moore, Edythe: "Systems Analysis: An Overview," *Special Libraries,* **58**: 87–90, Feb. 1967.

654. Moore, Evelyn A.: "Data Processing in the Washington University School of Medicine Library," *Institute on Information Retrieval, 1965, University of Minnesota, Information Retrieval with Special Reference to the Biomedical*

Sciences, Nolte Center for Continuing Education, University of Minnesota, Minneapolis, 1966, pp. 133–144.

655. Moore, Evelyn A., and Estelle Brodman: "Communications to the Editor: Circulation System Changes, Serial Record Changes (Washington University School of Medicine Library)," *Medical Library Association Bulletin,* 53: 99–101, Jan. 1965.

656. Moore, Evelyn A., Estelle Brodman, and Geraldine S. Cohen: "Mechanization of Library Procedures in the Medium-sized Library: III. Acquisitions and Cataloging," *Medical Library Association Bulletin,* 53:305–328, July 1965.

657. Morchand, Charles A.: *Preliminary Study for an Improved Information Transfer System for METRO Libraries,* METRO Miscellaneous Publication Series no. 2, New York Metropolitan Reference and Research Library Agency, New York, 1967, 9 pp. ED 017 301.

658. Morehouse, H. G.: *Equipment for Facsimile Transmission between Libraries: A Description and Comparative Evaluation of Three Systems,* University of Nevada Library, Reno, 1967, 30 pp. ED 021 566.

659. Morehouse, H. G.: *Telefacsimile Services between Libraries with the Xerox Magnavox Telecopier,* University of Nevada Library, Reno, 1966, 57 pp. ED 032 075.

660. Moreland, George: "Montgomery County Book Catalog," *Library Resources and Technical Services,* 8:379–389, 1964.

661. Morelock, Molete, and Ferdinand F. Leimkuhler: "Library Operations Research and Systems Engineering Studies," *College and Research Libraries,* 25:501–503, Nov. 1964.

662. Morozova, E. N.: "Some Trends in the Mechanization of Library and Bibliographical Operations at the State Public Library for Science and Technology of the USSR," *Libri,* 17:142–145, 1967.

663. Morse, Philip M.: *Library Effectiveness: A Systems Approach,* M.I.T., Cambridge, Mass., 1968, 207 pp.

664. Morse, Philip M.: "Probabilistic Models for Library Operations: With Some Comments on Library Automation," *Association of Research Libraries: Minutes of the Sixty-third Meeting, January 26, 1964,* pp. 9–19.

665. Morse, Philip M.: "The Prospect for Mechanization," *College and Research Libraries,* 25:115–119, Mar. 1964.

666. Moss, R.: "Minimum Vocabularies in Information Indexing," *Journal of Documentation,* 23:179–196, Sept. 1967.

667. Moyne, J. A.: "Information Retrieval and Natural Language," *Proceedings of the American Society for Information Science, 32nd Annual Meeting, San Francisco, California, October 1–4, 1969,* 6:259–263, Greenwood, Westport, Conn., 1969.

668. Muller, Robert H., and James W. Thomson: "The Computer-based Book Order System at the University of Michigan Library—A Review and Evaluation, *Clinic on Library Applications of Data Processing, 6th, University of Illinois, Urbana, 5–8 May, 1968, Proceedings,* in press, preprint, 19 pp.

669. Murdock, John W., and David M. Liston, Jr.: "A General Model of Information Transfer: Theme Paper 1968 Annual Convention," *American Documentation,* 18:197–208, 1967.

670. Murrill, Donald P.: "Production of Library Catalog Cards and Bulletin Using an IBM 1620 Computer and an IBM 870 Document Writing System," *Journal of Library Automation,* **1**:198-212, Sept. 1968.

671. McCabe, Charles E.: "Computer Applications in the Library of Congress Science and Technology Division," *Proceedings of the American Society for Information Science, 32nd Annual Meeting, San Francisco, California, October 1-4, 1969,* 6:63-67, Greenwood, Westport, Conn., 1969.

672. McCann, Anne: "Applications of Machines to Library Techniques: Periodicals," *American Documentation,* **12**:260-265, Oct. 1961.

673. McCaslin, O. R.: "The Book Catalog Program of the Austin Public Library: The Programmers Viewpoint," *Texas Conference on Library Mechanization, Proceedings,* Texas Library and Historical Commission, Austin, 1966.

674. McCormick, Jack: "The National Center for Atmospheric Research Library Automation Projects," *The LARC Reports,* **1**(31):1-34, Dec. 1968.

675. McCoy, Ralph E.: "Computerized Circulation Work: A Case Study of the 357 Data Collection System (Southern Illinois University)," *Library Resources and Technical Services,* 9:59-65, Winter 1965.

676. McCune, Lois C., and Stephen R. Salmon: "Bibliography of Library Automation," *ALA Bulletin* **61**:674-675, 678-694, June 1967.

677. McCurdy, May Lea: "The Book Catalog Program of the Austin Public Library: The Librarian's Viewpoint," *Texas Conference on Library Mechanization, Proceedings,* Texas Library and Historical Commission, Austin, 1966.

678. McCusker, Sister Mary Lauretta: "Implications of Automation for School Libraries," *School Libraries* **17**:23-27, Fall 1967.

679. McCusker, Sister Mary Lauretta: "Implications of Automation for School Libraries, Part 2," *School Libraries,* **18**:15-22, Fall 1968.

680. MacDonald, Ruth M.: "Book Catalogs and Card Catalogs," *Library Resources and Technical Services,* 6:217-222, 1962.

681. MacDonald, R. W.: "Serial Systems," *C.A.C.U.L. Workshop on Library Automation, University of British Columbia, 1967,* Canadian Association of College and University Libraries, Ottawa, 1967, pp. 43-48.

682. MacKenzie, A. Graham: "Systems Analysis of a University Library," *Program,* **2**:7-14, Apr. 1968.

683. McLaughlin, R. A.: "NASCOM: NASA's Communications Network for Apollo," *Datamation,* **14**:42, 44, 45, Dec. 1968.

684. McMurray, Glenn D.: "Film Library Use for the Computer," *Audio-visual Instruction,* **12**:314-320, Apr. 1967.

685. MacPherson, John F.: "Automated Acquisition at University of Western Ontario," *C.A.C.U.L. Workshop on Library Automation, University of British Columbia, 1967,* Canadian Association of College and University Libraries, Ottawa, 1967, pp. 37-42.

686. MacQuarrie, Catherine: "The Metamorphosis of the Book Catalogs (Los Angeles County Public Library)," *Library Resources and Technical Services,* 8:370-378, 1964.

687. MacQuarrie, Catherine: "A Report on the MARC Special Institute Held in Seattle, Washington, July 18-19, 1968," *The LARC Reports,* **1**(29):1-20, Sept. 1968.

688. Nance, Richard E.: "A Comparison of the Effects of Library Control Systems," doctoral thesis, Department of Industrial Engineering, Purdue University, Lafayette, Ind., 1967, 154 pp. PB 175 966.

689. Nance, Richard E.: "Systems Analysis and the Study of Information Systems," *American Documentation Institute: Levels of Interaction between Man and Information,* Thompson, Washington, 1967, pp. 70–74.

690. National Advisory Commission on Libraries: *Libraries at Large: Tradition, Innovation and the National Interest: The Resource Book Based on the Materials of the National Advisory Commission on Libraries,* Bowker, New York, 1969, 664 pp.

691. National Bureau of Standards: *Federal Information Processing Standards Series,* U.S. Department of Commerce.

692. National Library of Medicine: *The MEDLARS Story at the National Library of Medicine,* U.S. Public Health Service, 1963, 74 pp.

693. National Science Foundation: *Nonconventional Scientific and Technical Information Systems in Current Use,* no. 4, Dec. 1966.

694. "Nationwide Earth Science Computer Network Now Operational," *Communications of the ACM,* **11**:383, May 1968.

695. Neeland, Frances: *A Bibliography on Information Science and Technology,* Systems Development Corporation, Santa Monica, Calif. Published annually since 1965, in four parts each year. 1965 available as PB 169 040, PB 177 033, PB 177 034, and AD 648 562; 1966 available as AD 635 200, AD 640 572, AD 645 442, and AD 649 637. 1967 and 1968 available from the American Society for Information Science.

696. Nelson Associates, Inc.: *Centralized Processing for the Public Libraries of New York State: A Survey Conducted for the New York State Library,* in collaboration with The Theodore Stein Co., New York, 1966, 34 pp., appendices.

697. Nelson Associates, Inc.: *The Feasibility of Further Centralizing the Technical Processing Operations of the Public Libraries of New York City: A Survey Conducted for the Brooklyn Public Library, The New York Public Library, and the Queens Borough Public Library,* in collaboration with The Theodore Stein Co., New York, Nelson Associates, 1966, 45 pp.

698. Nelson, P. J.: "User Profiling for Normal Test Retrieval," *Proceedings of the American Documentation Institute, Annual Meeting, New York City,* vol. 4, 1967.

699. Nett, Roger, and Stanley A. Hetzler: *An Introduction to Electronic Data Processing,* Free Press, New York, 1959, 287 pp.

700. Newton, Gerald D.: *Statistical Report of Library Serials Mechanization for California, Oregon, and Washington,* presented at the Oregon Library Mechanization Workshop, University of Oregon, Eugene, 1968.

701. *The New York State Library's Pilot Program in the Facsimile Transmission of Library Materials: A Summary Report,* Nelson Associates, Inc., New York, June 1968, 93 pp. ED 022 501.

702. *The New York Times Thesaurus of Descriptors, a Guide for Organizing, Cataloging, Indexing, and Searching Collections of Information on Current Events,* New York Times Co., New York, *c* 1968, 15 pp.

703. Nicolaus, John J.: *The Automated Approach to Technical Information Re-*

trieval: Library Applications, Government Printing Office, 1964, 44 pp. NAVSHIPS 250-210-2.

704. Nodine, John H., and Frederic Rieders: "Poison Information by Digital Computer," *American Journal of Public Health and the Nation's Health,* 57: 1009–1014, June 1967.

705. Nolan, K. P., F. S. Cardinelli, and W. A. Kozumplik: "Mechanized Circulation Controls," *Special Libraries,* 59:47–50, Jan. 1968.

706. North, J. B.: "Look at the New COSATI (Committee on Scientific and Technical Information) Standard for the Descriptive Cataloging of Government Scientific and Technical Reports," *Special Libraries,* 58:582–584, Oct. 1967.

707. Nugent, William R.: "Compression Word Coding Techniques for Information Retrieval," *Journal of Library Automation,* **1**:250–260, Dec. 1968.

708. Nugent, William R.: "The Mechanization of the Filing Rules for the Dictionary Catalogs of the Library of Congress," *Library Resources and Technical Services,* **11**:145–166, Spring 1967.

709. Nugent, William R., *NELINET, the New England Library Information Network,* Inforonics, Inc., Cambridge, Mass., 1968, 4 pp.

710. Ofiesh, Gabriel D.: *State of the Art of Dial-access Information Retrieval,* Interim report on Library Research, Catholic University of America, Washington, Nov. 1967, 56 pp. ED 017 307.

711. Ohta, M.: "Comparison of Some Demand Subject Searches: Machine vs. Human," *Medical Library Association Bulletin,* 55:408–415, Oct. 1967.

712. *On-line Library Circulation Control System, Moffet Library, Midwestern University, Wichita Falls, Texas,* International Business Machines Corp., White Plains, N.Y., 1968, 14 pp. K-20-0271-0.

713. *On Research Libraries: Statement and Recommendations of the Committee on Research Libraries of the American Council of Learned Societies,* submitted to the National Advisory Commission on Libraries, Nov. 1967, M.I.T., Cambridge, Mass., 1969, 104 pp.

714. *An Operations Research and Systems Engineering Study,* Final Report, no. 5, Milton S. Eisenhower Library, Johns Hopkins University, Baltimore, 1968, 68 pp. PB 182 834.

715. *An Optical Character Recognition Research and Demonstration Project,* Los Angeles County Public Library, Los Angeles, 1968, 95 pp. ED 019 974.

716. Optner, Stanford L., and Associates: *Report on an Integrated Data Processing System for the Library Technical Services to the Public Library, City of Los Angeles,* Optner, Los Angeles, 1964, 71 pp.

717. Orlicky, Joseph: *The Successful Computer System: Its Planning, Development, and Management in a Business Enterprise,* McGraw-Hill, New York, 1969, 283 pp.

718. Ormsby, Jeanne: "Cuyahoga Automates!" *Ohio Library Association Bulletin,* **36**:19–21, Jan. 1966.

719. Ott, R. A.: "New Medical Communications System Being Introduced," *Illinois Medical Journal,* **133**:406–408, Apr. 1968.

720. Overhage, Carl F. J.: "Plans for Project Intrex," *Science,* **152**:1032–1037, May 1966.

721. Overhage, Carl F. J., and R. Joyce Harman, eds.: *Planning Conference on*

Information Transfer Experiments (INTREX), Woods Hole, Mass., 2 August-3 September, 1965, M.I.T., Cambridge, Mass., 1965, 276 pp.

722. Painter, Ann F.: "The Role of the Library in Relation to Other Information Activities: A State-of-the-art Review," TISA Project Report no. 23, Office of the Chief of Engineers, U.S. Department of the Army, 1968, 85 pp.

723. Palmer, Foster M.: "Computer Programming for the Librarian," *Drexel Library Quarterly,* **4**:197-213, July 1968.

724. Palmer, Foster M.: "Conversion of Existing Records in Large Libraries with Special Reference to the Widener Library Shelflist: Brasenose Conference on the Automation of Libraries, Oxford, England, 1966," John Harrison and Peter Laslett (eds.), *Proceedings of the Anglo-American Conference on the Mechanization of Library Services,* Mansell, London and Chicago, 1967, pp. 57-76.

725. Palmer, Foster M.: *Punch Card Circulation System for Widener Library-Harvard University,* Harvard University Libraries, Cambridge, Mass., 1965, 39 pp.

726. Palmerlee, Albert E.: "Automation and Map Libraries: Thoughts on Cooperative Cataloging," *Special Libraries Association Geography and Map Division Bulletin,* **69**:6-16, Sept. 1967.

727. Papazian, Pierre: "The Old Order and the New Breed: Or Will Automation Spoil Mel Dewey?" *ALA Bulletin,* **60**:644-646, June 1966.

728. Parker, Patricia E.: "The Preparation of MARC Bibliographic Data for Machine Input," *Library Resources and Technical Services,* **12**:311-319, Summer 1968.

729. Parker, Ralph H.: "Automation and the Library of Congress: Three Views: University Librarian," *Library Quarterly,* **34**:232-234, July 1964.

730. Parker, Ralph H.: "Book Catalogs," *Library Resources and Technical Services,* **8**:344-348, 1964.

731. Parker, Ralph H.: "Concept and Scope of Total Systems in Library Records," in John Harvey (ed.), *Data Processing in Public and University Libraries,* Drexel Information Science Series, vol. 3, Spartan, Washington, 1966, pp. 67-77.

732. Parker, Ralph H.: "Development of Automatic Systems at the University of Missouri Library," in Herbert Goldhor (ed.), *Clinic on Library Applications of Data Processing, University of Illinois, 1st, 1963, Proceedings,* Illinois Union Bookstore, Champaign, Ill. 1964, pp. 43-54.

733. Parker, Ralph H.: "Economic Considerations," in John Harvey (ed.), *Data Processing in Public and University Libraries,* Spartan, Washington, 1966, pp. 143-147.

734. Parker, Ralph H.: *A Feasibility Study for a Joint Computer Center for Five Washington, D.C., University Libraries,* Consortium of Universities of Metropolitan Washington, D.C., Washington, May 1968, 37 pp.

735. Parker, Ralph H.: "Library Records in a Total System: Brasenose Conference on the Automation of Libraries, Oxford, England, 1966," *Proceedings of the Anglo-American Conference on the Mechanization of Library Services,* Mansell, London and Chicago, 1967, pp. 33-45.

736. Parker, Ralph H.: "The Machine and the Librarian," *Library Resources and Technical Services,* **9**:100-103, 1965.

737. Parker, Ralph H.: "Not a Shared System: An Account of a Computer Operation Designed Specifically—and Solely—for Library Use at the University of Missouri," *Library Journal,* **92**:3967-3970, Nov. 1, 1967.

738. Parker, Ralph H.: "The Small Library Faces the Future," *ALA Bulletin,* **61**: 669-671, June 1967.

739. Parker, Ralph H.: "What a University Librarian Should Know about Computation," *Drexel Library Quarterly,* **4**:177-184, July 1968.

740. Parker, Ralph H.: "What Every Librarian Should Know about Automation," *Wilson Library Bulletin,* **38**:752-754, May 1964.

741. Patrinostro, Frank S.: "A Report on the Proceedings of Sessions 2 and 3 of the MARC Special Institute Held in Denver, Colorado, August 12-13, 1968," *The LARC Reports,* **1**(30):1-19, Sept. 1968.

742. Paxton, E. A., E. K. Bodie, and M. E. Jacob: "Integrating Major Library Functions into One Computer-oriented System," *Proceedings of the American Society for Information Science, Annual Meeting, Columbus, Ohio, October 20-24, 1968,* 5:141-149, Greenwood, New York, 1968.

743. Payne, Ladye Margarete, Louise Small, and Robert T. Divett: "Mechanization in a New Medical School Library: II. Serials and Circulation," *Medical Library Association Bulletin,* **54**:337-350, Oct. 1966.

744. Perreault, Jean M.: "Approaches to Library Filing by Computer," *Indexer,* 5:169-187, Autumn 1967.

745. Perreault, Jean M.: "The Computerized Book Catalog at Florida Atlantic University," *College and Research Libraries,* 25:185-197, May 1964.

746. Perreault, Jean M.: "Computerized Cataloging: The Computerized Catalog at Florida Atlantic University," *Library Resources and Technical Services,* 9:20-34, Winter 1965.

747. Perreault, Jean M.: "On Bibliography and Automation: Or How to Re-invent the Catalog," *Libri,* **15**:287-339, 1965.

748. Perreault, Jean M.: "The Computer and Catalog Filing Rules," *Library Resources and Technical Services,* **9**:325-331, 1965.

749. Perrine, Richard H.: "Catalog Use Difficulties," *RQ,* 7:169-174, Summer 1968.

750. Perry, J. W.: "Standardized Language in Document Selection," *Hawaii Library Association Journal,* **23**:41-59, June 1967.

751. Perry, P.: "Grouped Co-ordinate Index," *Journal of Documentation,* **22**: 329-333, Dec. 1966.

752. Peters, Claude, and Eugene Kozik: "Time-sharing Applications of Regional Data Handling," *American Society of Planning Officials National Planning Conference, Houston, Tex., April, 1967: Threshold of Planning Information Systems,* American Society of Planning Officials, Chicago, 1967, pp. 76-108.

753. Pfefferle, Richard A., and Theodore Hines: *Feasibility of a Cooperative Processing Center for Anne Arundel, Baltimore, Montgomery and Prince George's Counties, in Maryland,* Maryland State Department of Education Division of Library Extension, Baltimore, 1967, 66 pp. ED 024 428.

754. Pflug, Gunther: *Mechanisierung und Automatisierung in Amerikanischen Bibliotheken,* Vittorio Klostermann, Frankfurt am Main, *c* 1967.

755. Pflug, Gunther: "Problems of Electronic Data Processing in Libraries," *Libri,* **15**:35-49, 1965.

756. Phillips, Arthur H.: *Computer Peripherals & Typesetting,* Her Majesty's Stationary Office, London, 1968, 665 pp.

757. "Phototypeset Output versus Computer Printout Output in Book Catalog Production: Results of the First of a Series of Comparative Cost Studies Being Conducted," *The LARC Reports,* **1**(13):1–3, July 1968.

758. Pickford, A. G. A.: "FAIR (Fast Access Information Retrieval) Project: Aims and Methods (with discussion)," *ASLIB Proceedings,* **19**:79–95, Mar. 1967.

759. Pizer, Irwin H.: "Another Look at Printed Catalogs," *Special Libraries,* **55**: 119, Feb. 1964.

760. Pizer, Irwin H.: "Book Catalogs versus Card Catalogs," *Medical Library Association Bulletin,* **53**:225–238, Apr. 1965.

761. Pizer, Irwin H.: "A Mechanized Circulation System," *College and Research Libraries,* **27**:5–12, Jan. 1966.

762. Pizer, Irwin H., "A Regional Medical Library Network," *Bulletin of the Medical Library Association,* Apr. 1969.

763. Pizer, Irwin H., and Alexander M. Cain: "Objective Tests of Library Performance," *Special Libraries,* **59**:704–711, Nov. 1968.

764. Pizer, Irwin H., Donald R. Franz, and Estelle Brodman: "Mechanization of Library Procedures in the Medium-sized Medical Library: I. The Serial Record," *Medical Library Association Bulletin,* **51**:313–338, July 1963.

765. Pizer, Irwin H., Isabelle T. Anderson, and Estelle Brodman: "Mechanization of Library Procedures in the Medium-sized Medical Library: II. Circulation Records," *Medical Library Association Bulletin,* **52**:370–385, Apr. 1964.

766. *A Plan for a Library Processing Center for the State University of New York,* report to the Office of Education Communications, State University of New York, Arthur D. Little, Inc., Boston, 1967, 127 pp.

767. Popecki, Joseph T.: "A Filing System for the Machine Age," *Library Resources and Technical Services,* **9**:333–337, 1965.

768. "Potential Resources for EIN," *EDUCOM,* **3**:4–6, Nov. 1968.

769. Pratt, Allan: "Living with Computers," *California Librarian,* **29**:57–61.

770. Pride, Betty J.: "General Systems—Automated Book Ordering and Receiving," *Automation in Libraries: First ATLIS Workshop, 15–17 November, 1966,* Redstone Scientific Information Center, Redstone Arsenal, Ala., 1967, pp. 49–54. AD 654-766.

771. *Proceedings of the 6th Medical Symposium, 1964,* International Business Machine Corp., Poughkeepsie, N.Y., 1964, 653 pp.

772. Prodrick, R. G.: "Automation Can Transform Reference Services," *Ontario Library Review,* **51**:145–150, Sept. 1967.

773. *Progress Report on an Operation Research and Systems Engineering Study of a University Library, PB-168 187, NSF Grant GN-31,* Milton S. Eisenhower Library, Johns Hopkins University, Baltimore, 1965, 110 pp.

774. Ram, D.: "Automation in Libraries in India and the Role of Library Associations," *Herald of Library Science,* 5:304–307, Oct. 1966.

775. Randall, G. E., and Roger P. Bristol: "PIL (Processing Information List): or, a Computer-controlled Processing Record," *Special Libraries,* 55:82–86, 1964.

776. Rather, Lucia J.: "Special Characters and Diacritical Marks Used in Roman

Alphabets," *Library Resources and Technical Services,* **12**:285-295, Summer 1968.

777. Rauseo, M. J.: "Training Implications of Automated Personnel Systems," *American Documentation,* **18**:248-249, Oct. 1967.

778. *Recent Developments in Automation at British Columbia University Libraries: University of British Columbia, University of Victoria, Simon Fraser University,* no. 1, University of British Columbia, Vancouver, 1966.

779. Redd, Oliver F.: *An Experimental Investigation of Microprinting by the Offset Method,* Letterkenny Army Depot, Chambersburg, Pa., 1964. Also Supplement, Aug. 1965. AD 621479.

780. Rees, A. M.: "Evaluation of Information Systems and Services," *Annual Review of Information Science and Technology,* vol. 2, Interscience-Wiley, New York, 1967, pp. 63-86.

781. Rees, A. M., D. G. Schultz, et al.: *A Field Experimental Approach to the Study of Relevance Assessments in Relation to Document Searching,* 2 vols., Center for Documentation and Communication Research, Case Western Reserve University, Cleveland, Ohio, 1967, 475 pp. PB 170 080 and PB 176 079.

782. Reilly, Kevin D.: *Evaluation of Generalized File Management Systems,* Institute of Library Research, University of California at Los Angeles, Los Angeles, 1967, 46 pp.

783. Reimers, Paul: *Automation at the Library of Congress,* presented at the 15th International Meeting of the Institute of Management Sciences, Cleveland, Ohio, Sept. 11-13, 1968, Information Systems Office of the Library of Congress, Washington, 1968, 19 pp.

784. *Report on Serials Computer Project, University Library and USCD Computer Center, 1961/62,* 1 vol., University of California, San Diego, Library, 1962, various paging.

785. Resnikoff, H. L., and J. L. Dolby: "The Nature of Affixing in Written English," *Mechanical Translation,* 8:84-89, 1965.

786. Richmond, Phyllis A.: "Book Catalogs as Supplements to Card Catalogs," *Library Resources and Technical Services,* 8:359-365. 1964.

787. Richmond, Phyllis A.: "Commentary on Three Topics of Current Concern," *Library Resources and Technical Services,* **11**:460-467, Fall 1967.

788. Richmond, Phyllis A.: "General Advantages and Disadvantages of Using the Library of Congress Classification," *Institute on the Use of the Library of Congress Classification, New York, July 7-9, 1966, Proceedings,* American Library Association, Chicago, 1968, pp. 209-220.

789. Richmond, Phyllis A.: "Note on Updating and Searching Computerized Catalogs," *Library Resources and Technical Services,* **10**:155-160, 1966.

790. Richmond, Phyllis A., and Marcia K. Gill: "DYSTAL Programs for Library Filing," *American Documentation Institute: Levels of Interaction between Man and Information,* Thompson, Washington, 1967, pp. 197-201.

791. Roberts, Justine T.: "Mechanization of Library Procedures in the Medium-sized Medical Library: IV. Physical Characteristics of the Acquisitions—Cataloging Record," *Bulletin of the Medical Library Association,* **56**:59-70, Jan. 1968.

792. Roberts, Paul R.: "The Effective Use of Bibliographic Information and the Role of Automation in This Process," *Libri,* **17**:305-313, 1967.

793. Robinson, Charles W.: "The Book Catalog: Diving In (Baltimore County Public Library)," *Wilson Library Bulletin,* **40**:262-268, Nov. 1965.

794. Rocappi, Inc.: "Mechanized Procedures of ROCAPPI, Inc. (Research on Computer Applications in the Printing and Publishing Industries)," with commentary by Richard Goodwin, *The LARC Reports,* **1**(14):1-28, July 1968.

795. Rogers, Clara T.: "General Systems-patron Control System," *Automation in Libraries: First ATLIS Workshop, November 15-17, 1966,* Redstone Scientific Information Center, Redstone Arsenal, Ala., 1967, pp. 15-27. AD 654 766.

796. Rogers, Frank B.: "Costs of Operating an Information Retrieval Service," *Drexel Library Quarterly,* **4**:271-278, Oct. 1968.

797. Roper, Fred W.: "A Computer-based Serials Control System for a Large Biomedical Library," *American Documentation,* **19**:151-157, Apr. 1968.

798. Roper, Fred W.: "Information Retrieval, Mechanized Bibliographies, and Library Science," *Computer Studies in the Humanities and Verbal Behavior,* **1**:77-83, Aug. 1968.

799. Roper, Fred W.: *Preparation of Records for the Automated (Serials) System at the Biomedical Library, University of California at Los Angeles,* Los Angeles, 1964. 6 pp.

800. Rosenberg, K. C., and C. L. M. Blocher: "Comparison of the Relevance of Key-word-in-context versus Descriptor Indexing Terms," *American Documentation,* **19**:27-29, Jan. 1968.

801. Roy, Robert H.: "Utilization of Computer Techniques for Circulation and Inventory Control in a University Research Library (Johns Hopkins University)," *Association of Research Libraries, Minutes of the Sixty-third Meeting,* pp. 20-39, Jan. 26, 1964.

802. Ruby, Homer V.: "Computerized Circulation at Illinois State Library," *Illinois Libraries,* **50**:159-162, Feb. 1968.

803. Ruecking, Frederick: "Bibliographic Retrieval from Bibliographic Input: The Hypothesis and Construction of a Test," *Journal of Library Automation,* **1**: 227-238, Dec. 1968.

804. Ruecking, Frederick: *The Circulation System of the Fondren Library, Rice University,* Texas Library and Historical Commission, Austin, 1966.

805. Ruecking, Frederick: "Selecting a Circulation-control System: A Mathematical Approach," *College and Research Libraries,* **25**:385-390, Sept. 1964.

806. Russell, J. H.: "A Computer-produced Bibliography," in S. M. Cox and M. W. Grose (eds.), *Organization and Handling of Bibliographic Records by Computer,* Oriel Press, New Castle upon Tyne, England; Archon, Hamden, Conn., 1967, pp. 50-57.

807. Sackman, H.: *A Public Philosophy for Real Time Information Systems,* System Development Corp., Santa Monica, Calif., 1968. 27 pp. SP-3126.

808. Sage, C. R.: "Comprehensive Dissemination of Current Literature," *American Documentation,* **17**:155-177, 1966.

809. Sage, C. R., R. R. Anderson, and D. R. Fitzwater: "Adaptive Information Dissemination," *American Documentation,* **16**:185-200, 1965.

810. St. Pierre, Paul, Paul J. Fasana, and Russell Shank: *Elements of Information Systems,* student ed., Tutorial Subcommittee, American Society for Information Science, New York, 1968, 49 pp. PB 182 227.

811. Salmon, Stephen R.: "Automation of Library Procedures at Washington University," *Missouri Library Association Quarterly,* 27:11–14, Mar. 1966.

812. Salton, Gerard: *Automatic Information Organization and Retrieval,* McGraw-Hill, New York, 1968, 514 pp.

813. Sandt, Roger W.: "Micro-publishing at the Wall Street Journal," *Proceedings of the American Society for Information Science, 32nd Annual Meeting, San Francisco, California, October 1-4, 1969,* 6:329–331, Greenwood, Westport, Conn., 1969.

814. Saracevic, Tefko, et al.: *An Inquiry into Testing of Information Retrieval Systems,* Comparative Systems Laboratory Final Report, 3 parts, Center for Documentation and Communication Research, Case Western Reserve University, Cleveland, Ohio, 1968, 611 pp. PB 179 290; PB 180 951; and PB 180 952.

815. Saracevic, Tefko, and Alan M. Rees: "The Impact of Information Science on Library Practice," *Library Journal,* 93:4097–4101, Nov. 1968.

816. Sawyer, Thomas E.: *Preliminary Design for a Regional Information System as an Integral Part of a Statewide System,* prepared for the Southern California Association of Governments, TRW Systems, Redondo Beach, Calif., 1967, 43 pp.

817. Scantlebury, R. A., P. T. Wilkinson, and K. A. Bartlett: "The Design of a Message Switching Centre for a Digital Communication Network," *Congress of the International Federation for Information Processing (IFIP), 4th, Edinburgh, 5–10 August, 1968, Proceedings,* North-Holland Publishing, Amsterdam, 1968.

818. Schatz, Sharon: "Facsimile Transmission in Libraries: A State of the Art Survey," *Library Resources and Technical Services,* 12:5–15, Winter 1968.

819. Schieber, William D., and Ralph M. Shoffner: *Telefacsimile in Libraries: A Report on Experiment in Facsimile Transmission and an Analysis of Implications for Interlibrary Loan Systems,* Institute of Library Research, University of California at Berkeley, Feb. 1968, 139 pp. ED 019 106.

820. Schneider, John H.: "Experimental Trial of Selective Dissemination of Biomedical Information in an Automated System Based on a Linear Hierarchical Decimal Classification, *American Society for Information Science, Annual Meeting, Columbus, Ohio, 20–24 October, 1968, Proceedings,* vol. 5, Greenwood, New York, 1968, pp. 243–245.

821. Schultheiss, Louis A.: "Data Processing Aids in Acquisitions Work," *Library Resources and Technical Services,* 9:66–68, 1965.

822. Schultheiss, Louis A.: *System Analysis and Planning: Data Processing in Public and University Libraries,* Drexel Information Science Series, vol. 3, Spartan Books, Washington, 1966, pp. 92–102.

823. Schultheiss, Louis A., Don S. Culbertson, and Edward M. Heiliger: *Advanced Data Processing in the University Library,* Scarecrow Press, New York, 1962, 388 pp.

824. Schultz, Claire K.: "Automation of Reference Work," *Library Trends,* 12: 413–424, Jan. 1964.

825. Schwarz, P. J.: "Serials Record System for the College Library, Mountain-Plains," *Library Quarterly,* 12:7–17, Summer 1967.

826. Science Press, Inc.: "Mechanized Procedures of the Science Press, Inc.,"

with commentaries by George Watson and Helen Lockhart, *The LARC Reports,* **1**(15):1-10, July 1968.

827. *Scientific and Technical Communication: A Pressing National Problem and Recommendations for Its Solution,* National Academy of Sciences, Washington, 1969, 322 pp.

828. Scoones, M. A.: "Mechanization of Serial Records with Particular Reference to Subscription Control in Shell Centre," *ASLIB Proceedings,* **19**: 45-62, Feb. 1967.

829. Scott, Jack W.: "An Integrated Computer Based Technical Processing System in a Small College Library," *Journal of Library Automation,* **1**: 149-158, Sept. 1968.

830. Scott, James T.: "Economic and Regulatory Considerations in Data Networks," in Business Equipment Manufacturers Association, *The Computer: Tool for Management,* Business Press, Elmhurst, Ill., 1968, pp. 91-102.

831. Scribner, Mary L., and Curtis L. Brown: *Information Automation at the Institute of Paper Chemistry,* Institute of Paper Chemistry, Appleton, Wisc., 1968.

832. Segarra, Carlos O.: *An Approach to Cost Effectiveness of a Selective Mechanized Document Processing System,* Army Technical Library Improvement Studies (ATLIS), report no. 12, Technical Information and Library Branch, Army Engineer Research and Development Labs., Fort Belvoir, Va., Mar. 1967, 73 pp. AD 651 486.

833. Selig, Judith A., Robert D. Reinecke, and Lawrence M. Stolurow: *A Computer-based System Integrating Instruction and Information Retrieval: a Description of Some Methodological Considerations,* technical report, Harvard Computing Center, Cambridge, Mass., Feb. 1968, 44 pp. Report no. TR-5. AD-672 187.

834. *Seminar on Automation in British Columbia University Libraries,* University of British Columbia, Vancouver, 1966.

835. Shactman, Bella E.: "Other Federal Activities in Cooperative and Centralized Cataloging," *Library Trends,* **16**:112-126, July 1967.

836. Shactman, Bella, James P. Railey, and Stephen R. Salmon: "U.S. National Libraries Task Force on Automatic and Other Cooperative Services: Progress Report No.' 1," *Library of Congress Information Bulletin,* **42**: 65-73, Sept. 1967.

837. Shank, Russell: *Regional Access to Scientific and Technical Information: A Program for Action in the New York Metropolitan Area,* Report of the METRO Science Library Project, 1966-1967, METRO Miscellaneous Publications Series, Nov. 1, New York Metropolitan Reference and Research Library Agency, New York, 1968, 207 pp. ED 021 595.

838. Shaw, Ralph R.: "Control of Book Funds at the University of Hawaii Library," *Library Resources and Technical Services,* **11**:380-382, Summer 1967.

839. Shaw, Ralph R.: "Machine Application at the University of Hawaii," *College and Research Libraries,* **26**:381-382, 398, Sept. 1965.

840. Sheldon, R. C., R. A. Roach and S. Backer: "Design of an On-line Computer-based Textile Information Retrieval System," *Textile Research Journal,* **38**:81-100, Jan. 1968.

841. Shera, Jesse H.: "Librarians against Machines," *Wilson Library Bulletin,* **42**:65–73, Sept. 1967.

842. Shera, Jesse H.: "What Is Past Is Prologue: Beyond 1984," *ALA Bulletin,* **61**:35–47, Jan. 1967.

843. Shoffner, Ralph M.: "Implications of Technology on Library Processes—The Catalog," *C.A.C.U.L. Workshop on Library Automation, University of British Columbia, 1967,* Canadian Association of College and University Libraries, Ottawa, 1967, pp. 113–115.

844. Shoffner, Ralph M.: *Joint Design and Development of Library Systems,* Institute of Library Research, University of California at Los Angeles, 1967, 35 pp.

845. Shuart, Rodney A.: *Application of Information Processing Techniques to Library Systems (MARC Pilot Project),* American Institute of Aeronautics and Astronautics, 3rd Annual Meeting, Boston, 1966, Paper 66–832, AIAA, New York, 1966.

846. Siegel, S. J.: "Developing an Information System for a Hospital," *Public Health Reports,* **83**:359–362, May 1968.

847. Siegmann, Robert M.: *Information Systems in Universities,* School of Information Sciences, Georgia Institute of Technology, Atlanta, 1969, 89 pp. ED 032 098.

848. Sievers, Patricia T., and Paul J. Fasana: *Automated Routines in Technical Services: Research Report,* U.S. Air Force Cambridge Research Laboratories, Bedford, Mass., 1964. AD 435 615.

849. Simmons, P. A.: "An Analysis of Bibliographic Data Conversion Costs," *Library Resources and Technical Services,* **12**:296–311, Summer 1968.

850. Simmons, Peter: "Automation in American Libraries," *Computers and the Humanities,* **2**:101–113, Jan. 1968.

851. Simms, Daniel M.: "What Is a Systems Analyst?" *Special Libraries,* **59**: 718–721, Nov. 1968.

852. Simms, R. L., Jr.: "Trends in Computer/Communication Systems," *Computers and Automation,* **17**:22–25, May 1968.

853. Simonton, Wesley C.: "The Computerized Catalog: Possible, Feasible, Desirable?" *Library Resources and Technical Services,* 8:399–407, 1964.

854. Simonton, Wesley, and Charlene Mason, eds.: *Information Retrieval with Special Reference to the Biomedical Sciences, Institute on Information Retrieval, 1965, University of Minnesota,* Nolte Center for Continuing Education, University of Minnesota, Minneapolis, 1966, 199 pp.

855. Simpson, D. J.: "Before the Machines Come," *ASLIB Proceedings,* **20**: 21–33, Jan. 1968.

856. Simpson, Gustavus S., Jr.: "The Evolving U.S. National Scientific and Technical Information System," *Battelle Technical Review,* **17**:21–28, May-June 1968.

857. Slamecka, V.: "Information Science or Is It?" *Alabama Librarian,* **18**:3–4, Jan. 1967.

858. Slayden, Carolyn C.: "General Systems—Serials-basic System," *Automation in Libraries: First ATLIS Workshop, 15–17 November, 1966,* Redstone Scien-

tific Information Center, Redstone Arsenal, Ala., 1967, pp. 81-96. AD 654 766.

859. Smith, F. R., and S. O. Jones: "Card versus Book-form Printout in a Mechanized Library System," *Special Libraries,* 58:639-643, Nov. 1967.

860. Snyder, Samuel S.: "Automation at LC: Philosophy, Plans, Progress," *Library Journal,* **90**:4709-4714, Nov. 1965.

861. Somerfield, G. A.: "Next Hundred Weeks in Chemical Information," *ASLIB Proceedings,* **19**:255-259, Aug. 1967.

862. Sommerlad, M. J.: "Development of a Machine-readable Catalogue at the University of Essex," *Program,* 7:1-3, Oct. 1967.

863. Souter, Thomas A.: "Automated Procedures at Indiana University Library: Circulation Department," *Meeting on Automation in the Library—When, Where, and How, Purdue University, 1964, Papers,* Purdue University, Lafayette, Ind., 1965, pp. 43-45.

864. Sparks, David E., Mark M. Chodrow, and Gail M. Walsh: *A Methodology for the Analysis of Information Systems,* final report to the National Science Foundation, Information Dynamics, Wakefield, Mass., 1965, various paging. NSF-C-370.

865. *Specifications for an Automated Library System,* prepared for University of California, Santa Cruz, Computer Usage Company, Palo Alto, Calif., 1965, 122 pp.

866. Speer, Jack A.: *Libraries and Automation: A Bibliography with Index,* Teachers College Press, Emporia, Kans. 1967, 106 pp.

867. Spierer, M., and Robert D. Wills: *Applications of a Large-scale Time-sharing System,* System Development Corp., Santa Monica, Calif., 1968, 32 pp. SP-3062.

868. Spigia, Frances, Mary Taylor, and Michael A. Jennings: *A Pilot—An On-line Library Acquisition System,* Computer Center, Oregon State University, Corvallis, Ore., 1968, 117 pp. ED 024 410.

869. Sprenkle, Peter M., and Frederick G. Kilgour: "A Quantitative Study of Characters on Biomedical Catalogue Cards—A Preliminary Investigation," *American Documentation,* **14**:202-206, July 1963.

870. Spring, W. C.: "Applications of Information Science in Medicine," *Annual Review of Information Science and Technology,* vol. 2, Interscience-Wiley, New York, 1967, pp. 311-338.

871. Srygley, Ted F.: "Serials Record Instructions for a Computerized Serial System (Florida Atlantic University)," *Library Resources and Technical Services,* 8:248-256, 1964.

872. Stangl, Peter, and Frederick G. Kilgour: "Analysis of Recorded Biomedical Book and Journal Use in the Yale Medical Library: Part I. Date and Subject Relations," *Bulletin of the Medical Library Association,* 55:290-300, July 1967; "Part II. Subject and User Relations," *Bulletin of the Medical Library Association,* **56**:301-315, July 1968.

873. Stangl, Peter, Ben-Ami Lipetz and Kathryn F. Taylor: "Performance of Kilgour's Truncation Algorithm, When Applied to Bibliographic Retrieval from a Library Catalog," *Proceedings of the American Society for Information Science, 32nd Annual Meeting, San Francisco, California, October 1-4, 1969,* 6:125-127, Greenwood, Westport, Conn., 1969.

874. Stanley, W. J., and D. D. Cranshaw: "Use of a Computer-based Total Management Information System to Support an Air Resource Management Program," *Journal of the Air Pollution Control Association,* **18**:158–159, Mar. 1968.

875. Stegmaier, R. B.: "Data Banks Aid Defense," *Armed Force Management,* **14**:70–75, Aug. 1968.

876. Stein, Theodore: "Automation and Library Systems," *Library Journal,* **89**: 2723–2734, July 1964.

877. Stein, Theodore, Co.: *Centralized Book Acquisition for New York State: Proposed Computer System, Albany, New York State Library, 1967: Part I. System Definition,* 96 pp. ED 021 575; *Part II. System Design,* 136 pp. ED 021 576.

878. Stein, Theodore, Co.: *Proposed Computer System for Library Catalog Maintenance, Albany, New York State Library, 1967: Part I. System Definition,* 109 pp. ED 021 573; *Part II. System Design,* 123 pp. ED 021 574.

879. Steiner, W. A.: "The Use of Computers in Law Libraries," *International Association of Law Libraries Bulletin,* **19**:37–53, Apr. 1967.

880. Sternberg, V. A.: "Miles of Information by the Inch at the Library of the Bettis Atomic Laboratory, Westinghouse Electric Corporation," *Pennsylvania Library Association Bulletin,* **22**:189–194, May 1967.

881. Stevens, Mary Elizabeth, Vincent E. Giuliano, and Laurence B. Heilprin, eds.: *Statistical Association Methods for Mechanized Documentation, Symposium Proceedings, Washington, 1964,* National Bureau of Standards Miscellaneous Publication, no. 269, 1965, 261 pp.

882. Stevenson, C. L., and J. A. Cooper: "A Computerized Accounts System at the City University," *Program,* **2**:15–29, Apr. 1968.

883. Stewart, Bruce Warren: *A Computerized Serials Record for the Texas A&M University Library.* Library, Texas A&M University, College Station, Tex., 1965, 123 pp.

884. Stewart, Bruce Warren: "Data Processing in an Academic Library (Texas A&M University)," *Wilson Library Bulletin,* **41**:388–395, Dec. 1966.

885. Stimler, S., and K. A. Brons: "A Methodology for Calculating and Optimizing Real-time System Performance, *Communications of the ACM,* **11**:509–516, July 1968.

886. Stockton, Patricia Ann: "An IBM 357 Circulation Procedure," *College and Research Libraries,* **28**:35–40, Jan. 1967.

887. Stone, C. Walter: "The Library Function Redefined," *Library Trends,* **16**: 181–196, Oct. 1967.

888. Strieby, Irene M.: "Impact of Computerization on Indian Libraries," *Hawaii Library Association Journal,* **23**:8–15, June 1967.

889. Strom, Karen D.: "Software Design for Bio-medical Library Serials Control System," *American Society for Information Science, Annual Meeting, Columbus, Ohio, 20–24 October, 1968, Proceedings,* 5:267–275, Greenwood, New York, 1968.

890. Stuart-Stubbs, Basil: "Automation in a University Library from the Administrators' Viewpoint," *C.A.C.U.L. Workshop on Library Automation, University of British Columbia, 1967,* Canadian Association of College and University Libraries, Ottawa, 1967, pp. 124–134.

891. Stuart-Stubbs, Basil: *Conference on Computers in Candian Libraries, Université Laval, Quebec, March 21-22, 1966,* University of British Columbia Library, Vancouver, 1966, 13 pp.

892. Stuart-Stubbs, Basil: "Trial by Computer: A Punched Card Parable for Library Administrators," *Library Journal,* 92:4471-4474, Dec. 15, 1967.

893. *Subject Catalog,* 2d ed., Florida Atlantic University Library, Boca Raton, Fla., 1966, 817 pp.

894. Summit, Roger K.: "DIALOG: An Operational On-line Reference Retrieval System," *Proceedings of the 22nd National Conference of the Association for Computing Machinery,* Thompson, Washington, 1967, pp. 51-56.

895. Summit, Roger K.: *Remote Information Retrieval Facility: Ames Research Center and NASA Headquarters,* Lockheed Missiles and Space Co., Palo Alto, Calif., June, 1968, 44 pp. N-07-68-1.

896. Swanson, Don R.: "Dialogues with a Catalog," *Library Quarterly,* 34: 113-125, Jan. 1964.

897. Swanson, Don R.: "Library Goals and the Role of Automation," *Special Libraries,* 53:466-471, Oct. 1962.

898. Swanson, Rowena W.: *A Look at Technologies vis-a-vis Information Handling Techniques,* Air Force Office of Scientific Research, Arlington, Va., 1969, 22 pp. AD 688 558.

899. Swanson, Rowena W.: *Move the Information: A Kind of Missionary Spirit,* Air Force Office of Scientific Research, Arlington, Va., 1967, 203 pp. AD 657 794.

900. Swanson, Rowena W.: "SATCOM in Review, an Analysis of the Latest Government Initiated Report Setting Guidelines for Information Exchange," *Datamation,* 16:98-105, Feb. 1970.

901. Swenson, Sally: "Flow Chart of Library Searching Techniques," *Special Libraries,* 56:239-242, Apr. 1965.

902. System Development Corp.: *Reference Manual for Educational Information Service Centers,* technical memorandum, Falls Church, Va., 1968, 121 pp. TM-WD-521/000/01.

903. System Development Corp.: *Technology and Libraries,* Santa Monica, Calif., Nov. 15, 1967, 167 pp.

904. *Systems Study of the Cuyahoga County Public Library,* submitted by Computer Data Sciences, Inc., Sept. 10, 1969, 122 pp.

905. Takle, K. G.: "Operating Information Retrieval Satellite," *Special Libraries,* 58:644-650, Nov. 1967.

906. Tamaru, Takuji: "Prospects in Municipal Information Systems: The Example of Los Angeles," *Computers and Automation,* 17:15-18, Jan. 1968.

907. Tancredi, S. A., and O. D. Nichols: "Air Pollution Technical Information Processing, the Microthesaurus Approach," *American Documentation,* 19: 66-70, Jan. 1968.

908. Tanis, James R.: "A University Librarian Looks at Automation," *Drexel Library Quarterly,* 4:329-334, Oct. 1968.

909. Tate, F. A., and J. L. Wood: "Libraries and Abstracting and Indexing Services, a Study in Interdependency," *Library Trends,* 16:353-373, Jan. 1968.

910. Taylor, Robert S.: "Toward the Design of a College Library for the Seventies," *Wilson Library Bulletin,* **43**:44–51, Sept. 1968.

911. Taylor, Robert S., and Caroline E. Hieber: *Manual for the Analysis of Library Systems,* Center for Information Sciences, Library Systems Analysis, report no. 3, Lehigh University, Bethlehem, Pa., 1965, 44 pp.

912. Teare, Robert F.: "Experience to Date in Automated Acquisitions at Honnold Library," *Proceedings of the American Society for Information Science, 32nd Annual Meeting, San Francisco, California, October 1–4, 1969,* **6**:29–37, Greenwood, Westport, Conn., 1969.

913. *Technical Information Libraries,* Bell Telephone Laboratories, Murray Hill, N.J., n. d., 20 pp.

914. *Technical Proposal for an Automated Circulation-control System for the M. D. Anderson Memorial Library, University of Houston,* Hamilton Standard, Farmington, Conn., 1968, 65 pp. HSPC 68 U04.

915. "The Third Conversion of Book Catalogs for the Los Angeles County Library," with commentary by the Library Automation Research and Consulting, *The LARC Reports,* **1**(2):1–23, Apr. 1968.

916. Thomas, P. A., and H. East: "Comments on the Terminology of the Analysis of Library Systems and the Function of Forms Therein," *ASLIB Proceedings,* **20**:340–344, Aug. 1968.

917. Thomas, Sarah N.: "Planning for Computer Use in Library Situations," *Hawaii Library Association Journal,* **23**:26–36, June 1967.

918. Thompson, D. A., et al.: "Proposed Structure for Displayed Information to Minimize Search Time through a Data Base," *American Documentation,* **19**: 80–84, Jan. 1968.

919. Thompson, Evelyn, and George Forrester: "The Automatic Ordering of Replacement Titles for Libraries in Metropolitan Toronto," *Library Resources and Technical Services,* **11**:215–220, Spring 1967.

920. Thompson, G. K.: "Computerization of Information Retrieval and Index Production in the Field of Economic and Social Development," *UNESCO Bulletin for Libraries,* **22**:66–72, Mar.-Apr. 1968.

921. "Three National Libraries Approve an On-going Program for Systems Compatibility at the National Level," *Library of Congress Information Bulletin,* **26**:795–800, Nov. 30, 1967.

922. *The 3 R's Program—Meeting Industry's Informational Needs,* report to the Division of Library Development, New York State Library, Arthur D. Little, Inc., Boston, 1967, 78 pp. ED 022 500.

923. *Title Catalog,* Florida Atlantic University Library, Boca Raton, Fla., 1964, 471 pp.

924. *Title Catalog,* 2d ed., Florida Atlantic University Library, Boca Raton, Fla., 1966, 533 pp.

925. Tompkins, Mary L.: *Summary of Symposia on Mechanized Information Services in the University Library,* Institute of Library Research, University of California at Los Angeles, 1967, 91 pp.

926. Townley, H. M.: "A New Computer-based Current Awareness Service," *Program,* **3**:1–10, 1969.

927. Troutman, Joan C.: *Standards for Cataloging of Magnetic Tape Material,*

Institute of Library Research, University of California at Los Angeles, 1967, 34 pp.

928. Trueswell, Richard W.: "A Quantitative Measure of User Circulation Requirements and Its Possible Effect on Stack Thinning and Multiple Copy Determination," *American Documentation,* 16:20–25, Jan. 1965.

929. Trueswell, Richard W.: "Two Characteristics of Circulation and Their Effect on the Implementation of Mechanized Circulation Control Systems," *College and Research Libraries,* 25:285–291, July 1964.

930. Umstead, Charles R., and Fred E. Croxton: *Automated Library Control Systems,* American Data Processing, Inc., Detroit, *c* 1968, 168 pp.

931. Umstead, Charles R., and Fred E. Croxton: *Compatible Automated Library Circulation Control Systems,* Army Technical Library Improvement Studies, no. 14, Redstone Scientific Information Center, Redstone Arsenal, Ala., 1967, 177 pp. AD 653 591. RSIC-663.

932. United Aircraft Corporate Systems Center: *Initial Report on a Study to Plan Development and Implementation of a Connecticut Library Research Center,* a study supported by the Connecticut Research Commission for the Connecticut State Library, United Aircraft Corp., Farmington, Conn., 1966, 65 pp.

933. United Aircraft Corporate Systems Center: *Library Automation System,* submitted to Knollcrest Calvin Library, Calvin College, Grand Rapids, Mich., United Aircraft Corp., Farmington, Conn., 1967, 42 pp.

934. United Aircraft Corporate Systems Center: *Library of Congress Automation Program: Task I Report, Survey and Analysis of Bibliographic Apparatus: Appendix A, File Census,* prepared for Information Systems Office, Library of Congress, United Aircraft Corp., Farmington; Conn., 1967, 179 pp.

935. United Aircraft Corporate Systems Center: *Library of Congress Automation Program: Task I Report, Survey and Analysis of Bibliographic Apparatus: Appendix B, Analysis of Case Files,* prepared for Information Systems Office, Library of Congress. United Aircraft Corp., Farmington, Conn., 1967, 256 pp.

936. United Aircraft Corporate Systems Center: *Library of Congress Automation Program: Task I Report, Survey and Analysis of Bibliographic Apparatus: Appendix C, Sampling of Official Catalog,* prepared for Information Systems Office, Library of Congress, United Aircraft Corp., Farmington, Conn., 1967, 208 pp.

937. United Aircraft Corporate Systems Center: *Library of Congress Automation Program: Task I Report, Survey and Analysis of Bibliographic Apparatus: Appendix D, Survey of Gross Use of Major Catalogs,* prepared for Information Systems Office, Library of Congress, United Aircraft Corp., Farmington, Conn., 1967, 39 pp.

938. United Aircraft Corporate Systems Center: *Library of Congress Automation Program: Task I Report, Survey and Analysis of Bibliographic Apparatus: Appendix E, Functional Analysis and Statistics,* prepared for Information Systems Office, Library of Congress, United Aircraft Corp., Farmington, Conn., 1967, 299 pp.

939. United Aircraft Corporate Systems Center: *Library of Congress Automation Program: Task I Report, Survey and Analysis of Bibliographic Apparatus,* technical report prepared for Information Systems Office, Library of Congress, United Aircraft Corp., Farmington, Conn., 1967, 82 pp. SCR 320.

940. United Aircraft Corporate Systems Center: *Library of Congress Automation Program: Task II Report, System Requirements Analysis,* vol. I, Technical Report Appendix A, vol. II, prepared for Information Systems Office, Library of Congress, United Aircraft Corp., Farmington, Conn., 1967, 59 pp.

941. United Aircraft Corporate Systems Center: *Library of Congress Automation Program: Task II Report, System Requirements Analysis, System Requirements Data,* vol. II, Appendices A-E, prepared for Information Systems Office, Library of Congress, United Aircraft Corp., Farmington, Conn., 1967, 141 pp.

942. United Aircraft Corporate Systems Center: *Library of Congress Automation Program: Task II Report, System Requirements Analysis, System Requirements Data,* vol. III, Appendix F, prepared for Information Systems Office, Library of Congress, Farmington, Conn., United Aircraft Corp., 1967, 283 pp.

943. United Aircraft Corporate Systems Center: *Library of Congress Automation Program: Task II Report, System Requirements Analysis, System Requirements Data,* vol. IV, Appendix G, prepared for Information Systems Office, Library of Congress, United Aircraft Corp., Farmington, Conn., 1967, 181 pp.

944. United Aircraft Corporate Systems Center: *MEDLARS II, Management Summary and Cost Proposal,* vol. I, for the National Library of Medicine, United Aircraft Corp., Farmington, Conn., 1967, 53 pp.

945. United Aircraft Corporate Systems Center: *MARC Pilot Project: Final Technical Report: The MARC Pilot System, Fixed Field Codes Used in the MARC Pilot System,* Appendix C, Library of Congress Information Systems Office, United Aircraft Corp., Farmington, Conn., 1967, 274 pp.

946. United Aircraft Corporate Systems Center: *MARC Pilot Project: Final Technical Report: The MARC Pilot System, Manual for Participating Libraries Program Listings,* Library of Congress Information Systems Office, United Aircraft Corp., Farmington, Conn., 1967, 313 pp.

947. United Aircraft Corporate Systems Center: *MARC Pilot Project: Final Technical Report: The MARC Pilot System, MARC Master Tape of Bibliographical Information,* Appendix B, Library of Congress Information Systems Office, United Aircraft Corp., Farmington, Conn., 1967, 47 pp.

948. United Aircraft Corporate Systems Center: *MARC Pilot Project: Final Technical Report: The MARC Pilot System, Preparation of MARC Bibliographic Information—Computer Processing—Program Application,* Appendix F, vol. I, Library of Congress Information Systems Office, United Aircraft Corp., Farmington, Conn., 1967, 432 pp.

949. United Aircraft Corporate Systems Center: *MARC Pilot Project: Final Technical Report: The MARC Pilot System, Preparation of MARC Bibliographic Information—Computer Processing—Program Listings,* Appendix F, vol. 2, Library of Congress Information Systems Office, United Aircraft Corp., Farmington, Conn., 1967, 322 pp.

950. United Aircraft Corporate Systems Center: *MARC Pilot Project: Final Technical Report: The MARC Pilot System, Preparation of MARC Bibliographic Information—Editors' Procedure,* Appendix D, Library of Congress Information Systems Office, United Aircraft Corp., Farmington, Conn., 1967, 131 pp.

951. United Aircraft Corporate Systems Center: *MARC Pilot Project: Final Technical Report: The MARC Pilot System, Preparation of MARC Bibliographic Information—Input of Data for Computer Processing,* Appendix E,

Library of Congress Information Systems Office, United Aircraft Corp., Farmington, Conn., 1967, 123 pp.

952. United Aircraft Corporate Systems Center: *MARC Pilot Project: Final Technical Report: The MARC Pilot System, Manual for Participating Libraries,* Appendix A, vol. I, Library of Congress Information Systems Office, United Aircraft Corp., Farmington, Conn., 1967, 231 pp.

953. United Aircraft Corporate Systems Center: *Preliminary Job Description for Preparation of Union Catalog for CUNY,* technical proposal submitted to City University of New York, United Aircraft Corp., Farmington, Conn., 1967, 30 pp.

954. United Aircraft Corporate Systems Center: *A Study of Terminal Devices for Information Storage and Retrieval Systems,* United Aircraft Corp., Farmington, Conn., 1966, 131 pp. SCR 269.

955. United Aircraft Systems Corporation: *Development and Operation of a Technical Library System, Technical Proposal,* vol. I, submitted to National Aeronautics and Space Administration, Electronic Research Center, Cambridge, Mass., United Aircraft Corp., Farmington, Conn., 1967, 67 pp. SCP 66192-1.

956. United Aircraft Systems Corporation: *Technical Proposal for Analysis and Design of an Integrated Information Handling System,* submitted to U.S. Department of Agriculture. Washington, United Aircraft Corp., 1967, 259 pp.

957. U.S. Library of Congress: *Automation and the Library of Congress,* Washington, 1963, 88 pp.

958. U.S. Library of Congress: *The MARC Pilot Experience: An Informal Summary,* Washington, June 1968, 15 pp.

959. U.S. Library of Congress: *A Preliminary Report on the MARC Pilot Project,* Washington, 1966, 101 pp.

960. U.S. Library of Congress: *A Proposed Format for a Standardized Machine-readable Catalog Record,* Planning Memorandum, no. 3, a preliminary draft prepared by Henriette D. Avram, Ruth S. Freitag, and Kay D. Guiles, Washington, 1965, 110 pp.

961. U.S. Library of Cqngress: *Subscribers' Guide to the MARC Distribution Service,* Washington, Aug. 1968, 68 pp.

962. "U.S. National Libraries Task Force on Automation and Other Cooperative Services: Progress Report Number 1, November, 1967," *Library of Congress Information Bulletin,* 26:795–800, Nov. 30, 1967.

963. U.S. President's Science Advisory Committee: *Science, Government, and Information: The Responsibilities of the Technical Community and the Government in the Transfer of Information,* Weinberg Report, 1963, 52 pp.

964. U.S. Public Health Service, National Institute of Health Research Contracts Section: *Request for Proposal, MEDLARS II: Management Specifications, Functional Systems Specifications,* National Institute of Health, Bethesda, Md., 1967, 130 pp.

965. U.S. Veterans Administration: *Long-range Plan for a VA Total Information Processing System, Proposed Revision, January, 1967,* 1967. LRP-no. 30-01-00.

966. University of Chicago Library: *Development of an Integrated, Computer-based, Bibliographical Data System for a Large University Library,* University of Chicago, Chicago, 1968, 66 pp. PB-179 426.

967. University of Oxford: Chap. IV, *Report of the Committee on University Libraries:* Oxford University Press, London, 1966, pp. 295-306.

968. Vagianos, Louis: "Acquisitions: Policies, Procedures, and Problems," *C.A.C.U.L. Workshop on Library Automation, University of British Columbia, 1967,* Canadian Association of College and University Libraries, Ottawa, 1967, pp. 1-9.

969. Van Dam, A., and J. C. Michener: "Hardware Developments and Product Announcements," *Annual Review of Information Science and Technology,* vol. 2, Interscience-Wiley, New York, 1967, pp. 187-222.

970. Vann, Sarah K.: "Book Catalogs: Quo Animo? Members of the Black Gold Cooperative Library System Reply," *Library Resources and Technical Services,* **11**:451-460, Fall 1967.

971. Vdovin, George, et al.: *Serials Computer Project: Final Report,* University of California, San Diego, La Jolla, 1964, various paging.

972. Veaner, Allen B.: "The Application of Computers to Library Technical Processing," *College and Research Libraries,* **31**(1):36-42, Jan. 1970.

973. Ver Hulst, Jack: "An Approach to the Design of Computer-onto-microfilm (COM)," *Proceedings of the American Society for Information Science, 32nd Annual Meeting, San Francisco, California, October 1-4, 1969,* **6**:333-338, Greenwood, Westport, Conn., 1969.

974. Vickery, B. C.: "Bibliographic Description, Arrangement, and Retrieval," *Journal of Documentation,* **24**:1-15, Mar. 1968.

975. Vickery, B. C.: "The Future of Libraries," *Library Association Record,* **68**: 252-260, July 1966.

976. Voight, Melvin J.: "The Costs of Data Processing in University Libraries: In Serials Handling," *College and Research Libraries,* **24**:489-491, Nov. 1963.

977. Voight, Melvin J.: "LC and Automation," *Library Journal,* **89**:1022-1025, Mar. 1964.

978. Vorhaus, Alfred H., and Robert D. Wills: *The Time-shared Data Management System: A New Approach to Data Management,* System Development Corp, Santa Monica, Calif., 1968. SP-2747.

979. Wagman, Frederick H.: "Libraries in the Age of Automation," *Texas Library Journal,* 35:42-55, June 1959.

980. Waite, David P.: "Developing a Library Automation Program," *Wilson Library Bulletin,* **43**:52-58, Sept. 1968.

981. Waldron, R. K.: "Technology Revolution Cannot Be Ignored," *PNLA Quarterly,* **31**:216-222, Apr. 1967.

982. Wall, H. Duncan: *The Ontario Universities Bibliographic Center: A Program Plan,* Council of University Librarians, Toronto, 1968. 43 pp. OCUL-68-4.

983. Wall, H. Duncan: *The Ontario Universities Bibliographic Center: Major Functions, Summary Report, December, 1968,* Ontario Council of University Librarians, Toronto, 1968. 244 pp. OCUL-68-4. This report presents the major conclusions and recommendations of a study of possible innovations in the organization and technology of the University libraries of Ontario, through the creation of an Ontario Universities Bibliographic Centre. The study, conceived as part of a continuing program of system development, has been funded by the Committee of Presidents of Universities of Ontario, and has been prepared for OCUL chiefly by H. Duncan Wall.

984. Walsh, John: "Library of Congress: Automation Urged for Bibliographic Control but Not Prescribed as a Panacea," *Science,* **143**:452–455, 1964.

985. Warheit, I. A.: "Current Developments in Library Mechanization," *Special Libraries,* 58:420–426, July-Aug. 1967.

986. Warheit, I. A.: "File Organization of Library Records," *Journal of Library Automation,* **2**(1):20–30, Mar. 1969.

987. Warheit, I. A.: "Is EDP (Electronic Data Processing) Economically Feasible for Acquisition?" letter in reply to N. C. Batts, *Special Libraries,* 58:271, Apr. 1967.

988. Warheit, I. A.: "The Mechanization of Libraries," *1967 IEEE International Convention Record,* Institute of Electrical and Electronics Engineers, New York, 1967, pp. 44–47.

989. Washington Chapter Documentation Group: *Practical Problems of Library Automation,* Special Libraries Association, Washington, 1967, 52 pp. Available from Ellen Mahar, 4341 Nebraska Ave. N.W., Washington, 20016.

990. Wasserman, Paul: *The Librarian and the Machine,* Gale, Detroit, 1965.

991. Watson, William: "Library Automation: A Primer on Some of the Implications," *C.A.C.U.L. Workshop on Library Automation, University of British Columbia, 1967,* Canadian Association of College and University Libraries, Ottawa, 1967, pp. 135–146.

992. Weber, David C.: "Book Catalog Trends in 1966," *Library Trends,* **16**: 149–164, July 1967.

993. Wedgeworth, Robert: "Brown University Library Fund Accounting System," *Journal of Library Automation,* **1**(1):51–65, Mar. 1968.

994. Weil, Cherie B.: "Automatic Retrieval of Biographical Reference Books," *Journal of Library Automation,* **1**:239–249, Dec. 1968.

995. Weinstein, Edward A., and Virginia George: "Computer Produced Book Catalogs: Entry Form and Content," *Library Resources and Technical Services,* **11**:185–191, Spring 1967.

996. Weinstein, Edward A., and Virginia George: "Notes toward a Code for Computer-produced Printed Book Catalogs," *Library Resources and Technical Services,* **9**:319–323, 1965.

997. Weinstein, Edward A., and Joan Spry: "Boeing SLIP: Computer Produced and Maintained Printed Book Catalogs," *American Documentation,* **15**: 185–190, 1964.

998. Weinstock, Melvin: "Network Concepts in Scientific and Technical Libraries," *Special Libraries,* 58:328–334, May-June 1967.

999. Weisbrod, David L.: "An Integrated Computerized Bibliographic System for Libraries," *Drexel Library Quarterly,* **4**:214–232, July 1968.

1000. Weiss, Irvin J., and Emilie V. Wiggins: "Computer-aided Centralized Cataloging at the National Library of Medicine," *Library Resources and Technical Services,* **11**:83–96, 1967.

1001. Weiss, Rudi: "The State of Automation? A Survey of Machinery Used in Technical Services Departments in New York State Libraries," *Library Resources and Technical Services,* 9:289–302, 1965.

1002. Welch, H. M.: "Technical Service Costs, Statistics, and Standards," *Library Resources and Technical Services,* **11**:436–442, Fall 1967.

1003. Wells, A. J.: "The British National Bibliography: Brasenose Conference on the Automation of Libraries, Oxford, England, 1966," *Proceedings of the Anglo-American Conference on the Mechanization of Library Services,* Mansell, Chicago and London, 1967, pp. 24-29.

1004. Welsh, William J.: "Compatibility of Systems," in John Harvey (ed.), *Data Processing in Public and University Libraries,* Drexel Information Science Series, vol. 3, Spartan Books, Washington, 1966, pp. 79-93.

1005. Wesemael, A. L. Van: "Mechanisatie van de Catalogus," (Mechanization of the Catalog), *Bibliotheckleven,* **50**:593-603, Dec. 1965.

1006. Wessel, C. J.: "Criteria for Evaluating Technical Library Effectiveness," *ASLIB Proceedings,* **20**:455-481, Nov. 1968.

1007. Wessel, C. J., and B. A. Cohrssen: *Criteria for Evaluating the Effectiveness of Library Operations and Services, Phase I: Literature Search and State of the Art, Final Report,* Army Technical Library Improvement Studies (ATLIS), report no. 10, Thompson, Washington, 1967, 399 pp. AD 649 468.

1008. Wessel, C. J., K. L. Moore, and B. A. Cohrssen: *Criteria for Evaluating the Effectiveness of Library Operations and Services, Phase II: Data Gathering and Evaluation, Final Report,* Army Technical Library Improvement Studies (ATLIS), report no. 19, Thompson, Washington, 1968, 120 pp. AD 676 188.

1009. West, Leslie E.: "SPIRAL—Sandia's Program for Information Retrieval and Listing," *Proceedings of the American Society for Information Science, 32nd Annual Meeting, San Francisco, California, October 1-4, 1969,* **6**: 139-149, Greenwood, Westport, Conn., 1969.

1010. West, Lillian: "General Systems—Book Cataloging," *Automation in Libraries: First ATLIS Workshop, 15-17 November, 1966,* Redstone Scientific Information Center, Redstone Arsenal, Ala., 1967, pp. 55-70. AD 654 766.

1011. Weyhrauch, Ernest E.: "Automation in the Reserved Books Room," *Library Journal,* **89**:2294-2296, June 1964.

1012. White, Herbert S.: "To the Barricades! The Computers Are Coming!" *Special Libraries,* **57**:631-635, Nov. 1966.

1013. Wilhoit, G. Cleveland: "Computerized Indexing for Broadcast Music Libraries," *Journal of Broadcasting,* **11**:325-337, Fall 1967.

1014. Wilkinson, John P.: "A.A.U. (Association of Atlantic Universities) Mechanized Union List of Serials," *APLA Bulletin,* **29**:54-59, May 1965.

1015. Wilkinson, P. T., R. A. Scantlebury: "The Control Functions in a Local Data Network," *Congress of the International Federation for Information Processing (IFIP), 4th, Edinburgh, 5-10 August, 1968, Proceedings,* North-Holland Publishing, Amsterdam, 1968.

1016. Wilkinson, William A.: "The Impact of Automation on the Special Library," *Hawaii Library Association Journal,* **23**:15-21, June 1967.

1017. Wilkinson, William A.: "System for Machine-assisted Serials Control," *Special Libraries,* **58**:149-153, Mar. 1967.

1018. Willers, U.: "Automatik och Automatisering: Rapport fran landets Forskningsbibliotek 1963-1965 (Automation and Library Mechanization: Report from Sweden's Research Libraries 1963-1965)" *Biblioteksbladet,* **50** (8):538-545, 1965.

1019. Williams, B. J. S.: "Microforms in Information Retrieval and Communication Systems," *ASLIB Proceedings,* **19**:223–231, July 1967.

1020. Williams, William F.: *Principles of Automated Information Retrieval,* Business Press, Elmhurst, Ill., 1968, 475 pp.

1021. Wolters, P. H., and R. A. Green: "Union List of Scientific Serials in Canadian Libraries, 1967: Edition Design, Conversion, Computer Operations," *Canadian Libraries,* **24**:327–332, Jan. 1968.

1022. Wood, E. I.: *Report on Project History Retrieval: Tests and Demonstrations of an Optic-coincidence System of Information Retrieval for Historical Materials,* sponsored jointly by the Henry Francis du Pont Winterthur Museum and Drexel Institute of Technology, Graduate School of Library Science, Drexel, Philadelphia, 1966, 123 pp.

1023. Wood, R. G.: "Use of an ICT 1907 Computer in Southampton University Library: Report No. 3," *Program,* **2**:30–33, Apr. 1968.

1024. Yale University Library: Administrative Data Systems, Library Projects Staff: *The Kline (Science Library) Book Catalogues: A Progress Report,* Yale University Library, New Haven, Conn., 1965, 17 pp.

1025. Yerke, Theodor B.: "Adapting Library Computer Programs to Individual Documentation," *Second Annual American Water Resources Conference,* Chicago, Ill. 1966.

1026. Yerke, Theodor B.: "Computer Support of the Researcher's Own Documentation," *Datamation,* **16**:75–78, Feb. 1970. The Famulus system.

1027. Zaaiman, R. B.: "Provision of Technical Information in a Developing Region," *South African Libraries,* **33**:95-104, Jan. 1966.

1028. Zuckerman, Ronald A.: "Computerized Book Catalogs and Their Effects on Integrated Library Data Processing: Research and Progress at the Los Angeles County Public Library," *Clinic on Library Application of Data Processing, University of Illinois, 5th, 1967, Proceedings,* Graduate School of Library Science, University of Illinois, Urbana, Ill., 1967, pp. 70–89.

1029. Zuckerman, Ronald A.: *Optical Scanning for Data Collection, Conversion, and Reduction,* Los Angeles County Public Library, Los Angeles, 1967, 54 pp. PB 179 765.

BIBLIOGRAPHY SUBJECT INDEX

A.A.U. (Association of Atlantic Universities): 149, 650, 1014

Abstracting: 149, 650, 909

Accounting: 99, 882, 993

Acquisitions: 10, 44, 60, 134, 145, 162, 165, 231, 232, 243, 280, 297, 312, 368, 445, 588, 646, 668, 685, 770, 791, 821, 838, 868, 877, 912, 919, 968, 987

Administration (see also Accounting; Personnel): 189, 268, 279, 301, 380, 388, 519, 890, 892, 1024

Aerospace Research Applications Center: 235

Agriculture: 651

Air pollution: 874, 907

Airlie Foundation: 212

ALPHA (automated literature processing handling and analysis system): 186, 216, 239, 574

American Council of Learned Societies: 713

Analysis: 159

Anglo-American Conference on the Mechanization of Library Services: 47, 137

Apollo: 683

Architecture (see also Library buildings): 584

Archives: 166, 168, 178, 316, 317

Art: 450

Association of New York Libraries for Technical Services: 454

Atlantic Provinces Library Association (APLA): 1014

ATLAS (automation in libraries): 50, 186, 201, 216, 239, 574, 770, 795, 832, 858, 1008, 1010

AUDACIOUS: 330

Audio-visual materials: 106, 107, 481, 684

Auerbach Corp: 332

Austin Public Library: 673, 677

Australia: 156, 255

Authority lists (see also Thesauri): 385

Automated materials handling (see Materials handling)

AWRE: (atomic weapons research establishment): 219

BALANCE (Bay Area Libraries Associated Network for Cooperative Exchange): 63, 453

Baltimore County Public Library: 197, 503, 793

BELLREL: 496

Bettis Atomic Laboratory: 880

Bibliographic control: 31, 42, 47, 57, 64, 140, 155, 210, 228, 251, 254, 329, 336, 398, 438, 474, 531, 539, 618, 662, 728, 849, 974, 984, 994, 999

Bibliographies (of library automation): 35, 59, 66, 277, 317, 443, 545, 676, 695, 866

Bibliographies (mechanized): 618, 798, 803, 806
Biblios: 538
Biblioteca Nationale Centrale, Firenze: 84
Binding: 237, 396
Biological information: 222
Black Gold Cooperative Library System: 970
BNB (British National Bibliography): 225, 1003
Boeing: 997
Book catalogs: 82, 115, 144, 152, 185, 197, 291, 313, 341, 390, 391, 407, 420, 427, 428, 432, 453, 477, 479, 480, 484, 494, 503, 528, 557, 597, 632, 660, 673, 677, 680, 686, 730, 745, 757, 759, 760, 786, 793, 859, 915, 970, 992, 995, 996, 997, 1024, 1028
Book numbers: 133
Boston University: 253, 552
Bradford distribution: 563
Brasenose Conference on the Automation of Libraries: 47, 55, 137, 506, 724, 737, 1003
British National Bibliography: 225, 1003
Brooklyn Public Library: 697
Brown University Library: 993
Bryn Mawr College: 158

C.A.C.U.L. (see Canadian Association of College and University Libraries)
California: 700, 816
California State Library: 185
California Union Catalog: 185
CALMACQ: 10
Calvin College: 993
Canada: 38, 108, 115, 139, 168, 177, 205, 209, 265, 273, 280, 322, 410, 489, 681, 685, 778, 834, 843, 890, 891, 919, 968, 983, 991, 1021
Canadian Association of College and University Libraries (C.A.C.U.L.): 108, 179, 205, 265, 322, 410, 489, 681, 685, 843, 890, 968, 991
Card catalogs: 54, 171, 197, 286, 507, 552, 589, 631, 670, 680, 760, 786, 859
Case Western Reserve University: 12
Cataloging (see also Book catalogs; Conversion; Shelflist): 7, 38, 48, 55, 87, 98, 134, 145, 162, 182, 214, 215, 243, 269, 284, 285, 291, 308, 322, 324, 359, 373, 376, 377, 406, 426, 433, 434, 438, 445, 450, 482, 508, 511, 512, 515, 537, 542, 546, 561, 587, 592, 593, 625, 702, 706, 708, 726, 746, 747, 789, 791, 838, 843, 853, 862, 873, 878, 896, 923, 924, 934, 935, 936, 937, 938, 939, 1000, 1005
Cataloging of magnetic tape material: 927
Catalogs of old books: 451
Catholic University: 710
Centralized processing: 187, 339, 435, 696, 697, 766
Character sets: 111, 776, 869
Chemical information: 219, 861

Circulation: 3, 44, 85, 88, 108, 116, 134, 156, 162, 175, 176, 192, 201, 223, 231, 270, 318, 394, 408, 410, 429, 489, 520, 521, 523, 524, 556, 559, 562, 626, 655, 675, 705, 712, 725, 743, 761, 765, 801, 802, 804, 805, 862, 873, 886, 914, 928, 930, 931

Citation indexing: 42

City University of New York: 230, 581, 882, 953

Classification: 21, 27, 32, 129, 436, 788, 820

COBOL: 56

Coding: 98, 120, 287, 577, 707, 945

Colorado Academic Libraries Book Processing Center Study: 569

Columbia-Harvard-Yale Medical Libraries Computerization Project: 505

Columbia University: 387, 505

COM (Computer output to microfilm): 973

Communications: 4, 16, 69, 73, 79, 196, 247, 262, 272, 292, 342, 348, 358, 361, 471, 481, 490, 544, 603, 669, 683, 719, 817, 827, 852, 900, 1019

Computer centers: 71, 148, 158, 271, 274, 327, 571, 734, 742, 753

Computer programming (see Software)

Computers: 26, 238, 717 (see also Small computers)

Connecticut: 313, 333, 932

Control systems: 688, 795, 805, 914, 929, 930, 931, 1015

Conversion: 64, 190, 269, 398, 400, 482, 546, 591, 724, 849, 1021, 1029

Cooperative cataloging: 726

Cooperative processing: 753

Coordinate indexing: 35, 36, 221, 383, 751

COSATI (Committee on Scientific and Technical Information): 706

Cost effectiveness: 832

Costs: 65, 189, 190, 197, 206, 243, 279, 284, 285, 286, 335, 364, 420, 430, 507, 537, 572, 587, 591, 596, 642, 733, 757, 780, 796, 830, 832, 849, 976, 1002

Cranfield Research Project: 202

Cross referencing: 534

CUNY: 230, 581, 882, 953

Current awareness (see also SDI): 67, 702, 926

Cuyahoga County Public Library: 718, 904

Dartmouth College: 493

Data bases: 98, 264, 326, 331, 402, 478, 551, 648, 717, 875, 918

Data collection: 270, 408, 481, 675, 886

Data elements: 254

Data formats: 53, 254, 409, 471, 529, 595, 652, 945

Data management: 113, 118, 647

Descriptors: 577, 702, 800

Deutsche Bibliographie: 228

Dewey, Melvil: 727

Diacritical marks: 776

DIALOG: 894

Display facilities: 129, 130, 160, 405, 406, 894, 918
Dissemination (see Selective dissemination)
Document handling (see Materials handling)
Dorset County Library: 182
DYSTAL programs: 790

Earth science: 694
Economics: 920
Education: 323, 366, 624, 768
EDUCOM: 463, 786
Effectiveness: 1006, 1007, 1008
Equipment: 28, 76, 105, 362, 375, 452, 459, 469, 658, 699, 717, 954, 969, 1001
ERIC: 624
Essendon Public Library: 156

Facsimile transmission: 614, 658, 659, 701, 818, 819
FAIR (fast access information retrieval): 758
Famulus: 170, 1026
File census, Library of Congress: 934
File organization: 40, 61, 117, 118, 136, 204, 261, 271, 328, 402, 590, 594, 647, 782, 812, 986
Filing: 13, 246, 438, 590, 708, 744, 748, 767, 790, 934
Film library: 106, 107, 684
Five Associated University Libraries: 628
Fixed field codes: 945
Florida Atlantic University: 48, 93, 256, 423, 424, 426, 434, 745, 746, 871, 923, 924
Florida State Library: 187
Flowcharts: 122, 380, 823, 901
Franklin and Marshall College: 325
Future trends: 11, 74, 92, 123, 124, 138, 199, 241, 296, 349, 355, 365, 369, 371, 378, 567, 578, 585, 613, 645, 677, 842, 910, 975

General Electric Co.: 193, 456, 457
Geological Educational Research Center: 143
Georgia Tech Library: 495
Germany: 132, 228, 488, 754, 755
Gift and exchange: 558
Goodrich, B. F., Research Center Library: 188

Hardware (see Equipment)
Harvard University Library: 253, 266, 505, 553, 724, 725
Hatfield College of Technology Library: 59
Haverford College: 158
Health (see Medical sciences)

High schools (see School libraries)
History: 618, 1022
Honnold Library: 445, 912
Hospitals (see also Medical sciences): 846

ICL 1900 Series: 80
ICT 1907 Computer: 1023
Illinois State Library: 298, 393, 394, 435, 802
Indexes and indexing: 12, 24, 25, 29, 30, 31, 33, 35, 36, 41, 42, 65, 202, 221, 330, 383, 385, 438, 533, 557, 561, 587, 598, 600, 602, 605, 666, 702, 751, 800, 909, 920, 1013
India: 774, 888
Indiana: 2, 863
Information societies: 17
Information transfer: 16
Innovation: 163
Institute of Paper Chemistry: 831
Interlibrary loan: 819
INTREX: 98, 335, 464, 720, 721
Inventory control: 194, 801
Iowa: 465
Italy: 84

Japan: 504
Johns Hopkins University: 801
Junior College District of St. Louis: 484

Kilgour's truncation algorithm: 873
King County, Wash.: 391
KWIC (Key-Word-In-Context) Indexes: 315, 800
KWOC (Key-Word-Out-of-Context) Indexes: 479, 487

Language (see also Software): 121, 125, 141, 492, 574, 605, 667, 750
Laval Université: 273, 322, 891
Law: 292, 446, 447, 478, 491, 578, 879
Lawrence Radiation Laboratory: 134, 401, 494
Lehigh University: 318, 911
Librarians: 224, 294, 360, 418, 425, 607, 736, 739, 740, 841, 908, 990
Library buildings: 300, 584
Library of Congress: 21, 53, 54, 133, 413, 526, 527, 616, 620, 622, 623, 671, 708, 729, 783, 788, 836, 921, 934, 935, 936, 937, 938, 939, 940, 941, 942, 943, 957, 962, 977, 984
Library cooperation: 555
Links: 34
Lockheed-Georgia Company: 78

Los Angeles: 71, 341, 428, 432, 686, 716, 906, 915, 1028
Loungborough University of Technology: 306
LUCID: 326

Machine translation: 66
Magnetic tape: 109, 149, 439, 441
Management: 97, 257, 340, 370, 379, 384, 470, 547, 613, 640, 641, 717
Man-machine communication: 245, 644
Manuscripts: 38, 167, 168, 317
Map libraries: 298, 726
MARC: 43, 51, 52, 53, 55, 56, 57, 80, 161, 213, 214, 215, 226, 227, 229, 251, 495, 522, 529, 560, 615, 687, 728, 741, 845, 945, 946, 947, 948, 949, 950, 951, 952, 958, 959, 960, 961
Maryland: 388, 389, 660, 753
Massachusetts Institute of Technology: 502, 630, 721
Materials handling: 159, 183, 416, 569, 832
Mathematical models: 61, 387, 564, 664
Medical sciences: 70, 102, 145, 172, 173, 247, 248, 249, 250, 253, 264, 309, 319, 386, 505, 508, 573, 583, 608, 643, 654, 655, 719, 743, 762, 764, 765, 771, 791, 797, 799, 820, 854, 870, 872, 889
MEDLARS: 260, 332, 568, 692, 944, 964
Methodology: 345, 347, 415, 864, 885
Miami-Dade Junior College: 307
Michigan State University: 626
Microforms: 222, 535, 542, 973, 1019
Microprinting: 779, 813
Microthesaurus: 907
Midwestern University: 712
Mountain-Plains College: 825
Multiple copy determination: 928
Municipal information systems: 295, 606
Music: 392, 411, 1013

NAPALM: 216
NASA: 135, 136, 683, 895, 955
Nassau Library System: 339
National Advisory Commission on Libraries: 15, 713
National Agricultural Library: 314, 331, 462, 551, 648, 836, 921, 956, 962
National Catalog: 154, 228
National Center for Atmospheric Research: 674
National Libraries Task Force: 836
National Library of Medicine: 249, 332, 692, 832, 921, 944, 962, 1000
National Science Foundation: 236
National Science Library: 205

National Union Catalog: 382, 461
Natural Sciences: 440
NELINET, the New England Library Information Network: 7, 8, 9, 68, 709
Networks: 2, 7, 8, 11, 68, 69, 73, 89, 94, 95, 102, 106, 128, 138, 172, 173, 181, 184, 248, 249, 258, 262, 263, 271, 302, 325, 366, 463, 465, 468, 510, 514, 571, 576, 595, 637, 645, 651, 652, 683, 690, 694, 709, 734, 762, 816, 817, 819, 827, 830, 837, 998, 1015
New England State University Libraries: 274
New Haven: 612
New York City: 631, 657, 697, 837
New York State: 187, 272, 305, 454, 877, 878, 1001
New York *Times:* 702
Newcastle-upon-Tyne University: 368, 588
Nuclear science (see Physics)

Oakland University: 44, 45, 176
Ohio College Library Center: 510, 514
On-line processes: 73, 173, 216, 293, 330, 394, 414, 442, 492, 521, 523, 712, 840, 868, 894
Ontario: 115, 139, 140, 982, 983
Operations research: 565, 661, 714, 773
Optical scanning: 715, 1022, 1029
Oregon: 180, 597, 700, 868

Paper chemistry: 150
Patents: 142
Pennsylvania: 152, 646
Periodicals (see also Serials): 303, 307, 309, 483, 672
Personnel: 289, 381, 425, 437, 777
Pesticides Information Center: 314
Petroleum: 142
Pharmaceutical information: 222
Physics: 41, 159, 160, 330, 401, 449, 576
PIL (processing information list): 46, 775
Planning: 18, 97, 320, 439, 498, 583, 822
Poison information: 704
Printing: 120, 757, 794, 826
Programmers (see Software)
Public libraries: 37, 60, 71, 152, 391, 412, 435, 454, 536, 611, 673, 677, 696, 697
Purdue University: 20, 61, 99, 312, 396, 397, 565

Queen's University of Belfast: 524

Reclassification of libraries: 329
Reference services: 39, 164, 195, 208, 293, 319, 330, 474, 509, 604, 772, 824, 894, 994

Remote terminals (see also On-line processes): 64, 181, 710
Research libraries: 5, 15, 58, 134, 199, 269, 472, 631, 713, 801, 913, 1018
Reserved books: 1011
Retrieval: 43, 61, 67, 86, 105, 130, 136, 142, 150, 193, 194, 204, 260, 330, 343, 345, 378, 402, 446, 530, 550, 590, 593, 608, 609, 639, 667, 698, 711, 758, 784, 796, 833, 873, 894, 895, 901, 905, 920, 974, 994, 1007, 1009, 1019, 1020
Retrospective searching: 67
Rice University: 804
Role indicators: 34, 550

St. Louis Junior College District: 484
San Francisco Public Library: 208, 237
Sandia: 1009
SATCOM: 900
School libraries: 321, 678, 679
SDI (see Selective dissemination)
Searching: 119, 155, 204, 218, 283, 444, 502, 594, 781, 789, 901, 918
Security: 75
Selective dissemination: 19, 146, 217, 219, 448, 485, 487, 606, 808, 809, 820
Serials: 83, 101, 110, 113, 205, 236, 237, 242, 253, 265, 273, 288, 291, 303, 307, 309, 396, 397, 399, 483, 497, 553, 554, 583, 655, 672, 681, 700, 743, 764, 784, 797, 799, 825, 828, 858, 871, 883, 889, 971, 976, 1014, 1017, 1021
Shelflist: 153, 190, 267, 557, 724
Shell Oil Co.: 828
Simon Fraser University: 280, 778
SLA-LTP survey: 469
SLIP: 997
Small computers: 1, 511, 933
Social sciences: 440, 478, 575, 920
Software: 162, 331, 459, 633, 673, 723, 889, 949, 1025
South Africa: 1027
Southamptom University Library: 1023
Southern Illinois University: 270, 675
Specifications: 459, 579, 865, 964
SPIRAL: 1009
Stack thinning: 928
Standards: 210, 254, 304, 358, 373, 471, 595, 599, 652, 900, 927, 1002
Stanford University: 479, 480
State-of-the-art reviews: 22, 103, 104, 455
State University of New York: 556, 766
Statistics: 346, 562, 881, 1002
Storage (see File organization; Materials handling)

Subject indexes: 23, 230, 382, 403, 462, 609
SUNY Biomedical Communication Network: 173
Swarthmore College: 158
Sweden: 1018
Symposia: 925
SYNTOL: 32
Syracuse University: 628
Systems analysis: 9, 91, 126, 169, 191, 404, 417, 510, 549, 566, 653, 682, 689, 822
Systems concepts: 72, 76, 77, 90, 100, 114, 127, 207, 224, 259, 275, 278, 299, 374, 473, 476, 499, 500, 516, 517, 518, 525, 532, 543, 610, 617, 621, 629, 638, 661, 714, 731, 758, 773, 815, 844, 850, 855, 857, 889, 903, 979, 980, 981, 988, 989, 1012, 1016, 1020
Systems design: 9, 126, 143, 191, 415, 430, 510, 525, 548, 661, 714, 773, 889

TDMS: 117, 118
Teaching: 372, 810, 922
Technical libraries: 636, 703, 955, 1006
Technical processes: 14, 244, 289, 290, 363, 421, 442, 601, 697, 716, 775, 829, 848, 972, 1001, 1002
Technical reports: 67, 338, 570, 598, 706
TELEPORT: 357
Testing: 763, 814
Texas: 220, 673, 677, 883, 884
Thesauri: 33, 211, 302, 431, 702
Time and motion studies: 541
Time-sharing: 112, 467, 468, 493, 752, 807, 867, 978
TIP: 630
Toronto: 60, 919
Translation: 66
Typesetting: 756

UDC (Universal Decimal Classification): 174, 230, 330
UNESCO: 422, 572
Union Catalogs: 185, 309, 310, 311, 333, 382, 461, 953
Union Lists: 1014, 1021
University of British Columbia: 108, 179, 410, 778, 843, 891
University of California: 79, 419, 458, 635, 784, 799, 865, 971
University of Chicago: 3, 336, 337, 966
University of Essex: 862
University of Georgia: 181
University of Hawaii: 175, 838, 839
University of Houston: 914
University of Illinois: 244, 291, 350, 456, 475, 540, 557

University of Maryland: 231, 232
University of Michigan: 297, 668
University of Missouri: 732, 737
University of Oxford: 967
University of Pittsburgh: 582
University of Victoria: 778
University of Western Ontario: 685
User studies: 19, 193, 281, 282, 351, 352, 353, 354, 513, 535, 593, 595, 652, 698, 749, 792, 872, 928, 937
U. S. government: 6, 281, 282, 358, 460, 466, 501, 555, 561, 703, 835, 836, 848, 856, 875, 963, 964, 965
U.S.S.R.: 662
Utah State University: 192

Visuals: 62
Vocabularies: 462, 666

Washington, D.C.: 734
Washington (State): 94, 165, 700
Washington University: 145, 429, 654, 655, 811
Weinberg Report: 963
West Sussex: 81

Yale University: 505, 513, 872

INDEX

INDEX

Accession numbers, 31
Acquisition, 8, 25-35
Administrative processes, 7, 13, 93-103
Administrative services department, 95
Alternatives, 130
American Book Publishers Council, 32
American Documentation Institute (ADI), 61, 96
American Library Association (ALA), 9, 32, 39
American Medical Association (AMA), 63
American Society for Information Science, 9, 61, 96
Analysis, 109, 127
Analytics, 43
Anglo-American Cataloging Code, 39
Anglo-American Conference on the Mechanization of Library Services, 9
Art prints, 41
Audiovisual materials, 41
Authority files, 37, 41, 77, 78

Backlog listings, 28, 81
Bibliographic control, 27, 41, 54, 77-81
Binding, 43
Blanket orders, 26, 28
Book catalogs, 55, 80
Booklist (journal) 27
Books in print, 26
Boston University, 42
Branches, 68
British Museum, 9, 46
Browsing, 47, 106
Budgets, 28, 73, 80

Card numbers, 32, 39
Case Western Reserve University, 61
Cataloging, 8, 37, 51, 55, 79, 81
Character recognition, 62
Characteristics, 140
Choice (journal), 27
Circulation control, 12, 68, 87-89
City University of New York, 11, 44
Claiming, 30, 33
Classification, 42, 78, 79
Coding, 32, 44, 229
College catalogs, collections of, 57, 80
Communications, 94, 196
Component selection, 110
Computer center, 13, 93, 97, 98
Concepts, 159, 163, 215, 239
Conference proceedings, 43
Constraints, 236
Control processes, 7, 10-14
Conversion, 10, 43-45, 48, 191
Cooperation with other libraries, 31, 44, 56

Costs, 40, 44, 46, 47, 49, 59, 81
Council on Library Resources, 62
Criteria, 128
Critical reviews, 43
Cross reference, 41, 42, 83

Data banks, 57, 60, 72, 93, 94, 96, 98, 99
Data base (*see* Data management)
Data collection machinery (*see* Hardware)
Data management, 98, 243
Data services, 94
Data superstructure, 244
Debugging, 151
Definition, 109, 119, 124
Demand, 138
Description, 40, 123
Desiderata lists, 26
Design, 110, 135
Deutsche Nationalbibliothek, 9, 37
Development, 110, 120, 135, 146
Dewey classification, 42, 79
Dialog, 53, 63, 79
Dictionary catalog, 47
Direct-reading device, 69
Discovery, 25
Display, 199
Document control, 84
Documentation, 149
EDUCOM (Inter-University Communications Council), 99, 100
EDUNET, 100
Efficiency, 135
Electron-beam recording, 46
Engineers Joint Council (EJC), 78
Equipment (*see* Hardware)
Evaluation, 120
Exchange lists, 26
Expansion planning, 67
Experimentation, 120
Exposition, 132

Facsimile transmission, 85
Federal Libraries Committee, 99
Feedback, 58
Filing, 39, 40, 46, 47, 48
Financial records, 72
Finding lists, 47, 55
Florida Atlantic University, 10, 39, 45, 46
Ford Foundation, 62
Form of entry for serials, 83
Functional characteristics, 110, 140, 190

Gift listings, 28, 30
Glossary, 14–23, 113–117, 169–187
GRACE, 45
Great Britain, 9, 33, 37, 46

Hardware, 14, 68, 69, 145, 159, 162, 189, 239
Harvard University, 10

Identification, 31, 109, 119
Indexes, 54, 56, 73, 84
Information retrieval (*see* Reference service)
Information science, 61
Initiation request, 121
Input methods, 48
Installation, 110, 145, 153, 156
Interaction, 251
International Federation for Documentation, 9
Inventory control, 13, 68, 69, 81, 82, 85
Irregular journals, 30, 83

Jobbers, 26, 27, 29, 71, 80, 96
Journals (*see* Serials control)

Kent State University, 57
Kirkus (journal), 27
KWIC, 56, 62, 96

Legal records, 72
Liaison services, 95
Library of Congress, 9, 27, 37, 42, 63, 87, 101
Library of the U.S. Department of the Interior, 9
Logic, 110
Loss rate, 43

Machine Readable Cataloging (MARC), 9, 25, 26, 32, 37, 38, 42, 43, 48, 63, 99
Maintenance, 111, 158
Manuals, 147
Manuscripts, 41
Maps, 41, 48
Mechanization, 106, 136
Medical Literature Analysis and Retrieval System (MEDLARS), 42, 45, 48, 54, 60, 99
Methodology, 105
Microforms, 11, 31, 39, 41, 44, 46, 48, 68
Miniprint, 11, 46
Morgues, 57
Music, 41

National Agricultural Library, 9, 42, 61, 87
National Library of Canada, 9, 42
National Library of Medicine, 9, 48, 54, 78, 87, 99, 100
National Science Foundation (NSF), 62, 99
National Union Catalog, 26, 38
Near-print materials, 87
Need, 120, 215, 239
Networks, 56, 95, 100–101

New York state, 27
New York Times Information Bank, 57

Object processing, 164, 219
Ohio Colleges Library Center, 100
Ohio, 27
On-line applications, 31
Ontario Universities Bibliographic Center, 100
Operation, 96, 111, 153, 156
Opportunity, 120, 215, 239
Optical scanning, 62
Ordering, 29
Organization, 94–96
Orientation, 59, 97
Out-of-print materials, 26, 28
Output methods, 47, 49
Overdue books, 88
Overtime, 71

Performance characteristics, 110, 144
Periodicals (*see* Serials control)
Permutation on subject headings, 62
Personnel, 69–71, 148, 239
Phonodiscs, 41, 81
Photocomposition, 31
Physical condition of books, 43
Planning, 67, 68, 93
Presentation, 45
Prices of books, 43, 73
Print chains, 45, 46
Print-out, 31, 47, 60
Priorities, 107
Probationary period status, 71
Problem analysis, 122
Procedure, 39
Processing control, 11, 29, 77–92
Professional services department, 95
Profiles of users, 58
Programming, 38, 42, 150
Project control, 111
Proofreading, 44, 48
Prospects, 235
Publishers, 41, 56, 80

Quantification, 129
Query, 53, 55, 85

Readout, 31, 46, 60
Receiving, 29
Reference service, 10, 53–65
Release for production, 111
Remote access, 27
Research, 60
Reserve books, 47, 88–89
Resource control, 11, 67
Review, 120
Royal Library in Stockholm, 37
Rush status, 30, 81

Searching, 26, 27, 80
Selection, 10, 27, 131, 145

Selective dissemination of information (SDI), 58, 71, 86, 95
Serials control, 12, 33, 43, 54, 73, 83-86
Shelf list, 44, 82
Sick leaves, 71
Size identification, 41
Software, 94, 159, 162, 203
Space, 67
Special Libraries, 9
Special Libraries Association (SLA), 9
Specification, 109, 127
Staffing, 61, 70, 97
Standard Book Numbering (SBN), 32, 33
Standards, 37, 49, 67, 94
Stanford University, 10
Statistics, 29, 55, 80, 88
Storage, 194
Subject catalogs, 48
Subject headings, 42, 78
Suppliers, 71, 93
Symbols, 227
Systems approach, 93, 105

Teaching, 55, 59
Technical processes, 7, 8
Technical report literature, 60-62
Test, 110, 153
Thesauri, 42, 78, 99 (*See also* Authority files)
Traffic relationships, 67, 68
Training, 110

Ultramicrostorage, 84
United States Census Bureau, 72
United States Department of Defense, 78
United States government documents (*see* Document control)
University of British Columbia, 98
University of Chicago, 10
University of Illinois, 10, 39
University Library Information System (ULIS), 39, 62
University of Toronto, 45
Users, 46, 53, 58, 71
Utilization studies, 67

Vacation scheduling, 71
Vertical files, 55, 57
Vocabulary control, 59, 247

Western Union, 100
Work efficiency, 71, 80

Yale University, 45